BIG FLAVORS
OF THE
HOT SUN

ALSO BY

**Chris Schlesinger
and John Willoughby**

THE THRILL OF THE GRILL
(1 9 9 0)

SALSAS , SAMBALS ,
CHUTNEYS & CHOW CHOWS
(1 9 9 3)

CHRIS SCHLESINGER AND JOHN WILLOUGHBY

BIG FLAVORS
OF THE
HOT SUN

hot recipes and cool tips from the spice zone

■

PHOTOGRAPHY BY STEVEN ROTHFELD

ILLUSTRATIONS BY ALAN WITSCHONKE

WILLIAM MORROW AND COMPANY, INC.

NEW YORK

Library of Congress Cataloging-in-Publication Data

Schlesinger, Chris.
    Big flavors of the hot sun : hot recipes and cool tips from the spice zone / Chris Schlesinger and John Willoughby.
        p.   cm.
    ISBN 0-688-11842-9
    1. Condiments.   2. Cookery, International.   3. Spices.
I. Willoughby, John.   II. Title.
TX819.A1S337   1994
641.6'382—dc20   93-50757
                                                                  CIP

Printed in the United States of America

First Edition

1   2   3   4   5   6   7   8   9   10

BOOK DESIGN BY BARBARA BACHMAN

For my mom and dad—don't worry about the alligators and crocodiles.

—Chris

For my family.

—John

Acknowledgments

From Chris Schlesinger:

In some ways, being a cookbook author is a lot like being the chef of a restaurant—one person ends up getting credit for the work of many. In my case, I've been very fortunate in both efforts to work with many fine people. Owning a small business is an intense lifestyle, and to write a book along with it is quite a luxury, one that was possible only because of the skill and hard work of my associates: Nick Zappia, our general manager; Andy Husbands, chef at the East Coast Grill; Smiley and Tina from the front of the house; Bridget Batson, chef of the Blue Room; Lisa White, also from the Blue Room; Elmer, Amilcar, and the wild bunch at Jake & Earl's; Boone and Cathy up at HQ; and, of course, my partner Cary Wheaton, whose tireless work, dedication, and friendship continue to make hard work a hell of a lot easier and more pleasant.

Along the path of life and professional work there are many people whose impact is inseparable from one's own accomplishments. In my case, they include first of all my dad, who twenty years ago thought that having a son who wanted to be a cook was pretty neat, even though the only person he could relate it to was the character John Ritter played on the sitcom *Three's Company*; Pat Ricks, who gave me my first restaurant job as a dishwasher at Blue Pete's in Virginia Beach, Virginia; and Jimmy Burke and Bob Kinkead, at one time my chefs, now my close personal friends.

Then there is my friend and coauthor Doc (aka John). There is satisfaction in individual personal accomplishments, but to me it seems infinitely more fun and rewarding to participate in a collaboration, for this means that the bulk of the many hours of work are spent in the company of a true friend. These are the times that will be remembered long after the food is eaten. Thanks, Doc, for your tolerance, your humor, and your friendship.

From John Willoughby:

Writing can be a very solitary business. Having friends and colleagues who are ready to commiserate, celebrate, or just shoot the breeze on a daily basis makes it a lot more enjoyable. In this regard, I'd like to thank Mark Bittman for those endless hours of conversation and encouragement over the last several years. I'd also like to thank my colleagues at *Cook's Magazine*—Chris, Jack, Pam, and Maura—who put up with my preoccupation with this book.

Since much of the book is based on our travels over the years, I'd like to reach back and thank my high school Latin teacher, Miss Jo Thielen, who not only taught me the difference between various parts of speech but also encouraged me to "get out there and find out what the world is all about." In the same vein, thanks to my parents, who worked hard to make sure that I saw as much of the world outside my little hometown as possible.

And, of course, there is Chris. It is an unusual privilege to be able to work with someone who is also a close friend. It's even more of a treat when that friend has an outlook and a sense of humor that can make work seem just like a fun way to pass the time. Thanks, Chris, for your creative spirit, your patience, your loyalty, and most of all your friendship. I wouldn't trade the hours we spent working together on this book for any amount of vacation.

From Chris Schlesinger and John Willoughby:

Together, the two of us have spent a lot of time working in the food profession, and have been fortunate enough to be befriended along the way by many people who have gone out of their way to give us a helping hand.

Thanks to Barbara Haber, Curator of Books at the Schlesinger Library at Harvard, for being a good friend as well as a constant source of information and encouragement; to Joyce Toomre, for helping in the very beginning to clarify the focus of this book; to Alan Richman, for his humor, his irreverence, and his willingness to help out a couple of novices; to Lisa Ekus, for getting the word out there; to Steve Johnson, not only for his recipe contributions and his willingness to talk about food anywhere anytime but also for his unique personal style; to the guys who tested and retested the recipes, K.C., Andy, and Douglas; to Dahlia and Herb, for that wonderful day in New York; to our travel agent Gail, who takes it with good humor when at the last minute we change our destination from Bali to Singapore because hairy crabs are in season; to our many guides and hosts, particularly Moo Kan Fah in Kuala Lumpur, Mr. Truan in Ho Chi Minh City, and Ibrahim in Marrakesh, for putting up with our endless fascination with what to them was just everyday food; and to Salvatore, the quickest bartender in Costa Rica, for the many nights he kept the conversation lively and the glasses full.

We'd also like to thank the staff at William Morrow for their continued hard work and diligence, in particular the unflappable Chas Edwards and the incomparably talented designer Barbara M. Bachman. Steven Rothfeld's photos and Alan Witschonke's drawings also deserve grateful thanks.

Thanks also to Doe Coover, our literary agent, who not only does a superlative job with the business end of things but was also a participant in every aspect of the book, including many most excellent dinners.

And, of course, our coach, Maria Guarnaschelli, who, if she spends one-third as much time and energy on her other authors as she does on us, must have figured out a way to double the number of hours in the day. Her ability to glean the concept, hone the focus, and still pay attention to the smallest details is inspiring. We'd also like to thank Harriet Bell for her late-inning relief work.

And finally, most special thanks to our extended family, Susan, Rick, Lizzie, Tommy, Cary, and Jake, whose love, companionship, and ability to not only listen to our relentless blather but to eat our food, too, has made it all possible.

Contents

CONTENTS   i x

LOST IN THE SPICE ZONE AGAIN

■

Subtlety in food does not impress me. I like big, loud flavors—sweet, sour, hot, salty, aromatic, pungent, tingling—preferably all in the same bite. I'm the guy who always asks for salt and pepper in the fancy restaurants and who thinks that most dishes could benefit from a squeeze of lime or a shot or two of Tabasco.

Now, don't get me wrong. I don't mean to put down intricate or subtle food; I understand that my attraction to strong, intense, well-defined flavors is a personal choice. It's like preferring jazz to chamber music; shorts and flip-flops to tails and a black tie; or steamed crabs, glasses of beer, and bottles of hot sauce on a table covered with old newspapers to a damask tablecloth set with more silverware than I know what to do with and a plate of food that looks like a painting.

Over the years I have found that my type of food—casual, a little rough around the edges, and packed with big, bold tastes—is most easily found in places where the weather is hot. From Thailand to Brazil, from Singapore to Morocco to Mexico, I have continually discovered food with the vibrant flavors and direct, sensual appeal that excite and satisfy me.

It took me a while, though, to figure out that this hot-weather food could take its place alongside the classic creations of Escoffier and Carême that I was taught in culinary school.

I entered the world of professional cooking in the early 1970s, when the nouvelle cuisine wave was just washing over America. It was an incredibly exciting time to be a cook. Every day when I went to work, I was faced with ingredients I had never seen before and was given free rein to experiment with them, trying out my ideas on supportive co-workers and customers. Through sheer luck and good timing, I was participating in one of the most significant changes in the world of food since Columbus's voyages inaugurated the global food exchange of the 16th century. I quickly became addicted.

But in cooking as in the rest of life, it's hard to maintain an even course. Even the strange new ingredients couldn't hold my interest as the energy of nouvelle cuisine veered off into baby vegetables, fanned kiwi slices, and intricately constructed plate arrangements. It seemed to me that the rediscovery of creativity in cooking, at first fresh and exciting, was fast becoming precious and pretentious. So I resorted to the stratagem I most often employed during my twenties when faced with boredom: I took off in search of overhead waves and temperatures in the low eighties.

This time my pursuit of the beach bum existence evolved into an extended survey of the beaches of Barbados, Mexico, and Central and South America. As the months slipped by, I seemed to drift further and further from the world of professional cooking. I loved the food I was eating, but it was surely not the stuff of restaurant menus.

That perspective took a turn one day when I was hanging out at a beach shack in northern Costa Rica. I was monitoring the waves and tossing down a few beers from the comfort of my hammock when a fisherman pulled up in a boat and hauled out one of the weirdest fish I'd ever seen, a huge, iridescent-green creature with a giant flat head. Fascinated, I followed the fisherman as he carried this bizarre creature into the "kitchen" of the shack.

"¿Que pescado eso?" I asked the cook in my mutant Spanish, which usually reduced native speakers to helpless laughter. The fisherman was no exception, but he did manage to stop chuckling long enough to reply, "Es dorado, amigo."

He seemed amused as I watched him cut the fish into steaks and throw them on the open grill, so I bought him a beer and spent the next hour or so watching him prepare food for the lunchtime rush (a handful of other fishermen and a couple of tourists). Besides the dorado, his raw materials included an array of tropical ingredients that I knew little or nothing about, from yucca to plantains to habañero chiles, guavas, mangoes, and cilantro. As I watched this cook spritz lime juice into each dish just as I would add salt, I realized that he was using even the ingredients I was familiar with in unfamiliar ways.

When the fish came off the grill, accompanied by a fiery habañero-mango relish and grilled whole plantains, it was a revelation. Succulent and moist, the subtle, smoky dorado was perfectly countered by the bright, loud flavors of the relish and the mellow sweetness of the banana. Here was a guy who could really cook, who knew how to match ingredients and create food with intense culinary interest, yet could not have been less pretentious. As he chopped and mixed and threw things on the grill, he chatted with his customers, introducing each one to the Americano who was watching him so intently. The food was great, but in no way was it studied or overly refined or the center of too much attention.

It was a wonderful afternoon. I really liked the guy, I was learning something about his culture, and despite the language barrier I felt that we were becoming friends. This, I thought, was what food and cooking should be all about. It was a continuation of the excitement I had felt from the early stages of nouvelle cuisine, but on a more basic level. This was why I had decided to become a cook; the thrill of discovery was rekindled on a different fire.

This was a turning point in my culinary perspective, but it was only the first of many such scenes. Over the years, as I have continued to travel to the general vicinity of the tropics, I have been constantly amazed and fascinated by the foods and the people I have encountered. Eating fresh razor clams in a seafood market in Vietnam, spicy pork and peanut stew in a village in Peru, vinegary red snapper *escabeche* with mangoes in a beach shack on Barbados, fiery chile crabs in Singapore—the list goes on and on, and with each new eating experience my love for the food of hot-weather countries has been confirmed.

The foods I have tasted in these far-flung locales have provided my culinary inspiration, but I have not tried to duplicate individual dishes, re-creating the recipes of other cooks. Instead, I have tried to take the flavor dynamics and ingredient combinations that I have discovered and translate them into my own food while respecting the cultures in which they originated.

Actually, this is nothing new. Imagine the food that was put on the table by the first Spanish cook who was brought to the Americas and found himself working with Mexican ingredients. Then imagine the dishes that same cook might have come up with when he was reassigned to the Philippines and once again brought a Spanish cooking sensibility to bear on a whole new larder. What a great job! So you see that the concept is not new—but it sure is fun.

As I have traveled and learned about hot-weather cuisines, I have found that they not only share many basic character traits but also have a larder of common ingredients. These common foods include, first and foremost, the majority of the world's spices. A multitude of barks, flowers, berries, roots, buds, and seeds composing the spice lexicon is used throughout the hot-weather world with a sophistication and inventiveness that is both astonishing and richly rewarding. From the aromatic chile-lime combinations of Thailand to the intricate spice mixtures of India to the pungent and savory stews of North and East Africa, spices contribute mightily to the unique flavors of hot-weather cuisines.

This spice virtuosity is not by accident; spices are central to hot-weather cooking largely because most of them originated in the tropics and are still grown there. In his *Book of Spices* (Pyramid,1973), for example, Frederick Rosengarten points to the Asian tropics between 25° N latitude and 10° S latitude as the home of most spices. I call this narrow geographic band—which actually extends around the world to the American tropics where allspice, vanilla, and chile peppers originated—the Spice Zone. If I were told I could cook with nothing but ingredients found inside this little band for the rest of my life, I would feel like Brer Rabbit thrown into the briar patch.

In addition to spices, the common hot-weather larder encompasses a wide selection of starchy roots and tubers, from yucca to boniato to yams; vegetables ranging from squash that look like they are from outer space to aromatic greens of every description; a host of grains and legumes; and an overwhelming variety of fruit, from the familiar banana, pineapple, and coconut to mango, papaya, and guava.

Because the growing season in these areas lasts most of the year, and meat is relatively scarce, fruits and vegetables have occupied a much larger portion of the plate than in the U.S. This has naturally led to a tremendous inventiveness in cooking with them. After all, if you can stroll out to your backyard and pick a mango, you are far more likely to figure out that it not only can be treated as a fruit when ripe but can also be used as a vegetable in its green state.

There's a lot of ocean frontage in the tropics too, so the equatorial pantry also includes a truly amazing collection of sea dwellers, both finned and finless, that hang out in warm waters. Check out a fish market in most any tropical seaport, and you'll be blown away by the colors, shapes, and sizes; multicolored fish, squid, octopus, shrimp, weird shellfish, all kinds of crabs—the variety seems endless.

In addition to a common ingredient base, hot-weather cuisines share a devotion to a cooking method that is practically a religion to me: cooking over live fire. To me, the unpredictable, constantly changing dynamic of a wood-based fire makes cooking thrilling. Nothing ever cooks exactly the same way twice over a flame, which allows for cooking with a lot of personal character.

Nowhere do you find as much live-fire cookery as in the tropics. From the grilled satays on the streets of Malaysia to the tacos *al carbón* in Mexico, cooking outdoors with fire is not an occasion for funny aprons and elaborate tools. It's simply the way most people cook most of the time. Then, of course, there are also ritual feasts in which large animals are cooked whole using live fire—the luaus of Hawaii, the *charrascuria* of Brazil and Argentina, the whole grilled lambs of the Middle East, the huge spit-roasted fish on the beaches of Costa Rica.

Grilling is my number-one favorite cooking method, which is certainly no news to anyone who has read my first cookbook, *The Thrill of the Grill*. As a result, there are plenty of new grilling recipes in this book. However, I have found many other techniques in hot-weather regions that are fun, easy to do, and result in food with big, exciting flavors, and you'll discover them in this book, too.

Cooking fish in citrus, for example, is most familiar to us from the ceviche of Mexico and Latin America, but it is also a technique used in many parts of Asia, where citrus fruit originated. You couldn't ask for a cooler, easier way of taking food from raw to cooked, and the resulting dishes have a unique tart, summery flavor. Coating meat or fish with a spice rub before cooking is another very simple but ingenious technique that takes advantage of the myriad spice mixes of hot-weather cuisines. Rubbing spice mixes on the outside of food results in a crust of deep, concentrated flavor that contrasts with a moist, juicy interior.

That's not all in the technique department. Throughout the hot-weather world, cooks combine fresh fruits and vegetables with spices and chile peppers to make salsas, chutneys, and a whole range of other "little dishes" that add intense flavor to any simple meal. The pickling of fruits, vegetables, and even meat or fish—as in the vinegar-based *escabeches* found throughout Central America and the Caribbean—is another popular technique in hot climates. While pickling is no longer as necessary for preservation, it still creates dishes with wonderful, complex flavors.

There is another aspect of hot-weather food that, while kind of a side issue as far as I'm concerned, is very topical today: The food is very healthful. It was not consciously created to be healthful, but instead to be as tasty as possible using the available ingredients. Since these ingredients are primarily fruits, vegetables, grains, and legumes rather than meat and fowl, the food happens to be healthful as well, with almost no animal fat and in fact very little fat of any kind.

The reliance on starches as the central component of the diet is one of the factors that led to the intensity of flavor and the spiciness in hot-weather cuisines. A big pile of rice and beans tastes better with the addition of some salsa, and East Africa's millet and teff would become pretty monotonous on a daily basis without berberé spices.

The assertive flavor dynamics, wonderful and varied ingredients, healthful profile, and ingenious cooking techniques of hot-weather foods are enough to make me love them, but there is yet another compelling attraction—this food is the essence of casual dining.

I first learned this while growing up in the South: No jackets and ties were worn when my father and I served grilled food at the beach, and there were no fancy tablecloths at the local barbecue joint. People tend to avoid dressing up when it's hot and are generally looking for a beverage or two to help them cool off. This naturally leads to my type of meal—having fun, laughing a little too loud, and spilling stuff on your shirt, sharing relaxation with your friends and loved ones.

Sharing food with folks in this type of setting is a rewarding experience that I never seem to tire of; I'm ready for it anyplace, anytime. I have found that the ingredients, techniques, and customs surrounding food provide a unique insight into cultures and people all over the world, and you can always relate to someone over a plate of food and a bottle of the local booze. As is probably obvious by now, the direction I like to go is not matching china plates with delicate stemware but more like asking, "Hey, why don't you come on over tonight? I've got some fresh crabs and we can sit around and have a couple of beers and try to make that chile crab I had in Malaysia."

What it boils down to is that I am fascinated by visiting new lands and eating new foods, and in this book I have tried to translate what I have found into recipes that make sense in your kitchen. Of course, I should also point out that since these are the personal ideas of one cook, many different influences will inevitably peek through. This book is basically inspired by hot-weather cuisines, but my childhood in the American South and the bounty of my grandmother's table can't be overlooked, and both will always influence my food.

Finally, I would encourage you to cook the way I garden. I garden to relax. People come over to my house all the time and criticize my gardening style. They criticize me because I plant things in the wrong places and out of season; but the fact is, I do it for enjoyment, not because I want a perfect garden. And I notice that, somehow, everybody seems to have fun hanging out in my yard, however it may look.

I hope you enjoy the book. Above all, relax—enjoy the discovery of new foods and flavors, have a great time cooking, and may all your dinner companions be witty and kind.

THE SPICE
IS RIGHT

∎

This is my theory: Where the weather is hotter, the food is more intensely flavored.

To get a bit more technical, I think that hot-weather cuisines share a common method of presenting flavors. Unlike classical French sauces, for example, which build up a single taste by combining several flavors in what might be considered an ''architectural'' fashion, these tropical-inspired dishes lay out each of their several distinct tastes separately, in a kind of geographic presentation. From the first bite, you are presented with a range of loud, competing, individual flavors that light up every taste bud in your mouth like a gustatory machine gun.

A large part of this dynamic of flavor intensity comes from the way spices are used in these cuisines. The tropics are the original home of all spices, and they are deeply embedded in the foods of these regions, treated with great respect and care. An Indian cook creating a complex masala, or spice mixture, for example, must have the same level of skill, insight, and experience that a French chef needs to make a complex, subtle sauce.

I love the depth of flavor that spices add to food, and I have gradually become fascinated with everything about spices. In fact, not long ago my urge to learn more led me out of the kitchen and into the library. In the course of this foray into unfamiliar territory, my curiosity about food ended up getting me hooked on history, which I had totally ignored in school. For in many ways the story of spices is the history of commerce, discovery, and empire in the modern world.

Spices have been around since prebiblical times. At that point, they were valued not so much for their use in food but as medicines, poison antidotes, and ingredients in perfumes and incense. From their island homes in the Asian tropics, spices like cinnamon, cloves, and nutmeg were taken to coastal India, where black pepper was already growing. From there they were shipped across the Indian Ocean or hauled overland to Syria and Egypt via routes with such colorful monikers as the Silk Road. Next stop was Alexandria, where they were reloaded, shipped across the Mediterranean, then finally packed over the Alps to central and northern Europe.

That's a lot of traveling, so spices sold for major dollars in what was eventually to become Europe. As is usually the case when big bucks are involved, someone was making a huge profit—in this case, the middlemen who bought the spices from the East and sold them to the West.

To maintain this profitable situation, the wily spice dealers worked hard to maintain what Frederick Rosengarten, author of *The Book of Spices,* calls "the world's greatest trade secret." In true middleman fashion, the wheeling-dealing merchants concocted all manner of wild stories for their unsuspecting Roman customers. Some yarns included ferocious winged beasts that guarded the swamps and mountains where spices grew, while others told of spices being netted by bold fishermen at the misty headwaters of the Nile, where the spices had drifted via the rivers that flowed out of Paradise. All of this added more myth and mystery to spices and helped to drive their prices ever skyward. A true purveyor's dream.

The European love of spices continued to increase as the Middle Ages dawned, by which time spices were largely being used to flavor food. In fact, spices were so highly valued that they were sometimes used as currency or traded for gems, gold, and silver. Not surprisingly, their use in cooking served partially as a demonstration of wealth; it was not unusual for lavish banquets to include dishes in which the food was practically buried under mounds of spices, and in very wealthy households a silver platter bearing spices was passed around as a kind of relish tray.

Does all of this seem a bit strange to you? To me, it's very odd to look back from the vantage point of today's European cuisines, with their relative lack of spices, and find that medieval French cuisine used spices so heavily. Barbara Wheaton, in her wonderful book *Savoring the Past* (University of Pennsylvania Press, 1983), makes this point dramatically by comparing medieval French food to the modern cuisines of India and the Near East.

As I began to learn about the use of spices in medieval Europe, I found some ammunition to shoot down the often-repeated theory that spices were used mainly to cover up the taste of spoiled food. Let's face it, with spices being practically worth their weight in gold, does it make sense that folks would rub them on rotten meat? After all, they had plenty of salt to preserve meat, and they could use inexpensive herbs to disguise any "off" tastes if that's what was needed. As Wolfgang Schivelbusch says in his book *Taste of Paradise,* the idea of medieval Europeans using spices as preservatives or to mask the taste of rotten food is "like saying that champagne is a good thirst quencher."

In any case, the European craze for spices reached such a frenzy that it eventually led directly to the opening of trade routes to the East and to the European discovery of the Americas. Europeans carried out their fanatic search for new spice routes and sources with an intensity that Schivelbusch likens to today's search for alternative energy sources—although with considerably more success.

Ironically, as the Europeans became successful in finding new routes and discovering the true sources of spices, spices began to lose their cachet in Europe and started their slow fade from the cooking of that continent.

There are many economic and cultural reasons for this culinary sea change, which accompanied the other revolutions in taste brought by the Renaissance. There is one particular factor, however, that I find uniquely relevant today, when the economics of the Silk Road have long been supplanted by international jet transport. I think that spices disappeared from European cuisines partly because their randy history started to work against them.

What do I mean by "randy history"? Well, spices had long been associated with the exotic and mysterious East, with silk and jewels and sensuality. Also, whether as the result of some wild tale told by an old Phoenician spice trader to increase the value of his wares, or for some deeper reason, spices had always been considered potent aphrodisiacs. Intense in flavor, consumed not for sustenance but solely to add to the pleasure of eating, spices carried a strong whiff of lust, indulgence, and general wildness. This close association was no selling point in late medieval Europe, when sensuality as a trait was definitely not in favor.

Colin Spencer, a British writer who sometimes makes food his subject, laid out this argument very persuasively in a presentation at the Oxford Seminar on Food in 1992. Spencer theorized that there was always a subliminal fear that spices and herbs, being wild themselves, "might liberate the beast within and so despoil the fabric of civilization." I think Spencer is right on target, because that sounds like the same rot that certain people always start to drivel whenever they suspect something fun is going on.

You might think that I am stretching a point, or at least you might think that this association of spices and sensuality is a thing of the past. Well, if you want to check it out, just look in your trusty synonym finder under *spicy*; you'll find words like *racy, ribald, risky, suggestive,* and *vulgar*—and that's just a start. Check out *hot,* and the fun really begins: *sultry, torrid, passionate, libidinous, aroused, lustful.* I say, let's go! Maybe that's why the food revolution in the U.S. followed the sexual revolution? Maybe not.

In any case, to me this only increases the attraction of spices. While I started out just liking to cook and eat spicy food, I have ended up being deeply fascinated with the lore that surrounds spices, the epic quest to find them, and their generally exotic nature. And the hint that they might possibly cause me to lose control adds immeasurably to their gustatory appeal.

I guess the long and the short of it is that I think the spices that are liberally used in hot-weather food are wonderful. I also think the intense flavor dynamics that they add to food are underappreciated in America today. I would like the recipes in this book to serve as an introduction to spices and to spicy food. I would like to consider myself a kind of spice evangelist, trying to rekindle the lust once felt in the West for these awesome flavorings. Nowadays we know that spices aren't guarded by giant winged beasts or gathered from the rivers of Paradise, but that doesn't take a thing away from their ability to make every meal we eat a delicious, sensual, and slightly exotic experience. The way I see it, you gotta eat, so why not make it exciting?

THE PRACTICAL SPICE RAP

Now that I have pleaded the case for the importance and worth of culinary spices, let me pass on to you a few tips I have learned over the years about buying, storing, and preparing them.

So Exactly What Is a Spice, Anyway?

Unlike herbs—which, despite their variety, are all either leaves or stalks of green plants or trees—spices come in many guises. It's hard to pin them down to an exact definition, but I think it goes something like this: Spices are flavorings made from the nonleafy parts of plants and trees, including bark, as in cinnamon, the bark of a small evergreen tree; flowers, as in saffron, the stamen of the crocus flower; berries, as in allspice, the dried, unripe berry of the allspice tree; roots, as in ginger or galangal; buds, as in cloves, which are the dried, unopened buds of the clove tree; and seeds, as in cumin and coriander.

That may seem like a wide net to cast, but it simply points out the great variety of spices around the world. I'm sure that arguments can be made that this definition is not exactly correct, but it's the one I learned back at culinary school, and it seems like a good one to work with, so we're going with it.

Buying: Buy Whole

In countries such as India, where high-quality spices are crucial to good cooking, people buy them with the same care and enthusiasm that some American or French folks might devote to choosing wine. I think it makes sense to take a cue from these cultures and, whenever possible, buy spices whole. When you buy spices already powdered, their potency has a far shorter shelf life, so my suggestion is to buy whole and grind fresh. For grinding spices, you can purchase an electric spice mill or use a mortar and pestle, but I prefer an electric coffee grinder. (If you have previously used your coffee grinder for coffee, follow the advice of Corby Kummer of the *Atlantic Monthly* and whir a bit of sugar around in it to get rid of the coffee oils before you grind spices.)

Also, if you don't use a lot of spices, you should probably buy them in relatively small quantities. Dried spices do remain potent for months, but like most things in nature they lose some of their power over time.

Storing: Airtight, Dark, and Cool

Let's say that you have followed my advice and bought your spices whole, and the dish you have picked to make tonight calls for 2 tablespoons of ground cumin. While you're at it, you might as well grind up a larger batch and store it for future use. This makes the whole proposition easier—which means you're more likely to do it on a regular basis—and even if you store your ground spices for a few weeks, you're better off than you would be using the preground version you can buy in the store.

How should you store spices? Airtight, dark, and cool is the answer. I know that this kills the notion of those tidy rows of clear spice bottles lined up like soldiers on the rack, so here we are faced with the old dilemma of form versus content. If you ask me, grind the cumin and put it in a plastic bag with a tie or in a small jar, store it in a dark, cool place, and forget the spice display rack. The important thing about this stuff is not how it looks but how it tastes.

Preparing: Cook's Choice

Cooks use spices in hundreds of ways, but the people who have spent the most time thinking about this, as far as I can tell, are the cooks of India. In many ways, in that country dealing with spices is what being a cook is all about.

In Indian culture the options and variations in regard to using spices in food are legion. Spices are almost always cooked before they are added to a dish, but there are many ways to accomplish this. Sometimes whole spices are powdered and then sautéed in oil as the beginning of the cooking process; sometimes they are roasted whole in the oven, then powdered and added at the end of the cooking process; other times they may be sautéed whole and simply used that way.

Cooking spices releases their essential oils and therefore brings up their flavors. Because of this, in many recipes I call for spices to be cooked before they are used. In other recipes, however, they are added without being cooked first, because many of the cuisines of the Spice Zone regularly use uncooked spices. Since my cooking draws inspiration from hot-weather cuisines around the world, I like to stick with the spicing method appropriate to each individual dish. This means that in a dish like Cardamom Chicken Stew in the Indian Style (page 304), all the spices are sautéed right at the beginning of the cooking process, while in North African Lamb Stew with Sweet Potatoes and Couscous (page 323), some spices are sautéed and others not, and in Aromatic Southeast Asian Pork Stew (page 320), the spices are added uncooked to the pot.

When it comes to combining spices, there are very few hard-and-fast rules. Certain spices will overwhelm certain others, and there are clearly spice combinations that don't work well. But giving guidelines for combining spices is even more difficult than it is for combining herbs, where you can at least say, for example, that you should be wary of using rosemary with cilantro. In the case of spices, you have to learn by tasting and testing.

My advice is that you explore individual spices, use them often and heavily, get to know them, and then start combining them. To begin with, however, I recommend you use the spice mixtures in this book. Representing a wide range of tastes and techniques, they are the result of about 10 years of spice experimentation, for which I used the classic spice combinations of warm-weather cuisines as a jumping-off point. Once you have used these mixtures for a while, feel free to start making individual modifications and adjustments, either in proportion or composition. Always remember the golden rule of cooking: What is best is what tastes best to you.

A COOK'S NOTES: TOOLS, TECHNIQUES, AND A FEW TIPS

■

I cook for a living. I've been doing it for about 20 years. During that time I've worked in just about every kind of kitchen, from sub shops to banquet rooms, private yachts to cafeterias, fried-fish shacks to three-star restaurants. Along the way I managed to pick up some skills, and what I am trying to do here is transfer those skills so that you can make use of them without having to spend 20 years in professional kitchens. The vehicle for the transfer of this knowledge is the recipe, which functions as a blueprint does for a builder.

Duplicating a recipe can be difficult because the cooking process is full of variables, from the character of your ingredients to the heat of your fire. At the same time, as my friend and mentor, the outstanding chef from Washington, D.C., Bob Kinkead, used to say, "We're not talking about brain surgery here." It's not as if life and death were on the line.

After all, what are the worst things that can happen to you when you're cooking? Maybe the chicken thighs are not seared as perfectly as they might be, the onions are a bit undercooked, or the soup is a little watery. These are no great tragedies, and believe me when I tell you that you can go into any restaurant kitchen in the world any day of the week and see the same things happening.

So I advise you to relax with your cooking. Perfection is difficult to attain, and consistency is a constant struggle on any level. To my mind, cooking is a combination of trade and craft. When something is cooked properly, it may be wonderful and delicious and satisfying and entertaining and a whole host of other great qualities, but it is not a masterpiece of art like a great sculpture or painting. It is more like a well-crafted cabinet or a perfectly painted garage.

A recipe may result from individual creativity, but it is also governed by a body of scientific method and technique. What this means is that, to be a good cook, it helps to start with an understanding of the fundamentals. That helps you control the variables, which in turn will give you more confidence to let go and enjoy yourself.

First there are what we might call the individual physical variables—the freshness, girth, and juiciness of the tomatoes or peppers that you buy in your market, the size and composition of the pots and pans you cook with, the thickness of your cut of meat or piece of fish, the heat of your stove. All of these can have a great impact on the outcome of a dish.

Second, there are the variables of technique and experience. Someone who has grilled a thousand steaks can tell with a push of the finger when a sirloin is cooked to a perfect medium-rare; any cook from India or the Caribbean can peel, pit, and cut up a mango faster than most Americans can figure out where the pit is; a cook who has boned hundreds of chicken thighs will know precisely where to put the point of the knife to slide under the bone most easily.

In an effort to limit the variables as much as possible, I have provided some explanations of tools and techniques. I want you to feel comfortable enough to move a little within the framework of the recipe, leaving out an ingredient that you don't particularly like, for example. As always, remember that cooking should be relaxing and enjoyable and a meal should consist of much more than just food.

T O O L S

To be a good cook, you don't need a department store full of tools, just a few basic items. The following are the tools you will need to prepare the recipes in this book. We have also provided pictures and physical descriptions of the pots and pans we call for, so that when we say, for example, that something should be cooked in "a large stockpot," you will know what to use. Just cutting down on the variables.

Small Stuff

Heavy-duty spring-loaded tongs, both long- and short-handled. The long-handled version is essential for grilling; the short-handled one is great for hundreds of kitchen uses.

Three types of knives:

Paring

6-inch boning knife

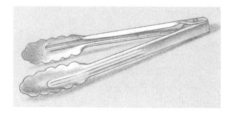

French chef's knife
(8 to 10 inches)

A handful of wooden spoons
Another handful of big metal spoons
Skewers, wooden and metal
Peelers
A whisk
A grater
A sturdy pepper mill
Measuring spoons
A measuring cup
A pastry brush
A small instant-read thermometer
A candy thermometer

Other Useful Items

Strainer
Colander
Heavy-duty cake or drying racks
Frying basket
Lots of little ceramic cups or glass bowls for holding ingredients, so you can have everything chopped and measured before you begin cooking.

Appliances

These are optional but definitely worth having:

Cuisinart or other food processor or good-quality blender

**Spice grinder
Mortar and pestle**
if you are a "back to the roots" type of cook

Pots and Pans

Obviously you don't need to have all of these. One stockpot is fine, for example. But since the cooking time in a recipe is directly related to the size of the pot in which the cooking is done, you will need to adjust your cooking times if you use a different size than the recipe specifies. For example, if a recipe says to cook for half an hour in a small stockpot and you use a large stockpot, you will have more surface area and therefore quicker liquid reduction, so you might need to add more liquid or cook for a shorter time. To guide you, here is what we mean:

Stockpots

Small: 8 quarts
Medium: 12 quarts
Large: 16 quarts

Sauté Pans and Cast-Iron Skillets

Small: 10-inch diameter
Medium: 12-inch diameter
Large: 14-inch diameter

Roasting Pans

Small: 14 inches long
Medium: 16 inches long
Large: 18 inches long

Saucepans

Small: 1 quart
Medium: 2½ quarts
Large: 4½ quarts
Wide-mouthed saucepan for braising: 6 quarts

A Pretty Grill Is Like a Melody

I am generally very agreeable about anything having to do with cooking—whatever works best for you is okay with me. When it comes to grills, however, I put on my game face and become uncompromising.

Grilling is a high-heat method of cooking. If you can't get intense heat, you can't get the quick, deep sear that gives grilling its unique, ineffable flavor. In my experience, gas grills are acceptable, but I prefer a live fire for its higher heat as well as the flavor it imparts. Stovetop grills are even further from what I like in grilling. They sound like a great idea—who wouldn't like to be able to grill inside in the winter without any mess or fuss? But these devices generate so little heat that you basically end up sautéing at best.

Besides, to my mind the best way to get a smoky, seared flavor is to use some form of wood or wood-based product. Gas is convenient, but it carries no flavor, the way wood smoke does. I also think that building and messing around with the fire is part of what makes grilling so much fun. So, I guess you could say that, in this one regard, I'm something of a purist: Grilling is best done over a live fire on a grill that lets you use a wood product as the fuel.

When it comes to selecting a particular grill, however, I revert to form: To a large extent the best grill for you is a matter of personal preference. There are all types of grills on the market, from tabletop hibachis you can pick up for about five dollars at any convenience store to sleek, architecturally significant models that sell for upward of a thousand. Any of them will do the job. The one critical factor is the size of the grilling surface; the larger the surface, the easier it is to move food around to hotter and cooler spots during cooking. I recommend that you buy the largest grill that will fit in your cooking area. Also, in general, covered grills such as the classic Weber kettle are somewhat more versatile than open grills because they allow you to simulate slow-cooking methods like roasting, smoking, and barbecuing.

Pass Me Those Dice

This is not about a tool, but I'm sticking it in here because it is another attempt to limit the variables having to do with size. In many recipes we refer to "dice," which are not the cubes with which you play Monopoly and games of chance, but the cubes into which you chop vegetables, fruits, and other ingredients. Just so we are playing the same game, you should know what we mean when we specify sizes.

Small, as in "1 red bell pepper, diced small," refers to pieces about this size:

Medium refers to pieces about this size:

Large refers to pieces about this size:

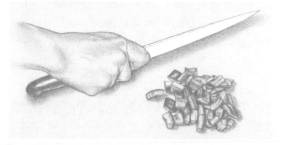

Recipes tell you how to cook something. As a part of this instruction, they usually specify a particular cooking technique, such as grilling, sautéing, or roasting, and leave it at that. Each of these techniques, however, has certain principles that will give the best result if followed. An improperly sautéed fish, for example, will be soggy and greasy rather than tender and crisp, and a steak grilled over a low fire will be tasteless and tough.

Although the dishes in this book are inspired by flavors and ingredients from many places around the world, the basic techniques remain the same. Here is a guide to the principal cooking methods we use in this book.

Grilling

I'm going to begin with grilling for two reasons: First, it is my favorite way to cook food and the most common cooking method in the countries whose food I like best, so lots of the recipes in this book call for it. Second, since grilling is such a dynamic method, in which you deal with the heat source as well as the actual cooking, there are more variables involved. This means it is particularly important to understand the technique, which can vastly improve the result, so there is a need for more detail than on the other methods.

In grilling, food is placed within a few inches of a very hot live fire and is quickly cooked by conduction, concentrating the juices in the middle of the food while searing the outside. During the searing process, the high heat produces a browning and a concentration of flavor that is the cornerstone of the taste of grilled food—the essence of what we all think of as grilled flavor. This complex browning reaction is known as the Maillard reaction.

For you scientifically minded folks, the Maillard reaction takes place when high heat is applied to a carbohydrate unit in the presence of sugar. The heat causes the carbohydrate to combine with a portion of an amino acid, all of which leads to the formation of an entirely new substance and a host of by-products. In this way the Maillard reaction is like another of my favorite chemical reactions, fermentation, which also creates a whole batch of new substances, each with its own taste, so that you get a very complex flavor overall.

More important from the point of view of the griller, the Maillard reaction creates what food scientist and author Harold McGee describes as "a full, intense flavor," the characteristic "browned" taste that cannot be achieved through any other process. The Maillard reaction takes place whenever food is browned, but to me it seems most intense—and therefore most flavorful—in grilling.

The Food: Because grilling is a means of cooking quickly over high heat, you should grill only foods that will cook to the desired degree of doneness on the interior before being turned to cinders on the exterior. Tender cuts of meat with little connective tissue, like steaks, chops, and smaller pieces of chicken, are excellent choices, as are firm-textured fish like tuna, swordfish, and mahimahi. In the crustacean department, shrimp, scallops, and lobster are great grill material. Just avoid trying to grill foods that are too mushy, such as tofu; too delicate, like cod, flounder, and sole; too tough, like stew beef; or too large, such as a roast beef.

Fuel for the Fire: Once you've selected your food, it's time to start the fire. There are several acceptable fuels, but my personal choice is lump hardwood charcoal. Because it is almost pure carbon, without any of the fillers and chemicals that are included in charcoal briquettes, hardwood charcoal starts more easily, burns hotter and cleaner, and responds more quickly to changes in oxygen, which means you can control your fire more easily.

Of course, you can always use the true original, plain old hardwood. This is a great fuel, but be aware that it burns unpredictably and does not always yield a proper bed of coals, so using it for fuel increases the ever-present danger of incinerating your dinner. It's exciting, but you may end up serving a plateful of ashes for dinner unless you know what you're doing.

Whichever fuel you choose, you should lay a bed that is about 3 inches deep at the center, tapers out to about 1½ inches at the edges, and is larger in surface area than the total surface area of the food you are planning to grill. This way, you will end up a very hot center and a cooler periphery, and can shift food between them to regulate its cooking.

Fanning the Flames: To ignite this well-laid fire, you have two good options. Oval-shaped electric fire starters are reliable, quick, and energy-efficient. Even better, however, is the fire chimney. You can buy one in most hardware stores, or you can easily make your own by taking both ends off a large coffee can and punching a few holes around the bottom rim. To use it, simply crumple up some newspaper and place it in the bottom of the chimney, fill the chimney to the top with charcoal, and light the newspaper. The laws of physics will send the flames sweeping up through the charcoal, and in about five minutes you will have a can full of blazing fuel. Spread this out in the center of your grill, top with other charcoal, and go have a cool one while you wait for the whole shebang to ignite.

Judging the Temperature: Once your fire is lit, it will take about forty minutes to work up to the fiery-red stage and then die down until all the coals are covered with a fine gray ash. When the fire has reached this point, test the temperature to make sure it is appropriate for the food you are cooking. Most seafood, for example, is happiest over a medium fire, while steak does best over a very high, searing heat.

To check the fire temperature, simply hold your hand about 5 inches above the cooking surface. If you can hold it there for 5 to 6 seconds, you have a low fire; 3 to 4 seconds, a medium fire; and 1 to 2 seconds, a hot fire.

That's basically all there is to it—you're ready to get out there and grill.

Sautéing

Like grilling, sautéing is a quick, high-heat cooking method. As such, it is also reserved for smaller, thinner, more tender cuts of meat or fish. Smaller and/or thinner because the high heat would cause a larger piece of meat or fish to burn on the outside long before being cooked on the inside; tender because the quickness of the process does not allow time for the collagen (the tough stuff) to break down during cooking. The goal of sautéing is to quickly drive the juices to the center of whatever you are cooking while the surface is attaining a flavorful browning—sort of like extended searing.

The key to success in this process takes place at the very beginning: heating a small amount of oil until it is "hot but not smoking" before you begin to sear. I have always wondered how you were supposed to know when the oil was *about* to start smoking, but there's really no better way to describe it. The problem, as usual, comes with the variables: Different oils have different "smoking points" and different points at which they burn. Since you can't stick your finger in the oil to find out if it's hot enough, the way to test it is to dip a corner of whatever you're cooking into the oil. You should see some heavy sizzling action if the oil is at the proper heat.

Basically, the two keys to successful sautéing are to use the right amount of oil, which is just enough to coat the bottom of the pan you're cooking in, and to make sure the oil is really hot before you begin.

Braising and Stewing

These two techniques are generally reserved for tough cuts of meat filled with lots of the connective tissues known as collagen. Both techniques are principally the same: Food is cooked with moist heat at low temperatures for long periods of time. This process allows the tough, stringy collagen in the meat to be turned into gelatin, which is tender.

Braising, which consists of cooking in a closed container with liquid that comes about halfway up the side of whatever you're cooking, is usually used for large cuts, like pot roast, lamb shoulder, or veal shanks. Stewing, which may be done covered or uncovered and in which the food is completely covered with liquid, is used for smaller pieces, such as stew beef or cut-up pork shoulder.

An important key to making good meat-based stews and braises is properly searing the meat before adding the liquid. Originally people thought that searing sealed the juices in the meat, but it turns out that is not true. What the process *does* do, however, is add a tremendous amount of flavor, once again through that complex chemical event known as the Maillard reaction. This flavor is transferred into the liquid during cooking.

So, to have a tasty, tender braise or stew, always sear heavily and cook at low temperatures, either at a simmer on top of the stove or at a low temperature in the oven for a long time. Stews and braises are done when the meat has become tender.

Frying

Frying has earned what I think is an undeserved bad reputation. This is partly the result of the healthy food movement, and partly the result of lazy fry cooks the world around who don't heat their oil properly or change it often enough. I maintain that a properly fried piece of food tastes great, is less filling, and really is not that high on the bad-for-you scale. Oil is simply a medium for cooking, and if you have that medium at the proper temperature, the resulting food will be crispy, not greasy.

The key, then, is beginning with and maintaining the proper oil temperature, which is around 350°F. If the oil is much hotter than that, the exterior of your food will fry while the interior remains raw; much cooler, and the oil will penetrate the surface of whatever you are cooking, making it soggy and greasy rather than crispy—which is where frying's bad reputation comes in. To keep the oil at a relatively uniform temperature, you should avoid crowding the pan. Better to cook in several batches than to have greasy food.

The type of oil you use is not really important as far as flavor is concerned because oil is just a cooking medium and, if you are frying right, not much of it will be absorbed. All you need is an oil that can reach and maintain the proper temperature without breaking down. Any vegetable oil has this capability. I recommend peanut or soy because they are less expensive than other types and do the job just as well.

Roasting

What is referred to as roasting today used to be called baking. In classic French culinary terms, *roasting* is defined as cooking large pieces of meat over live fire, while cooking something in an oven is baking. However, since it sounds a lot better to serve up a "roast pork loin" than a "baked pork loin," let's forget formality and stick with the common nomenclature.

The meats that are the best candidates for roasting are large cuts relatively free of tough connective tissues—lamb leg, pork loin, or rib roast, for example—so they don't have to cook for a long time to be tender. In fact, overcooking makes these cuts tougher as well as drier.

Roasts are generally seared at a high initial temperature, either on top of the stove or in the oven, and then cooked at a lower temperature in the oven. The sear is for flavor enhancement (there's Maillard again). I like to roast a little hotter than some folks—say, around 400°F rather than the usual 350°F—because it increases the surface sear.

The easiest way to test roasts for doneness is with a meat thermometer; because the cuts of meat are large, there is no other good way to tell what is happening inside them. Here is a chart showing you the temperatures at which beef is considered to be rare to well done. Remember that meat will rise an additional 5° to 7°F after you take it out of the oven, so remove the meat you are roasting when it is still a few degrees lower than the final temperature you want.

ROASTING CHART

Degree of Doneness	Appearance	Temperature at Which to Remove from Oven
Black and blue (very rare)	Cool center	118°F
Rare	Raw in center	122°F
Medium rare	Red in center, slightly warm	127°F
Medium	Pink in center	134°F
Well done	Gray in center	143°F

Cooking in Citrus Juice

This technique is much less familiar to most of us, but it is a widely used traditional method of cooking seafood in Central and South America and parts of Asia. Basically, it involves putting seafood into acidic citrus juice and leaving it there until the acid has "cooked" the protein in the food by causing the protein molecules to denature, or unwind. Lemon juice may be used as the cooking agent, but the more acidic lime juice is most often used.

It may seem odd to cook food without heat, but the chemical process that takes place is largely the same in both cases. In any case, to my mind, cooking with citrus juice is a lot less bizarre than microwaving, which cooks food from the inside out without heating up the plate you're cooking on!

Using Spice Rubs

Rubbing food with spice mixtures prior to cooking is a key technique in creating the spicy, high-flavor food in this book. When food that has been rubbed with a spice mixture is cooked, the rub creates a super-flavorful, slightly crunchy crust on the outside, while the interior retains its own distinct flavor. To me, there is no better way to achieve big flavor.

I first came across rubs at the barbecue pits of the South, where I grew up. Before a beef brisket or pork shoulder undergoes the long, slow cooking of the barbecue process, it is rubbed with a blend of spices that every pit master refers to as "mah special secret rub." I loved the contrast between the spicy crust and the rich, moist interior of the meat and became hooked on the idea of rubs at an early age.

As a result, when I began to discover the spice mixtures of hot-weather cuisines, it seemed only natural to me to rub them on the outside of food before I cooked it. If I was doing a North African–inspired dish, for example, I would make a rub inspired by the flavors of *ras al hanout,* the traditional Moroccan spice blend; if I was making a dish featuring Indian flavors and techniques, I would make a rub featuring the ingredients of an Indian masala. The inspiration provided by the wonderful spice mixtures of the world brought dry rubbing to a new level of intensity and taste.

As far as I have been able to discover, rubbing is not a traditional use for these spice combinations; for the most part, these mixtures were created as seasonings for soups or stews or as the base for condiment-like sauces and pastes to accompany grains and legumes. Some cuisines do have certain wet spice pastes that were traditionally used to coat food prior to cooking, such as the Yucatecan spice pastes that Rick and Deann Bayless included in their wonderful cookbook *Authentic Mexican* (Morrow, 1987). But as far as I can tell, the widespread use of dry rubs to coat food before cooking is a recently developed culinary technique.

I like to think of this technique as a kind of dry marinating. I find the use of rubs or spice pastes far preferable to traditional marinating because, in my experience, marinades only penetrate food a little bit, so they don't flavor the entire piece of meat or fish. On the other hand, they don't maintain their own taste very well either; the flavors of both the marinade and the food on which it is used become somewhat muddied.

With rubs—especially when you are using high-heat cooking techniques like grilling and sautéing—the spicy crust provides a great flavor contrast to the interior, which is largely unaffected and maintains the pure taste of the unadorned ingredient. Rubs also result in finished dishes with much stronger and more well-defined flavors than marinades, because the mixtures are most often composed of spices undiluted by liquids and because they adhere to the surface of foods better than marinades do. Finally, rubs are easier— all you have to do is rub them on and cook—and don't require a soaking time, as marinades do. (Since I don't think marinades really do much in the tenderizing department, there's no need to worry about losing that feature, either.)

SELECTED SPICE MIXTURES OF THE WORLD

MIXTURE	COUNTRY OF ORIGIN	TRADITIONAL USE	FORM	CHARACTERISTIC SPICES
BUMBU	Indonesia	Used to flavor rendangs and gulais, spicy dishes served with sauce	Dry spice mixture is combined with coconut milk prior to use	Ginger, turmeric, chiles, cinnamon, cloves, coriander, black peppercorns
RAS AL HANOUT	Morocco	All-purpose flavoring powder	Whole spices ground together	10 to 15 ingredients, usually including allspice, cloves, cumin, cardamom, chiles, ginger, peppercorns, mace, turmeric, and caraway seeds
BERBERÉ	Ethiopia	Cure for meats, added to condiments and stews	Ingredients are mixed together, then simmered prior to use	Chiles, cardamom, cumin, black pepper, fenugreek, allspice, ginger, cloves, coriander
HARISSA	Tunisia, Morocco, Algeria	All-purpose condiment, also used to flavor stews and sauces	Whole spices are ground together, then mixed with olive oil to moisten	Chiles, caraway, cumin, coriander, garlic
BAHARAT	Middle East (Lebanon, Syria, Gulf States, Saudi Arabia)	Whole spices ground together	Widely used to flavor all types of dishes, particularly soups and stews	Cloves, nutmeg, cinnamon, coriander, black pepper, paprika
CURRY POWDER	Southern India	Used to flavor thin, soupy sauces	Freshly ground spices are sautéed in oil at beginning of cooking process	Curry leaves, turmeric, chiles, coriander, black pepper, and sometimes cumin, ginger, fenugreek, cinnamon, cloves, nutmeg, and fennel seed

MIXTURE	COUNTRY OF ORIGIN	TRADITIONAL USE	FORM	CHARACTERISTIC SPICES
GARAM MASALA	Northern India	Usually added at end of cooking to complete seasoning	Spices are roasted whole, then ground into a powder	Cinnamon, cardamom, cloves, cumin seeds, coriander, black peppercorns, nutmeg, mace
PANCH PHORON (Indian 5-Spice Mix)	Eastern India—Bengal	All-purpose flavoring for vegetable dishes	Sautéed in hot oil prior to cooking	Whole cumin seeds, fennel seeds, fenugreek, parsley seeds, black mustard seeds
GAENG WAN (Green Curry Paste)	Thailand	All-purpose flavoring, widely used in soups and sauces	Ingredients are ground together in mortar and pestle to form a wet paste	Green chiles, turmeric, lemongrass, ginger, coriander, cumin, white peppercorns
MASSAMAN PASTE	Thailand	All-purpose flavoring, widely used in soups and sauces	Ingredients are ground together in mortar and pestle to form a wet paste	Chiles, coriander, cumin, cinnamon, cloves, star anise, cardamom, white peppercorns
RECADO	Yucatán Peninsula of Mexico	Rubbed on food prior to cooking, also used as all-purpose flavoring for sauces and stews	Spices are pounded to a paste in combination with vinegar, garlic, and herbs	Achiote, cloves, black pepper, chiles, allspice, cinnamon
FIVE-SPICE POWDER	China	Used as flavoring in wide variety of Chinese dishes; frequently used in marinades	Whole spices are ground into a raw powder	Anise, fennel seeds, cloves, cinnamon, peppercorns
QUATRE SPICES	France	Most often used in pâtés	Spices are combined and then ground into a powder	Pepper, nutmeg, cloves, ginger, sometimes cinnamon

MIXTURE	COUNTRY OF ORIGIN	TRADITIONAL USE	FORM	CHARACTERISTIC SPICES
PICKLING SPICES	Europe	Used to add flavor to pickles and certain liquids	Raw whole spices	Mustard seeds, cloves, coriander seeds, mace, black peppercorns, allspice, ginger, chiles
CAJUN BLACKENING SPICES	Louisiana, U.S.A.	Used to coat fish prior to cooking	Ground raw spices	Mustard seeds, cumin, paprika, cayenne pepper, black pepper
CRAB or SHRIMP BOIL	Chespeake Bay, U.S.A.	Thrown in water used for boiling crab or shrimp	Ground raw spices	Peppercorns, mustard seeds, coriander, salt, cloves, ginger, ground bay leaves
BARBECUE RUB	Southern and western United States	Rubbed on meats prior to cooking	Ground raw spices	Any combination of cumin, chiles, cloves, cinnamon, mustard seeds, paprika, and brown sugar

When you use a rub, take small handfuls (you have to use your hands for this—no other tool works as well) and coat the entire surface of the food you are about to cook. Use a little bit of pressure to rub the spices in (that's why they call it a rub, after all), mixing the spices slightly with some of the liquid from the flesh so they adhere. When you start to cook, don't worry when the rub turns dark brown; this is what happens to spices when they are cooked. As long as the rub doesn't begin to smoke, you are all right.

To give you an understanding of the origins of some of our spice rub inspirations, I have included above a table of several classic spice combinations of the world and their traditional uses. Because I think it's fun to know these things, I've also included information about their places of origin, the form in which they are usually found, and the range of ingredients that may be found in them. The main point to remember, however, is that this simple technique results in food with deep, intense, spicy flavors. It is a great way to explore the varied flavor footprints of Spice Zone cuisines, and I recommend that you use it often.

I think that in any field of endeavor there are a few very simple stratagems that make a huge difference in the outcome. I would bet this is true about lawyering or teaching. I know it's true about cooking.

These simple techniques are the ones that I plead with cooks on a daily basis to do. Although they might sound painfully obvious, they can really help make your cooking easier and your food better-tasting.

1. Salt and pepper just about everything. An integral part of every cook's set-up should be two bowls containing kosher salt and freshly cracked black pepper. It is with good reason that both of these have been used as currency at times in history. Salt is the flavor enhancer of choice in the West, and black pepper is the spice to which we most closely relate.

Now, I know that some of you will think that, for health reasons, it is rash to advise salting most everything. However, the latest research seems to indicate that salt is a danger only to that 10 to 15 percent or so of the population who have a genetic condition in which salt leads to high blood pressure. I certainly don't mean to minimize that, but I do think that we can relax a bit about eliminating salt from our diets. In any case, the best way to cut down on salt is to eat fewer processed foods, as they are usually heavily salted. I'm not suggesting you oversalt food, but I think it is very important to season meat and fish before cooking. It makes a tremendous difference in the final taste.

I prefer kosher salt or sea salt because I like the texture and, don't ask me why, I think it tastes better. As for pepper, there is no comparison between freshly cracked pepper-corns and stale pepper. Get yourself a good pepper grinder, or if you prefer you can crack large batches by putting them on a cutting board or other hard surface and rolling the edge of a sauté pan over them.

2. Buy good ingredients. Years ago a chef told me something that I have found to be consistently true: "If you buy good ingredients," he said, "all you have to do is keep from screwing them up and your food will be great."

In fact, buying ingredients of the best quality is the foundation of any good meal. It stands to reason that if you start out with lousy ingredients, you are severely restricting your chances of making it taste good. This is particularly important with seafood. There is no substitute for finding a good fishmonger, building a relationship with him or her, asking what is freshest when you go to buy, and building your meal around that product.

3. Learn how to check for doneness. "How long should I cook it?" is one of the toughest questions in all of cooking. The answer, of course, is "until it's done."

To provide you with a rough guideline, I have given cooking times with all the recipes in this book, but they are only approximate. There is no substitute for having an understanding of doneness and how to check for it. "Feeling for firmness" is the classic explanation of how this should be done, which is fine if you're someone who cooks 50 or 60 steaks a night. But since few of us are in that position, I'll let you in on a technique that all the pros use; it's known as the "Nick, peek, and cheat" method.

As the name implies, you simply pick up one piece of whatever you are cooking, cut it open, and check its state of doneness. I know people say that this lets all the juices run out, but it's not like we're talking about putting a hole in a water bottle or something. The small amount of juices you may lose pales in comparison to serving raw or burned food. In fact, this method really does not hurt the food, and if you feel that it mars its perfect appearance, keep the tested portion for yourself. Of course, if you prefer, you can adopt the attitude that prevents many men from asking directions while driving. To do so, however, is to run a distinct risk of serving raw chicken or shoe-leather pork.

What you see when you nick and peek will determine whether the food is done, but naturally it will differ with different foods.

Fish is easy. It is very malleable, so it's easy to get a look inside by bending or otherwise maneuvering it. What you are looking for is a consistent opacity—that is, the interior flesh should be completely white rather than translucent. Of course, remember that with a thicker piece of fish there will be a bit of carryover cooking after you remove it from the heat, so I would leave just a trace of translucence near the center to prevent overcooking.

With red meat, it's a matter of taste. Since opinions about what is "done" run the gamut from dead raw to completely gray, you simply need to look inside to see when the meat is to your liking. Just remember that carryover cooking will bring it up one degree of doneness after you remove it from the heat, so if you want it medium rare, remove it when it still looks rare, and so on. For large cuts of red meat, of course, you will need to use a meat thermometer and refer to the chart on page xxix.

Chicken and other fowl are like fish: You want the flesh to be opaque throughout. Duck is the exception, since many people like their duck breast rare. Prior to using the peek and cheat method with fowl, you can also cut into a piece at the joint and check to see if the juices run clear. If they do, it's a good indication that the bird is done.

4. Be prepared, organized, and clean. Yes, it's true, cooks and Boy Scouts have similar goals. The French call it *mise en place,* which roughly translates as "everything in its place." Before the meat hits the fire, the pan, or the roasting rack, you've gotta be ready. You can't stop to chop the parsley or grind the cumin in the middle of a fast sauté.

Before you start to cook, organize your tools and your ingredients. Little cups or bowls are perfect for setting out individual ingredients so they'll be at hand when you're ready for them. Believe me, the time you spend getting everything together will allow you to cook in a more relaxed atmosphere and enjoy both the cooking and any guests who happen to be around. As I always say, "Work smarter, not harder."

Finally, I know it's not really any of my business, but I can't help myself. Some call me compulsive, but I have to say it: "Keep your work area clean at all times." It makes cooking easier and more fun . . . at least for us compulsive types.

5. The Number-One Principle: Relax and have fun. Translation: Always have the pizza delivery guy's phone number handy. Seriously, what's the worst that can happen? After all, you can't get fired. I spent most of my early cooking days trying to fix food that I had screwed up, and it usually turned out okay. There's not a cook in the world who doesn't mess things up on a regular basis. So ignore all those pictures of food you see in books and magazines. It takes a whole crew of folks several hours to make the food look that good, and half the time you can't even eat it.

Don't worry if the dish you're cooking doesn't come out perfect; you're off work and you're supposed to be having fun. Put on some music, fix your favorite beverage, and make the food a part of the celebration, not the be-all and end-all. I think you'll find that it tastes great even if it doesn't look like the cover of a magazine.

Musky Mellow Gazpacho ▪ Shrimp and Sweet Potato Soup ▪ Aromatic Grilled Shrimp Broth with Lemongrass ▪ Shrimp and Corn Chowder with Yucca ▪ Clear Soup with Pan-Seared Scallops and Lime ▪ Smoked Eggplant and Tomato Soup with Rosemary-Garlic Butter ▪ Lemon-Garlic Grouper Ceviche ▪ Lime-Cooked Rare Tuna with Southeast Asian Flavors ▪ Spice-Rubbed Grilled Giant Shrimp Skewers with Peaches and Hot Chiles ▪ Escabeche of Mackerel with Mangoes and Potatoes ▪ Red Snapper Cooked in Lemon with Coconut Milk and Shredded Green Mango ▪ Corn-Crusted Panfried Shrimp with Sweet and Hot Seared Onions ▪ Molasses-Glazed, Peanut-Crusted Grilled Shrimp with Napa Cabbage and Sesame Vinaigrette ▪ Grilled Scallops with Green Bread Sauce ▪ Grilled Squid with Spicy Almond Sauce ▪ Tommy's Complicated Grilled Spicy Thai Chicken Sticks with Coconut-Peanut Dipping Sauce ▪ Grilled Chicken Thighs with Persian-Style Nut Rub ▪ Grilled Chicken-Chipotle Quesadillas with Cheddar ▪ Barbecued Duck Legs with Basil, Coconut Milk, Chiles, and Green Peppercorns ▪ Raw Beef with Ginger and Cardamom and Grilled Chile-Garlic Toast ▪ Beer-Battered Fried Clams with Ginger-Soy Dipping Sauce ▪ Sweet Potato–Onion Pancakes ▪ Southeast Asian Shrimp and Pork Salad ▪ Warm Barley Salad with Smoked Salmon and Grapes ▪ Chile-Yucca Fritters ▪ Black-eyed Pea Fritters with Joey's Seared Collards ▪ Grilled Pork- and Shrimp-Stuffed Chiles with Sweet Soy Glaze ▪ Fried Shrimp and Pork Toasts ▪ Grilled Regular Mushrooms on Cornmeal Mush ▪ Grilled Foie Gras on Toast ▪ Smoky Eggplant Dip with Yogurt and Grilled Pita ▪ Spicy Roasted Red Pepper Dip with Grilled Pita ▪ Spicy Pumpkin Dip ▪ Grilled Figs and Tomatoes with Olives and Feta

SOUPS, SMALL DISHES, AND APPETIZERS

What some people call appetizers, I have always thought of as "small dishes." To me that is a real difference, because the ones I like best have more in common with the street food you can find all over the world—roasted corn in Peru, brothy seafood soups in Thailand, noodles with pickled mango in Malaysia—than with the laboriously constructed first courses you get in fancy restaurants.

No matter what you call these small dishes, today there is a trend toward creating a meal out of several of them rather than having a classic appetizer-entrée progression. This makes perfect sense to me: You can sample more dishes that way, you can more easily get just enough to suit your appetite of the moment, and for some reason these smaller dishes seem to inspire the most adventurous combinations of ingredients and flavors.

Of course, any one of these little dishes is also great by itself or in the classic appetizer role. As usual, the only rule should be to do what best fits your mood and desires.

Musky Mellow Gazpacho

Gazpacho started out in Spain as a bread-based soup but has evolved into a tomato-based soup with a kind of chopped-up salad in it. My version takes advantage of the common tropical practice of using fruits as vegetables when they're underripe. I use papayas and avocados, both of which have a rich kind of muskiness that is cut by the acidity of the tomato and lime juices.

METHOD

In a large bowl, mix all the ingredients gently. Allow to stand, covered and refrigerated, for at least 2 hours—4 to 6 hours is ideal. Will keep for up to 4 days, covered and refrigerated.

Serving Suggestion:

This makes a wonderful summer starter for just about any grilled dinner.

6 cups tomato juice

²/₃ cup papaya juice (you may substitute mango or pineapple juice)

2 slightly underripe papayas, peeled, seeded, and diced medium (you may substitute slightly underripe mangoes)

2 avocados, peeled, pitted, and diced medium

½ red bell pepper, diced small

½ green bell pepper, diced small

½ red onion, diced small

3 tablespoons lime juice (about 1½ limes)

4 dashes Tabasco sauce

3 tablespoons chopped fresh cilantro

Salt and freshly cracked black pepper to taste

Shrimp and Sweet Potato Soup

This quick, brothy soup is light and aromatic in the tropical tradition of hot soups for a hot day. Keeping the cooking time relatively short allows the components to retain their separate identities, which is why the shrimp are added at the last minute.

METHOD

1. In a large stockpot over medium-high heat, heat the oil until hot but not smoking. Add the onions and sauté, stirring occasionally, until translucent and just beginning to take on some color, 5 to 7 minutes. Add the chiles, garlic, chili powder, cumin, and paprika and continue to sauté, stirring constantly, for 1 minute.

2. Add the clam juice, water, and sweet potatoes, bring to a boil, reduce the heat to very low, and simmer for 20 to 30 minutes, or until the potatoes are easily pierced by a fork but still offer some resistance.

3. Add the shrimp, remove from the heat, and stir in the ¼ cup of oregano. Garnish each bowl with shredded cabbage, diced red onion, and a sprinkling of oregano.

1 tablespoon vegetable oil

2 yellow onions, diced small

2 tablespoons minced fresh red or green chile pepper of your choice

3 tablespoons minced garlic

2 tablespoons chili powder

2 tablespoons ground cumin

1 tablespoon paprika

1 quart bottled clam juice

1 quart water

3 large sweet potatoes, peeled and diced small

1½ pounds medium-size (16/20 count) shrimp, shelled, deveined, and sliced in half lengthwise

¼ cup chopped fresh oregano plus 2 tablespoons for garnish

½ head green cabbage, shredded, for garnish

1 red onion, finely diced, for garnish

Salt and freshly cracked black pepper to taste

Peeling and Deveining Shrimp

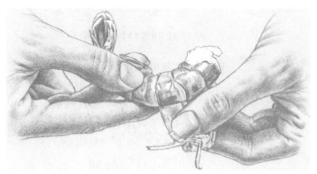

Peeling shrimp

Finishing peeling tail

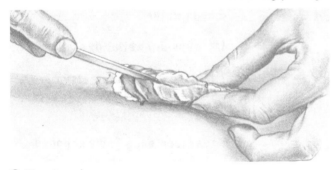

Cutting to vein

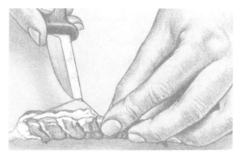

Discarding vein

Aromatic Grilled Shrimp Broth with Lemongrass

In the tropics people tend to drink hot liquids as a way to cool off from the intense heat. Hot tea, for instance, is favored over cold sodas or beers as a lunch drink by those in the know. In that mode, this heady broth is outstanding for a hot day. The unique Southeast Asian flavor of lemongrass combines with the equatorial standards of lime and cilantro, and the slightly smoky dimension of the grilled shrimp makes a nice contrast to the flowery broth.

4 teaspoons sesame oil

2 stalks lemongrass, tough upper leaves and outer stalk removed and reserved, inner portion of bulb (bottom ⅓ of stalk) very finely minced

12 ounces medium-size (16/20 count) shrimp (about 12), shelled and deveined, with shells reserved

1 tablespoon minced garlic

1 teaspoon minced ginger

1 teaspoon minced fresh red or green chile pepper of your choice

3 cups water

1½ cups dry white wine

1 tablespoon tomato catsup

½ cup bottled clam juice

1 teaspoon each finely chopped fresh mint, cilantro, and basil

Salt and freshly cracked white pepper to taste

1 lime, halved

METHOD

1. In a large saucepan, heat the sesame oil over medium-high heat until hot but not smoking. Roughly chop the upper leaves and outer stalk of the lemongrass and add to the pot along with the shrimp shells. Sauté until the shells turn red, 1 to 2 minutes. Add the garlic and ginger and sauté an additional 2 minutes, stirring occasionally.

2. Add the chile, water, wine, and catsup, bring just to a boil, and simmer over low heat for 45 minutes. Remove from heat, strain, discard solids, and add the clam juice to the broth.

3. Meanwhile, grill the shrimp over a medium-hot fire for 3 to 4 minutes per side. If a grill is not available, you may sauté the shrimp over medium heat for 4 to 5 minutes, turning occasionally.

4. Remove the shrimp from the heat, cut them in half lengthwise, and add them to the clear hot broth. Stir in the minced lemongrass bulb, mint, cilantro, basil, salt, and pepper and add a squeeze of lime juice just before serving.

Peeling lemongrass

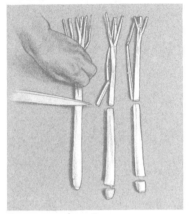

Sectioning lemongrass

Chopping lemongrass

Serving Suggestions:

For a perfect lunch on the hottest day of the summer, I would serve this spicy broth with Sweet and Hot Sesame-Spinach Condiment (page 362) and Red Potato and Cucumber Salad with Mango (page 202).

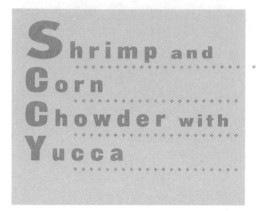

Shrimp and Corn Chowder with Yucca

1 quart milk

1 quart bottled clam juice

2 cups water

2 tablespoons paprika

2 pounds medium-size (16/20 count) shrimp, shelled, deveined, tails removed, and cut in half lengthwise, with shells reserved

4 slices bacon, cut into bite-size pieces

1 yellow onion, diced small

2 stalks celery, diced small

1 tablespoon minced garlic

1 cup corn kernels (from about 3 ears corn)

1 cup peeled and diced yucca (about 2 yuccas; you may substitute sweet potatoes)

Salt and freshly cracked black pepper to taste

Okay, okay, so this isn't your traditional chowder. But in some ways it actually is. I mean, how do you define a chowder? Lots of people will tell you that it is a milk-based corn or shellfish soup that also contains bacon, onions, and a starchy vegetable of some sort. If we accept that general definition, this dish qualifies.

Anyway, I think this is a good example of a dish that uses a traditional form with unusual ingredients. It's easy once you know the rules, and the melding of the rich flavors of shrimp and bacon with the freshness of corn and the starchy yucca is fantastic.

METHOD

1. In a large stockpot, combine the milk, clam juice, water, paprika, and shrimp shells. Bring to a boil over medium-high heat, reduce the heat to low, and simmer for 20 minutes. Strain, discarding the shrimp shells, and reserve the liquid.

2. In the same stockpot, cook the bacon over medium-high heat until crisp, about 7 minutes, then remove and drain on paper towels or brown paper bags.

3. Drain all but about 2 tablespoons of bacon fat from the pot. Add the onion and celery and cook, stirring frequently, until the onion is transparent, 5 to 7 minutes. Add the garlic and cook, stirring frequently, for 1 minute more.

4. Add the corn, yucca, and reserved liquid and bring to a boil. Reduce the heat to low and simmer for 30 minutes or until the yucca is tender but not mushy. During the last 4 minutes of simmering, add the shrimp and cooked bacon to the pot. Season with salt and pepper and serve.

Serving Suggestions:

Try this one with Avocado and Orange Salad with Black Olive Dressing (page 199) and Chile Quesadilla Bread (page 396).

Clear Soup with Pan-Seared Scallops and Lime

This very simple broth spotlights the delicate nature of scallops. Soups of this type, most often featuring seafood, are common in Myanmar (Burma) and Southeast Asia and provide a good illustration of how, in that part of the world, fish is combined with pungent, aromatic ingredients in a way that doesn't overwhelm the fish. This soup can also be done just as successfully with shrimp or oysters.

1 tablespoon sesame oil

½ pound sea scallops

Salt and freshly cracked white pepper to taste

1 teaspoon minced garlic

1 teaspoon minced ginger

2 cups water

1 cup bottled clam juice

1 cup dry white wine

2 scallions, thinly sliced

1 tablespoon each chopped fresh cilantro, basil, and mint

Juice of 1 lime

Lime rounds for garnish (optional)

METHOD

1. In a large sauté pan, heat the sesame oil over high heat until hot but not smoking. Sprinkle the scallops with salt and pepper, place in the pan, and stir vigorously for about 30 seconds. Add the garlic and ginger and stir an additional 30 seconds, or until the scallops are just browned on the exterior. Remove from heat and set aside.

2. Combine the water, clam juice, and wine in a medium-size saucepan and bring to a boil. Add the scallions along with the seared scallops, ginger, and garlic and cook for 1 minute.

3. Remove from heat and add the cilantro, basil, mint, and lime juice. Stir well and serve at once, garnished with lime rounds if desired.

Serving Suggestions:

I would serve this as a semi-exotic appetizer to be followed by an Asian-flavored entrée such as Faux Hokien-Style Ginger Roast Chicken (page 172) or Grilled Pork- and Shrimp-Stuffed Chiles with Sweet Soy Glaze (page 55).

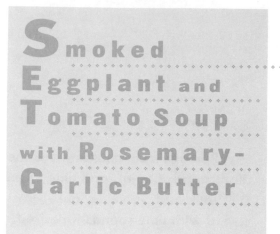

Smoked Eggplant and Tomato Soup with Rosemary-Garlic Butter

Serves 6 as appetizer

Throughout the Mediterranean world, the long-standing and happy relationship between eggplant and an open fire has resulted in many classic culinary gems, like babaganoush and caponata. This smoky soup, which also takes advantage of that fortuituous combination, is good cold as well as hot. If you're serving it cold, use the rosemary-garlic butter on a chunk of crusty bread instead of putting in the soup, and add another 1½ cups of stock to adjust the soup's consistency.

2 medium eggplants, unpeeled, each sliced lengthwise into 3 pieces

3 tomatoes, halved

2 yellow onions, halved

¼ cup vegetable oil

Salt and freshly cracked black pepper to taste

1 teaspoon minced garlic

2 quarts chicken stock

ROSEMARY-GARLIC BUTTER:

½ cup butter, softened

½ teaspoon minced garlic

1 tablespoon rosemary needles

Salt and freshly cracked black pepper to taste

M E T H O D

1. Rub the eggplants, tomatoes, and onions with oil, sprinkle with salt and pepper, and grill over a medium-low fire until dark golden brown. The eggplant should take 4 to 5 minutes per side, the tomatoes 3 to 4 minutes per side, and the onions 5 to 6 minutes per side.

2. Remove the vegetables from the grill and purée (leaving the skins on) with the garlic in a food processor or blender.

3. Transfer the vegetable purée to a large saucepan, add 3 cups of the chicken stock, and heat over medium heat until very hot but not quite boiling. Adjust the consistency to your liking with the remaining chicken stock and season with the salt and pepper.

4. Meanwhile, make the rosemary-garlic butter: In a food processor or blender, purée the butter with the garlic, rosemary needles, and salt and pepper, then roll it into a log in waxed paper and place in the refrigerator.

5. Just before serving the soup, add a chunk of the rosemary-garlic butter to each serving.

Serving Suggestions:

For a meal in itself, serve this with Grilled Hearthbread Johnson (page 406) and Arugula Salad with Oven-Dried Tomatoes, Olives, and Blue Cheese (page 214).

Lemon-Garlic Grouper Ceviche

The active ingredient in Latin-style raw fish preparations is usually lime, but in this recipe we substitute lemon, then add some ginger, the old stand-bys chile and cilantro, and some carrots to provide a textural background. In a departure from many ceviche recipes, which simply combine all the ingredients, here we "cook" the fish in the lemon juice first, then remove it and combine it with the other ingredients. This guarantees tender, firm, tasty fish (not at all mushy or soft from over-long exposure to the acid).

If you can't locate grouper, you may substitute halibut, flounder, or mahi-mahi.

2 pounds grouper fillets, skins removed, cut into little-finger-size strips

1 red onion, diced small

2 cups lemon juice (8 to 10 lemons)

1 carrot, cut into matchstick strips

2 tablespoons minced fresh red or green chile pepper of your choice

1 teaspoon minced ginger

2 tablespoons minced garlic

¼ cup chopped fresh cilantro

Salt and freshly cracked black pepper to taste

½ head green cabbage, very thinly sliced

M E T H O D

1. Layer the fillets in a loaf pan into which they fit rather snugly in a single layer. Pour the lemon juice over the fillets, cover, and allow to sit for 2 to 3 hours, or until the fillets are opaque throughout. Remove the fillets and discard the lemon juice.

2. Combine all remaining ingredients except the cabbage and mix well. When the fillets are ready, place them on top of a bed of thinly sliced cabbage and pour the carrot-herb-spice mixture over them.

Serving Suggestions:

Serve this flavorful, light dish before a heavy meat course like London Broil "Smoke Gets in Your House" Style (page 148).

Slicing carrots

Carrots into matchsticks

Lime-Cooked Rare Tuna with Southeast Asian Flavors

1½ pounds sushi-quality tuna

1 cup fresh lime juice (about 8 limes)

1 small red onion, thinly sliced

1 tomato, diced small

1 tablespoon minced ginger

1 cup coconut milk, unsweetened canned, or prepared by method on page 458

¼ cup chopped fresh cilantro

Salt and freshly cracked black pepper to taste

Although the Latin American ceviche seems to be better known, the practice of "cooking" fish in citrus juices is found in Asia as well. Here the fish takes on the lime juice, then is combined with coconut milk and ginger for some sweetness to balance the sour. This will not be a totally cooked tuna dish, as the short time in the lime juice leaves the fish with a great sushi-like interior.

METHOD

1. Cut the tuna into thin slices about the size and thickness of a matchbook. Lay the tuna slices in a shallow pan in a single layer and pour the lime juice over them; make sure the juice covers the tuna completely. Cover and soak for 2 hours, moving the tuna slices around and turning them over to be sure that all surfaces are exposed to the lime juice. At the end of 2 hours, the tuna should be a milky gray on the exterior but pink to red in the interior.

2. Remove the tuna, discard the lime juice, and combine the tuna with all remaining ingredients in a medium-size bowl. Mix well and serve.

Spice-Rubbed Grilled Giant Shrimp Skewers with Peaches and Hot Chiles

Serves 4 as appetizer

SPICE RUB:

2 tablespoons whole cumin seeds

1 tablespoon crushed coriander seeds

1 teaspoon red pepper flakes

1 teaspoon salt

1 tablespoon freshly cracked black pepper

16 very large (less than 12 to a pound) shrimp, shelled and deveined

2 peaches about the size of baseballs, each peeled and cut into 6 wedges

8 red jalapeño peppers (you may substitute any fresh red or green chile pepper of your choice)

With the heat of the peppers, the intensity of the spices, and the rich, smoky flavor of the shrimp, this dish has a lot going for it. Because of that, you can substitute chunks of red bell pepper for the jalapeños if grilled chiles ignite too hot a fire in your mouth. On the other hand, I think the coolness of the peaches is a nice balance for the peppers' fire, so you might want to give it a try.

METHOD

1. Combine all the spice rub ingredients and toast lightly in a small sauté pan over medium heat until the spices just begin to smoke, 3 to 4 minutes. Allow to cool to room temperature.

2. Rub the shrimp generously with the spice mixture. Thread the shrimp onto skewers along with the peaches and jalapeños.

3. Grill over medium-high heat for 4 to 5 minutes per side, or until the shrimp are completely opaque throughout. Serve at once.

Escabeche of Mackerel with Mangoes and Potatoes

Latin American cooks have been pickling fish as a means of preservation for hundreds of years. Although the process is known by different names—escovitch, caveached, escabeche—it is basically the same throughout the region and involves putting fish and other tasty ingredients in vinegar. These days it is done more for reasons of flavor than for preservation.

This particular recipe was inspired by a West Indian version of escabeche I found in Barbados. The potatoes and mangoes provide textural contrast to the fried fish, and the spices, lime, and cilantro give an aromatic quality to the rich mackerel.

1 potato, peeled and cut into ½-inch cubes

1 large ripe mango, peeled, pitted, and cut into ½-inch cubes

½ red bell pepper, diced small

½ green bell pepper, diced small

½ red onion, diced small

1 cup white vinegar

1 tablespoon minced garlic

1 tablespoon sugar

1 teaspoon ground cumin

1 teaspoon prepared curry powder

4 dashes Tabasco sauce

1 cup water

Salt and freshly cracked black pepper to taste

½ cup all-purpose flour

1 teaspoon each salt and freshly cracked black pepper

1 pound mackerel fillets

¼ cup vegetable oil

¼ cup chopped fresh cilantro

2 limes, halved

METHOD

1. Cook the potato cubes in boiling water to cover until they are easily pierced with a fork but still offer some resistance, about 8 minutes.

2. In a shallow serving dish, combine the potato, mango, bell peppers, and onion and set aside.

3. In a saucepan, combine the vinegar, garlic, sugar, cumin, curry powder, Tabasco, water, and salt and pepper to taste. Bring to a boil, remove from the heat, and pour over the potato-mango mixture.

4. Combine the flour with 1 teaspoon each of salt and pepper and dredge the mackerel in the mixture. In a large sauté pan, heat the oil until hot but not smoking. Place the fillets in the pan and cook until golden brown on the outside and completely opaque on the interior, 3 to 4 minutes per side.

5. Remove the fish from the pan and place on top of the potato-mango mixture. Sprinkle with the cilantro, squeeze the limes over the top, and serve hot or cold. This dish will keep, covered and refrigerated, for 2 or 3 days.

Serving Suggestions:

I would serve this as part of a meal of small dishes, along with Deep-Fried Plantain Rounds (page 253), Amilcar's Grilled Shrimp and Avocado Salad (page 226), and Elmer's Salvadoran Pickled Cabbage (page 273).

Red Snapper Cooked in Lemon with Coconut Milk and Shredded Green Mango

1 pound whole red snapper fillets, skins removed

MARINADE:

1 tablespoon minced garlic

1 tablespoon minced ginger

1 teaspoon minced fresh red or green chile pepper

1 cup lemon juice (about 4 lemons)

2 green or semi-ripe mangoes, peeled, seeded, and shredded

1 red bell pepper, thinly sliced

1 red onion, thinly sliced

1 tablespoon minced ginger

¼ cup chopped fresh cilantro

½ cup coconut milk, unsweetened canned, or prepared by method on page 458

½ cup fresh orange juice

¼ cup lemon juice (about 1 lemon)

Salt and freshly cracked black pepper to taste

Any tropical area worth its culinary salt has some version of raw fish cooked in citrus, and here's a West African–style entry. The lemon is offset a bit by the mellow coconut milk, but then the green mango adds back a bit of sour, which is then countered by the pungent, sweet ginger and the citrus sweetness of the orange. With so many flavors happening here, no one can accuse this dish of being boring.

You may substitute halibut, ocean perch, or rockfish for the snapper.

METHOD

1. Find a small loaf pan into which the pieces of snapper fillets will just fit in a single layer and place them in it.

2. In a small bowl, combine the garlic, ginger, chile, and lemon juice. Pour this mixture over the snapper, cover, and refrigerate for 4 to 6 hours.

3. Remove the snapper from the pan, slice against the grain into pieces about the size of a finger, and discard the liquid.

4. In a large bowl, combine all remaining ingredients and toss well. Arrange on a platter or individual dishes and top with the sliced snapper.

Serving Suggestions:

This makes part of an all-cold, no-meat summer buffet, along with Pumpkin Salad with Cilantro and Toasted Cumin (page 206), Avocado and Orange Salad with Black Olive Dressing (page 199), and Red Potato and Cucumber Salad with Mango (page 202).

Corn-Crusted Panfried Shrimp with Sweet and Hot Seared Onions

Serves 4 as appetizer

Panfrying has somewhat of a bad name these days, but if you cut down on the amount of oil, it's really not unhealthy. Here we coat shrimp with a bit of cornmeal, fry them until they are crispy, and serve them on top of seared onions that have a chutney-like tang.

¾ cup yellow cornmeal

1 tablespoon ground cumin

1 tablespoon chili powder

Salt and freshly cracked black pepper to taste

3 tablespoons virgin olive oil

16 medium-size (16/20 count) shrimp, shelled and deveined

2 yellow onions, thinly sliced

½ cup pineapple juice

¼ cup white vinegar

2 tablespoons cracked coriander seeds

¼ cup molasses

1 tablespoon minced fresh red or green chile pepper of your choice

¼ cup chopped fresh cilantro

1 lime, quartered (optional)

METHOD

1. In a large bowl, combine the cornmeal, cumin, chili powder, salt, and pepper. Lightly dredge the shrimp in this mixture.

2. In a large sauté pan, heat the olive oil over medium heat until hot but not smoking. Add the shrimp and fry until a peek inside shows that they are opaque throughout, 3 to 4 minutes per side. Remove the shrimp with a slotted spoon and set on several layers of paper towel.

3. Heat the oil remaining in the pan for a minute. Throw in the onions and stir vigorously until they begin to turn dark brown (not black), 7 to 9 minutes.

4. Add the pineapple juice and vinegar and cook, stirring frequently, for 4 minutes. Add the coriander, molasses, chile, and cilantro and remove from the heat. Stir, season to taste, and serve the shrimp on top of the onions, garnished with lime quarters if desired.

Serving Suggestions:

This goes well with Bob's Quick-Cooked Lettuce (page 232), Grilled Onion Rings (page 246), and Grilled Peppered Tomatoes with Lemon and Garlic (page 247).

Molasses-Glazed, Peanut-Crusted Grilled Shrimp with Napa Cabbage and Sesame Vinaigrette

VINAIGRETTE:

¼ cup sesame oil

¼ cup virgin olive oil

¼ cup lime juice (about 2 limes)

2 tablespoons white vinegar

2 tablespoons soy sauce

1 teaspoon sugar

1 teaspoon minced fresh red or green chile pepper of your choice

Salt and freshly cracked black pepper to taste

1 small head Napa cabbage

1 carrot, thinly sliced

5 scallions, including green, thinly sliced diagonally

2 tablespoons each chopped fresh mint, basil, and cilantro

½ cup bean sprouts

1 pound medium-size (16/20 count) shrimp, shelled and deveined

¼ cup molasses

½ cup unsalted roasted peanuts, roughly chopped

Crunchy, aromatic, pungent, sweet, sour, healthy, easy to prepare—that describes a lot of the food from just about any part of Southeast Asia. The concept of crunchy vegetable salads served with portions of meat or fish is widespread in this area, from Singapore to Vietnam. The base for these dishes may be cabbage, carrots, green papayas, cucumber, or any combination of them. Here we use Napa cabbage and carrots, toss in the Southeast Asian aromatic herb trio of mint, basil, and cilantro, and dress the whole affair with a sour-sweet-chile combination. Topped with sweet shrimp, this makes a great salad course or substantial appetizer.

METHOD

1. In a small bowl, combine all vinaigrette ingredients and whisk together well. Set aside.

2. Remove the thick veins from the bottom portion of the cabbage leaves. Cut the remaining cabbage into thin strips (you should have about 4 cups) and put into a large bowl along with the carrot, scallions, mint, basil, cilantro, and bean sprouts. Cover and refrigerate.

3. Thread the shrimp onto skewers and grill over a medium-hot fire until opaque throughout, 3 to 4 minutes per side.

4. Remove the shrimp from the skewers, brush with molasses, and sprinkle liberally with chopped pea-

nuts; the molasses should cause the peanuts to stick to the shrimp.

5. Pour the vinaigrette over the reserved cabbage mixture and toss well. Put ¼ of this mixture onto each plate, top with 4 or 5 shrimp, and serve at once.

Serving Suggestions:

I would serve this in front of a spicy dish like Gingered Crab in Chile Sauce (page 294) or Grilled Fiery White-Peppered Chicken Wings (page 290), or with a meat dish like Skewered Steak with Guava-Soy Glaze and Grilled Pineapple (page 146).

Grilled Scallops with Green Bread Sauce

When grilling scallops, I always find it easier to blanch them quickly first so that they firm up a bit and don't stick to the grill. Also, be sure to keep a close eye on them because, although they are as easy to grill as hot dogs, they become tough if overcooked. Fortunately, there's a very easy method of testing them: When they start to look like they're done, pop one in your mouth and see.

The Latin-flavored sauce that we pair with the scallops here is similar to a mayonnaise but uses stale bread instead of egg yolks as a binder. Tastes great and is a lot better for your health, too. Peasant cuisines to the rescue once again.

SAUCE:

3 cloves garlic

1 tablespoon kosher salt

1 teaspoon freshly cracked black pepper

¼ cup bread crumbs, either from stale bread or from fresh bread toasted in a 250°F oven for 10 to 15 minutes

2 tablespoons grainy Dijon mustard

1 tablespoon ground cumin

¼ cup chopped fresh parsley

4 dashes Tabasco sauce

6 tablespoons lime juice (about 3 limes)

½ cup extra-virgin olive oil

1 pound sea scallops

2 tablespoons virgin olive oil

Salt and freshly cracked black pepper to taste

METHOD

1. Make the sauce: In a food processor or blender, combine all the sauce ingredients except the olive oil and blend until well mixed. With the motor running, add the olive oil in a slow, steady stream. Set aside.

2. Blanch the scallops in boiling salted water for 1 minute. Drain and allow to cool.

3. While the scallops are cooling, check to be sure that your grilling surface is very clean, then allow it to heat up over the fire. Rub the scallops lightly with olive oil, sprinkle with salt and pepper, and thread onto skewers. Grill over a medium fire until brown and slightly crispy on the exterior and opaque throughout the interior, 2 to 3 minutes per side. Remove from the grill and serve topped with the green bread sauce.

Serving Suggestions:

Serve this as the appetizer in a Latin-style meal of Skinless Chicken Thighs with Latin Flavors (page 187), Señor Rossi's Cuban-Style Yucca (page 256), and Quick and Easy Sautéed Leafy Greens with Lime and Chiles (page 231).

Grilled Squid with Spicy Almond Sauce

Grilling squid is a very Mediterranean thing to do. In the United States squid qualifies as the most underused seafood around, but if more people tasted it grilled, I'm sure it wouldn't hold the title for long. Here we grill the squid quickly over high heat so that it doesn't become chewy, then serve it with a sauce that combines almonds and red peppers, a variation of the classic Spanish mixture known as romesco.

SAUCE:

2 tablespoons plus 1 cup virgin olive oil

1 yellow onion, thinly sliced

1 tablespoon minced garlic

1 tablespoon minced fresh red or green chile pepper of your choice

4 roasted red bell peppers

¼ cup blanched almonds, toasted in a 350°F oven in a baking pan until just brown, 5 to 7 minutes

2 tablespoons dry sherry

2 tablespoons red wine vinegar

3 tablespoons chopped fresh parsley

Salt and freshly cracked black pepper to taste

1 pound cleaned squid, including tentacles

1 tablespoon vegetable oil

Salt and freshly cracked black pepper to taste

METHOD

1. Make the sauce: Heat the 2 tablespoons of olive oil in a medium-size sauté pan over medium heat until hot but not smoking. Add the onion and sauté, stirring occasionally, until just translucent, 5 to 7 minutes. Add the garlic and cook 1 minute longer. Add the chile, bell peppers, almonds, sherry, and vinegar, reduce heat to low, and simmer for 5 minutes, stirring occasionally.

2. Remove the mixture from the heat and purée in a food processor or blender. With the motor running, add the 1 cup of olive oil in a steady stream. Fold in the chopped parsley, season to taste, and set aside. This mixture should have the texture of wet sand, kind of goopy, and should hold together well enough to throw at your fellow cook.

3. Rub the squid with vegetable oil and sprinkle with salt and freshly cracked pepper. Place the squid bodies on the grill over a hot fire, cover them with a clean brick or other large, heavy object, and grill for 1½ to 2 minutes per side. Remove the brick and use your tongs to roll the bodies around on the grill for another 30 seconds or so, then remove them from the grill.

4. Place the tentacles on the grill and cook for about 2 minutes, or until they are brown and crispy, rolling them around with your tongs as they cook so that they brown evenly. Remove them from the grill, place on a platter with the bodies, and serve with the spicy almond sauce for dipping.

Serving Suggestions:

This goes well with other sunny Mediterranean-derived dishes like Grilled Hearthbread Johnson (page 406), and Grilled Regular Mushrooms on Cornmeal Mush (page 60).

SQUID YOU BE MY NEIGHBOR?

Grilling squid is a real trip. It's basically easy, and grilling works very well with this sea creature because the fast cooking time gives you a finished dish that is tender instead of rubbery. The two crucial elements here are very high heat and (as usual) very fresh seafood. If you can't get high-quality fresh squid in your area, you are better off using best-quality frozen rather than second-rate fresh. As for size, the choice is up to you; the smaller ones are a bit more tender, but the larger ones are easier to handle on the grill.

Tommy's Complicated Grilled Spicy Thai Chicken Sticks with Coconut-Peanut Dipping Sauce

MARINADE:

¼ cup vegetable oil

1 teaspoon minced garlic

1 tablespoon minced fresh red or green chile pepper of your choice

1 teaspoon fish sauce (available in Asian markets) (optional)

1 cup orange juice

12 chicken tenderloins (you may substitute 1 pound boneless chicken breast cut into Band-Aid-size strips about ¼ inch thick)

DRY SPICE MIX:

(You may substitute ½ cup Simple Dry Masala, page 203.)

1 tablespoon ground coriander

1 tablespoon ground cumin

2 tablespoons dried Thai chiles (you may substitute red pepper flakes)

1 tablespoon mustard seeds

1 tablespoon crushed fenugreek seeds

1½ teaspoons anise seeds

Chicken tenderloins are the small but shapely pieces that are attached just underneath the breast. What we do in the restaurant is save them until we have a bunch, then skewer 'em up and grill 'em. If you don't feel like waiting until you have accumulated enough tenderloins, you can achieve the same effect by cutting small strips from a boneless breast of chicken, then pounding them a bit if they are more than ½ inch thick.

In this recipe we bathe the tenderloins in a spicy hot marinade, grill them, then hit them with a sweet chile glaze and finish them off with a sprinkling of incendiary spice mix. I developed the recipe with my eleven-year-old nephew, Tommy, because one of his favorite ways to spend an afternoon is messing around in the kitchen mixing a bunch of stuff together for rubs and glazes and other preparations. He says it's like doing science experiments.

1½ teaspoons crushed
cardamom seeds

1 tablespoon freshly cracked
white pepper

SWEET CHILE GLAZE:

Makes about 1 cup

½ cup apricot preserves

½ cup white vinegar

1 tablespoon Vietnamese chile-
garlic paste (you may
substitute 1½ teaspoons
minced garlic combined
with 1½ teaspoons minced
fresh chile pepper)

Removing chicken tenderloins

METHOD

1. In a small bowl, combine all the marinade ingredients and mix well. Lay the tenderloins or chicken breast strips in a small shallow pan, pour the marinade over them, cover, and refrigerate for 3 hours.

2. Make the dry spice mix: In a small bowl, combine all the ingredients and mix well.

3. Make the chile glaze: In a small saucepan, combine all the glaze ingredients and heat over medium-low heat, stirring, until the preserves have melted and all the ingredients are well blended, 3 to 4 minutes.

4. Thread the tenderloins onto skewers, discard the marinade, and grill the tenderloins over a medium-hot fire until they are completely opaque, 3 to 4 minutes per side.

5. Immediately after you remove the skewers from the grill, brush them with the sweet chile glaze and sprinkle them liberally with the dry spice mix. Serve accompanied by Coconut-Peanut Dipping Sauce.

(continued)

Coconut-Peanut Dipping Sauce

Makes about 2 cups

In a small bowl, combine all the ingredients and mix well. This sauce should have the consistency of soft ice cream; if it is too thick, add up to ¼ cup of warm water to thin it a bit.

⅓ cup peanut butter

¼ cup white vinegar

2 tablespoons lime juice (about 1 lime)

¼ cup coconut milk, unsweetened canned, or prepared by method on page 458

¼ cup tamarind water (page 466)

¼ cup sugar

SOUTHEAST ASIA'S HOT DOGS

I have taken to calling satays the hot dogs of Southeast Asia. People always give me a strange look when I say this, but all I mean is, in that part of the world, satays are the daily street food of everyday people, just as hot dogs are here. In cities like Bangkok, any place there is room enough to set up a small grill, from a vacant lot to the street outside National Stadium during Thai boxing matches, someone will be grilling and selling these little skewers of meat, usually accompanied by a spicy peanut sauce.

Grilled Chicken Thighs with Persian-Style Nut Rub

Serves 8 as appetizer

8 chicken thighs

Salt and freshly cracked black pepper to taste

¼ cup honey

¼ cup lemon juice (about 1 lemon)

1 tablespoon ground cumin

¼ cup Persian-Style Nut Rub (page 35), warmed in a sauté pan over medium heat to perk up the flavor

2 lemons, quartered

I first came across the technique of dry rubbing when I encountered the Texas method of rubbing beef briskets before setting them to cook for long periods over smoke. That's right, I'm talking about barbecue, where every pit master has a secret spice rub mixture.

Anyway, as a creative kind of guy, I took this freedom to combine spices any way you want and went with it—all the way to North Africa and parts of the Middle East, where you find a spice mixture known as *zaatar*. I took this mix as a base, substituted a few ingredients that are easier to get hold of in the U.S., then rubbed it on some chicken thighs. While zaatar is commonly used to flavor yogurt dips in the Middle East, I think using it as a rub produces a unique and delicious grilled chicken.

THE THIGHS HAVE IT

As I've said before, chicken thighs are made for grilling. Let me count the ways:

- They are small enough to grill relatively quickly without too much flare-up.
- They are more flavorful than the bland breast.
- They are tenderer than the leg, without nearly as much sinew.
- They are easy to find, adaptable, and convenient to serve: 1 per person makes an appetizer, 2 or 3 become an entrée.

(continued)

METHOD

1. Sprinkle the thighs with salt and pepper, then grill, skin side down, over a medium-low fire until the skin is crispy, 8 to 10 minutes. Flip over and cook an additional 4 to 6 minutes. To make sure the thighs are fully done, make an incision close to the bone and check for redness; if you see any, return to the grill for another minute or so.

2. Meanwhile, mix together the honey, lemon juice, and cumin in a small bowl. Brush this mixture on the chicken thighs immediately after removing them from the grill and then sprinkle generously with the nut rub. Return the thighs to the grill for 1 more minute, turning once, or just until the nut mixture has crisped up. Serve with lemon quarters for garnish.

Serving Suggestions:

Try this with another set of Middle Eastern flavors, like Turnip and Bread Salad with Minted Yogurt Dressing (page 208). I also think Lime-Raisin Chutney (page 347) or Cucumber-Tomato Relish with Oregano and Cinnamon (page 353) goes nicely with this.

SOUR GRAPES

There is no clearer illustration of how different cultures develop a liking for different tastes than the predominance of "sour" in the cuisine of Iran.

As in much of the rest of the world, cooks in Iran use lemons as a souring agent. Their sour larder extends much further than that, however. It also includes such items as dried limes, sour oranges (quite a different fruit from the sweet oranges we are used to), rhubarb, sour green plums (which children dip in salt and eat as a special treat), sour cherries, tamarind, sumac powder, dried sour yogurt, Persian pomegranates, and . . . yes, it's true . . . sour grapes.

Persian-Style Nut Rub

Makes about 1 cup

This is a variation on the zaatar spice and nut mixture that is used in the Middle East for a variety of culinary purposes. When I went to the house of my friend Jimmy Burke, who is Lebanese, his mother sprinkled this rub on her own fresh-baked pita bread.

I've left out the sumac, a woody, earthy-tasting spice that is quite difficult to find in the U.S., and have substituted fresh herbs for the dried thyme commonly used in Middle Eastern versions. I like the way the fresh herbs interact with the nuts.

¼ cup sesame seeds

¼ cup ground pistachios

2 tablespoons ground almonds

¼ cup finely chopped fresh oregano

1 tablespoon ground allspice

Salt and freshly cracked black pepper to taste

1. In a medium-size sauté pan, roast the sesame seeds, pistachios, and almonds separately over medium heat, shaking the pan frequently to prevent burning, until they are just browned, 4 to 5 minutes each.

2. When all the nuts are roasted, combine them with the remaining ingredients and, using a coffee grinder or blender, process until fine, about the consistency of coarse meal.

Grilled Chicken-Chipotle Quesadillas with Cheddar

This dish is yet another creative way to use tortillas, thought up by former *jefe del* East Coast Grill, K. C. O'Hara. Here the heat from the grill melts the cheese, which binds the other three elements together. This recipe has a fairly high degree of difficulty but, when pulled off with style, is definitely worth the effort. If you grill the chicken on a medium fire, and have all the other ingredients prepared, then you hustle it up a bit, the fire will be ready for grilling the quesadillas just when you finish assembling them. Otherwise you're going to end up building two fires.

3 tablespoons vegetable oil

1 red onion, finely diced

1 red bell pepper, thinly sliced

1 green bell pepper, thinly sliced

1 to 4 finely minced chipotle chiles (see Pantry, page 457), depending on your taste for heat

¼ cup lime juice (about 2 limes)

Salt and freshly cracked black pepper to taste

6 small chicken thighs, boned

20 6-inch corn or flour tortillas

½ pound Vermont Cheddar cheese, grated

¼ cup packed cilantro leaves and stems, finely chopped

OPTIONAL GARNISHES:

2 cups sour cream

3 limes, quartered

Salsa of your choice

METHOD

1. In a large saucepan, heat the oil over medium-high heat until hot but not smoking. Add the onion and cook until slightly wilted, 4 to 5 minutes. Add the bell peppers and sauté for another 4 minutes, stirring occasionally. Add the chipotles and lime juice, season to taste with salt and pepper, and remove from the heat. The vegetables should be just coated with liquid, not swimming in it; if the mixture is too wet, drain off a bit of the liquid. Cover and set aside.

2. Sprinkle chicken lightly with salt and pepper and grill over a medium fire until cooked through, 7 to 8 minutes per side. Remove from the fire and set aside to cool. When cooled, slice into strips about the size of your little finger and set aside.

3. Assemble the quesadillas: Lay out 10 tortillas and cover each one lightly with grated cheese. Add a layer of chicken strips, then a layer of the pepper-onion mixture, then sprinkle each with ¹⁄₁₀ of the remaining cheese and a teaspoon or so of chopped cilantro. Place the other 10 tortillas on top and press down firmly.

4. Grill the quesadillas in a covered grill over a medium-low fire for about 3 minutes per side, or until well browned and crispy on the outside. Be careful when you flip the quesadillas—you need a large spatula for this task. When both sides are well browned, remove the quesadillas from the grill, cut into wedges, and serve with sour cream, limes, and the salsa of your choice.

Serving Suggestions:

Serve this with Pickled Shrimp with Avocado (page 114) and Grilled Onion Rings (page 246), Fried Green Tomatoes with Sweet and Hot Dressing (page 234), and All-Purpose Rice and Beans (page 262).

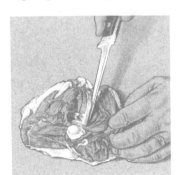

Boning chicken thigh   Removing bone

Barbecued Duck Legs with Basil, Coconut Milk, Chiles, and Green Peppercorns

1 tablespoon kosher salt

1 tablespoon freshly cracked white pepper

1 teaspoon crushed star anise

1 teaspoon crushed cardamom seeds

4 duck legs, trimmed of excess fat

SPICE RUB:

1 tablespoon sesame oil

1 teaspoon minced garlic

1 tablespoon minced ginger

1 tablespoon prepared curry powder or curry spice mix of your choice

1 tablespoon minced fresh red or green chile pepper of your choice

2 tablespoons green peppercorns

¾ cup coconut milk, unsweetened canned, or prepared by method on page 458

¼ cup chopped fresh basil

Salt to taste

In this dish we apply the indirect barbecue method of cooking to duck (incidentally providing a solution for those of you who have lots of recipes for duck breast but none for the legs). Duck is not commonly thought of as barbecue material, but the rich dark meat goes great with a smoky barbecue flavor. The crispy, crunchy skin is wonderful with smooth coconut milk and spicy green peppercorns.

Now, you might wonder what gives a chef the right to combine duck, coconut milk, and green peppercorns, three ingredients that may seem completed unrelated. As it turns out, raw green peppercorns—not canned or dried or pickled, but raw and on the stem—are commonly used in Thai dishes along with chicken and coconut milk. Try it and I'm sure you'll agree it's a fantastic combination.

METHOD

1. In a small bowl, combine the salt, white pepper, anise, and cardamon and mix well. Rub the duck legs generously with this spice mixture.

2. Build a very small fire in one side of your kettle grill and place the duck legs on the rack on the opposite side. Cover and cook for about 2 hours, refueling the fire with a couple of handfuls of charcoal every half hour or so to maintain a slow, low fire. After 2 hours, test for doneness: The leg bone should twist easily, the juices should run clear when the meat is pierced with a knife, and the meat itself should be free of redness.

3. Meanwhile, make the spice rub: Heat the sesame oil in a saucepan over medium heat until hot but not smoking; add the garlic, ginger, and curry powder and cook, stirring constantly, for 1 minute. Add the chiles, peppercorns, and coconut milk and bring to a boil. Reduce the heat to low and simmer for 30 minutes. Remove from heat, add the basil, adjust the seasoning, and spoon over the grilled duck legs.

Serving Suggestions:

I would serve this as an appetizer in front of Jennie's Crab Cakes

GREEN PEPPERCORNS

I first discovered fresh green peppercorns in Bangkok in a phony trattoria called Maria's, appropriately decorated with gaudy murals of Venetian gondolas and the leaning tower of Pisa. I had stopped there in desperation because I had been unable to find any "authentic" Thai restaurants in the immediate vicinity. It turned out that, in addition to pizza and calzone, they also had fantastic Thai regional food.

One of the dishes I enjoyed that day was chicken served in a sauce rich with giant basil, bird chile peppers, and spicy, piquant, uniquely flavorful bunches of fresh green peppercorns, still on the stem. You may have a hard time finding fresh green peppercorns in your neighborhood store, so feel free to use canned ones in this dish. But if you ever get to a place where you see fresh peppercorns, give them a try. They are amazing in appearance and taste, a great example of something we eat all the time but never see in their original, unprocessed state.

with Funny Red Tartar Sauce (page 126) for an exotic duck-crab combo. If you're having a hard time trying to pair a beverage with this, I'd recommend Watermelon Daiquiris (page 447).

Raw Beef with Ginger and Cardamom and Grilled Chile-Garlic Toast

1 pound very lean top round, with all fat trimmed off

1 teaspoon extra-virgin olive oil

1 tablespoon minced garlic

1 tablespoon minced ginger

3 scallions, finely chopped

2 tablespoons minced fresh red or green chile pepper of your choice

¼ cup lemon juice (about 1 lemon)

1 tablespoon crushed cardamom pods

For this particular raw beef treatment, we look to East Africa, one of many places where raw meat in some form is used as an appetizer. To give the dish an East African flavor, we punch up the raw beef with lemon, ginger, and cardamom. I've given two ways to prepare this recipe. The first is the classic tartare/hamburger method, and the second resembles the Italian method for carpaccio, in which the meat is frozen to facilitate very thin slicing.

I like to use top round steak for this dish because it is so lean, has good flavor, and is much more economical than sirloin or fillet, which is usually called for in this type of dish. A crunchy, slightly spicy toast is served with the meat for a nice contrast in texture.

EAT IT RAW

I'm not sure how it started, but at a very early age I got into eating raw meat. As a kid, I would always grab some raw hamburger and down it with a little salt and pepper before my mom could cook the burgers. When I grew older, I was delighted to discover steak tartare—no longer could I be shamed by family and friends who thought it was gross to eat raw meat. As it turns out, many cultures have raw beef dishes. I'm always searching for acceptable new ones so that when somebody gives me a hard time about eating raw meat, I can defend myself more easily.

Tartare Method:

1. Using your sharpest knife, cut the top round into very small pieces, then chop it with that same sharp knife until it resembles coarse hamburger.

2. In a large bowl, mix together all the remaining ingredients.

3. Add the chopped beef and mix together well. Chill and serve on top of Grilled Chile-Garlic Toast.

Serving Suggestions:

For a collection of appetizers, I would serve this with Pickled Shrimp with Avocado (page 114) and Grilled Regular Mushrooms on Cornmeal Mush (page 60).

Carpaccio Method:

For those who think ahead and don't like to chop a lot or who don't have a really sharp knife.

1. In a small bowl, mix together all the ingredients except the steak.

2. Coat steak with the mixture and work it in well with your hands.

3. Place the steak on a double sheet of plastic wrap, wrap very tightly, and freeze for at least 8 hours.

4. Remove the steak from the freezer, unwrap, and slice paper thin. Serve on top of Grilled Chile-Garlic Toast.

Grilled Chile-Garlic Toast

1. Grill the bread over a medium-hot fire until golden brown and crispy, approximately 2 minutes per side.

2. In a small bowl, combine the olive oil, garlic, and chili powder and mix well. Remove the bread from the grill, brush it with the olive oil–garlic mixture, and top with raw beef.

1 baguette, cut into slices ½ inch thick

⅓ cup extra-virgin olive oil or to taste

1 tablespoon finely minced garlic

1 tablespoon chili powder

Beer-Battered Fried Clams with Ginger-Soy Dipping Sauce

I live fairly close to Ipswich, Massachusetts—fried clam epicenter of the universe—so I have become partial to this way of preparing these little mollusks. The beer batter I use here is considerably lighter than the breading used on traditional New England fried clams; it actually bears more resemblance to tempura batter. Continuing in the light theme, we trade in tartar sauce for a lighter soy-ginger concoction.

The keys to this preparation are fresh clams and proper oil temperature. If the oil is not hot enough, the clams will have to spend too long in it and will emerge greasy. When a clam hits the oil, you should see immediate, intense frying action. If you don't, remove that clam and wait until the oil is hotter. It also helps to keep the batter cold. Slip an ice cube into the batter to ensure this.

DIPPING SAUCE:

1/2 cup soy sauce

2 tablespoons rice wine vinegar (you may substitute white vinegar)

2 tablespoons sugar

3 dashes Tabasco sauce

1 tablespoon minced ginger

1 1/2 pounds shucked cherrystone or littleneck clams

3/4 cup cornstarch

3/4 cup all-purpose flour

1 tablespoon salt

1 tablespoon baking powder

1 cup beer of your choice

3 cups peanut or vegetable oil for frying

METHOD

1. Combine all the dipping sauce ingredients, mix, cover, and set aside.

2. Dredge the clams lightly in ¼ cup of the cornstarch.

3. Make the beer batter: In a large bowl, combine the remaining ½ cup of cornstarch, flour, salt, and baking powder and mix well. Whisk in the beer.

4. In a large saucepan, heat the oil over medium heat to about 350°F. (If you do not have a fat or candy thermometer, test the oil by dropping a small bit of batter into it; when it is hot enough, you will see considerable frying action.)

5. You want to cook the clams about 10 or 11 at a time, so dip that many into the batter. Shake off any excess so that the clams are just lightly coated, and drop them into the oil. They should sink, then rise immediately to the surface of the oil, surrounded by a ring of bubbles. (If the clams do not immediately rise to the surface, your oil is not hot enough. Turn up the heat slightly and/or allow additional time.) Cook the clams for 2 to 3 minutes, or until golden brown. Remove to a baking sheet covered with a triple layer of paper towels and allow to drain for 2 to 3 minutes. Repeat until all the clams have been cooked, making sure that the oil does not cool off too much during the process.

6. Serve the clams in a bowl lined with absorbent paper and accompanied by the ginger-soy sauce for dipping.

Serving Suggestions:

For an exotic Eastern appetizer combination, try this with Raw Beef with Ginger and Cardamom and Grilled Chile-Garlic Toast (page 40), Sweet and Hot Sesame-Spinach Condiment (page 362), and Bob's Quick-Cooked Lettuce (page 232).

(continued)

Slicing ginger

Mincing ginger slices

I used to think that clams were unique to the East Coast of the U.S., but that was before I visited the awesome seafood markets of Asia. There I witnessed a mind-blowing variety of shellfish, among which were clams of all sizes, types, and colors, from giant geoducks to svelte razors. But let's make it a bit easier on ourselves and just stick with American clams, which are readily available on the East Coast.

In this department there are two basic varieties, softshell (aka steamers) and hardshell. The hardshell are named according to their size: If there are around 500 in a bushel, they're called littlenecks; 300 to a bushel makes them cherrystones; a bushel of 180 is known as topnecks; and when you get only 120 to a bushel, they become chowder clams, also called quahogs. For the recipes in this book that call for clams, littlenecks and cherrystones will do the trick.

Sweet Potato–Onion Pancakes

Cute and tasty, these ones can be made ahead and held in a 200°F oven for up to an hour. Chances are that you will have the ingredients on hand, so you can whip them up whenever you need a special treat for breakfast. They also make an excellent side dish.

METHOD

1. Mix together the onions and sweet potatoes in a large bowl. Add the olive oil, flour, and eggs and mix well. Add the milk and parsley and mix once more. Season to taste with salt and pepper.

2. Pour the peanut oil into a 10-inch cast-iron skillet; it should be about ¼ inch deep. Heat over medium heat until very hot but not smoking.

3. Drop about ¼ cup of the pancake mixture into the hot oil and press into a pancake shape with a spatula or wooden spoon. Continue to do this until the pan is full but not crowded. Fry the pancakes 1½ to 2 minutes per side, or until golden brown on both sides. Remove and drain on paper towels.

2 yellow onions, halved, and thinly sliced (about 1½ cups)

1½ pounds sweet potatoes, peeled and grated using the large holes of a kitchen grater (about 4½ cups)

3 tablespoons virgin olive oil

1 cup all-purpose flour

3 large eggs, lightly beaten

½ cup milk

¼ cup chopped fresh parsley

Salt and freshly cracked black pepper to taste

¾ cup peanut or vegetable oil

Southeast Asian Shrimp and Pork Salad

Pork and shrimp seem to find their way together into a lot of Southeast Asian preparations. Here they mix it up in an aromatic salad that traces its roots directly to Vietnam, with that country's ubiquitous nuoc cham serving as a vinaigrette. Don't be put off by the fish sauce; before long, it will take its place alongside soy sauce in your condiment rack.

You can cook the shrimp and pork for this dish ahead of time—even the night before, when the grill is still hot from your dinner cooking. Just mix all the ingredients together as close to serving time as possible.

1 pound medium-size (16/20 count) shrimp, shelled and deveined

Salt and freshly cracked black pepper to taste

1 pork tenderloin, 10 to 12 ounces, exterior fat trimmed

1 small head Napa cabbage, split, cored, and cut into thin strips

1 red bell pepper, cut into thin strips

1 cup bean sprouts

1 bunch scallions, thinly sliced diagonally

1 bunch fresh cilantro, leaves picked from stems and well washed

1½ cups Vietnamese Dipping Sauce

2 tablespoons sesame seeds, lightly toasted in a 250°F oven for 12 to 16 minutes, or until lightly browned

½ cup crushed roasted unsalted peanuts

2 limes, quartered

M E T H O D

1. Season the shrimp with salt and pepper, thread them onto skewers, and grill them over a medium-hot fire for approximately 2 minutes per side or until opaque throughout. Remove the shrimp from the fire, split them in half lengthwise, and set aside.

2. Sprinkle the pork tenderloin with salt and pepper and grill it over a medium-hot fire for 12 to 15 minutes, rolling it every 3 to 4 minutes to ensure even cooking. Remove the tenderloin from the fire and check for doneness by cutting into the center with a thin knife; it should be slightly pink and juicy in the center. Allow the tenderloin to sit for 10 minutes so the juices are evenly distributed, then slice it into rounds about ⅛ inch thick, then slice the rounds in half. Set aside.

3. In a large bowl, combine the cabbage, bell pepper, bean sprouts, scallions, and cilantro. Pour enough Vietnamese Dipping Sauce over the mixture to moisten, toss lightly, and sprinkle with sesame seeds and chopped peanuts. Place on a serving platter, top with shrimp and pork, and serve with lime quarters for squeezing.

Serving Suggestions:

If you are going to use this as an appetizer, try backing it up with some heavy red meat experience like London Broil "Smoke Gets in Your House" Style (page 148) or a game dish like Grilled Quail with Cardamom, Ginger Sauce, and Grilled Scallions (page 192).

Vietnamese Dipping Sauce

Makes about 2 cups

In a small bowl, combine all the ingredients and mix together well. This mixture will keep, covered and refrigerated, for 3 to 4 weeks.

½ cup fish sauce (available in Asian markets)

¼ cup lime juice (about 2 limes)

¼ cup sugar

1 teaspoon minced garlic

¼ cup grated carrots

½ cup warm water

1 teaspoon red pepper flakes

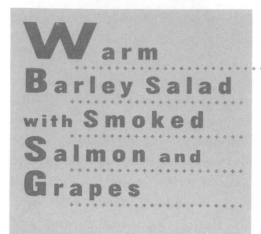

Warm Barley Salad with Smoked Salmon and Grapes

Serves 4 as appetizer

1 cup medium pearl barley

2 cups chicken stock or water

1/2 red onion, diced small

1/2 red bell pepper, diced small

1/2 cup seedless grapes (red or green or a mixture of both), halved

1/4 cup chopped fresh basil

1/4 cup extra-virgin olive oil

1 teaspoon minced garlic

1/4 cup lemon juice (about 1 lemon)

Salt and freshly cracked black pepper to taste

1/2 pound smoked salmon, thinly sliced

The pressure is on to increase grain consumption in our diets, and barley, although unfamiliar to most of us except as an ingredient in soups and Scotch, is a grain that is good to get to know. It has a pleasant, unaggressive flavor, comes equipped with all the healthful attributes of other grains, and is an apparent antidote to high blood cholesterol. It also has an unrivaled history, being the world's most ancient cultivated grain, at least as far as anthropologists can tell. There are many forms of barley, but the easiest to deal with is pearl barley. In this dish we use it as a kind of pleasing blank canvas against which we feature strong, smoky salmon and sweet, juicy grapes.

METHOD

1. Rinse and drain the barley and place in a small saucepan along with the chicken stock or water. Bring to a boil over medium-high heat. Reduce the heat to low and simmer, covered, for about 40 minutes or until all the stock or water has been absorbed. Remove from the heat and allow to sit, covered, for 10 minutes. Cool to room temperature.

2. In a large bowl, combine the cooked barley and all the remaining ingredients except the salmon.

Mix gently but thoroughly. Put ¼ of the mixture on each of 4 plates and top with slices of salmon.

Serving Suggestions:

Try this with Grilled Swordfish Steaks with Green Grape–Parsley Relish (page 76), Spice-Rubbed Grilled Bluefish with Green Olive Relish, Smoked Tomatoes, and Grilled Fennel (page 90), or Grilled Shell-On Giant Shrimp with Hot Peanut-Chile Butter (page 284).

Chile-Yucca Fritters

Yucca, also known as cassava or manioc, is one of the most popular starchy tubers in the tropical world, along with malanga and yams. Its original home is Brazil, and there it is used in many forms. In one form it is made into a toasted meal that is then sprinkled over a variety of foods. It is also used fresh, mashed like a potato or grated and made into fritters, which is what we have done here. This is starch with a bite; think of French fries with chili powder sprinkled over them, and you begin to get the idea.

Makes about 20 fritters

2 pounds yucca, peeled

1 yellow onion

3 tablespoons all-purpose flour

2 large eggs, beaten

2 tablespoons minced garlic

2 tablespoons mild curry powder or ground dried chile of your choice

6 tablespoons chopped fresh cilantro

1 tablespoon minced fresh red or green chile pepper of your choice

Salt and freshly cracked black pepper to taste

About 1 cup vegetable or peanut oil for frying (enough to fill a 12-inch skillet about ¼ inch deep)

METHOD

1. Using the largest holes on your grater, grate the yucca and onion and combine in a large bowl.

2. Add the flour and beaten eggs and mix well.

3. Add all the remaining ingredients except the oil and mix well again. The batter should have the consistency of wet sand.

4. In a large cast-iron skillet, heat the oil over medium heat until it is very hot but not smoking. Using a serving spoon or ice cream scoop, scoop up about 3 tablespoons of the yucca mixture, then press down on it lightly to form a round or oval patty about ¼ inch thick. Repeat with remaining mixture.

5. Place the fritters in the hot oil until the pan is full but not crowded, and cook until brown on both sides, about 2 minutes per side. As each fritter is done, remove and drain on paper towels, then add another fritter until all have been cooked. If the oil gets very brown, replace it and cook the remaining fritters. You can make these fritters in advance and keep them in a 200°F oven for 30 to 45 minutes.

Serving Suggestions:

You might want to serve this with Escabeche of Mackerel with Mangoes and Potatoes (page 18) or Scrambled Eggs with Fresh Oysters and Chiles (page 296) for an exotic dinner. Or pair it with "The Greatest": Grill-Roasted Prime Rib (page 144) to add exotic to classic.

Black-eyed Pea Fritters with Joey's Seared Collards

Makes 16 to 20 fritters

1 cup dried black-eyed peas

5 scallions, roughly chopped

1 tablespoon garlic, minced

¼ cup lime juice (about 2 limes)

¼ cup chopped fresh cilantro

Salt and freshly cracked black pepper to taste

About ¾ cup cold water

About 1 cup peanut or vegetable oil for frying (enough to fill a 12-inch skillet about ¼ inch deep)

Fritters show up in many cultures, including the American South of my childhood. They go by different names in different countries, but whatever they are called, these mixed, molded, and fried things are a great way to turn staples like black-eyed peas into creative dishes featuring tastes from just about anywhere.

The combination of black-eyed peas and collard greens covers a lot of territory, from Africa, where they both originated, to the islands of the Caribbean and the shores of Brazil, where both are used in traditional fritter preparations. The combination makes sense to me because the slightly bitter greens are a great contrast to the musty fritters.

METHOD

1. Soak the peas in 2 cups cold water for at least 4 hours and up to 8 hours. Rub the peas roughly to remove the skins, drain, cover with water, and rub again. Repeat this 3 or 4 times or until most of the skins have floated off. (This is a bit time-consuming, but the more skins you rub off, the better the taste of the final dish.) Rinse one last time with cold water and drain.

2. Put the peas, scallions, garlic, lime juice, cilantro, salt, and pepper in a food processor or blender and purée until smooth. Add ½ cup cold water and purée again, then add enough additional water to make the mixture the consistency of mayonnaise.

3. Scrape the mixture into a large bowl and beat with a wooden spoon for 5 minutes or until your arm is tired—the more you beat, the fluffier the fritters will be. (Those of you who are into modernism can use your electric mixer here.)

4. In a large cast-iron skillet, heat the oil over medium heat until it is very hot but not smoking. Using a serving spoon or ice cream scoop, scoop up about 3 tablespoons of the pea mixture, then press down on it lightly to form a round or oval patty about ½ inch thick. Repeat until all of the mixture has been used.

5. Place the fritters in the hot oil until the pan is full but not crowded, and cook until brown on both sides, 2 to 3 minutes per side. As each fritter is done, remove and drain on paper towels, then add another fritter until all have been cooked. If the oil gets very brown, replace it and cook the remaining fritters. Place the fritters in a 200°F oven while you prepare Joey's Seared Collards, then serve on top of a bed of the collards.

Serving Suggestions:

In a continuum of making everyday foods taste good and unusual, I would pair this with Cumin-Crusted Braised Bluefish (page 92) and Uncommon Carrot-Raisin Slaw (page 212). You might want to serve Chunky Corn and Tomato Salsa (page 340) alongside.

(continued)

Joey's Seared Collards

Serves 4 to 6 as side dish

This method of cooking collards is radically different from the southern method of boil, boil, and boil some more. This method was shown to me by my pal Dr. Joey Knauss, former chef at the East Coast Grill, who was lucky enough to live in Brazil for a while. Here the greens are cooked quickly over high heat and become tender without the hours of cooking in the southern style.

1. In a wok or the largest sauté pan you have, heat the olive oil over high heat until it just begins to smoke.

2. Quickly throw in the greens, add the salt and pepper, and stir madly for 30 seconds, turning the greens over and over until they have all wilted slightly and have turned a rich, bright green. Remove from heat, add the lime juice, Tabasco, and additional salt and pepper to taste, and stir well.

3 tablespoons olive oil

3 cups collard greens, washed, dried, stems removed, and leaves cut into ribbons about the width of your little finger

Pinch of salt and freshly cracked black pepper

2 tablespoons lime juice (about 1 lime)

3 to 10 dashes Tabasco sauce, depending on your taste for heat

Grilled Pork- and Shrimp- Stuffed Chiles with Sweet Soy Glaze

Stuffing chiles has always seemed a distinctively Latin American technique to me, but somehow I wasn't surprised to find that it is also done in parts of Southeast Asia. Passing by a little noodle shop in downtown Kuala Lumpur one day, I came upon a guy grilling chiles stuffed with shrimp and pork. I chatted with him about Michael Jordan for a while and then began to nose around, looking for some guidelines about the filling. It turned out to be a fairly straightforward forcemeat bound with egg whites. It has become one of my favorites in the slightly complicated preparation department. The sweet and slightly sour glaze is a great complement to the mellow shrimp and pork mixture.

This dish is a little painstaking. Removing the seeds from the chiles and pushing in the forcemeat are both tedious tasks, but when you're done, you can bask in the glow of your accomplishment while accepting kudos from friends and family. The first time or two that you cook this, it will probably be

Serves 10 as appetizer

3 large egg whites

½ pound ground pork sausage of your choice

½ pound shrimp (any size), shelled, deveined, and finely chopped

1 teaspoon minced garlic

1 teaspoon minced ginger

2 tablespoons chopped fresh cilantro

2 tablespoons sesame oil

1 tablespoon vegetable oil

Salt and freshly cracked black pepper to taste

10 Anaheim chiles, each 4 to 6 inches long

(continued)

pretty sloppy, but the more you try it, the better you'll get. If you want to make your on-site preparation a bit easier, you can always prepare the chiles ahead, then heat them up on the grill.

In this dish your chile pepper selection is key. Anaheim peppers, slightly shorter than a banana and having a uniform thickness, are best, but you can substitute other mild fresh chile peppers if Anaheims aren't available.

METHOD

1. Preheat the oven to 400°F. Place all the ingredients except the chiles on a cutting board and kind of mince everything up some more, half chopping, half mixing, until the mixture is gooey and well mixed.

2. Lightly oil the chiles, place them on a baking sheet, and put in the preheated oven for about 12 minutes, or until they have softened but are not yet mushy.

3. Remove the chiles from the oven and make a small slit along the side of each one, starting at the top and going about ¾ of the way down. Slide your fingers into the slit and remove the seeds. (You may want to wear rubber gloves while doing this. If you don't and your fingers start to burn from the capsaicin in the seeds, rinse them in a mild bleach solution.)

4. Using a teaspoon, fill the chile cavities with the pork-shrimp mixture, adding enough so that the chiles are rather firm to the touch.

5. Grill the stuffed chiles over a medium-low fire for about 10 minutes, rolling them around to ensure even cooking. To check for doneness, cut one open and check the sausage-shrimp mixture; it should be firm all the way through—no signs of color in the juice.

6. Remove the chiles from the heat, coat them lightly with Sweet Soy Glaze, and serve while hot.

Serving Suggestions:

I would serve this along with a couple of other appetizers, like Raw Beef with Ginger and Cardamom and Grilled Chile-Garlic Toast (page 40) and Cold Grilled Tuna Salad with Spinach, Cashews, and Five Spices (page 230).

Sweet Soy Glaze

Makes about 1½ cups

This recipe can easily be doubled or tripled. If I were you, I'd make up a big batch and keep it in the refrigerator. That way, when you need a quick entrée, you can always break this out and brush it over grilled chicken or fish during the last minute of cooking.

1 cup soy sauce

1 teaspoon minced ginger

2 tablespoons brown sugar

5 dashes Tabasco sauce

2 tablespoons lime juice (about 1 lime)

1 teaspoon cornstarch

1. Place the soy sauce, ginger, and brown sugar in a small saucepan and bring to a boil. Boil for 10 minutes.

2. Meanwhile, in a small bowl, combine the Tabasco and lime juice. Add the cornstarch and whisk until it is completely dissolved in the liquid.

3. Add the cornstarch mixture to the soy sauce mixture and simmer for another 10 minutes. Spoon over the chiles. This sauce will last, covered and refrigerated, about 1 month.

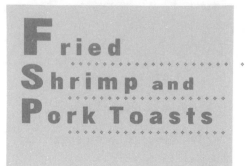

Fried Shrimp and Pork Toasts

This is my attempt to re-create the shrimp toasts that I had as a child at our neighborhood Polynesian restaurant in Virginia Beach. They were served along with spareribs, egg rolls, and teriyaki chicken on that South Seas classic (they really do have them there), the pupu platter. The best part, though, was the Sterno-fired flaming volcano in the center of the platter that provided children with a dynamic new way to play with their food.

8 medium-size (16/20 count) shrimp, shelled, deveined, and tails removed

6 ounces boneless pork (cutlet or other), diced

1 teaspoon minced garlic

1 tablespoon minced ginger

1 teaspoon chopped fresh cilantro

1 tablespoon lemon juice

2 tablespoons sugar

1 tablespoon fish sauce (available in Asian markets) (optional)

1 tablespoon soy sauce

1 teaspoon freshly cracked white pepper (you may substitute black)

5 to 7 dashes Tabasco sauce or 1 teaspoon Vietamese chile-garlic paste

2 large eggs

1 cup vegetable oil

About 1 foot of baguette, sliced about ½ inch thick

METHOD

1. Combine all the ingredients except the vegetable oil and bread slices and purée in a food processor until reduced to a smooth paste.

2. Spread each slice of bread with about 1 tablespoon of the shrimp-pork mixture. You may use more or less according to taste, but do not make the layer of shrimp-pork mixture more than 2 times thicker than the bread.

3. In a large sauté pan, heat the vegetable oil over medium heat until hot but not smoking. Place a single layer of toasts in the oil, shrimp-pork side down, and fry until light golden, about 1 minute. Flip over with tongs or a spatula and cook for 45 seconds on the other side, until the bread is light golden.

Remove the toasts to a baking sheet covered with paper towels or a brown paper bag and sprinkle with salt and pepper. Repeat until all the toasts have been fried, and serve hot.

Serving Suggestions:

For your Pseudo-Neo-Postmodern Pupu Platter, I recommend serving this with Deep-Fried Plantain Rounds (page 253), Lime-Cooked Rare Tuna with Southeast Asian Flavors (page 16), Tommy's Complicated Grilled Spicy Thai Chicken Sticks (page 30), and Grilled Fiery White-Peppered Chicken Wings (page 290).

Grilled Regular Mushrooms on Cornmeal Mush

If you have some high-toned guests coming over for dinner, you can substitute fancy mushrooms for the white button variety called for here, serve them this dish, and tell them they're eating wild mushrooms and polenta. If your guests are friends or family, call it what I do—grilled mushrooms on fried mush. Whichever mushroom you use, this dish tastes just as good, the earthy mushrooms making an excellent partner to the slightly grainy polenta. In fact, I suggest that you double the recipe because you are probably going to have people asking for seconds. If they are too shy to ask, or want to save room for the main course, don't worry—this stuff keeps well for a day or two, covered and refrigerated, and makes a great light lunch when reheated.

CORNMEAL MUSH:

2 cups water

1 teaspoon salt

Pinch of freshly cracked black pepper

¾ cup yellow cornmeal

1 tablespoon butter

2 pounds medium-size mushrooms, stems trimmed

¼ cup virgin olive oil

Salt and freshly cracked black pepper to taste

¼ cup butter, melted

2 tablespoons dry sherry

¼ cup chopped curly parsley

2 dashes Tabasco sauce

1 teaspoon minced garlic

Serving Suggestions:

Try serving this as an appetizer followed by Smoked Roasted Leg of Lamb with Chile-Garlic Rub (page 138) and Spinach, Avocado, and Papaya Salad with Orange-Cumin Dressing (page 198).

METHOD

1. Lightly oil a baking sheet or small baking pan. Set aside.

2. In a large saucepan, bring the water, salt, and pepper to a boil. Add the cornmeal in a slow, steady stream, whisking constantly to prevent lumps. Reduce the heat to low and cook, stirring constantly, until the mixture has become quite thick and pulls away from the sides of the pan, 15 to 20 minutes.

3. Spread the mush on the oiled baking sheet, making a layer about ½ inch thick, which corresponds to a square about 8" × 8". Cover and refrigerate for at least a half hour, then cut into 4 squares.

4. Melt the tablespoon of butter in a skillet over low heat. Turn the heat to medium and fry the squares of mush until lightly browned, about 4 minutes per side.

5. Meanwhile, combine the mushrooms and olive oil in a medium bowl, sprinkle with salt and pepper, and toss well. Thread the mushrooms onto a skewer and grill over a medium fire until they are brown and soft, 4 to 5 minutes. Remove the mushrooms from the fire and, when cool enough to handle, cut them into quarters.

6. Combine the [mush]rooms quarters wi[th but]ter, sherry, parsley, [Tabasco,] garlic and mix well. Spoon over hot squares of mush and serve.

THAT'S POLENTA TO YOU, JACK

When I came north as a young cook, I was easily intimidated by all the new food items I was exposed to and shied away from trendy things with names I didn't recognize, like polenta. Well, one day while at work in the kitchen of a large restaurant, I noticed that the cook next to me was cooking cornmeal and water. When asked him what he was making, he said it was polenta. "Polenta, shmolenta," I said with my usual tact, "that's cornmeal mush. Even my sister can make that stuff."

From then on, the specials coming off my station always contained polenta, and I began to realize that it's a mistake to be intimidated by food. First of all, it interferes with your ability to enjoy all kinds of different dishes, and secondly, intimidating foods with fancy names are very often just the everyday foods of regular folks from other countries.

Grilled Foie Gras on Toast

Serves 6 to 12 as appetizer

1 baguette, cut into about 20 thin slices

1 lobe of foie gras (grade B is okay) cut into slices ¼-inch thick and about the diameter of an egg

Salt and freshly cracked black pepper to taste

Okay, now, I know you're saying to yourself, "What's this foie gras stuff doing in a book inspired by equatorial flavors, and what's the idea of grilling it?" It's not often I work with such a lofty ingredient, but as part of the April Fools' dinner at the East Coast Grill, I decided to give it a go.

The results blew everybody away. The high heat of the grill quickly seared the surface of the foie gras and drove the juices to the center.

So, in the event that you ever come across some foie gras, you can surprise people by telling them that you're going to prepare it in the equatorial fashion. Nothing fancy here, just a straight-ahead preparation that is creamy and rich, with a little toast to help it move more quickly from plate to mouth. One tip, though: Make sure your grill grid is super clean to avoid problems with sticking.

One final note: I know we should be cutting down on the fat in our diets, but this is really great fat, right up there with marrow in the taste and texture departments. You'll notice that there is a wide range in how many we say this recipe will serve—that's to give you some leeway in deciding how much of your daily fat quotient you want to use up on this one dish.

METHOD

1. Lightly toast the bread slices over a medium-hot fire until just browned, 1 to 2 minutes per side.

2. Sprinkle the foie gras with salt and pepper and grill over a medium-hot fire until it acquires a nice, light sear, 1 to 2 minutes per side. At this point, it will be reddish and juicy on the inside.

3. Remove the liver from the grill, slice, place on toast, and savor.

LET THEM EAT FOIE GRAS

Foie gras is the liver from a goose or duck that has been force-fed and fattened over a period of 4 to 5 months. After the liver is taken from the fowl, it is soaked overnight in milk, water, or port, then marinated in a mixture made of armagnac, port, or madeira and seasonings. The result is incredibly rich and silky smooth, the kind of haute ingredient that I usually shy away from.

When I decided to grill foie gras just as an April Fools' joke on the customers at the East Coast Grill, the results were amazing. Could it be, I thought, that this method had not been attempted before? Well, here's another proof of the maxim that, with food, just about everything has been done before by somebody somewhere. To my joy and amazement, a little research uncovered the fact that grilled foie gras is a common street food in Israel, that country being a large producer of foie gras. I was also told that in parts of France vendors grill foie gras and duck kebabs outside bullrings, just as we do hot dogs outside baseball parks.

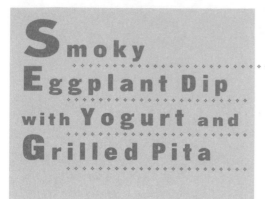
Smoky Eggplant Dip with Yogurt and Grilled Pita

There are hundreds of recipes for eggplant in Middle Eastern cooking, and a great many of them involve this particular method, which might seem strange if you've never done it before. When grilled to the proper state, the eggplant resembles a soft, mushy, burned black bag. Sounds a bit odd, but the combination of fire and eggplant results in a wonderful smoky, charred eggplant flavor.

Here we embellish the Middle Eastern classic babaganoush with some yogurt, and grill the pita to make it a little stiff for easy scooping. I also suggest you cut the pita into small pieces to counter the inevitable tendency toward hogging the dip.

3 large eggplants

1 large yellow onion, sliced ½ inch thick

1 cup plain yogurt

2 tablespoons minced garlic

¼ cup lemon juice (about 2 lemons)

¼ cup tahini (see Pantry, page 464) (optional)

Salt and freshly cracked black pepper to taste

¼ cup chopped fresh parsley

¼ cup chopped tomatoes

¼ cup virgin olive oil

GRILLED PITA:

6 pita rounds

¼ cup olive oil

2 tablespoons ground cumin

METHOD

1. Over a medium fire, grill the eggplants, turning occasionally, until the skins are well blistered and the pulp begins to soften, 12 to 15 minutes. Over the same fire, grill the onion slices until light brown, about 5 minutes per side.

2. Split the grilled eggplants in half lengthwise and scrape out the pulp, trying to avoid the charred skin. Place the pulp and the grilled onion slices in a blender or food processor and blend until smooth.

3. Add the yogurt, garlic, lemon juice, and tahini and purée well. Season with salt and pepper.

4. Transfer the mixture to a serving bowl, sprinkle with parsley and tomatoes, and pour the olive oil over the top.

5. Meanwhile, brush the pita rounds with olive oil, sprinkle with cumin, and grill over a medium fire until lightly browned, about 1 minute per side. Remove from the grill, cut into quarters, and serve with the dip. The dip will keep, covered and refrigerated, for about 3 days.

Spicy Roasted Red Pepper Dip with Grilled Pita

Serves about 8 as a dip

¼ cup virgin olive oil

1 yellow onion, thinly sliced

2 tablespoons ground cumin

1 teaspoon minced garlic

2 tablespoons minced fresh red or green chile pepper of your choice

¼ cup molasses

6 roasted red bell peppers

¾ cup extra-virgin olive oil

6 tablespoons chopped fresh parsley

¼ cup lime juice (about 2 limes)

Salt and freshly cracked black pepper to taste

Pomegranate molasses for drizzling, if you can find it—best bet, Middle Eastern or Indian markets

One cool fall day in New York City, I had the pleasure of being shown around the spice markets of the city by a local cookbook collector, Dalia Carmel, and her husband, Herb. We spent the entire afternoon going from shop to shop, with me asking questions about the spices and Dalia in turn interrogating the merchants, who were used to her questions from her many visits to their shops. The merchants were constantly giving us things to try, and the variety of spices and spice mixtures that we sampled was intense. Of course, Dalia would often criticize the products, chiding the poor merchants for leaving out an essential ingredient or switching to lower-grade ingredients to save money. It seemed to be an entertaining ritual for all concerned.

One of the most remarkable things I tasted that day was a spicy-sweet-hot roasted red pepper preparation known as m'hammara. Its sweetness came from pomegranate molasses, a Middle Eastern staple. This is my version of that dip—sweet, smoky, spicy, and hot. Just grill some pita bread, and you've got a great beginning to your meal. Serve this one anytime, anyplace.

METHOD

1. In a large sauté pan, heat the olive oil over medium-high heat until hot but not smoking. Add the onion and cook, stirring occasionally, until translucent, 5 to 7 minutes.

2. Add the cumin, garlic, and chile pepper and continue to cook, stirring frequently, for 1 minute.

3. Transfer the mixture to a food processor or blender, add all the remaining ingredients except the salt, pepper, and pomegranate molasses, and purée until very smooth. Season with salt and pepper and drizzle with pomegranate molasses if you have it. This mixture will last, covered and refrigerated, for 1 week.

Grilled Pita Bread

This couldn't be simpler: Cut store-bought pita rounds into quarters or eighths, depending on how large you like your dipping medium, brush lightly with melted butter or olive oil, and grill over a low fire until well browned and a bit crispy, 2 to 3 minutes per side. If you don't feel like starting a fire, you can achieve somewhat the same effect (minus the smoky taste) by putting the cut and oiled pita on a baking sheet in a 450°F oven for about 5 minutes.

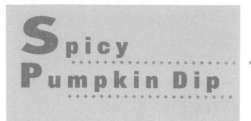
Spicy Pumpkin Dip

Makes about 2 pints

6 cups pumpkin flesh, cleaned, seeded, and cut into 1-inch cubes

2 tablespoons caraway seeds

¼ cup lime juice (about 2 limes)

6 tablespoons lemon juice (about 1½ lemons)

¼ cup extra-virgin olive oil

1 tablespoon minced garlic

½ cup chopped fresh parsley

1 tablespoon minced fresh red or green chile pepper of your choice

Salt and freshly cracked black pepper to taste

One process that cooks use to come up with new and exciting ideas is to take a familiar form and substitute a different set of ingredients. This dish illustrates that process. What I'm doing here is taking the Middle Eastern eggplant dip babaganoush as a model, exchanging pumpkin for eggplant as the central ingredient, then adding chile peppers and lime to complement the pumpkin flavor.

METHOD

1. Bring a stockpot of water to a rolling boil, add the pumpkin, and cook until they are easily pierced by a fork but still offer some resistance, 6 to 8 minutes.

2. Meanwhile, toast the caraway seeds in a small sauté pan over medium heat, watching carefully and shaking frequently to prevent burning, until they just begin to release a little smoke, 2 to 3 minutes.

3. Drain pumpkin, allow to cool to room temperature, combine with caraway seeds and remaining ingredients, and purée in a food processor or blender. Serve with grilled pita (page 67) for dipping.

Grilled Figs and Tomatoes with Olives and Feta

Big appetizer platter for
4 to 6

8 ripe fresh figs

8 plum tomatoes

6 tablespoons virgin olive oil
(approximately)

1 teaspoon minced garlic

1 tablespoon finely chopped
fresh oregano

Salt and freshly cracked black
pepper to taste

1/2 head romaine lettuce, thinly
sliced

1 pound Kalamata or other black
olives

1/2 pound feta cheese, crumbled

1/4 cup extra-virgin olive oil

1 lemon, halved

1/4 cup chopped fresh basil

The idea of salads prepared ahead of time, laid out on a table, and shared with friends over drinks in the fading evening sun is perhaps one of the main reasons I'm into warm-weather cuisines. I mean, you don't really picture the cuisines of northern Europe on a patio with a pitcher of sangria or margaritas. The antipasto-type dishes of Italy, however, do lend themselves to this scene. In this dish figs and tomatoes catch a little smoke on the grill and then join other Mediterranean flavors on a platter to make a very pleasant snack before dinner.

METHOD

1. Cut the figs and plum tomatoes into quarters, rub them with olive oil and garlic, sprinkle with oregano, salt, and pepper, and grill over a low to medium fire until they have some color, 2 to 3 minutes per side.

2. Place the lettuce on a platter and arrange the figs, tomatoes, olives, and cheese on top. Drizzle with olive oil, squeeze the lemon halves, sprinkle with basil, and serve with crusty bread.

Grilled Swordfish Steaks with Green Grape–Parsley Relish ▪ Grilled Swordfish with Spicy Shrimp Salsa ▪ Grilled Mahimahi with Honey-Macadamia Crust and Pineapple-Ginger Relish ▪ Grilled Spice-Rubbed Loup with Tomato-Cucumber Salad ▪ Grilled Striped Bass with Sweet Tomato Salsa and Glazed Mango ▪ Grilled Salmon with Chile-Honey Glaze and Ginger–Red Onion Relish ▪ Grilled Pompano with Lemon-Cinnamon Sauce ▪ Spice-Rubbed Grilled Bluefish with Green Olive Relish, Smoked Tomatoes, and Grilled Fennel ▪ Cumin-Crusted Braised Bluefish ▪ Regulation Breaded Flounder with Spicy Latin Tartar Sauce ▪ Panfried Cod with Tomato-Mint Yogurt Sauce ▪ Sautéed Trout Stuffed with Garlic, Chile, and Toasted Pecans with Garden Tomato Relish ▪ Grilled Spice-Rubbed Tuna with Pineapple Glaze ▪ Grilled Tuna with Sesame-Ginger Relish ▪ Grilled Tuna, Cabbage, and Pineapple Skewers with Hoisin Glaze ▪ Grilled Peppered Tuna Sandwiches with Sweet Smoked Onion Relish and Fresh Horseradish ▪ Citrus-Cooked Rare Tuna over Green Olives, Radishes, and Potatoes ▪ Grilled Red Snapper with Napa Cabbage and Ginger-Lime Vinaigrette ▪ Fried Red Snapper Fingers in a Sour Orange–Mango Pickle ▪ Pickled Shrimp with Avocado ▪ Grilled Chile Corn-Crusted Shrimp with Tropical Fruit Relish ▪ Grilled Shrimp with Green Mangoes and Red Lime Sauce ▪ Grilled Shrimp Skewers on Grilled Eggplant with Tomato-Feta Relish ▪ Sautéed Scallops with Bacon-Corn-Chile Relish ▪ Scallop and Nectarine Skewers with Grilled Red Pepper–Lime Sauce ▪ Jennie's Crab Cakes with Funny Red Tartar Sauce ▪ Pineapple Steamed Clams with Simple Coconut Curry ▪ Grilled Spice-Rubbed Squid with Lime ▪ Spicy Grilled Squid Salad with Peanuts and Chiles

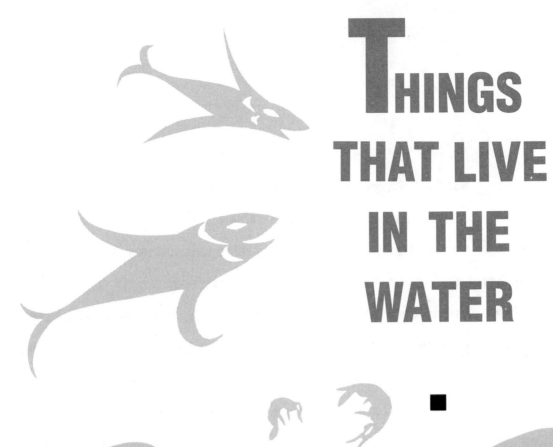

THINGS THAT LIVE IN THE WATER

When you're trying to decide what to make for dinner, it might help to remember one of those little factoids we all learned in grade school: Three-quarters of the earth's surface is covered with water. For us grown-ups, this translates into an incredible variety of great food.

Some cultures learned this lesson a long time ago. There are some countries in Southeast Asia, for example, where the per capita consumption of seafood is more than 100 pounds per year; in the U.S., it's hovering right around 15 pounds. But the recent pressure on Americans to turn away from red meat has caused us to gain a greater appreciation for seafood because, in addition to its variety, versatility, and great taste, seafood is also very healthful, low in the bad stuff and high in the good stuff.

Now, I don't mean to say that we never ate fish or shrimp or lobster in this country until now, but I do think that we are branching out in several important ways. First, we are starting to eat varieties of seafood, such as squid and skate, that many of us would have grimaced at before. Second, we no longer think that fish can only be broiled or poached or fried; people are getting used to alternative ways of cooking seafood, such as grilling, which I think is an excellent way to prepare it. Finally, we are starting to understand that, if prepared properly, seafood can stand up to other strong tastes, which makes for more interesting dishes.

This last point is particularly important to me. Fish has a reputation for being so delicate that you can't combine it with spices or it will be overwhelmed. Like many bad raps, this one is greatly exaggerated. It's true that you have to be aware of the delicacy of many types of seafood, but if you think you can't spice it, just take a look at the equatorial regions of the world. If you've ever had a chile crab in Thailand or a skewer of shrimp with habañero salsa in the Yucatán peninsula of Mexico, you know that seafood can be paired with hot chile peppers and assertive spices to tremendous effect.

Of course, there is nothing wrong with serving seafood in an unadorned state; sometimes there is nothing better. I just think both options should be made available, and another myth about spicy food should be put to rest.

Whichever way you prepare your seafood, you will have a much better chance of success if you pay attention to the three basic rules for cooking seafood: Start with fresh fish, start with fresh fish, and start with fresh fish.

The single most important requirement for preparing outstanding seafood is to start with a good product. I learned a lot about this during my travels in Asia. The difference between how fish is treated there compared to here is incredible. Even in developing countries like Malaysia and Vietnam, where the general standard of living is light-years behind the U.S., the quality of fish eaten by most people is far superior to what we eat; the poorest person in the market would not accept fish of the quality that we buy daily. Over there the fish comes directly to the market from small boats, and a lot of it is still kicking when it arrives in the market. As a result, some of the best seafood dishes I have ever had were consumed in little joints in Southeast Asia and Hong Kong.

I'll say it again—there is no substitute for freshness in seafood. The best way to check it is to smell it; if it smells like fish, don't buy it, period. A corollary of this rule, of course, is never to buy seafood in a place where they won't let you smell it. If you're buying a whole fish, you should check to make sure the gills are red or pink (not gray) and the eyes are clear and at least a little bulged out. For fish cut into fillets or steaks, though, there's no substitute for smelling. Shrimp should pass the smell test, and clams and oysters should have tightly closed shells. Lobsters and crabs have to be fully alive when you buy them—don't be fooled by a fishmonger who tells you a lobster is just sleeping.

But, you might say, how do I find fresh fish? What I suggest is that you find a local fish store, get to know the owners, and develop a personal relationship with them. Think of them the same way you think of your lawyer, doctor, or psychiatrist—although this will probably be an infinitely more rewarding relationship. An honest fishmonger can always tell you what is best and freshest on any given day. My advice is to follow his or her suggestion rather than insisting on buying what you had in mind when you went to the store.

Once you've bought your fish, you need to avoid the bête noire of the seafood cook—overcooking. Far more fish has been ruined by being cooked too long than by any other error. Don't be afraid to pick up a piece of the fish you're cooking, bend it, and look into the interior to check for doneness, even long before you think it is really done. It will hardly affect the appearance of the fish, and you'll be sure to catch it before it gets dry and tasteless.

Finally, it always pays to explore and experiment. Today's trash fish—underutilized species—is often tomorrow's delicacy, so don't be afraid to try out wolffish or eel or squid or whatever else might find its way to your fishmonger's counter. You might find something great.

In this chapter I use lots of different kinds of seafood, a range of cooking methods, and flavor combinations from around the hot-weather world. Some of them are a little "out there," like Fried Red Snapper Fingers in a Sour Orange–Mango Pickle or Citrus-Cooked Rare Tuna over Green Olives, Radishes, and Potatoes, but I urge you to give them a try because I think you'll really love them. Others are old-fashioned dishes with a little Spice Zone twist, like Regulation Breaded Flounder with Spicy Latin Tartar Sauce. Then, of course, there are the spice-rubbed dishes, such as Grilled Spice-Rubbed Loup or Cumin-Crusted Braised Bluefish, and (among my favorites) the dishes featuring grilled shrimp, like Grilled Shrimp with Green Mangoes and Red Lime Sauce. Whatever the best seafood in your fish market today, I'll bet there's a recipe or two for it here. So remember what you learned in grade school, head down to your fishmonger, and get cooking.

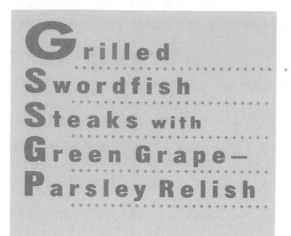

Grilled Swordfish Steaks with Green Grape—Parsley Relish

Serves 4 as entrée

∙∙∙∙∙∙∙∙∙∙∙∙∙∙∙∙∙∙∙∙∙∙∙∙∙∙∙∙∙∙∙∙∙∙

2 8-ounce swordfish steaks, each ½ to ¾ inch thick

----

2 tablespoons vegetable oil

Salt and freshly cracked black pepper to taste

Swordfish is an outstanding fish for grilling, right up there with tuna. The meat is firm and steaklike, its relatively high oil content keeps it moist, and its flavor is mild but distinctive. As always when grilling fish, you should be careful not to overcook. Don't be afraid to probe into the swordfish looking for doneness—these steaks can be bent without any serious damage, allowing you a clear view into the center to check for opacity—and remember to leave just a tiny trace of translucence because there will be some carryover cooking after you remove the fish from the grill.

Because of its distinctive taste, I'm not afraid to match swordfish with some fairly strong flavors. Here I pair it with a relish in which everyday ingredients with very distinct tastes are combined in a kind of exotic way.

SEAFOOD PHANTASM

Until the last decade or so, Americans thought of swordfish mainly as a trophy fish. You know, the kind that the millionaire sportsman in the movies always had mounted on the wall in his billiards room. This was largely the result of the unique phantasmal shape of this sea creature, with its saillike dorsal fin and its snout like a sword. Over the past few years, though, we have come to appreciate the culinary virtues of this fish.

These guys can grow as big as half a ton, but the ones that make it to the market average around 300 pounds. Spain is the world's leading harvester of swordfish, but the U.S. catches its fair share in summer and fall off both the East and West coasts.

METHOD

Rub the swordfish lightly with vegetable oil, sprinkle liberally with salt and pepper, and grill over a medium fire for 4 to 5 minutes per side, turning once, until almost completely opaque. Remove from the grill and serve, accompanied by the relish.

Serving Suggestions:

Serve this with **New Potato Hash Browns with Caramelized Onions (page 236)**, **Grilled Onion Rings (page 246)**, and **Hobo Pack Vegetables (page 248)**.

Green Grape–Parsley Relish

Makes about 1½ cups

This relish is one of those funny things that happens every once in a while: You come up with an idea that looks and sounds really strange, then when you make it, the flavor turns out to be not only unique but truly tasty. The mixture is very strong with vinegar and garlic, but when you bite into the grapes, the resulting bursts of sweetness balance the flavor. To my mind, that's what a relish is all about. I would use this with anything from fish to fowl to meat.

Mix 'em all together. That's it. This relish will keep, covered and refrigerated, for 3 or 4 days.

1 cup seedless green grapes, halved

¼ cup red wine vinegar

¼ cup virgin olive oil

1 teaspoon minced garlic

¼ cup chopped fresh parsley

Salt and freshly cracked black pepper to taste

Grilled **S**wordfish with **S**picy Shrimp **S**alsa

4 6-ounce swordfish steaks,
    about 1 inch thick

3 tablespoons vegetable oil

Salt and freshly cracked black
    pepper to taste

Here we're double-dipping, seafood with a seafood salsa. I've cut down on the amount of swordfish per portion, then made it up with the shrimp in the salsa. My understanding of food-beverage pairings is a bit sketchy, but I usually serve a gewürztraminer with this. My wine fanatic friends always say it's a good match.

SALSA:

Makes about 1½ cups

½ pound medium-size (16/20
    count) shrimp, shelled and
    deveined

Salt and freshly cracked black
    pepper to taste

1 ripe tomato, diced small

½ red onion, diced small

½ cup lime juice (about 4 limes)

1 teaspoon ground cumin

1 teaspoon ground coriander

7 dashes Tabasco sauce

1 tablespoon virgin olive oil

¼ cup chopped fresh cilantro

METHOD

1. Rub the swordfish lightly with the vegetable oil, sprinkle with salt and pepper, and grill over a medium-hot fire for 6 to 7 minutes per side, or until a peek inside shows that the fish is opaque throughout.

2. Meanwhile, make the salsa: Season the shrimp with salt and pepper, thread them onto skewers, and grill over the same medium-hot fire for 3 to 4 minutes per side, or until they are opaque throughout.

3. Remove the shrimp from the heat, slide them off the skewers, and chop into small pieces. Put into a medium-size bowl, add all the remaining ingredients, season with salt and pepper, and mix well. Serve each swordfish steak topped with a generous helping of the salsa.

Serving Suggestions:

I'd serve Spicy Roasted Red Pepper Dip with Grilled Pita (page 66) before this, and Watercress Salad with Grilled Asparagus and Red Onion (page 218) and All-Purpose Rice and Beans (page 262) alongside it.

Grilled Mahimahi with Honey-Macadamia Crust and Pineapple-Ginger Relish

Serves 4 as entrée

4 8-ounce mahimahi fillets, cut diagonally ½ inch thick

----

1 teaspoon vegetable oil

Salt and freshly cracked black pepper to taste

----

3 tablespoons honey

½ cup toasted macadamia nuts, crushed

If you have ever seen a mahimahi taken out of the water, you will remember its chameleonlike color changing from blue to green. Although mahimahi is its Hawaiian name, this sweetly moist, mild-tasting, white-fleshed fish is known by other names throughout the tropical world. In Spanish-speaking countries it is known as dorado, while elsewhere it is called dolphinfish—not to be confused with dolphin the mammal, as in Flipper. Sticking with the Hawaiian interpretation, here we combine mahimahi with macadamia nuts and pineapple.

METHOD

1. Rub the fillets lightly with oil and sprinkle with salt and pepper. Place the fillets on the grill over a medium-hot fire and cook for 5 to 6 minutes per side.

2. While the second side is cooking, coat the exposed side lightly with honey and sprinkle with crushed macadamia nuts. Flip and cook 1 more minute, coating the second side with honey and nuts. Flip again, and cook another minute, or until the crust is golden brown. Check for doneness by cutting into a piece; it should be completely opaque all the way through.

3. Remove the fillets from the grill, cut each in half, and serve accompanied by Pineapple-Ginger Relish.

Serving Suggestions:

This goes well with Coconut Rice (page 272) and Hobo Pack Vegetables (page 248).

Pineapple-Ginger Relish

Makes about 1½ cups

Combine all the ingredients in a small bowl and mix well.

1 cup diced fresh pineapple

½ cup pineapple juice

1 tablespoon minced ginger

2 tablespoons thinly sliced scallion

¼ cup lime juice (about 2 limes)

1 teaspoon minced fresh red or green chile pepper of your choice (optional)

Grilled Spice-Rubbed Loup with Tomato-Cucumber Salad

TOMATO-CUCUMBER SALAD:

4 ripe garden tomatoes, chopped small

1 cucumber, peeled and sliced very thin

1 red onion, sliced very thin

¼ cup olive oil

¼ cup lemon juice (about 1 lemon)

¼ cup red wine vinegar

¼ cup chopped fresh mint

¼ cup chopped fresh parsley

1 tablespoon sugar

1 teaspoon minced garlic

Salt and freshly cracked black pepper to taste

4 8-ounce ocean catfish fillets

2 tablespoons vegetable oil

½ cup Sweet and Hot Masala #7 (page 388), or Simple Dry Masala (page 376), or prepared curry powder

Lemon quarters for garnish (optional)

Whole mint leaves for garnish (optional)

I always take pleasure in trying to figure out ways to get people to try foods that they wouldn't ordinarily think of eating. In this case, my efforts are on behalf of the lowly wolffish, renamed ocean catfish by some American marketing genius in an image improvement measure that didn't really pan out. Since this fish is popular in Europe, I've attempted to help it out by referring to it by the name under which it sells in France. People might disagree about its name, but nobody is going to deny that this is one ugly fish. If you ever come across one in its whole state, you will probably write me a letter asking how I could possibly try to get you to eat it.

But the important thing is, what does it taste like? Well, I would describe it as a more tender, more densely textured monkfish. Mild, white, and adaptable, it lends itself well to strong preparations. Here we're laying on a strong spice rub to form a flavorful crust, then pairing it with a minty, summery relish.

METHOD

1. In a medium-size bowl, gently toss all the salad ingredients together and set aside.

2. Rub the fillets lightly with vegetable oil, then rub generously with Sweet and Hot Masala #7. Grill over a medium-hot fire for 3 to 4 minutes per side, or until just opaque throughout.

3. Meanwhile, divide the salad among 4 plates. Remove the fillets from the grill and serve on top of the salad, garnished with lemon quarters and whole mint leaves if desired.

Serving Suggestions:

Serve this one with Couscous with Raisins and Parsley (page 276), Indian-Style Grill Bread (page 400), and Quick and Easy Sautéed Leafy Greens with Lime and Chiles (page 231).

Grilled Striped Bass with Sweet Tomato Salsa and Glazed Mango

Because of overfishing and pollution, there has been a ban on commercial fishing of striped bass for some time. Fortunately, the aquaculture folks acted quickly, and there are now more than 100 fish farms throughout the U.S. They have developed a farm-raised product that is very good, and so we can enjoy the sweet taste of striped bass once again. Here we give it a Caribbean twist by serving it with a simple tomato salsa and a sweet, grill-glazed mango.

SALSA:

2 ripe tomatoes about the size of baseballs

1 small red onion, diced

¼ cup lime juice (about 2 limes)

¼ cup chopped fresh cilantro

1 teaspoon cayenne pepper

1 teaspoon toasted cumin seeds (toast in a small sauté pan over medium heat, shaking frequently to prevent burning, until they just begin to smoke, 2 to 3 minutes)

Salt and freshly cracked black pepper to taste

4 8-ounce striped bass fillets

2 tablespoons vegetable oil

Salt and freshly cracked black pepper to taste

METHOD

1. In a medium-size bowl, combine all the salsa ingredients, mix well, cover, and refrigerate until the fish is done.

2. Sprinkle the fillets with salt and pepper and grill over a medium fire for 3 to 4 minutes per side, or until just opaque throughout. To check for doneness, slide a knife into the center of one of the fillets, lift it open, and check to be sure that there is no remaining translucence. Remove from the grill and serve, accompanied by Glazed Mango and a generous portion of sweet tomato salsa.

Serving Suggestions:

Try this with Your Basic Cornbread (page 393), All-Purpose Rice and Beans (page 262), Brazilian-Style Gin and Tonic (page 444), and Banana-Papaya Fool (page 421).

DOWN ON THE FISH FARM

Although it is certainly very sad to see a wild fish stock depleted, there are certain advantages to farm-raised seafood. Because the fish are raised in a controlled atmosphere, there is little danger of pollution. Also, they do not go through the trauma of being caught, with the accompanying enzymatic reactions that speed up deterioration of the fish's texture. Finally, the fish can be processed more quickly and brought to market with a consistently high level of freshness. As a result, you have a good chance of getting a high-quality fish these days.

(continued)

Glazed Mango

The mango is just about my favorite fruit, but it can be a pain to pit and peel. The method illustrated here is the best I have found in many years of trying. Once you have turned the large side portions of the mango into little porcupines, you can slice off the sections to use in any dish. Or you can serve the mangoes whole or halved and let people slice off their own sections, as we do in this simple preparation. The lush sweetness of the fruit picks up a little smoky taste here, which I think makes a nice complementary flavor.

1. In a small bowl, combine the glaze ingredients and mix well.

2. Slice the 2 large side portions from each side of the mango pit (see illustration). Score these portions deeply in a cross-hatch pattern, cutting down to but not through the skin. Place the mango halves on the grill, cut sides down, and cook for 2 minutes. Turn over, brush the flesh liberally with the glaze, cook for an additional 30 seconds, and remove from the heat.

3. When the mangoes have cooled to room temperature, push them from the skin side to turn them inside out—they should resemble thick-quilled porcupines—and serve.

GLAZE:

2 tablespoons tomato catsup

1 tablespoon sugar

1 tablespoon white vinegar

2 ripe mangoes

Slicing mango

Cross-hatching mango

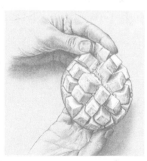
Turning mango inside out

Grilled Salmon with Chile-Honey Glaze and Ginger-Red Onion Relish

GLAZE:

¼ cup orange juice

¼ cup honey

1 tablespoon ground cumin

1 tablespoon chili powder

1 teaspoon minced fresh red or green chile pepper of your choice

4 8-ounce salmon fillets

2 tablespoons sesame oil

Salt and freshly cracked white or black pepper to taste

I like salmon for grilling for a couple of reasons. First, it is very versatile. Cut as either a boneless fillet or a steak, it has the heavy texture needed to hold together during the grilling process. It also has a range of flavor from rich to mild, which can take on a char and still come through.

Here we use salmon in yet another dish that disproves the old maxim that chiles and seafood don't match because the heat of the peppers will overpower the delicate taste of the fish. In this case, we're going with a sweet and hot Asian-flavored glaze in combination with a simple onion-based relish flavored with lime and ginger.

METHOD

1. Combine all the glaze ingredients in a small saucepan. Heat over medium-low heat, stirring, for 2 or 3 minutes or until all the ingredients are well combined. Set aside.

(continued)

2. Rub the salmon lightly with sesame oil and sprinkle with salt and pepper. Grill the salmon over a medium-hot fire for 6 to 8 minutes per side, or until it is opaque throughout. During the last 30 seconds of grilling, brush the fish with the chile-honey glaze. (Be careful not to leave the fish on the grill too long after you apply the glaze, or the sugar in the glaze will burn.) Serve accompanied by Ginger–Red Onion Relish.

Serving Suggestions:

I think this is particularly nice with Grilled Spring Onions with Fried Garlic-Ginger Sauce (page 244), New Potato Hash Browns with Caramelized Onions (page 236), and Hobo Pack Vegetables (page 248).

Ginger–Red Onion Relish

Makes about 1½ cups

1 red onion, thinly sliced

1 tablespoon minced ginger

¼ cup lime juice (about 2 limes)

1 tablespoon chopped fresh cilantro

Salt and freshly cracked white or black pepper to taste

Combine all the ingredients and mix well.

GOIN' FARMIN'

There are many types of salmon. Atlantic salmon account for about 25 percent of the world's salmon catch. The chinook or king salmon, which hang out in the North Pacific and can weigh in at several hundred pounds, are the monarchs of the salmon clan. Other varieties include the chum, coho, and pink sockeye. Although they all have their own characteristics, they can be used interchangeably.

Over the past few years, salmon has come on strong in popularity, thanks largely to its many culinary virtues, from its heavy texture to its rich taste. This fish's star-level popularity also owes a great deal to the expansion in American aquaculture, or fish farming. Because of this farming, your chances of locating consistently fresh salmon have increased exponentially. Purists will say that farmed fish don't have the same character as wild-caught fish, and I agree. But the rather subtle difference in flavor is more than offset by the ability to bring the farmed fish to market in good shape.

Grilled Pompano with Lemon-Cinnamon Sauce

SAUCE:

¼ cup lemon juice (about 1 lemon)

⅓ cup extra-virgin olive oil

3 pinches ground cinnamon *or* ⅛ stick cinnamon, crushed

1 tablespoon chopped fresh oregano

1 teaspoon minced garlic

Salt and freshly cracked black pepper to taste

4 pompano fillets, 8 to 10 ounces each

2 tablespoons vegetable oil

Salt and freshly cracked black pepper to taste

Pompano is the best-eating member of the jack family, which also includes amberjack and horse mackerel. This fish generally hangs out in the Caribbean, so you see it a lot in Florida. If you happen across a fresh one in your local market, snap it up and you will have one of the finest-eating fish around. Its flesh is firm and delicate, and its flavor clean and subtle but also just a little buttery.

In order not to overpower the fine flavor of the pompano, we use a very light sauce here, with the lemon-oregano-cinnamon combination common to Greek cooking.

METHOD

1. In a small bowl, combine all the sauce ingredients, mix well, and set aside.

2. Rub the pompano fillets lightly with the vegetable oil and sprinkle with salt and pepper. Place the fillets, skin sides up, over a medium-hot fire and grill for 3 to 4 minutes. Flip them and cook for an additional 2 to 3 minutes, or until the fish is opaque all the way through. Remove the fillets from the fire, drizzle fairly heavily with the lemon-cinnamon sauce, and serve.

Spice-Rubbed Grilled Bluefish with Green Olive Relish, Smoked Tomatoes, and Grilled Fennel

Serves 4 as entrée

In this robust dish each flavor is overpowered by the next, so that you taste in succession the spice-crusted, slightly oily bluefish, the lemony olives, and the seared, licorice-scented fennel. Subtle it's not, but I really like this combination of strong flavors.

The key here is getting high-quality bluefish, which is no problem in the late summer when they're running. If you're not fairly close to where the blues are being caught, you might want to substitute mackerel, kingfish, or tuna, and vary the cooking time accordingly.

SPICE RUB:

1 tablespoon fennel seeds

1 tablespoon coriander seeds

1 tablespoon freshly cracked pepper (white if available)

1 teaspoon ground cinnamon

1 teaspoon ground turmeric

1 teaspoon cayenne pepper

1 tablespoon dry mustard

2 tablespoons kosher salt

4 8-ounce pieces of bluefish, each 1½ to 2 inches thick

3 tablespoons vegetable oil (approximately)

4 ripe plum tomatoes, cut in half lengthwise

2 fennel bulbs, sliced ½ inch thick from top to bottom, each bulb making 5 slices lengthwise

Salt and freshly cracked black pepper to taste

METHOD

1. Make the spice rub: Toast the fennel seeds and coriander seeds in a small sauté pan over medium heat until they just begin to smoke, 2 to 3 minutes. Grind the seeds in a spice mill or coffee grinder or crush them under the bottom of a sauté pan. In a small bowl, combine the ground seeds with all the other spice rub ingredients and mix well.

2. Rub the bluefish lightly with the vegetable oil and sprinkle with a light dusting of the spice rub. Make sure your grill surface is very clean, then heat it up over the coals. Grill the bluefish over a medium fire for 5 to 8 minutes per side, depending upon the thickness of the fish, or until the flesh is completely opaque throughout. To check for doneness, slide a sharp thin knife into one of the pieces of fish and peek inside.

3. Meanwhile, rub the tomato halves and fennel slices lightly with the remaining vegetable oil and sprinkle them with salt and pepper. Place on the grill, tomatoes with cut sides down, and grill until the vegetables are slightly charred. This will take about 2 minutes per side for the tomatoes and 3 minutes per side for the fennel.

4. Put several tablespoons of Green Olive Relish on each plate, place the bluefish on top of the relish, and top with 2 tomato halves and a couple of slices of fennel. Serve hot.

Serving Suggestions:

Serve this with Big Sky's Grilled Sweet Lemon Salad with Parsley (page 222) or Avocado and Orange Salad with Black Olive Dressing (page 199).

Green Olive Relish

❖ ❖

Makes about 1 1/2 cups

1/2 cup pitted green olives of your choice

1 teaspoon minced garlic

1/2 red onion, diced small

1/4 cup chopped fresh parsley

1/4 cup virgin olive oil

1/4 cup lemon juice (about 1 lemon)

Salt and freshly cracked black pepper to taste

In a medium-size bowl, combine all the ingredients and mix well. This relish will keep, covered and refrigerated, about 4 days.

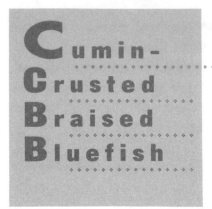

Cumin-Crusted Braised Bluefish

Serves 4 as entrée

¼ cup cumin seeds

2 tablespoons paprika

1 tablespoon kosher salt

1 tablespoon freshly cracked black pepper

4 8-ounce bluefish fillets, 1 inch thick, skins on

¼ cup vegetable oil for frying

1 yellow onion, thinly sliced

2 tablespoons minced garlic

1 tomato, diced medium

1 cup fresh orange juice (about 3 oranges)

¼ cup lime juice (about 2 limes)

1 tablespoon minced chipotle chile (see Pantry, page 457)

1 tablespoon ground cinnamon

¼ cup roughly chopped fresh oregano

¼ cup raisins

When I was a kid growing up on the beach in Virginia, my best friend's dad was an avid surf caster who rightly insisted on eating whatever he caught. Unfortunately for his family, in late summer that meant a lot of bluefish. My friend's mom, who was a pretty good cook, was always trying different ways to deal with Mr. Bluefish. One year, heavily browning the fish and then pan-braising it in a lemon-tomato sauce was a favored method, and I recall that dish here. Whenever I cook bluefish, I use the heaviest flavors I can, and it always amazes me how the flavor of the fish still manages to poke its head through. In this particular preparation, we challenge the bluefish with citrus and chipotle chile.

METHOD

1. Preheat the oven to 350°F. In a small bowl, combine the cumin seeds, paprika, salt, and pepper and mix well. Rub the bluefish fillets well with this mixture.

2. In a large sauté pan, heat the vegetable oil over medium heat until hot but not smoking. Add the fillets, skin sides up, and sauté for 2 to 3 minutes on one side only, until the cumin seeds just begin to color. Remove the fish and set aside.

3. Place the onion in the same pan and cook, stirring occasionally, until some color begins to appear, about 6 minutes. Add the garlic and tomato and cook 1 minute more. Add the orange juice, lime juice, chipotle, cinnamon, oregano, raisins, and browned fish and bring to a simmer.

4. Cover the pan and put it in the oven for 10 to 15 minutes, or until a peek inside one of the fillets reveals no translucence. Serve at once.

Serving Suggestions:

This dish is good with Rice Pilaf with Lime Zest and Almonds (page 270). My friend's dad insisted that bluefish and India Pale Ale were a match made in heaven, so if I were you I would give that a try, too.

Regulation Breaded Flounder with Spicy Latin Tartar Sauce

Serves 4 as entrée

This frying method—in which a classic flour-egg-flour coating interacts with hot oil to form a crispy golden jacket—was permanently imprinted on my brain as the cooking method of choice for seafood when I was growing up. That imprint was deepened when I started my restaurant career as the fry guy at Blue Pete's Seafood Restaurant in Pungo, Virginia. Maybe I am partial, but I think that fried fish has been hit with somewhat of a bad rap recently. To beat the rap, you need to use outstanding fresh fish and have your oil hot enough (around 350°F) to quickly seal the fish so the oil is not absorbed. Check the temperature of the oil by hanging a piece of fish in it; you should see some heavy frying action. Also, don't crowd the pan because that draws too much heat from the oil.

My deep regard for good old fried fish doesn't mean I am a stickler for every tradition; I like to spice up classic tartar sauce by adding some bold Latin flavors.

TARTAR SAUCE:

1 cup mayonnaise

¼ cup chopped fresh cilantro

¼ cup chopped sweet pickles or sweet pickle relish

8 dashes Tabasco sauce

2 tablespoons lime juice (about 1 lime)

1 tablespoon chili powder

1 tablespoon ground cumin

Salt and freshly cracked white or black pepper to taste

1 cup all-purpose flour

2 large eggs

1 cup milk

Salt and freshly cracked pepper to taste

1 yellow cup cornmeal

1 teaspoon red pepper flakes

1 cup peanut or other vegetable oil for frying

2 pounds boneless, skinless flounder (4-ounce pieces work best in this recipe)

METHOD

1. In a medium-size bowl, combine all the tartar sauce ingredients and mix well. Cover and refrigerate.

2. Set up 3 small baking pans or bowls for breading the fish. Put the flour in the first; in the second, combine the eggs, milk, salt, and pepper and beat well; in the third, combine the cornmeal and red pepper flakes.

3. In a large, heavy sauté pan, heat the oil over medium heat until moderately hot. (Test by dropping a bit of the egg-milk mixture in; you should see considerable bubbling action.)

4. Lightly dredge each piece of fish through the flour, then the egg-milk mixture, and finally the corn-meal–red pepper mixture. Place the fish in the sauté pan and cook for about 2 minutes per side, or until crispy, golden brown and completely opaque throughout. (You can get a view of the interior by sliding a sharp thin knife into a piece of the fish.) Remove from the pan and drain briefly on a paper towel.

5. Serve the flounder accompanied by the spicy tartar sauce.

Serving Suggestions:

For a return to my days as the fry cook at Blue Pete's, I would serve this with Fried Green Tomatoes with Sweet and Hot Dressing (page 234) and New Potato Hash Browns with Caramelized Onions (page 236).

Panfried Cod with Tomato-Mint Yogurt Sauce

Whether fresh or salted and dried, cod is found in cuisines all over the world. I use Atlantic cod in this dish, since its mild taste and fine, flaky texture match up well with frying. You can easily substitute Pacific cod or even haddock, hake, or pollock, all of which are members of the extensive cod family. In this dish we perk up the mellow cod with a cornmeal crust and a lemony mint-yogurt sauce.

Serving Suggestions:

With its Middle Eastern flavors, this goes very well with Uncommon Carrot-Raisin Slaw (page 212) and/or Parsley Salad with Bulgur, Mint, and Tomatoes (page 216).

YOGURT SAUCE:

¾ cup plain yogurt

1 ripe tomato, finely chopped

1 tablespoon lemon juice (about ¼ lemon)

¼ cup chopped fresh mint

1 tablespoon ground cumin

1 teaspoon minced garlic

Salt and freshly cracked black pepper to taste

½ cup yellow cornmeal

Salt and freshly cracked black pepper to taste

4 8-ounce cod fillets, each about 1 inch thick

1 cup peanut or vegetable oil

M E T H O D

1. In a small bowl, combine all the yogurt sauce ingredients and mix well. Cover and refrigerate.

2. Mix the cornmeal with the salt and pepper, dredge the cod lightly in this mixture, then shake lightly to remove any excess.

3. In a large sauté pan, heat the oil over medium heat until hot but not smoking. Place the cod in the pan and cook slowly, 4 to 5 minutes per side, or until the fish is opaque throughout. (You can get a view of the interior by sliding a sharp thin knife into one of the fillets. If the fish becomes well browned on the exterior but the interior is still not done, remove the fillets from the pan, place them in a baking pan in a 375°F oven, then check for doneness every 5 minutes until they become completely opaque in the interior.)

4. Remove the fish from the pan, drain briefly on several layers of paper towels, and serve with a generous helping of tomato-mint yogurt sauce.

IS COD REALLY DEAD?

Cod has long been one of the most popular and widespread fish in the world. In fact, cod was an important part of the so-called trading triangle of the American colonies. Ships loaded with rum and salt cod sailed to Spain and Portugal, then proceeded empty to Africa to pick up slaves, then sailed to the West Indies, where the slaves were exchanged for sugar and molasses, the latter to be made into rum, and the triangle began again.

The importance of this fish is due largely to two factors: the cod's prolific nature and its greedy appetite. Because each female lays almost 10 million eggs, a good number of them survive to populate the great fishing banks of the world. And because the cod swallows anything that comes within reach, including baited hooks, it has always been easy prey for commercial fishers.

Amazingly enough, modern fishing methods have actually resulted in a depletion of the worldwide stock of cod, and this inexpensive staple of ethnic diets from Africa to Europe to the United States is becoming rare and increasingly expensive.

Sautéed Trout **S**tuffed with **G**arlic, **C**hile, and **T**oasted **P**ecans with **G**arden **T**omato Relish

Serves 4 as entrée

RELISH:

3 large ripe garden tomatoes, finely chopped

1 small red onion, finely chopped

1 tablespoon minced garlic

2 tablespoons lime juice (about 1 lime)

3 tablespoons chopped fresh parsley

2 tablespoons virgin olive oil

Salt and freshly cracked black pepper to taste

¼ cup plus 2 tablespoons virgin olive oil

1 tablespoon minced garlic

2 tablespoons minced fresh red or green chile pepper of your choice

2 tablespoons chopped fresh cilantro

¼ cup pecans, toasted in a 400°F oven for 4 minutes, then roughly chopped

4 12-ounce trout, cleaned and totally boned or semi-boned with heads and tails on

½ cup all-purpose flour

Salt and freshly cracked black pepper to taste

Trout is a sweet, supple fish, so satisfying that it is a perfect match for quick, simple cooking techniques like grilling and sautéing. Here we stuff the trout with a rather hot mixture of chiles, nuts, and herbs, and accompany it with a tomato relish that relies on Italian flavorings.

METHOD

1. In a medium-size bowl, combine all the relish ingredients. Set aside.

2. Combine the 2 tablespoons of olive oil, garlic, chile, cilantro, and pecans. Spread each trout open and stuff ¼ of the chile-pecan mixture into the cavity.

3. In a large bowl or baking pan, mix the flour, salt, and pepper well. Dredge the trout lightly in this flour mixture, shaking off any excess.

4. In your largest sauté pan, heat the ¼ cup of olive oil over medium-high heat until hot but not smoking. Place the trout gently in the pan (they are rather fragile), turn the heat down to medium, and cook for 4 to 5 minutes per side, or until golden brown and opaque throughout.

5. Remove the trout from the pan and serve topped with a generous helping of the garden tomato relish.

Serving Suggestions:

I would serve this accompanied by something like Green Bean Salad with Corn, Basil, and Black Olives (page 200) or Parsley Salad with Bulgur, Mint, and Tomatoes (page 216).

Grilled Spice-Rubbed Tuna with Pineapple Glaze

It's hard to go wrong with tuna on the grill. Its sturdy texture makes it a natural for grilling, and its distinctive flavor allows it to stand up to spicy tastes, as in this dish. Here the tuna is coated in spices, grilled, and served with a kind of Americanized Pacific islands sauce.

SPICE RUB:

1 tablespoon crushed star anise

1 tablespoon minced ginger

1 tablespoon ground turmeric

1 tablespoon ground cinnamon

1 teaspoon ground cloves

1 tablespoon red pepper flakes

1 tablespoon salt

1 tablespoon crushed cardamom

1 tablespoon cumin seeds

GLAZE:

1 cup pineapple juice

½ cup white vinegar

1 tablespoon minced ginger

¼ cup soy sauce

¼ cup packed brown sugar

½ cup tomato catsup

¼ cup lime juice (about 2 limes)

¼ cup finely chopped cilantro

1 tablespoon freshly cracked white pepper

4 8-ounce tuna steaks, about
1½ inches thick

4 slices pineapple, 1 inch thick,
with peel left on

Lime quarters for garnish

METHOD

1. Make the spice rub: Combine all the spice rub ingredients in a large sauté pan, mix well, and heat over medium heat, shaking frequently, until they just begin to smoke, 2 to 3 minutes. Remove from the heat, allow to cool, then grind in a coffee grinder, spice mill, or mortar and pestle until fine.

2. Make the glaze: Combine the pineapple juice, vinegar, ginger, soy sauce, and brown sugar in a small saucepan and bring to a boil. Reduce the heat to low and simmer until the volume is reduced by half, about 30 minutes. Add the catsup and cook an additional 5 minutes. Remove from the heat, add the lime juice, cilantro, and white pepper, and mix well.

3. Rub the tuna steaks on all sides with the spice rub. Grill the tuna over a medium fire for 4 to 5 minutes per side, or until a peek into the interior shows some pink. (This is for medium rare, which is the way I like tuna; if you prefer it more well done, keep cooking until it reaches the stage you like.)

4. Spoon some of the glaze over each tuna steak and serve with a slice of pineapple, garnished with a lime quarter.

Serving Suggestions:

This one is great with Coconut Rice (page 272), Quick and Easy Sautéed Leafy Greens with Lime and Chiles (page 231), and Cucumber-Ginger Relish (page 354).

Grilled Tuna with Sesame-Ginger Relish

Serves 4 as entrée

4 8-ounce tuna steaks, 1½ to 2 inches thick

2 tablespoons vegetable oil

Salt and freshly cracked black pepper to taste

If you're new to grilling fish, tuna is a good starter. It almost never sticks to the grill, and actually cooks like a steak. Here we combine the tuna with an Asian-flavored relish featuring the crunchy texture of water chestnuts in a spicy-sweet-sour sauce.

METHOD

1. Rub the steaks lightly with oil, sprinkle with salt and pepper, and grill over a medium-hot fire 4 to 5 minutes per side, being careful not to overcook. Check for doneness by bending a steak gently and peering inside, looking for just a trace of translucence in the center.

2. Remove the tuna steaks from the grill, cut each in half, and serve accompanied by the Sesame-Ginger Relish.

Serving Suggestions:

This makes a good combination with Sweet and Hot Sesame-Spinach Condiment (page 362) and Hobo Pack Vegetables (page 248) or Coconut Rice (page 272).

Sesame-Ginger Relish

Makes about 1½ cups

In a small bowl, combine the water chestnuts and scallions. Add the sugar, ginger, sesame oil, and sesame seeds and toss well. Add the soy sauce, orange juice, vinegar, chile-garlic paste, and pepper, and toss again. Serve at once. (Because of the scallions, this relish does not store well and is best used the day it is made.)

¼ cup fresh water chestnuts, sliced (you may substitute canned)

1 cup very thinly sliced scallions (both white and green parts)

2 teaspoons sugar

1 tablespoon minced ginger

1 teaspoon sesame oil

4 tablespoons sesame seeds, toasted in a single layer in a 350°F oven for 20 minutes

2 tablespoons soy sauce

2 tablespoons orange juice

2 tablespoons rice wine vinegar

1 teaspoon Vietnamese chile-garlic paste (you may substitute 1½ teaspoons minced garlic combined with 1½ teaspoons fresh chile pepper)

Freshly cracked white pepper to taste

Grilled Tuna, Cabbage, and Pineapple Skewers with Hoisin Glaze

Serves 4 as entrée

This one is for those of you who haven't experienced the thrill of grilled cabbage. This everyday veggie takes on a new personality with the smoky taste, and its crunchy texture provides a great complement to the silky tuna and the sweet pineapple. If you want to take it to the next level, top the finished skewers with crushed toasted peanuts and a squeeze of lime.

GLAZE:

3 tablespoons hoisin sauce (available in Asian markets)

2 tablespoons tomato catsup

1 tablespoon sugar

1 tablespoon white vinegar

1 1-pound tuna steak, ¾ to 1 inch thick

1 small head green cabbage

1 pineapple, peeled and cored

About ¼ cup vegetable oil

Salt and freshly cracked black pepper to taste

M E T H O D

1. In a small bowl, mix all the glaze ingredients thoroughly and set aside.

2. Cut the tuna steak into ¾-inch to 1-inch cubes. Cut the cabbage in half and remove the core. Cut the cored cabbage halves into wedges about 2 inches long. Cut the pineapple into 1-inch cubes.

3. Thread the tuna, cabbage, and pineapple onto 4 skewers, making sure all leaves on the cabbage wedges are skewered. Use 2 pineapple cubes and 1 cabbage wedge for each piece of tuna.

4. Brush the skewers lightly with the oil, sprinkle with salt and pepper, and grill over a medium-hot fire until the tuna is just opaque through, about 5 minutes per side.

5. Brush the skewers lightly with the hoisin glaze during last minute of cooking, turning once; be careful not to let the glaze burn.

6. Remove the skewers from the grill and serve them either on or off the skewer, as you prefer.

Serving Suggestions:

For a light meal I might serve these accompanied by plain steamed rice or Rice Pilaf with Lime Zest and Almonds (page 270), then finish with Banana-Guava Bread Pudding with Rum Sauce (page 424).

Grilled Peppered Tuna Sandwiches with Sweet Smoked Onion Relish and Fresh Horseradish

Sandwiches for 4

4 4-ounce very fresh tuna steaks, each about 1 inch thick

2 tablespoons vegetable oil

1 tablespoon salt

6 tablespoons freshly cracked black pepper

8 slices good bread

¼ cup freshly grated horseradish

¼ cup lemon juice (about 1 lemon)

I am always amazed by the number of customers in the East Coast Grill who, when the tuna steak they ordered arrives at their table, confuse it with a steak steak. Its heartiness is very much like beef, and in this recipe we take advantage of that quality to create a seafood version of the classic steak sandwich. If you're really ambitious, use Grilled Hearthbread Johnson (page 406) as the sandwich bread.

METHOD

1. Rub the tuna steaks with the oil and sprinkle all over with salt and pepper, using the full amount of both.

2. Over a medium-hot fire, grill the tuna steaks for 2 to 3 minutes per side, or until the interior is pink. (This is for medium rare, which is the way I like tuna; if you prefer it more well done, keep cooking until it reaches the stage you like.)

3. While the tuna is cooking, toast the bread and combine the grated horseradish with the lemon juice and mix well.

4. Let your guests build their own sandwiches, using as much of the fresh horseradish and Sweet Smoked Onion Relish as they like.

Serving Suggestion:

This makes a great dinner along with the Arugula Salad with Oven-Dried Tomatoes, Olives, and Blue Cheese (page 214).

Sweet Smoked Onion Relish

❖ ❖

Makes about 1½ cups

1 large yellow onion, quartered

½ red bell pepper, quartered

1 tablespoon virgin olive oil

Salt and freshly cracked black pepper to taste

2 tablespoons sugar

2 tablespoons balsamic vinegar

2 tablespoons cider vinegar

3 tablespoons chopped fresh parsley

1. Brush the onion and bell pepper with the olive oil and grill over a medium fire until well browned, 4 to 5 minutes. Remove the vegetables from the grill, allow them to cool to room temperature, then chop them rather small.

2. Add the sugar, vinegars, and parsley, mix well, and adjust the seasonings.

Citrus-Cooked Rare Tuna over Green Olives, Radishes, and Potatoes

Here is a Peruvian-style addition to the "citrus-cooked" line of seafood dishes generally known as ceviche and found throughout the tropical world. Removing the tuna from the citrus juices while it is still raw in the middle allows it to retain the firm texture and pure flavor that it would lose if you let it sit until it was completely cooked. Just be sure that you have super fresh tuna when you make this dish.

Since both potatoes and green olives are native to Peru, I combine them with radishes and onions to make a bed of veggies on which the tuna is served. Chiles, basil, and coriander seeds are sprinkled on top for a final layer of intense flavor.

2 pounds super fresh sushi-quality tuna, about ½ inch thick, cut into pieces the size of a matchbook

1½ cups lime juice (about 10 limes)

½ cup lemon juice (about 2 lemons)

6 Red Bliss potatoes, skins left on, cut into slices about the size of half dollars

½ cup pitted cured green olives

1 red onion, thinly sliced

3 large red radishes, thinly sliced, about ⅛ inch thick

2 tablespoons extra-virgin olive oil

Salt and freshly cracked black pepper to taste

1 tablespoon chopped fresh red or green chile pepper of your choice

1 tablespoon thinly sliced fresh basil

1 tablespoon coriander seeds, toasted in a small sauté pan over medium heat until they just begin to smoke, 2 to 3 minutes, then finely crushed

METHOD

1. Place the tuna pieces in a shallow pan that is large enough to hold all of them in a single layer. Pour the lime juice and lemon juice over the tuna, cover with plastic wrap, and allow to marinate for 2 to 4 hours. The tuna should have a milky whitish color on the surface but still be a little raw on the inside.

2. Meanwhile, bring enough salted water to a boil to cover the potato slices, and set a large bowl of ice water in the sink. Blanch the potato slices in the boiling water for about 1 minute, then immediately drain and plunge into the ice water to stop the cooking. They should still have some crunch to them.

3. In a large bowl, combine the potatoes, olives, onion, radishes, and olive oil, sprinkle with salt and pepper, and mix well.

4. Transfer the mixed vegetables to a large platter, lay the tuna on top, and sprinkle with the chile, basil, and coriander.

Serving Suggestions:

This would go easy with some Chile-Yucca Fritters (page 50) or any dish containing grilled lamb or beef.

THE WONDERFUL LIME

Throughout most of the tropical world, limes are an essential flavoring ingredient, almost as prevalent as salt in European and American cooking. The lime has achieved this position of culinary prominence not only because of its fresh, distinctive taste but also because it shares with salt the uncanny ability to enhance the flavors of other ingredients.

Cooks in Central and South America as well as Southeast Asia also take advantage of the fact that, with a sugar content of less than 1 percent, limes are the most acidic of all fruits. Because of this, lime juice can be used to "cook" fish and other seafood in preparations known in South America as ceviches.

Grilled Red Snapper with Napa Cabbage and Ginger-Lime Vinaigrette

This tasty dish shows you that healthy food doesn't have to be diet food. Here we feature the Southeast Asian practice of using lots of greens with grilled seafood, including the aromatic trio of cilantro, basil, and mint. The dressing might seem a bit spicy, but to me its bright floral quality promotes the snapper instead of masking it.

Serves 4 as entrée

DRESSING:

¼ cup virgin olive oil

2 tablespoons sesame oil

2 tablespoons chopped ginger

1 teaspoon minced fresh red or green chile pepper of your choice

6 tablespoons lime juice (about 3 limes)

1 tablespoon sugar

Salt and freshly cracked black pepper to taste

2 cups Napa cabbage, cut into very thin strips

½ cup grated carrots

1 red bell pepper, cut into thin strips

½ cup loosely packed fresh cilantro, stems included

2 tablespoons chopped fresh basil (optional)

2 tablespoons chopped fresh mint (optional)

4 7- to 9-ounce red snapper fillets

2 tablespoons virgin olive oil

Salt and freshly cracked black pepper to taste

METHOD

1. In a small bowl, combine all the dressing ingredients and whisk together well. Set aside.

2. In a large bowl, combine the cabbage, carrots, bell pepper, cilantro, basil, and mint and toss lightly.

3. Rub the snapper fillets lightly with the olive oil, sprinkle with salt and pepper, and grill over a medium-hot fire for 5 to 6 minutes per side, or until they are just opaque throughout.

4. Add the dressing to the cabbage mixture and toss thoroughly. Place the greens on a large platter or individual plates and top with the grilled fillets.

Serving Suggestions:

I would serve this with **Red Potato and Cucumber Salad with Mango** (page 202), **Coconut Rice** (page 272), and **Grilled Spring Onions with Fried Garlic-Ginger Sauce** (page 244).

IT'S ALIVE!

In the New Territories of Hong Kong, there's a village called Lei Yen Mun, which consists of virtually nothing but a maze of seafood restaurants sitting cheek by jowl (or maybe gill by fin) to shops selling live fish out of huge tanks. Like a Cousteau casting call, the seawater tanks contain just about any seafood you could want, from giant grouper to geoduck clams to abalone. You point out what you want, they haul it out of its tank, weigh it, and then carry it into the kitchen of the restaurant of your choice, where it is cooked to order. Unless you're going to go out in a boat equipped with fishing tackle and a portable grill, there's no way to have a fresher, more delicious seafood meal.

Fried Red Snapper Fingers in a Sour Orange–Mango Pickle

This is a variation of the time-honored pickle-like preserving technique often called escabeche, which is used in many different cultures. This version was developed by Amilcar Buruca, our lead line cook at the East Coast Grill. Amilcar claims that it's close to something his grandma makes back in El Salvador, but he smiles a sly smile when he says this, so nobody is sure whether he's telling the truth or just making up a good story to justify his idea. In any event, if his grandma doesn't make it, maybe she should, because it is very tasty and has become a favorite of customers at the Grill. If the concept seems a bit strange to you, try thinking of it as a fish pickle, like a wild Latin version of pickled herring.

Serving Suggestions:

This goes well with All-Purpose Rice and Beans (page 262), Skinless Chicken Thighs with Latin Flavors (page 187), and Chile Quesadilla Bread (page 396).

1 cup all-purpose flour

1 tablespoon cayenne pepper

1 tablespoon ground cumin

1 tablespoon salt

1 tablespoon freshly cracked black pepper

2 pounds red snapper fillets, skins on, cut into strips about the size of a finger

½ cup vegetable oil for frying

PICKLE:

2 tablespoons virgin olive oil

1 yellow onion, thinly sliced

1 red bell pepper, thinly sliced

2 green mangoes, peeled, pitted, and cut into bite-size chunks

1 tablespoon minced garlic

3 tablespoons minced fresh red or green chile pepper of your choice

2 cups fresh orange juice (about 6 oranges)

1 cup red wine vinegar

⅓ cup chopped fresh oregano

Salt and freshly cracked black pepper to taste

METHOD

1. In a large bowl or brown paper bag, combine the flour, cayenne, cumin, salt, and pepper and mix well. Dredge the strips of snapper in this mixture, either by dragging them through it in the bowl or shaking them gently in a paper bag. Shake gently to remove excess flour mixture.

2. In a large sauté pan, heat the vegetable oil over medium heat until hot but not smoking. Add as many snapper strips as will fit in a single layer with space between them, and fry until lightly browned and opaque throughout, 3 to 4 minutes per side. Remove, set aside on several thicknesses of paper towels, and repeat until all snapper strips have been fried.

3. Make the pickle: Wipe the sauté pan clean, add the olive oil, and heat over medium heat until hot but not smoking. Add the onion and cook, stirring frequently, until transparent, 5 to 7 minutes. Add the bell pepper and mangoes and cook, stirring frequently, for 5 minutes. Add the garlic and chile peppers and cook, still stirring, for 1 more minute. Add the orange juice and

vinegar. Bring to a boil, reduce the heat to low, and simmer for 5 minutes. Remove from heat, add the oregano, salt, and pepper, and mix well. You can pour the sauce over the fish and serve it hot, or you can allow the mixture to cool a bit, pour it over the fish, and serve it as a room-temperature dish.

RED SNAPPER

Often imitated, never duplicated, the real American red snapper is truly a world-class eating fish. This finny delicacy, which makes its home mostly off Florida and on into the Gulf of Mexico, has firm flesh and a sweet, distinctive, light flavor that is hard to beat. There are many other delicious members of the snapper family—mutton snapper and grax shapper in the American branch, blood snapper and humpback snapper on the Asian side, and yellowtail snapper and silk snapper among the Caribbean brethren. To my taste, however, the American red is still the shining light of this extended clan.

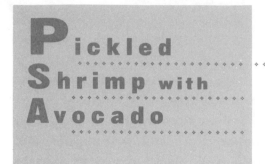

Pickled Shrimp with Avocado

Serves 3 to 4 as entrée or
6 to 8 as side dish

This flavorful shrimp dish is another one inspired by escabeche, a vinegar-based dish popular throughout Central and South America. Escabeche originated as a way of preserving food, but today's versions are valued for their flavors rather than their preservative qualities. In this recipe I have added avocado because I think its richness, along with the mellow shrimp, makes a good foil for the acidity of the vinegar and lime juice, the sweetness of the brown sugar, and the aromatic cilantro.

4 teaspoons virgin olive oil

1½ pounds medium-size (16/20 count) shrimp, shelled and deveined

3 teaspoons ground cumin

½ cup white vinegar

¼ cup lime juice (about 2 limes)

1 tablespoon brown sugar

1 teaspoon minced garlic

¼ cup chopped fresh cilantro

Salt and freshly cracked black pepper to taste

1 ripe but firm avocado, peeled, pitted, and diced small

½ red onion, diced small

1 red bell pepper, diced small

METHOD

1. In an extra-large sauté pan, heat the oil over medium-high heat until hot but not smoking. Add the shrimp in a single layer, in 2 batches if necessary, and sauté until they are well browned, about 3 minutes per side. To check for doneness, slide a thin knife into the center of one of the shrimp and peek at the interior; it should be opaque throughout.

2. Remove the shrimp to a medium-size bowl and add the cumin, vinegar, lime juice, brown sugar, garlic, cilantro, salt, and pep-per. Mix well, cover, and allow to sit in the refrigerator for 4 to 6 hours, stirring once in a while.

3. Just prior to serving, add the avocado, red onion, and red bell pepper and mix well.

Serving Suggestions:

You could serve this with All-Purpose Rice and Beans (page 262), Pumpkin Salad with Cilantro and Toasted Cumin (page 206), and Uncommon Carrot-Raisin Slaw (page 212).

Grilled Chile Corn-Crusted Shrimp with Tropical Fruit Relish

GLAZE:

1/2 cup apricot preserves

1/4 cup Vietnamese chile-garlic paste (you may substitute 2 tablespoons minced garlic combined with 2 tablespoons minced fresh red or green chile pepper)

2 tablespoons white vinegar

2 tablespoons water

CORN CRUST:

1 cup stale cornbread

1/2 teaspoon salt

1 teaspoon ground cumin

1 teaspoon paprika

2 teaspoons cayenne pepper

2 pounds medium-size (16/20 count) shrimp, shelled and deveined

Latin West Indies in style, this particular dish was developed by our former dauntless East Coast Grill chef K. C. O'Hara. K. C. claims that Escoffier used to do lots of grilling with bread crumbs. In any case, the crunch of the crust works well with the limey fruit mixture. K. C. also likes to pull the starfruit out of the fruit relish and put it on the rim of the plate for a dramatic tropical presentation.

METHOD

1. Make the glaze: Place all the glaze ingredients in a small heavy saucepan and heat over medium heat, stirring constantly, until boiling. Remove from the heat and set aside to cool.

2. Make the corn crust: Place the cornbread in a food processor or blender and process until fine. Add the salt, cumin, paprika, and cayenne and process until just mixed. Dump out onto a cookie sheet. Bake 10 minutes at 350°F; allow to cool, and place in a small bowl.

3. Thread the shrimp onto skewers and grill over a medium-hot fire for 3 to 4 minutes per side, or until opaque throughout.

4. Remove the shrimp from the fire, brush both sides with the glaze, and dip into the bowl of corn crust so that they are well covered. Return the shrimp to the fire and toast briefly, about 15 seconds per side.

5. Arrange the fruit relish on a serving tray and place the shrimp on top, skewered or unskewered as you wish.

Serving Suggestions:

Try this with Mexican Corn Pudding (page 398), Señor Rossi's Cuban-Style Yucca (page 256), and an Equatorial Wine Cooler Blanco (page 451).

Tropical Fruit Relish

◆ ◆

I realize that salt and pepper on fruit might sound kind of "out there." But long before I ran into the spiced-up fruits of tropical cuisines, I had seen my Grandfather Wetzler happily sprinkling salt and pepper on his slice of watermelon at lunch during my summer visits. Dutifully playing my role as grandson, I copied him, much to the dismay of my mother and sister and to my own delight. Partly because of this experience, I have always like fruits with seasonings, and I was not as surprised as some to find this a common preparation around the world.

In a large bowl, mix together all the ingredients for the fruit relish. Cover and refrigerate.

½ pineapple, peeled and diced into ½-inch cubes

1 ripe mango, peeled and diced into ½-inch cubes

1 starfruit (carambola), sliced ⅛ inch thick

1 pound watermelon, peeled and diced into ½-inch cubes

½ cup lime juice (juice of 2 limes)

6 tablespoons chopped fresh cilantro

½ cup orange or pineapple juice

Salt and freshly cracked black pepper to taste

Grilled Shrimp with Green Mangoes and Red Lime Sauce

Grilled shrimp are a specialty of the thatched-roofed, open-sided beach shacks on the Pacific coast of Mexico, and to me there is nothing that tastes better. Here we combine them with green mangoes, which have a firm texture that makes them ideal for grilling, and then coat everything with a sauce that features the flavors of Mexico and Central America.

GLAZE:

1 teaspoon ground achiote seeds (you may substitute paprika)

1 teaspoon minced garlic

1 teaspoon ground cumin

1 teaspoon chili powder

¼ cup white vinegar

2 tablespoons molasses

¼ cup orange juice (about 1 orange)

¼ cup finely chopped fresh cilantro

Salt and freshly cracked black pepper to taste

¼ cup lime juice (about 2 limes)

3 large slightly green mangoes (you may substitute green tomatoes)

2 red onions

36 medium-size (16/20 count) shrimp, shelled and deveined

METHOD

1. Make the glaze: Combine all the glaze ingredients except the lime juice in a saucepan, bring to a boil, and simmer over low heat for 2 minutes. Remove from the heat, stir in the lime juice, and set aside.

2. Dice the mangoes and onions into ½-inch chunks and thread them onto skewers alternately with the shrimp.

3. Grill the skewers over a medium fire until the shrimp are just opaque, 3 to 4 minutes per side. Right before you remove the skewers from the grill, brush both sides generously with the glaze. Leave the skewers over the fire just long enough for the glaze to color, then pull them off. Serve over rice and beans and spoon excess glaze over the top.

Serving Suggestions:

I recommend you serve these skewers on top of All-Purpose Rice and Beans (page 262), accompanied by Hobo Pack Vegetables (page 248). Warm tortillas make a nice accompaniment.

Grilled Shrimp Skewers on Grilled Eggplant with Tomato-Feta Relish

This dish is part of a summer meal I like to prepare that is sort of a buffet of modified bar food. I just put out plates of this, along with Grilled Artichokes Johnson (page 242) and Grilled Eggplant and Pepper Sandwiches with Basil and Black Olive Spread (page 266), and let people help themselves. We stagger the cooking, so it's kind of freestyle summer eating, drinking, and sharing good fellowship without too much concern about anything in particular.

RELISH:

2 ripe garden tomatoes, roughly chopped

½ pound feta cheese

⅓ cup extra-virgin olive oil

2 tablespoons balsamic vinegar

Juice of 1 lemon

¼ cup chopped fresh basil

2 tablespoons capers (optional)

2 pounds medium-size (16/20 count) shrimp, shelled and deveined

1 large eggplant, sliced ½ inch thick just prior to grilling

1 tablespoon vegetable oil

Salt and freshly cracked black pepper to taste

METHOD

1. Combine all the relish ingredients, mix well, and set aside.

2. Thread the shrimp onto skewers, rub the eggplant slices lightly with the vegetable oil, and sprinkle with both salt and pepper.

3. Over a medium-hot fire, grill the shrimp until they are completely opaque, 3 to 4 minutes per side. At the same time, grill the eggplant slices until golden brown, also 3 to 4 minutes per side.

4. Remove the eggplant from the grill and put 2 slices on each plate. Remove the shrimp from the grill and place on top of the grilled egg-plant, either skewered or unskewered, as you prefer. Accompany each serving with a generous helping of the tomato-feta relish.

Serving Suggestions:

If you want to make the full not-too-concerned-about-it buffet extravaganza, add Middle Eastern–Style Crisp Bread with Toasted Sesame Seeds (page 404), Lemon-Garlic Grouper Ceviche (page 14), Beer-Battered Fried Clams with Ginger-Soy Dipping Sauce (page 42), and Spicy Roasted Red Pepper Dip with Grilled Pita (page 66).

Sautéed Scallops with Bacon-Corn-Chile Relish

I like to cook sea scallops hard and fast, providing a flavorful sear on the outside and driving the juices inward without overcooking. Both grilling and sautéing are good ways to produce these results. Here we sauté the silky, mellow scallops and serve them with corn and bacon in a chowderesque preparation without the milk.

¼ cup virgin olive oil

2 pounds (20 to 30) medium-size scallops (about the size of golf balls)

RELISH:

5 slices bacon, diced small

½ red bell pepper, diced small

½ green bell pepper, diced small

½ red onion, diced small

4 ears sweet corn, husked, blanched in boiling water 1 minute, and kernels sliced off (you may substitute 2 cups frozen corn)

1 tablespoon minced garlic

1 tablespoon chili powder

1 tablespoon ground cumin

¼ cup chopped fresh cilantro

2 tablespoons lime juice (about 1 lime)

Salt and freshly cracked black pepper to taste

METHOD

1. In a large sauté pan, heat the olive oil over medium-high heat until hot but not smoking. Add just enough scallops so the pan is not crowded and cook, turning occasionally, 3 to 4 minutes. Remove the scallops from the pan and set aside. Repeat with remaining scallops.

2. Make the relish: Add the diced bacon to the pan, reduce heat to medium, and cook until crisp, 4 to 5 minutes. Remove bacon and set aside. Drain all but about 3 tablespoons of fat. Turn heat to medium high, add peppers and onions, and cook for 4 to 5 minutes, stirring occasionally. Add the corn and cook an additional 2 minutes, stirring occasionally; add the garlic, chili powder, and cumin and cook 2 minutes more, stirring occasionally.

3. Remove the mixture from the heat. Add the cilantro, lime juice, salt, and pepper and mix well.

4. Place a generous helping of the relish on each plate and top with ¼ of the scallops.

Serving Suggestions:

This dish is great with Quick and Easy Sautéed Leafy Greens with Lime and Chile (page 231), Mexican Corn Pudding (page 398), and a pitcher of Nick's Sangria 22 (page 450).

GO FOR THE BIG BOYS

There are two basic types of scallops, sea and bay. The bay variety are smaller, more delicate, and, many think, tastier than their meatier cousins. Because the largest scallop-producing seaport in the U.S. is located in New Bedford, Massachusetts, about 30 miles south of Boston, I have had the opportunity to work closely with these fellows over the years, and I like the big ones. In my opinion, their size makes them easier to cook properly. In fact, the small guys might taste better in theory, but it's hard to tell because they are so often overcooked.

Scallop and Nectarine Skewers with Grilled Red Pepper–Lime Sauce

Scallops on the grill are super easy if you firm them up with a quick blanch first. In this case, we skewer the blanched scallops with nectarines, which take on a slight char by the time the scallops are cooked through. Then we finish off the dish with a smoky sauce heavy on grilled peppers and lime juice. This makes a colorful dish for a summer lunch.

SAUCE:

1 large yellow onion, sliced ½ inch thick

3 red bell peppers, halved

2 tablespoons vegetable oil

1 clove garlic

½ cup chicken stock

¼ cup lime juice (about 2 limes)

¼ cup chopped fresh cilantro

Pinch red pepper flakes

Salt and freshly cracked black pepper to taste

¼ cup virgin olive oil

2 pounds (20 to 30) medium-size sea scallops (about the size of pinball balls)

Salt and freshly cracked black pepper to taste

4 nectarines, peeled and cut into 8 wedges (you may substitute peaches)

METHOD

1. Make the sauce: Rub the onion slices and bell pepper halves lightly with vegetable oil and grill over a medium-hot fire until golden brown, 3 to 4 minutes per side. Remove from the grill.

2. In a food processor or blender, combine the grilled peppers and onions with all the remaining sauce ingredients except the olive oil and purée. With the food processor or blender still running, add the olive oil in a steady stream. Set the sauce aside.

3. Grill the skewers: Blanch the scallops in boiling water for 1 minute, drain, and sprinkle with salt and pepper. Thread the scallops onto skewers alternately with pieces of nectarine. You should have about 8 skewers.

4. Over a medium-hot fire, grill the skewers for 2 to 3 minutes per side, or until the scallops are light brown on the outside and just opaque throughout. Serve with the red pepper–lime sauce.

Serving Suggestions:

I would serve this with Grilled Hearthbread Johnson (page 406), Quick and Easy Sautéed Leafy Greens with Lime and Chiles (page 231), and Grilled Peppered Tomatoes with Lemon and Garlic (page 247).

Jennie's Crab Cakes with Funny Red Tartar Sauce

RED TARTAR SAUCE:

¼ cup mayonnaise

¼ cup catsup

2 tablespoons prepared horseradish

¼ cup lemon juice (about 1 lemon)

2 tablespoons pickle relish

2 tablespoons capers

2 tablespoons chopped fresh basil (optional)

1 pound backfin crabmeat

½ cup finely ground toasted bread crumbs

2 large eggs

¼ cup chopped fresh parsley

1 tablespoon lemon juice

2 tablespoons grainy mustard such as Dijon

7 dashes Tabasco sauce

4 dashes Worcestershire sauce

Salt and freshly cracked black pepper to taste

1 cup yellow cornmeal

¼ cup virgin olive oil

I have a close friend, Jennifer, to whom I recently lost a wager. The stakes in this case included a home-cooked meal of the winner's choice, and she chose crab cakes. Since I am not only a professional cook but also a son of Tidewater Virginia, I naturally assumed that the type of preparation would be up to me. No way. Jennifer had crab cakes on her mind, and she knew exactly how she wanted them to be prepared.

In a way I'm sorry that the crab cakes she dreamed up turned out so well—after all, I cook for a living, so I like to think it takes a special skill—but in fact, her recipe was fantastic. So here are her crab cakes, just as ordered, accompanied by a sauce that has, to my knowledge, never been produced anywhere before, a concoction that came to life in the mind of a person who has been eating and loving seafood all her life.

METHOD

1. In a medium-size bowl, combine all the tartar sauce ingredients and mix well. Cover and refrigerate until ready to use.

2. In a large bowl, combine all the crab cake ingredients except the cornmeal and olive oil and mix well. Form the mixture into 4 round or oval patties, each about 1½ inches thick. Roll the patties in cornmeal to cover lightly.

3. In a large sauté pan, heat the olive oil over medium heat until hot but not smoking. Fry the crab cakes until well browned, 3 to 4 minutes per side. Serve accompanied by tartar sauce.

Serving Suggestions:

Serve this with **Savory Watermelon and Pineapple Salad (page 220)**, **Green Bean Salad with Corn, Basil, and Black Olives (page 200)**, and **Uncommon Carrot-Raisin Slaw (page 212)**.

Pineapple Steamed Clams with Simple Coconut Curry

Serves 4 as appetizer or
2 as entrée

COCONUT CURRY:

3 tablespoons coconut milk, unsweetened canned, or prepared by method on page 458

2 tablespoons ground cumin

2 tablespoons paprika

1 teaspoon ground turmeric

1 tablespoon crushed coriander seeds

1 teaspoon cayenne pepper

1 tablespoon minced ginger

1 tablespoon ground cinnamon

1 teaspoon dry mustard

1 cup pineapple juice

1 cup water

2 dozen hyperfresh clams

¼ cup lime juice (about 2 limes)

¼ cup chopped fresh cilantro

¼ cup unsalted peanuts, roughly chopped

Having grown up on Chesapeake Bay and then lived for many years in Boston (Fried Clam Capital of the World), I considered myself somewhat of a seafood expert. But my mind was totally blown by the incredible shapes and forms of shellfish that I encountered in Southeast Asia, from Malaysia to Hong Kong.

One night we had dinner in a restaurant in Bangkok that had huge tanks with live seafood; you picked out the particular fish or shellfish you wanted to devour. I was starving, so I ordered two dozen of a type of clam that resembled littlenecks. The waiter recommended the coconut curry preparation, which I got. I was once again completely stunned by the ability of Thai cooks to lay heavily assertive flavors on seafood without overpowering it.

Here I've tried to re-create the spirit of that dish. You can use any type of clam, and in fact any type of edible mollusk will do, from steamers to oysters to mussels. Since there are many other flavors in this dish, you can get away with a simple spice mix; to come closer to the original dish, though, substitute Coconut-Ginger Wet Spice Mix (page 389).

METHOD

1. In a small bowl, combine all the curry ingredients and mix well.

2. In a small stockpot, combine the pineapple juice, water, and curry mixture and mix well. Place over high heat, add the clams, cover, and bring to a boil.

3. Allow to steam until all the clams have opened, 5 to 7 minutes. (Discard any clams that fail to open after 7 minutes.)

4. Remove from the heat, add the lime juice, cilantro, and chopped peanuts, and serve at once.

Serving Suggestions:

Try this with Malaysian Fruit Salad (page 223) and plain steamed rice or Coconut Rice (page 272).

Grilled Spice-Rubbed Squid with Lime

Cheap, high in protein, and able to hold its own against other intense flavors, squid is a champion in Asian and Mediterranean cuisines. Over the past few years, it has begun to make inroads into American cooking, too. Here we rub it with an Asian-flavored spice mix, then cook it quickly over the intense heat of a hot fire, which results in a flavor-packed crust that covers the entire squid. This treatment avoids the rubbery quality that has given squid somewhat of a bad name among many Americans.

SPICE RUB:

1 teaspoon chili powder

1 teaspoon ground cinnamon

1 teaspoon ground white pepper

1 teaspoon ground cloves

1 teaspoon ground star anise

1 teaspoon cayenne pepper

1½ pounds squid, including tentacles, cleaned

2 limes, halved

M E T H O D

1. In a small bowl, combine all the spices and mix well. Rub the squid all over with the mixed spices.

2. Place the squid bodies on the grill over a hot fire, cover with a clean brick wrapped in foil, and cook 1½ to 2 minutes. Flip, cover with the brick again, and cook an additional 1½ minutes. Remove the brick and roll the bodies around on the grill for another 30 seconds. Remove from the grill and slice into thin rounds.

3. Meanwhile, place the squid tentacles on the grill and cook for about 2 minutes, rolling them around with your tongs so that they cook evenly; they should get quite brown and crispy. Remove the tentacles from the grill, squeeze limes over the tentacles and bodies, and serve.

Serving Suggestions:

This goes quite well before a heavy meat course like Smoked Roasted Leg of Lamb with Chile-Garlic Rub (page 138) or "The Greatest": Grill-Roasted Prime Rib (page 144). And—don't laugh now, I actually had this once and found it to be a great combination—try it with Grilled Bologna and Bacon Sandwiches (page 164).

Cleaning Squid

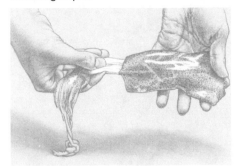

Removing squid guts

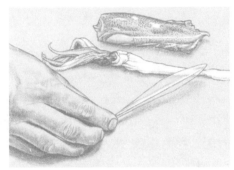

Removing cartilage

Severing tentacles

Peeling bodies

Spicy Grilled Squid Salad with Peanuts and Chiles

In this dish is the crown prince of the underutilized seafood world, the most excellent squid (the king in my mind being the gruesome wolffish, aka ocean catfish, aka loup; see page 82). This strange-looking but delicious-tasting sea creature travels through many cultures and lends itself beautifully to a variety of preparations and flavors. The high heat of grilling is well suited to take on the unique texture of squid, making it chewy but not tough, crispy but not burned.

Serves 4 as appetizer

1 pound medium-size squid, including tentacles, cleaned (see illustrations, page 131)

Salt and freshly cracked black pepper to taste

¼ cup roughly chopped unsalted roasted peanuts

1 teaspoon minced garlic

1 tablespoon minced fresh red or green chile pepper of your choice

¼ cup lemon juice (about 1 lemon)

¼ cup chopped fresh parsley

1 tablespoon molasses

METHOD

1. Sprinkle the squid bodies and tentacles with salt and pepper.

2. Combine all the remaining in-gredients in a large bowl.

3. Place the squid bodies on the grill over a hot fire, cover them with a clean brick or other large, heavy object wrapped in foil, and grill for 1½ to 2 minutes per side. Remove the brick, and use your tongs to roll the bodies around on the grill for an additional 30 seconds or so, then remove them from the grill.

4. Place the tentacles on the grill and cook for about 2 minutes, or until they are brown and crispy, rolling them around with your tongs as they cook so that they brown evenly. Remove them from the grill.

5. Add the bodies and tentacles to the bowl with the other ingredi-ents, toss well, and serve.

MEATS

Smoked Roasted Leg of Lamb with Chile-Garlic Rub ▪ Grilled Lamb Chops with Sweet Mint-Chile Glaze ▪ Spicy Grilled Peppered Lamb Skewers ▪ Rosemary-Cumin Grilled Lamb Skewers ▪ "The Greatest": Grill-Roasted Prime Rib ▪ Skewered Steak with Guava-Soy Glaze and Grilled Pineapple ▪ London Broil "Smoke Gets in Your House" Style with Lime-Marinated Red Onions and Chunky Pineapple Catsup ▪ Gingered Beef Jerky ▪ Roast Pork Tenderloin with Orange–Red Onion Salsa ▪ Grilled Pork and Pineapple Skewers with Spicy Hoisin Glaze ▪ Grilled Pork Chops with Green Apple–Chipotle Salsa ▪ Fried Pork Salad with Cabbage and Avocados ▪ Stewed Greens with Potatoes and Grilled Kielbasa ▪ Grilled Shrimp BLTs with Smashed Avocados ▪ Grilled Bologna and Bacon Sandwiches ▪ Fenway Sausage Bombs—Fully Loaded in the Style of George ▪ Grilled Orange Rabbit with Green Sauce and Toasted Pecans from Hell

BIRDS

Grilled Chicken in the Style of Vulcan ▪ Faux Hokien-Style Ginger Roast Chicken ▪ Barbecued Whole Chicken with Rosemary and Garlic ▪ Grilled Chicken Breasts with Red Cabbage Slaw and Cilantro-Pecan Pesto ▪ Spice-Rubbed Grilled Chicken Breasts with Sweet and Hot Peach Relish ▪ Chile-Soaked Grilled Chicken with Indonesian Catsup ▪ Smoked Chicken and Chickpea Salad with Walnut-Cilantro Vinaigrette ▪ North African Roast Chicken Thighs with Raisins, Almonds, and Apricots ▪ Big Jim's Grilled Chicken Thighs with Garlic and Herbs ▪ Skinless Chicken Thighs with Latin Flavors ▪ Grilled Turkey Steaks with Two New World Salsas ▪ Chile-Rubbed Grilled Turkey Sandwich with Smoky Red Onion Salsa ▪ Grilled Quail with Cardamom, Ginger Sauce, and Grilled Scallions

MEAT AND FOWL MAIN COURSES

■

Traveling in Southeast Asia not long ago, I was having the culinary time of my life. I was sitting down four or five times a day to super fresh seafood of every possible variety, wild noodle preparations, inventive rice dishes, the strangest and most delicious fruit I had ever encountered. Despite all this, one night about three weeks into the trip, I slipped out to a glitzy tourist restaurant in a five-star hotel and had a cheeseburger. It was not a great cheeseburger by any stretch of the imagination, but it was exactly what I wanted.

The point is, sometimes what really tastes best to you is what you are used to. In America the tradition has always been that if a meal didn't include a big steak, a thick pork chop, a large bird, or something else in the meat-fowl line, then it wasn't really a meal. At best it was a snack, at worst a tease.

I have long been an advocate of that line of reasoning, but over the past few years I have changed my tune. Although I'm not into health food, I think the evidence has become too strong to ignore that a diet high in red meat or any kind of animal fat (if you think prime rib is fatty, try a duck!) is bad for your health. A whole range of modern ailments seems to bear some relationship to continuous heavy meat consumption.

Fortunately, there are many other models of eating from areas around the world where meat is less plentiful. In fact, throughout most of the rest of the world, meat has traditionally been used more as a flavoring than as a main course, and most of the recipes in this book follow along that model.

But let's be honest: Sometimes nothing else will satisfy except a great big rare steak or a fat, juicy bird. To my mind, there's nothing wrong with indulging that craving, as long as it isn't a daily occurrence. And if you're going to do it, really do it. Instead of eating a "light" burger that has been steamed to remove the fat, go ahead and indulge in the red meat religious experience—but worship at that altar twice a week instead of twice a day. I guess what I am really saying is that, although I believe we should all shift our diets so that we rely more on grains, fruits, and vegetables, it doesn't make sense to me to eliminate meat entirely at this point.

To that end, here is a chapter with everything from the total fill-your-plate American meal of Grill-Roasted Prime Rib to the Big Bird experience of Faux Hokien-Style Ginger Roast Chicken. I've included a lot of pork and chicken dishes because I love the flavor of pork and the adaptability of chicken, but there are also some meat and fowl choices that are a little more unusual, like rabbit (as in Grilled Orange Rabbit with Green Sauce and Toasted Pecans from Hell) and quail (try Grilled Quail with Cardamom, Ginger Sauce, and Grilled Scallions).

After all, it is part of our culinary heritage to reserve the center of the plate for meat or fowl, and even if it is only on occasion, every once in a while you gotta come back home.

Smoked Roasted Leg of Lamb with Chile-Garlic Rub

Serves 6 to 8 as entrée

3 tablespoons minced garlic

¼ cup chopped fresh cilantro

3 tablespoons chili powder

3 tablespoons crushed coriander seeds

3 tablespoons ground cumin

3 tablespoons minced fresh red or green chile pepper of your choice

Salt and freshly cracked black pepper to taste

1 4- to 5-pound boneless butterflied leg of lamb

Hot weather, lamb, grilling—a unique relationship exists among these three. Here we use a cooking technique that I think is a particularly excellent way to deal with a whole leg of lamb. Half grilling, half roasting, it makes for a crusty exterior and a juicy, rare interior. The spice rub is heavy with chile and garlic, but you can substitute any other dry rub that you like. Middle East Spice Rub (page 383), East African Spice Mix #3 (page 380), and Sweet and Hot Masala #7 (page 388) are all good choices.

MAKING BUTTERFLIES

A butterflied leg of lamb is easy to find, but if the leg you get is boned out but not butterflied, it's easy enough to do yourself. Simply make one cut almost completely through the lamb, lay it open on a counter, then cover it with plastic wrap. Next take a mallet or heavy frying pan and whack it a couple of times, keeping in mind that your object is to flatten the meat to make it cook more quickly. You're looking for a uniform thickness of 2 to 3 inches.

METHOD

1. In a food processor or blender, combine all the ingredients except the lamb and process until puréed. Massage this paste into the lamb thoroughly. (You may refrigerate it in a plastic bag for a couple of hours at this point or go on and cook it right away.)

2. Build a fire on one side of your covered grill. When the fire is hot, put the lamb directly over the coals and sear both sides until very well browned, 4 to 5 minutes per side.

3. Move the lamb to the side of the grill with no coals, put the cover on, and cook for 15 to 20 minutes for medium rare. To avoid cooking the lamb past the stage at which you like it, open the grill at the 10-minute mark and check the doneness by nicking a piece off the lamb. When the lamb is done to your liking, remove it from the grill and allow it to rest for 5 to 10 minutes before slicing.

Serving Suggestions:

Try accompanying this with All-Purpose Rice and Beans (page 262) and Your Basic Cornbread (page 393) and serving Green Grape–Parsley Relish (page 77) alongside.

Butterflying a Leg of Lamb

Trimming fat from leg of lamb

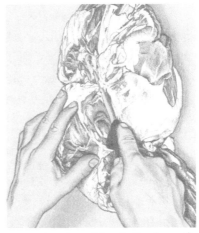

Spreading leg of lamb like butterfly

Slicing into leg of lamb

Grilled Lamb Chops with Sweet Mint-Chile Glaze

Serves 4 as entrée

GLAZE:

¼ cup red wine vinegar

¼ cup orange juice

¼ cup molasses

1 tablespoon minced fresh red or green chile pepper of your choice

1 tablespoon ground cumin

¼ cup finely chopped fresh mint

¼ cup lime juice (about 2 limes)

Salt and freshly cracked black pepper to taste

8 loin lamb chops, each 1½ to 2 inches thick

Salt and freshly cracked black pepper to taste

I clearly remember the day my father handed me some lamb chops and told me to grill them up for dinner. At the tender age of 12, going solo on the family meal was an awesome burden, and somehow I became momentarily distracted and torched the chops completely. I was crushed, but you should let the sad tale of the young boy be a lesson about the give and take of grilling. If you grill, at some point you will ruin dinner.

The fat here is highly combustible, and the thick chops call for a slightly lower fire than you would usually use for red meat. If you have a flare-up from fat dripping into the fire, remove the chops, allow the fire to cool, and then return them to the grill.

M E T H O D

1. Make the glaze: Combine the vinegar and orange juice in a small saucepan, bring to a boil over high heat, reduce the heat to low, and simmer until reduced by half, about 35 minutes.

2. Add the molasses, chiles, and cumin and simmer another 10 minutes or so. Remove the mixture from the heat, add the mint and lime juice, and stir well. Season with salt and pepper and set aside.

3. Sprinkle the lamb chops with salt and pepper and grill over a medium fire for 6 to 7 minutes per side.

During the last 30 seconds or so of the cooking time, brush with the glaze. Remove the chops from the grill, brush again with the glaze, and serve.

Serving Suggestions:

Serve this with Rice Pilaf with Lime Zest and Almonds (page 270), Mangoes, Cucumbers, and Red Onion in Vinegar with Toasted Sesame Seeds (page 350), Parsley Salad with Bulgur, Mint, and Tomatoes (page 216), and A Peach Shortcake for Lizzie (page 430).

Spicy Grilled Peppered Lamb Skewers

Serves 4 as entrée

¼ cup olive oil

1 tablespoon minced garlic

¼ cup freshly cracked black pepper

2 tablespoons salt

1 tablespoon red pepper flakes

2 pounds boneless leg of lamb, cut into 1-inch cubes (slightly smaller than golf balls)

2 red bell peppers, each cut into 8 chunks

3 red onions, quartered

In this version of the classic lamb cubes on a skewer with vegetables, we crank up the heat with two peppers—cracked black pepper and red pepper flakes. Mixed with oil and garlic, the peppers should turn into a crusty coating on the lamb, just the thing for those who need some kick in everything they eat.

METHOD

1. In a small bowl, combine the olive oil, garlic, black pepper, salt, and red pepper flakes and mix well. Pour this mixture over the lamb cubes, coating well.

2. Thread the lamb, red bell peppers, and red onions alternately on 4 skewers, and grill over a medium-hot fire 5 to 7 minutes per side for medium-rare lamb.

Serving Suggestion:

Try it with my personal favorite relish for lamb, Green Grape-Parsley Relish (page 77).

Rosemary-Cumin Grilled Lamb Skewers

ROSEMARY-CUMIN RUB:

2 tablespoons virgin olive oil

2 tablespoons ground cumin

1 teaspoon ground cinnamon

¼ cup finely chopped fresh rosemary

1 tablespoon minced garlic

1 tablespoon kosher salt

2 tablespoons freshly cracked black pepper

2 pounds boneless leg of lamb, cut into ½-inch chunks

Lamb, with its wonderful, distinctive flavor, is a grilling natural. Here we are combining it with a very heavy, moist spice rub with lots of garlic, rosemary, and cumin. Because the rub tends to get overly charred if it stays on the grill too long, we cut the lamb into smaller chunks than usual before skewering and grilling.

METHOD

1. In a medium-size bowl, combine all the rub ingredients and mix well.

2. Rub the lamb chunks lightly with the rosemary-cumin mixture, thread onto skewers, and grill over a medium-hot fire for 4 to 5 minutes per side for medium rare. If you prefer your red meat more well done, just grill longer, until it is one category less well done than you prefer.

3. Remove and allow to stand for 5 minutes, then serve.

THE BIRTH OF BRIQUETTES

Among the many accomplishments of Henry Ford—whether for good or evil—is the invention of the charcoal briquette. Looking for a way to sell the wood remaining from forms used to assemble automobile bodies, Ford hooked up with scientist Charles Kingsford. Kingsford converted the scrap wood into a convenient compressed form of charcoal that also contained sawdust, camphor, petroleum products, and binders.

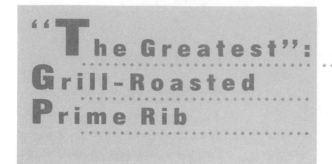

"The Greatest": Grill-Roasted Prime Rib

Serves 8 to 12 as entrée

1 12- to 15-pound capless prime rib (aka export rib), bone in

1 cup kosher salt

1 cup coarsely cracked black pepper

At one time the prime rib ruled as the most impressive cut of meat of all. But now, largely due to its high fat content (read tenderness and flavor), it has taken a slight fall from grace—except, of course, in towns like Las Vegas and Kansas City. But back when I was a young, growing eater, fat was not much of a concern, and there were any number of family stories about my regular habit of taking four or five trips back to the prime rib section of a local restaurant's buffet table. Yes, I have cut way back on my red meat consumption now, but once a year or so I get back in touch with my roots and go hunting for a serious, high-level red meat experience. This is it.

Here we take this large hunk of meat and do a slow roast on the covered grill. This means the type of fuel you use is going to have a big impact on the flavor. Hardwood charcoal is good, but chunks of wood are even better. If you've got a fruit tree getting in the way in your backyard, this is the time to chop it down and throw chunks of green fruit wood on the fire instead of charcoal.

METHOD

1. Rub the prime rib all over with salt and pepper.

2. In a large kettle grill, start a fire well over to one side. When the coals are well lit, place the rib on the grill grid on the side opposite the coals, being careful that no part of the rib is directly over the coals. Put the lid on the kettle with the vents ¼ open. Cook for approximately 2 hours, adding a handful of fresh charcoal every 30 minutes or so.

3. At the 2-hour point, check the rib with a meat thermometer to determine doneness; remove from the fire at 118°F for very rare, 122°F for rare, 126°F for medium rare, and so on, adding 4°F for each degree of doneness. Allow to rest for 30 minutes before slicing.

Serving Suggestions:

You might want serve this with Hobo Pack Vegetables (page 248) Señor Rossi's Cuban-Style Yucca (page 256), and Nick's Sangria 22 (page 450), and put out your Homemade Worcestershire Sauce (page 356) to pour on.

SKEWER MAGIC

- - - - - - - - - - - - - - - - - - -

Prior to the advent of the meat thermometer as a standard tool in the professional chef's tool kit, there was an alternate method of testing meat for doneness that used a steel (not aluminum) skewer. It's pretty easy once you get your confidence up, and it's an impressive feat for your guests. Here's how it works:

- Take the lid off the grill and stick the skewer through the roast; sticking it all the way through is the most impressive, of course.
- Allow the skewer to remain for 30 seconds, then place your hand around the skewer with your thumb marking the point at which the skewer meets the meat.
- Pull the skewer out, figure out the point that is about ⅓ of the way down the section that was actually in the meat, then rub this part of the skewer across the underside of your bottom lip, right where jazz musicians grow little goatees, running it back and forth to sense the temperature.
- If you want your meat rare, this section should be neither cool (that indicates raw) nor hot (that indicates medium), but just warm. Whether you have guessed right or not, it helps to nod your head sagely; then either put the meat back in the oven or set it aside to rest before carving, as indicated.

- - - - - - - - - - - - - - - - - - -

Skewered Steak with Guava-Soy Glaze and Grilled Pineapple

Serves 4 as entrée or 8 as appetizer

Bring out the leis and the blender drinks for this one. No, we're not talking Trader Vic's here—this is my version of the steak skewers I used to enjoy after work in a small bar on the island of Maui in Hawaii. The sweet and tart glaze features the distinct, heavy sweetness of guava juice and caramelizes easily when painted on the skewers just before they are taken off the heat.

2 pounds top round beef, 1½ to 2 inches thick

Salt and freshly cracked black pepper to taste

GUAVA-SOY GLAZE:

½ cup soy sauce

½ cup guava juice (you may substitute pineapple juice)

¼ cup packed brown sugar

¼ cup white vinegar

2 tablespoons minced ginger

1½ tablespoons cornstarch dissolved in 1 tablespoon water

¼ cup lime juice (about 2 limes)

½ pineapple, sliced into 4 rounds 1 inch thick, peel left on

METHOD

1. Cut the steak against the grain into 16 2-ounce slices, pound it lightly, thread it onto skewers, and sprinkle it lightly with freshly cracked black pepper.

2. Make the glaze: In a small saucepan, combine the soy sauce, guava juice, brown sugar, vinegar, and ginger. Bring the mixture to a boil over medium-high heat, reduce the heat to low, stir in the cornstarch-water mixture, and simmer for 5 minutes. Remove from heat, add the lime juice, and mix well.

3. Over a very hot fire, cook the skewered meat for 2 minutes per side, brushing the glaze on each side for the final 30 seconds of cooking.

4. At the same time, grill the pineapple slices for 2 to 3 minutes per side, brushing each side with glaze for the last 15 seconds or so. Remove the pineapple from the grill, cut it into thick wedges, and serve with the grilled steak skewers.

Serving Suggestions:

Try this with New Potato Hash Browns with Caramelized Onions (page 236), Hobo Pack Vegetables (page 248), Banana-Papaya Fool (page 421) for dessert, and Watermelon Daiquiris (page 447) alongside.

AMERICAN EXOTIC

While most of the more exotic tropical fruits seem to come from equatorial Asia, the guava is an American native. Originally from Brazil, it now can be found all over the tropical world. It is hard to get hold of in the United States, however, because it doesn't travel well and is extremely susceptible to infestation by fruit flies, so we must usually make do with guava nectar or paste.

The guavas that we do see in the flesh are usually green on the outside and pink on the inside. Since there are almost 150 varieties of this fruit, however, the interior may range from white to yellow to red, while the outside may be yellow as well as green. Related to cloves and allspice, guavas have a very distinctive, intense aroma and a sweet-tart taste.

London Broil "Smoke Gets in Your House" Style with Lime-Marinated Red Onions and Chunky Pineapple Catsup

Serves 4 as entrée

2 red onions, very thinly sliced

¼ cup lime juice (about 2 limes)

2 to 3 dashes Tabasco sauce

¼ cup freshly cracked black pepper

2 tablespoons salt

1 2-pound London broil (aka top round), about 1 inch thick

4 tablespoons all-purpose flour

If you're not into getting your kitchen and your entire house smoky, then stop right here. This is a variation of the way my grandma taught me to cook this particular cut of meat, marketed as London broil. Most of the time it is top round, a piece of meat cut from the leg of the cow that is less than super tender but quite flavorful. If cooked properly and sliced very thin, it loses much of its toughness while retaining that good flavor.

My grandma would make this dish in the winter, when the grill was parked away in the garage for the season but the family was hankering for that characteristic grilled char. This preparation comes close to grilling but has one important side effect: mucho fumo, amigo. Grandma didn't serve it with this pineapple catsup, but in combination with the lime-marinated onions, it is an excellent cure for winter doldrums.

METHOD

1. Combine the onions, lime juice, and Tabasco and allow to sit, covered and refrigerated, for at least 2 hours.

2. Rub the black pepper and salt into the meat, sprinkle 2 tablespoons of flour on each side, and sear over high heat in a large skillet (with no oil) until well browned, 5 to 7 minutes per side for rare. If you prefer your meat more well done, cook until it is almost the way you like it but not quite there, since it will cook a little bit more after you take it off the heat.

3. Remove from the heat and serve in thin-as-possible slices, accompanied by the marinated onions and Chunky Pineapple Catsup.

Serving Suggestions:

Try this with Grilled Artichokes Johnson (page 242) as an appetizer, then accompany it with New Potato Hash Browns with Caramelized Onions (page 236), Hobo Pack Vegetables (page 248), and Spinach, Avocado, and Papaya Salad with Orange-Cumin Dressing (page 198).

TAMARIND TREES

Tamarind trees, which can reach heights of up to 70 feet, grow in both dry and wet tropics throughout the world. Only India, however, has mature tamarind plantations. Some plantations have recently been planted in Mexico, but throughout the rest of Latin America, Asia, and Africa the trees grow wild in backyards, along roadsides, and in the midst of fields of other crops.

Wherever tamarinds grow, the pulp that is contained in the tree's rust-colored pods is valued for its tangy, sweet-sour taste and its excellent keeping qualities. It is eaten fresh from the pod, but is also used in chutneys, curries, stews, confections, syrups, and drinks of all varieties.

(continued)

Chunky Pineapple Catsup

Makes about 2½ cups

1. In a large sauté pan, heat the oil over medium-high heat until hot but not smoking. Add the onion and sauté until translucent, 5 to 7 minutes.

2. Add the pineapple and continue to cook, stirring, for an additional 3 minutes.

3. Add the remaining ingredients and continue to cook, stirring, for an additional 5 minutes. Remove from the heat. Serve this hot (with the London broil) and then cover and refrigerate for up to 2 weeks.

2 tablespoons vegetable oil

1 yellow onion, very thinly sliced

½ pineapple, peeled, eyes removed, cored, and cut into bite-size chunks

¼ cup orange juice

¼ cup packed brown sugar

¼ cup tamarind water (page 465) (you may substitute ¼ cup white vinegar)

Pinch ground cloves

Salt and freshly cracked black pepper to taste

Gingered Beef Jerky

When I was young, an important activity among the group of kids I used to run with was a daily trip to the store for a quart of soda, some gum balls, potato chips, and beef jerky. So, for an important part of my life, this food was right there on my training table.

I rediscovered this snack on a trip to Malaysia, and upon my return to the U.S., I was inspired to give it a go. I call for a double quasi-curing process here, not only a brine cure but a dry cure as well. This flavor-packed meat is delicious by itself, or you can cut it up and use it as you might use bacon, in a salad or pasta, or as a bar food similar to salted peanuts.

1 pound lean top round, cut against the grain into very thin (⅛-inch) slices

MARINADE:

½ cup soy sauce

¼ cup white vinegar

1 tablespoon minced ginger

1 teaspoon minced garlic

6 dashes Tabasco sauce

2 tablespoons sugar

SPICE RUB:

1 teaspoon ground cumin

1 teaspoon chili powder

1 teaspoon salt

2 tablespoons freshly cracked black pepper

Pinch of ground cinnamon

(continued)

METHOD

1. Place the slices of top round in a baking pan. (It's okay if they overlap each other somewhat.) Combine all the marinade ingredients and pour over the beef strips, making sure all the strips are covered with liquid. Allow to sit, covered and refrigerated, for 10 to 12 hours.

2. Remove the beef strips and discard the liquid. Lay the strips on a cake rack or other wire rack, placing a cookie sheet underneath the rack. In a small bowl, combine all spice rub ingredients and mix well. Sprinkle the beef strips liberally with the rub.

3. Place the rack of beef strips in a 160°F oven, close the door, and go on about your other business. Start checking the strips after about 8 hours; they should be very dry. To check for doneness, remove a piece and allow it to cool to room temperature, then bend it—it should break, not bend. If the meat is not totally dry when you check it, but you are bored with the process and think the meat is okay, you can remove it. Unless you have dried it to a brittle texture, however, you need to store it in the refrigerator.

Roast Pork Tenderloin with Orange–Red Onion Salsa

Citrus, chiles, cumin, cilantro—this classic combination of hot-weather ingredients goes great with lean, clean pork tenderloin. I enjoy working with the tenderloin, not only because it is healthful but also because it is a good portion size and is very versatile, good for grilling or roasting, whole or shaped into scallops. If you want to grill this instead of baking it, grill over a medium-hot fire for 5 to 8 minutes per side or until done to your liking.

SALSA:

1 orange, peeled, seeds removed, and divided into sections

1 red onion, diced small

1 teaspoon minced garlic

5 tablespoons lime juice (about 3 limes)

1 teaspoon minced fresh red or green chile pepper of your choice

1 teaspoon ground cumin

2 tablespoons chopped fresh cilantro

1 teaspoon chili powder

Salt and freshly cracked black pepper to taste

2 pork tenderloins, each 10 to 12 ounces

Salt and freshly cracked black pepper to taste

2 tablespoons vegetable oil

(continued)

METHOD

1. Make the salsa: Combine all the salsa ingredients, mix well, and set aside. (This mixture will keep, covered and refrigerated, for 3 or 4 days.)

2. Preheat the oven to 500°F. Sprinkle the tenderloins with salt and pepper and heat the oil in a large sauté pan until hot but not smoking. Add the tenderloins and sear them well, 2 to 3 minutes per side.

3. Place the tenderloins in a very lightly oiled baking pan and bake for 10 to 12 minutes, or until a peek inside shows just a trace of pink at the center. (If you like your pork more well done, just leave it in the oven another 2 to 3 minutes.)

4. Remove the tenderloin from the oven, allow it to sit for 5 to 10 minutes, cut it into inch-thick slices, and serve with the orange–red onion salsa.

Serving Suggestions:

Serve this quick and easy dish with that Latin classic, All-Purpose Rice and Beans (page 262), and try Amilcar's Grilled Shrimp and Avocado Salad (page 226) as a starter.

HOG HEAVEN

Pork has always been a big number in the American diet. In fact, 19th-century visitors from England complained of being served pork for breakfast, lunch, and dinner, and one of them went so far as to call the United States the Republic of Porkdom. In those days hogs were bred with an eye toward increasing their yield of lard, which was used not only in cooking but as fuel for lamps, as a lubricant, and even in munitions, so a "good" hog was virtually half fat. In recent years, however, America's pork producers, in line with the evidence indicting fat in many modern diseases, have worked to reverse the goal of their forebears and breed leaner hogs. The pork tenderloin, the leanest part of the pig, now contains no more fat than a boneless, skinless chicken breast.

Grilled Pork and Pineapple Skewers with Spicy Hoisin Glaze

Serves 4 as entrée

GLAZE:

¼ cup hoisin sauce (available in Asian markets)

¼ cup tomato catsup

1 tablespoon minced fresh red or green chile pepper of your choice

Salt and freshly cracked black pepper to taste

2 pounds boneless lean pork fillets, cut into ½-inch cubes

Salt and freshly cracked black pepper to taste

1 small pineapple, peeled, cored, and cut into 1-inch cubes

Skewers allow you to move the food around easily and also let each person eat exactly as much or as little as he or she wants. Here we combine flavorful pork with the typically Asian tastes of pineapple and hoisin.

METHOD

1. Make the glaze: In a small bowl, combine all the glaze ingredients, mix thoroughly, and set aside.

2. Make the skewers: Sprinkle the pork cubes with salt and pepper and thread the pork and pineapple chunks alternately onto skewers. Place the skewers on the grill over high heat and sear well. This should take 5 to 6 minutes per side.

3. Just before you pull the meat off the grill, brush it with the glaze. Leave the skewers over the fire just long enough to take on some good color, about 30 seconds per side, then pull them off. Brush with the remaining glaze and serve.

NEO-POSTMODERN PUPU PLATTER

Fried Shrimp and Pork Toasts (page 58)

Deep-Fried Plaintain Rounds (page 253)

Lime-Cooked Rare Tuna with Southeast Asian Flavors (page 16)

Tommy's Complicated Grilled Spicy Thai Chicken Sticks (page 30)

Grilled Fiery White-Peppered Chicken Wings (page 290)

Grilled Pork Chops with Green Apple—Chipotle Salsa

Serves 4 as entrée

4 loin pork chops, bone in, each 10 to 12 ounces

Salt and freshly cracked black pepper to taste

The practice of sitting down and eating large pieces of meat has begun to come under fire of late because of the high fat content of red meat. So it's more important than ever to make your meat count. I don't eat meat consistently as much as I used to, but neither do I deprive myself of the occasional meaningful big meat experience. And when I indulge, a big grilled pork chop is always on my short list. Here we take the Old World pork-apple combo and put a New World chile twist on it with the salsa.

METHOD

Sprinkle the chops with salt and pepper and grill them over a medium-hot fire for 6 to 8 minutes per side, or until the center of the chop is just a bit pink. If you prefer your pork more well done, continue to cook another 2 to 3 minutes. Remove from grill, allow to sit for 5 minutes, and serve with the Green Apple–Chipotle Salsa.

Green Apple–Chipotle Salsa

Makes about 4 cups

1. In a large sauté pan, heat the oil until hot but not smoking, add the onion, and cook over medium heat for 2 minutes. Add the apples, cover, and continue to cook over medium heat, stirring occasionally, for an additional 8 minutes, or until the apples are a bit soft on the exterior. Remove from heat and set aside to cool.

2. Meanwhile, combine the chipotles and vinegar in a blender or food processor and purée. Transfer to a medium-size bowl, add the cumin, lemon juice, molasses, oregano, salt, and pepper, and mix well.

3. Add the apples and onions to the chipotle mixture and stir well. Allow to sit in the refrigerator, covered, overnight or for at least 2 hours.

2 tablespoons vegetable oil

1 large yellow onion, diced small

6 Granny Smith apples, unpeeled, cored, and chopped into bite-size pieces

2 canned chipotle peppers (see Pantry, page 457)

1 tablespoon white vinegar

1 tablespoon ground cumin

1 tablespoon lemon juice

2 tablespoons molasses

2 teaspoons chopped fresh oregano

Salt and freshly cracked black pepper to taste

Fried Pork Salad with Cabbage and Avocados

I know "fried pork salad" doesn't sound very healthful, but in fact this Mexican-inspired salad is a good example of unconscious healthfulness. Instead of the 8-ounce pork chop of earlier days, here we use only about 3 ounces of pork per person, combining it with other strong flavors in what becomes largely a vegetable dish. The meat adds another great taste to the whole but is a flavoring, not a centerpiece. Who said you had to give up meat to be healthy?

Serves 6 as entrée

RUB:

¼ cup crushed cumin seeds

3 tablespoons chili powder

1 tablespoon salt

1 tablespoon freshly cracked black pepper

1 pound boneless pork loin

¼ cup olive oil

1 large head green cabbage, thinly sliced

½ cup lime juice (about 4 limes)

2 tablespoons minced fresh red or green chile pepper

1 red onion, finely diced

1 tablespoon minced garlic

2 ripe avocados, peeled, pitted, and cut into bite-size chunks

1 cup freshly squeezed orange juice (about 2 oranges)

¼ cup red wine vinegar

½ cup chopped fresh cilantro

¼ cup pumpkin seeds, toasted in a sauté pan over medium heat until they begin to pop

Salt and freshly cracked black pepper to taste

METHOD

1. Make the rub: In a small bowl, combine the cumin seeds, chili powder, salt, and pepper and mix well. Rub the pork rounds thoroughly with this mixture.

2. In a large sauté pan, heat the olive oil until hot but not smoking. Slice the pork into rounds about ½ inch thick, add to the sauté pan, and cook over medium-high heat until well browned, 3 to 4 minutes per side. Remove and cut into thin slices.

3. In a large bowl, combine all the remaining ingredients and toss well. Lay the pork strips over the top of the salad and serve.

Serving Suggestions:

You might serve this with Mangoes, Cucumbers, and Red Onion in Vinegar with Toasted Sesame Seeds (page 350), Hobo Pack Vegetables (page 248), or Sweet and Spicy Lo Mein Noodles (page 274).

Stewed Greens with Potatoes and Grilled Kielbasa

Like most things that are slightly sour or bitter, "cooking greens" are an acquired taste for most people. In my case, after a childhood spent fleeing the assertive flavor of these greens, I seem to be spending an adulthood admiring them. I liken the strong, bitter flavor to a shot of whisky—strong, rough, and really good. There are many cooking greens to choose from, and those that are attached to root vegetables like turnips and beets are tossed out by many cooks. So in addition to getting great taste, you can feel good about using food ordinarily wasted.

In this Portuguese-style soup, we throw some potatoes and grilled spicy sausage in with the greens.

Serves 4 to 6 as entrée

2 tablespoons virgin olive oil

1 yellow onion, thinly sliced

1 tablespoon minced garlic

1 tablespoon red pepper flakes

2 pounds cooking greens of your choice, chopped into bite-size pieces (see page 162)

½ cup white vinegar

2 quarts chicken stock

4 potatoes, peeled and halved

1 pound precooked spicy sausage (kielbasa, linguica, andouille, or chorizo)

Salt and freshly cracked black pepper to taste

METHOD

1. In a large soup pot, heat the olive oil over medium-high heat until hot but not smoking. Add the onion and sauté, stirring occasionally, until transparent, 5 to 7 minutes.

2. Add the garlic, red pepper flakes, and greens and cook, stirring, for 2 to 3 minutes; the greens should be bright green at this point.

3. Add the vinegar and chicken stock, bring to a boil, and add the potatoes. Reduce the heat to low and simmer, uncovered, for 1 hour.

4. Meanwhile, grill the sausages over a medium-hot fire for 5 to 8 minutes, or until they are well browned on the exterior. When the soup has cooked for 1 hour, slice the sausages thinly and add them to the soup. Continue to cook for 5 minutes. Adjust seasoning with salt and pepper and serve.

Serving Suggestions:

Serve this with big hunks of Your Basic Cornbread (page 393) and a bottle of aggressive red wine.

(continued)

WHEN A GREEN IS NOT A SALAD

Cooking greens are also called potherbs, a not-very-descriptive name that is used to distinguish them from milder, more tender greens that are usually eaten raw. Greens shrink a lot during cooking—most lose a quarter or more of their volume—so don't think that you are using way more than you need when you start out with a giant bunch of greens for 4 or 5 people.

Cooking greens need to be washed particularly well before being used, and if they are mature, you may want to remove the tough stems and ribs before cooking.

The following are some of the more popular cooking greens.

BEET GREENS: Deep green with red stems and veins, these greens have a nice, earthy flavor, with a trace of the richness of the beets they top.

COLLARDS: The classic green of the South, collards are a member of the cabbage family and are milder than many other greens.

ESCAROLE: The crisp, broad, pale green leaves of escarole have a milder flavor than their cousin, curly endive.

KALE: Another member of the cabbage family, this cousin to collards has gained great popularity lately, after decades of being used in the U.S. only in Portuguese and Creole cooking. It has a mild, cabbagelike flavor.

MUSTARD GREENS: These greens have a bite to them, with a distinct peppery flavor. The most common variety is bright green with a fuzzy texture and frilly-edged leaves.

SWISS CHARD: Like its relative the beet green, chard has red stems and veins, but the leaves that top the stems are darker and more crinkled, kind of like large spinach leaves. There is also a variety with silvery stalks, which is somewhat less flavorsome. Both types have a rich, earthy, sweetish taste.

TURNIP GREENS: Another member of the mustard family, these are among the most bitter of the potherbs. They are dark green, with a rough texture and a particularly tough central rib, which should be removed even on young specimens.

Grilled Shrimp BLTs with Smashed Avocados

Here it is, the Cadillac of summer sandwiches. BLTs have always been one of my favorites, but when you add a rich mixture of shrimp, avocados, and onions, you've got a sandwich that will put a smile on your face. Make sure you use sturdy bread so that you can stuff all the ingredients inside; but even if things fall out, it's still great.

METHOD

1. Sprinkle the shrimp with salt and pepper and thread onto skewers. Grill over a medium-hot fire for 3 to 4 minutes per side, or until opaque throughout. Remove from the grill, cut each into 4 small pieces, and place in a bowl.

2. Add the avocados, onion, lime juice, Tabasco, salt, and pepper and mix together roughly with a large spoon. The mixture should form a thick and chunky kind of paste.

3. Put a generous amount of this mixture on each of 4 pieces of bread, top with bacon, lettuce, and tomato, put the other pieces of bread on top, and eat.

Makes 4 big, hearty sandwiches

1 pound medium-size (16/20 count) shrimp, shelled, deveined, tails removed

Salt and freshly cracked black pepper to taste

2 ripe avocados, peeled, pitted, diced medium

1 small red onion, diced small

¼ cup lime juice (about 2 limes)

3 dashes Tabasco sauce

8 slices bread of your ohoice, lightly toasted

12 slices bacon, cooked until just crisp

4 leaves romaine lettuce, well cleaned

2 large ripe tomatoes, sliced ½ inch thick

Grilled Bologna and Bacon Sandwiches

12 slices bologna

½ cup barbecue sauce of your choice

12 slices bread of your choice, toasted

12 slices bacon, cooked until just crisp

6 leaves lettuce

6 thick slices tomato

1 onion, sliced ¼ inch thick

Sweet pickle relish to taste

I usually save this recipe for close friends, as some people find it difficult to appreciate. I've found it to be particularly popular with kids and my dog Jake. If you have any chili hanging around, or other pork products that you are looking to use up, throw them in. In this case, more is more.

METHOD

Grill the bologna slices over a medium-hot fire until marked with grill marks, about 1 minute per side. Remove from the grill, paint thickly with barbecue sauce, and pile 2 slices between each 2 slices of toast, along with ⅙ of each of the other ingredients. Serve and get out of the way.

Serving Suggestions:

Serve this with a bag of potato chips, a quart of cola, and a subscription to a health magazine.

ON THE STREETS OF GOLD

Whenever I go to a new town, I try to find someone who knows about those unpolished restaurant gems that tend to go unnoticed. On a recent trip to Los Angeles, I was fortunate enough to make contact with Jonathan Gold, who supplies just this kind of information to the public in his role as a wonderfully amusing and informative food writer for the *Los Angeles Times*.

We were just winding down after a day of L.A. ethnic restaurant cuisine, ready to go home fully loaded with everything from Korean steamed beef stomach to world-class El Salvadorean pupusas (stuffed masa cakes), when Gold spotted a rundown joint and insisted that we end the day with an "Okie dog." I've eaten everything from real dog in Vietnam to beef hearts in Peru, but in all my travels I never encountered anything that remotely prepared me for this eating experience. Pushing the outer edge of the taste and health envelope, we sat down to something that I can only describe as some sort of hot dog bomb: An extra-large hot dog was wedged into a bun and then topped with bacon, onions, relish, a bunch of other stuff I didn't even recognize, and finished off with a huge helping of chili. This baby was impressive.

At a time when most people are backing off from meat products loaded with fat, here was a concept running in the opposite direction. I was particularly taken by the combination of bacon and hot dog, being a big fan of both products, and looked to put it in a place that is accessible so that everyone who wishes to can enjoy this unique culinary experience. Being no stranger to bologna as a main-course meat, I did not find it hard to put this together. Here's the result, a sandwich inspired by the fabulous Okie dog itself.

Fenway Sausage Bombs— Fully Loaded in the Style of George

Subs for 8

3 red bell peppers, halved

2 green bell peppers, halved

3 red onions, halved

¼ cup virgin olive oil

Salt and freshly cracked black pepper to taste

¼ cup balsamic vinegar or lemon juice (about 1 lemon)

1 tablespoon red pepper flakes

2 tablespoons minced garlic

¼ cup chopped fresh herbs (oregano, basil, thyme, or sage, alone or in any combination)

¼ cup Home-Style Inner Beauty Hot Sauce (page 355) (you may substitute your favorite hot sauce or Tabasco)

16 3- to 4-ounce link sausages of your choice *or* 8 extra-large sausages such as kielbasa or linguica

8 sub rolls, each 8 to 12 inches long

This dish is a tribute to my friend George, who works a sausage cart in front of Fenway Park before Red Sox games. Maybe it has something to do with the outdoor location or the frenzy involved in scoring a bomb before the game begins, but to my mind George serves the finest sausage bombs known to humankind. If he moved his stand, I would definitely be seeing fewer Red Sox games.

George is also unique because his is the only food stand, among the hundreds around Fenway, that provides Inner Beauty Real Hot Sauce, which I make, with his sandwiches. It is one of my proudest moments when I see his customers happily splashing this sauce on their sandwiches.

George sells a gazillion subs before and after each ball game, and the regulars always call out whether they want theirs "loaded" or not. In this version you get it fully loaded, which I think is the only way to go. The only thing you need to serve with this is a quart of beer, for that real ball park feeling, even if you can't be there.

METHOD

1. Rub the bell pepper and onion halves lightly with about 2 tablespoons of the olive oil, sprinkle with salt and pepper, and grill over a medium-hot fire for 3 to 4 minutes, or until slightly charred. (In this case, it's better to have the vegetables slightly undercooked rather than too charred.) Remove from the grill and slice into thin strips.

2. In a large bowl, combine the grilled peppers and onions with the remaining olive oil, vinegar, red pepper flakes, garlic, herbs, and Inner Beauty and mix well. This is your "load."

3. Over a medium to medium-low fire, grill the sausages slowly for 10 to 15 minutes, or until a peek inside shows no traces of pink. While the sausages are cooking, slit open the rolls and toast lightly on the grill for a minute or two, until lightly browned.

4. Remove the sausages and rolls from the grill and make people line up and walk by as you furiously hustle to put the sausages in the rolls, asking if they want them loaded or not. The loaded get heaping spoonfuls of the vegetable mixture on the bun before the sausage goes in.

Grilled Orange Rabbit with Green Sauce and Toasted Pecans from Hell

If you have a good source for rabbit but haven't tried grilling any yet, have a little faith and give it a try. In order to avoid those annoying "tastes like chicken" remarks from fellow diners, we're going to throw a few curve balls here, adding a pungent cilantro purée, hot spiced pecans, and an oil infused with annatto or paprika to give the meat an unusual orange color.

Notice that the rabbit stays on the grill a long time, so be patient here. The key is a nice, low fire so the rabbit can get cooked through without burning on the exterior. When the rabbit comes off the grill and is ready to carve, your basic whole-chicken breakdown technique works pretty well, except you have to deal with a loin and four legs instead of two.

When you're tired of that same old chicken for dinner, check this out. This is a pretty swanky (and great-tasting) dish for special times and special friends.

½ cup vegetable oil

¼ cup annatto seeds *or* achiote paste (you may substitute 6 tablespoons paprika)

2 tablespoons cumin seeds

2 tablespoons coriander seeds

1 tablespoon chili powder

Salt and freshly cracked black pepper to taste

GREEN SAUCE:

2 cups packed cilantro stems and leaves

¼ cup olive oil

½ cup lime juice (about 4 limes)

2 teaspoons minced garlic

Salt and freshly cracked black pepper to taste

PECANS FROM HELL:

¼ cup Home-Style Inner Beauty Hot Sauce (page 355) or other hot sauce

1 tablespoon olive oil

1 teaspoon white sugar

Salt to taste

½ cup shelled pecans

2 3½-pound rabbits, quartered, with loin cut in half (your butcher can do this for you)

METHOD

1. Combine the vegetable oil and the annatto seeds, achiote paste, or paprika in a saucepan and cook over low heat for about half an hour; this should cause the oil to turn bright orange. Cool, strain, discard the seeds if used, and set oil aside.

2. While the oil is cooling, toast the cumin seeds, coriander seeds, and chile powder in a small sauté pan over medium heat, watching carefully and shaking frequently to prevent burning, until the seeds just begin to release a little smoke, 2 to 3 minutes. Crush the toasted seeds in a spice mill, coffee grinder, or using the bottom of a heavy pan. Add the spice mixture, salt, and pepper to the cooled oil and mix well.

3. Make the green sauce: Purée the cilantro in a food processor or blender with the oil and lime juice. Add the garlic, purée again, and season with salt and pepper. Set aside.

4. Make the pecans from hell: Preheat the oven to 350°F. In a medium-size bowl, combine the hot sauce, olive oil, sugar, and salt. Mix well, add the pecans, and toss until well coated. Toast the pecans in a single layer on a baking pan in the oven until slightly browned, 8 to 10 minutes. Set aside.

5. Rub the rabbits well with the oil mixture and place them on the grill over a low fire. Cover and cook for 10 to 12 minutes per side, or until the meat is opaque throughout. The meat should look just like cooked chicken, although you may want to leave it a little pink at the center, which is the way I like it.

6. To serve, pour a few tablespoons of green sauce on each plate, top with rabbit, and sprinkle some of the spicy pecans over the top.

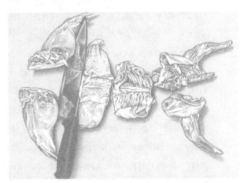

Rabbit in six parts

Serving Suggestions:

To make this a really special dinner, before the rabbit I would serve the unusual Warm Barley Salad with Smoked Salmon and Grapes (page 48), and along with the rabbit I would serve Chile Quesadilla Bread (page 396) and Grilled Sweet Potatoes with Molasses Glaze (page 240). For drinks try Nick's Sangria 22 (page 450), and for a light dessert, the Banana-Papaya Fool (page 421).

(continued)

LIPSTICK SPICE

Annatto is the name of a small evergreen tree that grows throughout the Caribbean, Mexico, and South and Central America. The tree is so brightly colored that the English called it the lipstick tree. Annatto is also the name of a spice made from the seeds and the pulp surrounding the seeds of the annatto tree. It is sort of a strange spice because, while it does have some taste, its flavor pales in importance compared to its brilliant orange-red color.

In pre-Columbian times, annatto was used by Carib Indians and the Maya of Guatemala and Mexico to make a dye with which they painted their bodies prior to battle. Today it is widely used in Caribbean cooking, particularly in Puerto Rico, Jamaica, and Cuba, where it is sautéed in oil or lard which is then used in many dishes. In fact, this process—sautéing oil or lard with a substance that adds more color than taste—is popular throughout South America. Peruvian cooks use an herb called palillo for the purpose, Chilean cooks go for paprika, and Brazilians have palm oil.

Annatto is also known as achiote, but this word may also describe a paste made from ground annatto to which herbs and other ingredients, such as sour orange, are sometimes added.

Grilled Chicken in the Style of Vulcan

Although this dish features the classic Greek flavors of garlic, lemon, cinnamon, and oregano, we named it after our favorite Roman god, who happens to be in charge of fire. In any case, this is a flavor combo that travels back thousands of years and will no doubt still be pleasing palates hundreds of years into the future. There's really nothing more satisfying than a simple combination of basic flavors.

MARINADE:

1 cup lemon juice (4 to 6 lemons)

2 tablespoons minced garlic

1 tablespoon ground cinnamon

1 tablespoon tomato purée

2 tablespoons chopped fresh oregano (you may substitute basil, rosemary, or thyme)

1 tablespoon minced fresh red or green chile pepper of your choice

Salt and freshly cracked black pepper to taste

4 8- to 10-ounce whole boneless chicken breasts

METHOD

1. In a small bowl, combine all the marinade ingredients and mix well. Lay the chicken breasts in a flat, shallow baking pan and pour the marinade over them. Allow to sit, covered and refrigerated, for 2 to 3 hours, turning a couple of times.

2. Remove the chicken breasts and discard the marinade. Grill the chicken breasts over a medium-hot fire for 7 to 9 minutes per side, or until the juices run clear when the chicken is pierced, and a peek at the thickest part of one of the breasts shows no translucence. Remove from the grill and serve.

Faux Hokien-Style Ginger Roast Chicken

Serves 6 to 8 as entrée

2 3-pound whole roasting chickens

4 tablespoons minced ginger

2 tablespoons sesame oil

1 tablespoon vegetable oil

4 tablespoons minced scallions

3 tablespoons freshly cracked white pepper

1 tablespoon ground star anise

1 tablespoon red pepper flakes

2 tablespoons kosher salt

There is a huge Chinese population in Malaysia today. A great many of them are descended from Hokien Chinese brought from southern China to build the railroads for British colonists. While Chinese food of all kinds is prevalent in Malaysia, perhaps the most widespread single dish is "chicken rice," available from stands in every corner of the Malay Peninsula. It's pretty simple—you get a plate of roast chicken, chicken broth, and white rice—but it tastes fantastic.

This is my tribute to those many chicken-rice meals I consumed as daily snacks while traveling in Malaysia. If you are Hokien or Malaysian, please forgive my unworthy attempt to honor this dish, which feeds millions daily. If you are not, check it out—it's easy and tastes great.

METHOD

1. Preheat the oven to 425°F. Lift the skin away from the meat at the breastbone of one bird, right at the top of the cavity into which you would put stuffing if you were doing that. With a sharp knife, cut the membrane that holds the skin to the flesh along the center of the bird, then slide your fingers under the skin and probe around on top of the breast down to about the ribs, separating the skin from the meat. Repeat this process with the second bird.

2. In a small bowl, combine the ginger, oils, and scallions and mix well. Spread half of this mixture evenly underneath the skin of the breast of each bird, trying not to poke through the skin in the process.

3. In a small bowl, combine the white pepper, anise, red pepper flakes, and salt and mix well. Rub this mixture all over the outside of the chickens.

4. Place the birds on a rack in a roasting pan and roast in the preheated oven for 40 to 50 minutes. Check for doneness by piercing the area between the leg and thigh with a fork. If the juices run clear, the bird is done; if not, return it to the oven and check again in 10 minutes or so.

Putting Spices under Chicken Skin

Lifting skin of chicken

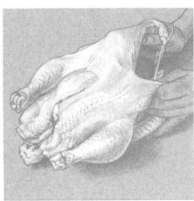

Stuffing spices under skin

Barbecued Whole Chicken with Rosemary and Garlic

Serves 4 to 6 as entrée

2 3- to 3½-pound whole chickens

¼ cup fresh rosemary needles

2 tablespoons minced garlic

Salt and freshly cracked black pepper to taste

This recipe uses your Basic Barbecue Technique—covered indirect cooking. The key here, as with all barbecuing, is to be patient and keep the fire low. Before you begin, you should review your mantra—"slow and low"—and be sure you remember the timer for measuring the intervals between adding small handfuls of coals: roughly the amount of time it takes an average human being to consume 12 ounces of beer. On a large covered grill, you can do two whole chickens of this size without any problem. Any more is pushing it.

BARBECUED CHICKENS OF THE WORLD

The method used in this recipe—rubbing the chicken inside and out with flavoring agents—can be done using any herb combination you like or any dry or wet spice mixture in this book.

For Middle Eastern barbecued chicken, for example, rub the bird inside and out with Middle Eastern Spice Rub (page 383). Sweet and Hot Masala #7 (page 388) will give you a North Indian barbecued chicken; Latin-Style Spice Rub (page 379) results in a Mexican-flavored barbecued chicken. For a truly wild taste, try using Tangerine Chile Oil (page 365) as the rub. Check out the spice rubs on pages 371–389 and use whatever strikes your fancy.

I really like this idea because it lets you cook the same basic dish dozens of times with a very different result in terms of flavor. No matter what oil or rub you use, the cooking time and technique remain the same.

METHOD

1. Starting at the tip of the breast-bone, loosen the skin from the breasts of the chickens, being careful not to tear the skin. Gently rub the rosemary and garlic under the skin. Sprinkle the outside of the chickens with salt and pepper.

2. In a covered grill, build a small fire off to one side, making sure that all of the fuel becomes completely engulfed in flames. When the flames have died down and you are left with flickering coals, place the chickens on the grill surface over the side with no fire. It is important that the chickens not come in contact with the flames at any time during cooking.

3. Cover the grill and vent slightly. You will need to check the fire every 20 minutes or so as the chickens cook, adding a bit more fuel as necessary to keep the fire going. The key here is to go slow and low.

4. After 2 hours, check the chickens for doneness by piercing the thigh with a fork. When the juices run clear, the birds are done.

Serving Suggestions:

I would serve this with Green Bean Salad with Corn, Basil, and Black Olives (page 200), Roast Beet and Carrot Salad with Lemon-Mint Dressing (page 204) and Couscous with Raisins and Parsley (page 276). For dessert, try the Banana-Papaya Fool (page 421).

Grilled Chicken Breasts with Red Cabbage Slaw and Cilantro-Pecan Pesto

CILANTRO-PECAN PESTO:

1 cup loosely packed fresh cilantro (stems may be included)

1 tablespoon minced garlic

¼ cup chopped pecans

6 tablespoons virgin olive oil

¼ cup lime juice (about 2 limes)

6 dashes Tabasco sauce

Salt and freshly cracked black pepper to taste

4 8- to 10-ounce boneless chicken breasts

¼ cup vegetable oil

Salt and freshly cracked black pepper to taste

This lively chicken breast dish has a Latin slant to it, featuring a strong cilantro purée along the lines of basil pesto, with pecans filling in for the pine nuts. The crunchy, sweetish-sour coleslaw has a little kick to it, and the dish as a whole has a lot of vibrant colors going on.

METHOD

1. Make the pesto: Combine all the ingredients in a food processor or blender and process until a rough paste is formed. Cover and set aside.

2. Coat the chicken lightly with oil on both sides and sprinkle with salt and pepper.

3. Grill the chicken over a medium fire, 7 to 9 minutes per side. To check the level of doneness, simply cut into one of the breasts and peek inside to be sure it has no pink.

4. Remove the chicken from the fire, top each breast with a generous tablespoon of the cilantro-pecan pesto, and serve accompanied by Red Cabbage Slaw.

Serving Suggestions:

This is good cold the next day; try it with Mexican Corn Pudding (page 398).

Red Cabbage Slaw

1. Combine the cabbage and red pepper in a large bowl.

2. In a small bowl, combine all the remaining ingredients and whisk together well.

3. Pour the dressing over the cabbage and pepper and toss well.

1 small head red cabbage, thinly sliced

½ red bell pepper, thinly sliced

¼ cup virgin olive oil

⅓ cup mayonnaise

¼ cup pineapple juice

¼ cup golden raisins

3 dashes Tabasco sauce

Salt and freshly cracked black pepper to taste

Spice-Rubbed Grilled Chicken Breasts with Sweet and Hot Peach Relish

Serves 4 as entrée

In this chicken preparation, we remove the skin from the breast—a maneuver that more and more health-conscious eaters are doing—and replace it with a spice paste, which provides a nice, crusty exterior much like that of the skin. You will also find that skinless chicken is considerably easier to grill, since the danger of flare-up is completely removed.

SPICE PASTE:

1 tablespoon each minced garlic, ground cumin, chili powder, curry powder, crushed coriander seeds, paprika, and brown sugar

1 teaspoon ground allspice

¼ cup red wine vinegar

¼ cup white wine

Salt and freshly cracked black pepper to taste

4 8- to 10-ounce boneless, skinless chicken breasts

2 tablespoons vegetable oil

Salt and freshly cracked black pepper to taste

METHOD

1. In a small bowl, combine all the spice paste ingredients and mix well.

2. Rub the chicken lightly with the vegetable oil, sprinkle with salt and pepper, and grill over a medium fire for 7 to 9 minutes per side.

3. Brush on the spice paste and cook 1 additional minute per side; the paste should be brown and crusty but not burned and the chicken should be opaque through-out. Serve accompanied by Sweet and Hot Peach Relish.

Serving Suggestions:

I would serve this with a selection of Middle Eastern–inspired salads, like Turnip and Bread Salad with Minted Yogurt Dressing (page 208), Parsley Salad with Bulgur, Mint, and Tomatoes (page 216), and Roast Beet and Carrot Salad with Lemon-Mint Dressing (page 204), along with Middle Eastern–Style Crisp Bread (page 404).

Sweet and Hot Peach Relish

This relish is fairly hot, but it also has a mellow sweetness that contrasts nicely with the spicy, crunchy exterior of the chicken breasts.

In a large bowl, combine all the ingredients and mix well. This relish will keep, covered and refrigerated, for about 4 days.

4 large ripe or semi-ripe peaches, pitted and thinly sliced

1 red bell pepper, cut into thin strips

½ cup orange juice

1 tablespoon lime juice (about ½ lime)

1 tablespoon molasses

1 tablespoon minced fresh red or green chile pepper of your choice

¼ cup chopped fresh parsley

Salt and freshly cracked black pepper to taste

Chile-Soaked Grilled Chicken with Indonesian Catsup

2 pounds boneless, skinless chicken breasts

CHILE MARINADE:

¼ cup minced fresh red or green chile pepper of your choice

¼ cup lime juice (about 2 limes)

¼ cup soy sauce

½ cup water

1 tablespoon freshly cracked pepper (white if available)

This is a version of satay, the hot dog of Southeast Asia. I call it that because, whether you're in Malaysia, Indonesia, Thailand, or Singapore, you will find street vendors selling these little snacks in every vacant lot, train station, and thoroughfare. The general rule is, if there's room to set up a charcoal grill, someone will be there cooking something on a skewer.

Here I turn up the heat on the chicken with a soy-lime-chile bath prior to cooking, so it's going to be spicy. But the sweet catsup (actually *kejap* in Indonesia) balances the heat.

METHOD

1. Cut the chicken breasts into slices about ½ inch thick and 3 inches long (like a thin finger) and thread onto skewers. Place the skewers in a single layer in a large shallow pan.

2. In a large bowl, combine all the marinade ingredients and mix well. Pour the marinade over the chicken skewers and allow to sit for 3 to 4 hours, covered and refrigerated, turning once or twice.

3. Remove the chicken skewers, discard the marinade, and grill the skewers over a medium-hot fire un-til nicely browned on the outside and completely opaque on the interior, 2 to 3 minutes per side. Just before removing from the grill, brush the chicken with Indonesian Catsup. Remove from the heat and serve, with a bowl of the catsup for dipping.

Serving Suggestions:

Green Mango Slaw (page 213), Coconut Rice (page 272), and this dish make an excellent trio.

Indonesian Catsup

Makes about 2 oups

In a medium-size saucepan, combine all the ingredients, bring to a boil, reduce the heat to low, and simmer for 7 to 10 minutes, stirring frequently, until the mixture has thickened slightly. Remove from the heat. The mixture may seem liquid, but it thickens considerably after refrigeration. It will keep, covered and refrigerated, for several months.

½ cup molasses

½ cup soy sauce

½ cup packed brown sugar

2 tablespoons minced fresh ginger

1 teaspoon nutmeg (freshly grated if possible)

2 tablespoons freshly cracked black pepper

Smoked Chicken and Chickpea Salad with Walnut-Cilantro Vinaigrette

4 8- to 10-ounce boneless, skinless chicken breasts

Salt and freshly cracked black pepper to taste

VINAIGRETTE:

¼ cup walnuts

1 teaspoon minced garlic

½ cup lemon juice (about 2 lemons)

¼ cup roughly chopped fresh cilantro

¾ cup virgin olive oil

Salt and freshly cracked black pepper to taste

1 16-ounce can chickpeas, drained and rinsed well (about 2 cups)

2 ripe tomatoes, diced small

2 cucumbers, diced small

1 red onion, diced small

½ cup chopped fresh parsley

1 tablespoon ground cinnamon

1 head romaine lettuce, washed well, dried, and leaves torn in thirds

This is a great way to use any leftover grilled chicken from last night's dinner. However, in my experience grilled chicken is so good that there is rarely any left over, so what you might want to do is just toss a chicken breast on the side of the grill while you're grilling tonight's steak, then save it for tomorrow's lunch.

The walnuts, lemon, and cinnamon in this dish put the inspirational source somewhere in the Middle East, so grilled pita is a nice accompaniment.

METHOD

1. Sprinkle the chicken breasts lightly with salt and pepper and grill over a medium fire for 7 to 9 minutes per side, until the meat is opaque throughout when you slice into it. Remove the chicken from the grill, set aside to cool, then slice into strips about the thickness of your little finger.

2. While the chicken is cooling, make the vinaigrette: Toast the walnuts in a single layer on a baking sheet in a 350°F oven until light golden brown, 15 to 20 minutes. Roughly chop the toasted walnuts and mix them in a small bowl with the garlic, lemon juice, and cilantro. Whisk the olive oil into this mixture and season with salt and pepper.

3. In a large bowl, combine the chickpeas, tomatoes, cucumbers, red onion, parsley, cinnamon, and lettuce and toss well. Top with the sliced chicken and drizzle with as much vinaigrette as you like.

Serving Suggestions:

If you're serving this as a dinner appetizer, you might follow it up with Panfried Cod with Tomato-Mint Yogurt Sauce (page 96), Salty Persian-Style Pickled Turnips and Onions (page 254), and Grilled Pita Bread (page 67).

North African Roast Chicken Thighs with Raisins, Almonds, and Apricots

In this dish we see a commonly used technique for cooking with spices, which is to add them at the sauté stage and sweat them to bring out their flavors.

12 skinless chicken thighs (bones in)

Salt and freshly cracked black pepper to taste

2 tablespoons virgin olive oil

1 yellow onion, thinly sliced

1 tablespoon minced garlic

2 small to medium-sized sweet potatoes, peeled and cut into bite-size chunks

1 tablespoon minced ginger

1 tablespoon ground cumin

1 tablespoon ground cinnamon

1 tablespoon ground coriander

1 teaspoon ground turmeric

1 teaspoon paprika

2 teaspoons salt

4 cups chicken stock

2 tablespoons lemon juice (about ½ lemon)

¼ cup raisins

¼ cup dried apricots, chopped

¼ cup blanched almonds, roughly chopped

1 tablespoon minced fresh red or green chile pepper of your choice

METHOD

1. Heat the oven to 350°F. Sprinkle the chicken thighs with salt and pepper. In a large sauté pan, heat the olive oil over medium heat until hot but not smoking; add the chicken thighs and cook, moving around every couple of minutes, until well browned on all sides, 5 to 7 minutes. Remove and set aside.

2. Add the onion slices to the sauté pan and sauté over medium heat, stirring frequently, until they begin to brown, 5 to 7 minutes. Add the garlic and cook, stirring frequently, 1 additional minute. Add the sweet potatoes, ginger, spices, and salt and cook, still stirring frequently, for 1 more minute. Add the stock, reserved chicken thighs, and all the remaining ingredients and bring to a boil.

3. Cover the sauté pan, put it in the preheated oven, and cook until the chicken thighs are tender and cooked through, 20 to 25 minutes. Season with salt and pepper and serve.

Serving Suggestions:

This North African–slanted combo is great with Rice Pilaf with Lime Zest and Almonds (page 270), Roast Beet and Carrot Salad with Lemon-Mint Dressing (page 204), North African Chile Pepper Condiment (page 360), and Eggplant Chutney (page 348).

Big Jim's Grilled Chicken Thighs with Garlic and Herbs

8 6- to 7-ounce chicken thighs (bones in)

Salt and freshly cracked black pepper to taste

VINAIGRETTE:

6 tablespoons extra-virgin olive oil

2 tablespoons balsamic vinegar

1 teaspoon minced garlic

1 tablespoon capers

2 tablespoons chopped fresh herbs of your choice (rosemary, basil, oregano, or thyme, alone or in combination)

Lemon quarters for garnish (optional)

Jimmy Burke, my long-time friend and the first real chef I worked for, taught me one of the golden rules of cooking: Sometimes less is more. From him I learned that simple flavors presented in a clear, uncluttered way are really good. He always said, "Whatever you're going to do, whether it's a hamburger or foie gras, use the best stuff and do it right." Heeding his advice, here we stay simple and feature the classic Italian combination of fresh herbs, garlic, olive oil, and balsamic vinegar.

METHOD

1. Sprinkle the chicken thighs with salt and pepper and grill, skin side down, over medium-low fire for 8 to 10 minutes.

2. Flip the thighs and grill for an additional 4 to 6 minutes. To make sure they are done, make an incision close to the bone and check that there is no redness.

3. Meanwhile, combine the vinaigrette ingredients in a bowl and mix well.

4. Remove the thighs from the grill and ladle the vinaigrette over them. Serve with lemon quarters for garnish.

Shrimp and Corn Chowder with Yucca (page 8)

Scallop and Nectarine Skewers with Grilled Red Pepper-Lime Sauce (page 124); Grilled Sausage Skewers with Fresh Apricots, Jalapeños, and Chipotle Vinaigrette and Whole Grill–Roasted Banana (page 288); Skewered Steak with Guava-Soy Glaze and Grilled Pineapple (page 146); Tommy's Complicated Grilled Spicy Thai Chicken Sticks with Coconut Peanut Dipping Sauce (page 30); Grilled Shrimp with Green Mangoes and Red Lime Sauce (page 118)

Grilled Chicken Thighs with Persian-Style Nut Rub (page 33), served with Big Sky's Grilled Sweet Lemon Salad with Parsley (bottom)(page 222) and Parsley Salad with Bulgur, Mint, and Tomatoes (page 216)

Neo-Postmodern Pupu Platter (clockwise from top left): Fried Shrimp and Pork Toasts
(page 58), Grilled Pork- and Shrimp-Stuffed Chiles with Sweet Soy Glaze (page 55),
Watermelon Daiquiris (page 447), Fried Sweet Plantains (page 260), Grilled
Mahimahi with Honey-Macadamia Crust and Pineapple-Ginger Relish (page 80),
Grilled Pork and Pineapple Skewers with Spicy Hoisin Glaze (page 155)

Grilled Foie Gras on Toast
(page 62)

Smoky Eggplant Dip with
Yogurt (page 64), Spicy
Roasted Red Pepper Dip
(page 66), and Spicy
Pumpkin Dip (page 68),
all served with
Grilled Pita (page 67)

Grilled Swordfish with Spicy Shrimp Salsa (page 78)

Grilled Peppered Tuna Sandwiches with Sweet Smoked Onion Relish and Fresh Horseradish (page106)

Citrus-Cooked Rare Tuna over Green Olives, Radishes, and Potatoes (page108)

Grilled Red
Snapper with
Napa Cabbage
and Ginger-Lime
Vinaigrette
(page 110)

Lava-Soaked Very Rare
Steak Salad with
Grilled Cabbage
and Galangal
(page 282)

Grilled Fiery White-Peppered Chicken Wings (page 290)

Smoked Roasted Leg of Lamb with Chile-Garlic Rub (page 138) accompanied by Green Grape–Parsley Relish (page 77)

Faux Hokien-Style Ginger Roast Chicken (page 172)

Watercress and Crab Salad with
Mangoes and Fish Sauce
(page 221)

Grilled Quail
with Cardamom,
Ginger Sauce, and
Grilled Scallions
(page 192)

Cardamom Chicken Stew in the Indian Style (page 304)

Indian-Style Grill Bread (page 400), surrounded by (clockwise):
Mangoes, Cucumbers, and Red Onion in Vinegar with Toasted Sesame
Seeds (page 350); Red Onion–Chile Relish with Lime and Basil (page 351);
Eggplant Chutney (page 348); Apricot-Anise Chutney (page 342); Lentil Salad
with White Grapes and Carrots (page 210)

Panfried Banana Fritters
with Molasses-Rum
Sauce (page 428)

Grilled Peaches with Blue Cheese
and Sweet Balsamic Glaze
(page 412)

Banana-Papaya Fool (page 421)

Skinless Chicken Thighs with Latin Flavors

It is becoming more and more popular to remove the skin from chicken as people try to avoid as much fat as possible in their diets. This is a little problematic for me because the semi-burned, crispy skin of grilled chicken is my favorite part. Here I use a paste of herbs and spices to try to re-create the crusty texture of the skin. This particular paste is rather loose when first made; if you prefer a thicker mixture, put it in the refrigerator for a couple of hours and it will firm up. If you use it right after making it, soak the chicken in it for 5 to 10 minutes before grilling; if you let it chill and firm up, just slap it on the chicken and grill away.

CITRUS-HERB PASTE:

1 teaspoon each minced garlic, ground cumin, chili powder, paprika, ground coriander, salt, and freshly cracked black pepper

2 tablespoons chopped fresh cilantro

3 tablespoons each orange juice and pineapple juice

2 tablespoons lime juice (about 1 lime)

4 to 8 dashes Tabasco sauce

1 tablespoon olive oil

6 boneless, skinless chicken thighs

METHOD

1. Combine all the paste ingredients in a food processor or blender and purée. Rub the boned thighs with the paste.

2. Grill the chicken thighs over a medium-hot fire for 4 to 5 minutes per side, or until a peek inside shows no trace of red.

Grilled Turkey Steaks with Two New World Salsas

Serves 4 as entrée

1 tablespoon ground cumin

1 tablespoon red pepper flakes

1 tablespoon ground coriander

Salt and freshly cracked black pepper to taste

4 10-ounce turkey breast steaks, ½ to 1 inch thick

Here's a combination of dishes featuring New World ingredients. The Spaniards may have brought chickens to Mexico, but the Aztecs had domesticated turkeys long before that. Of course, they were also eating insect tamales with earth cheese (algae grown on canals), but then taste is a funny thing.

Not many of us think of turkey fillets on the grill or in the sauté pan, but they react well to the high heat of quick-cooking methods, seared on the outside and juicy and tender in the interior. To accompany the fillets, we provide a smooth, limey Avocado Salsa and a spicy Chile-Corn Salsa.

METHOD

1. In a small bowl, combine cumin, red pepper flakes, coriander, salt, and pepper.

2. Rub the turkey steaks well with this mixture and grill over a medium-hot fire for 5 to 6 minutes per side, or until the turkey is lightly browned on the exterior and, when cut into with a knife, opaque throughout. Serve each turkey steak accompanied by a generous helping of the Avocado Salsa and Chile-Corn Salsa.

Avocado Salsa

In a large bowl, combine all the ingredients, mix well, and adjust seasonings to taste.

2 ripe avocados, peeled, pitted, and diced medium

½ cup lime juice (about 4 limes)

¼ cup chopped fresh cilantro

2 teaspoons finely minced garlic

1 tablespoon sour cream

1 red onion, diced small

2 teaspoons ground cumin

Salt and freshly cracked black pepper to taste

Chile-Corn Salsa

1. Rub the corn lightly with vegetable oil and sprinkle lightly with salt and pepper. Grill over a low fire, rolling the ears around with your tongs to be sure they cook evenly, until the corn is slightly charred, 7 to 10 minutes.

2. Remove the corn from the grill and, as soon as it is cool enough to handle, slice the kernels off the cobs. In a large bowl, mix together with all the remaining ingredients and season with salt and pepper. This salsa will keep, covered and refrigerated, for 3 to 4 days.

4 ears corn, husked and desilked

1 tablespoon vegetable oil

Salt and freshly cracked black pepper to taste

4 scallions, thinly sliced

1 red bell pepper, diced small

2 tablespoons minced fresh red or green chile pepper of your choice

2 tablespoons sugar

¼ cup cider vinegar

Chile-Rubbed Grilled Turkey Sandwich with Smoky Red Onion Salsa

3 tablespoons chili powder

1 tablespoon ground cumin

1 tablespoon freshly cracked black pepper

4 4- to 5-ounce turkey fillets, each 1 to 1½ inches thick

8 slices bread of your choice

SALSA:

1 small red onion, sliced into 4 large rounds

1 ripe tomato, sliced into 4 large rounds

6 tablespoons lime juice (about 3 limes)

¼ cup chopped fresh cilantro

4 to 10 dashes Tabasco sauce, depending on your taste for heat

Salt and freshly cracked black pepper to taste

Turkey fillets are great—fast and easy to cook when you don't feel like putting a lot of effort into dinner, low in fat, and high in protein. They are also perfect for grilling because the quick-cooking method keeps the interior moist while the sear adds flavor to the meat. Here we use a simple spice rub to pep up the rather bland turkey meat and, since the fire is already built, we take advantage of it to add a smoky red onion–tomato salsa as the condiment of choice. A flavorful sandwich that's quick and healthful, this one is just right for a weekend picnic.

METHOD

1. In a small bowl, combine the chili powder, cumin, and black pepper and mix. Rub the turkey fillets with this spice mixture.

2. Over a medium-hot fire, grill the turkey fillets until they are lightly browned on the exterior and cooked through, 6 to 7 minutes per side. Check for doneness by nicking one of the fillets and peeking inside; it should be completely cooked, with no trace of red.

3. While the fillets are cooking, lightly toast the bread on the outer part of the grill until golden, about 1 minute per side.

4. To make the salsa: Over the same medium fire, grill the onion and tomato slices until slightly seared, about 2 minutes per side. Remove from the grill and put in a medium-size bowl. Add all the remaining ingredients and mix well.

5. Serve the cutlets sandwiched between 2 slices of the toast with a generous portion of salsa.

Grilled Quail with Cardamom, Ginger Sauce, and Grilled Scallions

Butterflying quail for the grill is a bit tricky, but I think it's worth the effort. You end up with a great-tasting little item that takes to the grill well, is flavorful in its own right, makes a good foil for many other flavors, and can be served as appetizer or entrée. This particular dish uses a dry rub featuring cardamom, the world's second most costly spice (after saffron). The pungency of this costly little pod goes great with the orangy, sweet, Asian-style barbecue sauce.

SWEET GINGER SAUCE:

1 tablespoon sesame oil

2 tablespoons olive oil

2 tablespoons minced ginger

1/2 cup freshly squeezed orange juice (about 1 orange)

1/4 cup rice wine vinegar

1/4 cup hoisin sauce (available in Asian markets)

3 tablespoons freshly ground cardamom

3 tablespoons freshly cracked white pepper

2 tablespoons salt

1 teaspoon red pepper flakes

10 quail, butterflied and backbone removed

10 scallions, trimmed, leaving 5 or 6 inches of green

1 tablespoon sesame oil

Salt and freshly cracked white pepper to taste

METHOD

1. Make the sauce: In a sauté pan over medium heat, heat the sesame and olive oils until hot but not smoking. Add the ginger and cook, stirring frequently, for 2 minutes. Add the orange juice and rice wine vinegar and cook for 5 minutes, stirring occasionally. Add the hoisin sauce and cook 1 minute more, still stirring occasionally. Remove from the heat and set aside.

2. In a small bowl, mix together the cardamom, white pepper, salt, and red pepper flakes. Rub the quail all over with this mixture.

3. Grill the quail over a medium-hot fire for 4 to 6 minutes per side. They should be cooked through, but the meat should still have a somewhat pinkish appearance.

4. Meanwhile, rub the scallions with sesame oil, sprinkle with salt and white pepper, and grill for 3 to 4 minutes, or until they are golden, rolling them over once or twice so that they cook evenly.

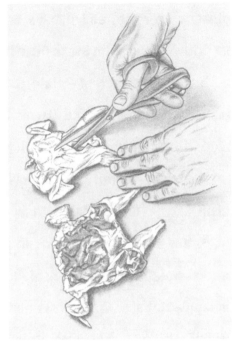

Butterflying quail

5. Serve each quail with a couple of tablespoons of sweet ginger sauce and a grilled scallion. For appetizers, serve 1 quail per person; for an entrée, serve 2 or 3 quail per person, depending on the appetites of your guests.

SALADS

Spinach, Avocado, and Papaya Salad with Orange-Cumin Dressing ▪ Avocado and Orange Salad with Black Olive Dressing ▪ Green Bean Salad with Corn, Basil, and Black Olives ▪ Red Potato and Cucumber Salad with Mango ▪ Simple Dry Masala ▪ Roast Beet and Carrot Salad with Lemon-Mint Dressing ▪ Pumpkin Salad with Cilantro and Toasted Cumin ▪ Turnip and Bread Salad with Minted Yogurt Dressing ▪ Lentil Salad with White Grapes and Carrots ▪ Uncommon Carrot-Raisin Slaw ▪ Green Mango Slaw ▪ Arugula Salad with Oven-Dried Tomatoes, Olives, and Blue Cheese ▪ Parsley Salad with Bulgur, Mint, and Tomatoes ▪ Watercress Salad with Grilled Asparagus and Red Onion ▪ Savory Watermelon and Pineapple Salad ▪ Watercress and Crab Salad with Mangoes and Fish Sauce ▪ Big Sky's Grilled Sweet Lemon Salad with Parsley ▪ Malaysian Fruit Salad ▪ Sesame Shrimp and Mango Salad with Ginger-Soy Vinaigrette ▪ Amilcar's Grilled Shrimp and Avocado Salad ▪ Grilled Shrimp and Black Bean Salad with Papaya ▪ Cold Grilled Tuna Salad with Spinach, Cashews, and Five Spices

VEGETABLES

Quick and Easy Sautéed Leafy Greens with Lime and Chiles ▪ Bob's Quick-Cooked Lettuce ▪ Fried Green Tomatoes with Sweet and Hot Dressing ▪ New Potato Hash Browns with Caramelized Onions ▪ Orange-Glazed Carrots and Mangoes ▪ Arabian Summer Vegetables with Feta ▪ Grilled Sweet Potatoes with Molasses Glaze ▪ Grilled Artichokes Johnson ▪ Grilled Spring Onions with Fried Garlic-Ginger Sauce ▪ Grilled Onion Rings ▪ Grilled Peppered Tomatoes with Lemon and Garlic ▪ Hobo Pack Vegetables ▪ Braised Cabbage with Ginger, Soy, and Quince ▪ Spicy Pumpkin and Tomato Dish ▪ Deep-Fried

THE NO-MEAT CHAPTER: SALADS, VEGETABLES, AND GRAINS

Style Yucca ▪ Deep-Fried Plantain Rounds ▪ Salty Persian-Style Pickled Turnips and Onions ▪ Black Bean Dip with Fried Sweet Plantains ▪ Basic Black Beans ▪ All-Purpose Rice and Beans ▪ Mashed Turnips with Lemon, Garlic, and Yogurt ▪ Grilled Eggplant and Pepper Sandwiches with Basil and Black Olive Spread ▪ Your Favorite Real Grilled Cheese Sandwich

GRAINS

Rice Pilaf with Lime Zest and Almonds ▪ Coconut Rice ▪ Elmer's El Salvadoreon Pickled Cabbage ▪ Sweet and Spicy Lo Mein Noodles ▪ Couscous with Raisins and Parsley

To start off, let me say that this chapter is for everybody, not just vegetarians. I think it's important to say that because I like meat and I eat it regularly. Over the past few years, however, I have found that more and more of my meals consist of vegetables and grains and unusual salads. Meat is still part of my diet, but it's no longer the bedrock of every meal.

While this change has been motivated partly by health concerns, it has not meant adopting some rigid "diet program" or making phony hamburgers out of grains or using fake fats in my food. All of that stuff strikes me as antithetical to the enjoyment of food and therefore bound to fail. Go far enough down that path, and you end up like the Jetsons, eating a pill for a meal. I think fun and enjoyment are an essential part of healthfulness in eating, so that road is not for me.

I am hooked on excitement and adventure and big, loud tastes in food. By looking to other cultures where grains, vegetables, and fruits have long played a more prominent role than in the heavily carnivorous American diet, I've learned a lot about how to use these ingredients. As a result, I've come up with a variety of salads and vegetable dishes that fill the center of the plate where meat used to be the king, and also provide the range of tastes and textures to satisfy both my "feed me, I'm hungry" appetite and my appetite for culinary adventure.

Some of the dishes in this chapter are American classics to which I've given a little warm-weather twist, like Fried Green Tomatoes with Sweet and Hot Dressing; Spinach, Avocado, and Papaya Salad with Orange-Cumin Dressing; or

New Potato Hash Browns with Caramelized Onions. Others are a bit more exotic, such as Green Mango Slaw; Braised Cabbage with Ginger, Soy, and Quince; or Big Sky's Grilled Sweet Lemon Salad with Parsley. A handful contain seafood, like Grilled Shrimp and Black Bean Salad with Papaya. Many are side dishes that can be served as accompaniments or put together for a meal, and others—All-Purpose Rice and Beans, for example, or Grilled Eggplant and Pepper Sandwiches with Basil and Black Olive Spread—are excellent as main courses by themselves.

So, whether you include meat in your diet often, occasionally, or not at all, I encourage you to graze through this chapter. You won't find any meat, but you will find plenty of exotic tastes and big, satisfying flavors. I guarantee that if you spend a little time getting acquainted with the dishes here, you'll just naturally find yourself eating less meat, not willfully depriving yourself of it. Food will continue to play a rich, warm, and rewarding role in your life, and you'll improve your health at the same time. That's what unconscious health-fulness is all about.

Spinach, Avocado, and Papaya Salad with Orange-Cumin Dressing

DRESSING:

½ cup virgin olive oil

2 tablespoons red wine vinegar

6 tablespoons orange juice (about 1½ oranges)

2 tablespoons lime juice (about 1 lime)

1 tablespoon ground cumin

Salt and freshly cracked black pepper to taste

1½ pounds spinach, peeled, stems removed, washed well, and dried

2 ripe avocados, peeled, pitted, and sliced ⅛ inch thick

2 tablespoons lime juice (about 1 lime)

1 medium-size *or* 2 small ripe papayas, peeled, seeded, and diced into ½-inch cubes

1 red onion, thinly sliced

This is a great salad for summertime, when both avocados and papayas are at their musky best. It's fairly large, so it can work either as a light lunch or as a dinner in combination with something like Grilled Shell-On Giant Shrimp with Hot Peanut-Chile Butter (page 284), Grilled Hearthbread Johnson (page 406), and Salty Persian-Style Pickled Turnips and Onions (page 254). I might also have a sandwich with this, like Grilled Eggplant and Pepper Sandwiches with Basil and Black Olive Spread (page 266).

METHOD

1. In a medium-size bowl, whisk all the dressing ingredients together until well mixed.

2. Place all the salad ingredients in a large bowl, pour the dressing over, and toss lightly.

Avocado and Orange Salad with Black Olive Dressing

Serves 4 as salad

This Arab-inspired fruit and vegetable salad contains all kinds of flavors—the richness of avocados, the tart-sweetness of oranges, the bite of onions, the loamy flavor of black olives.

DRESSING:

¼ cup chopped cured black olives

6 tablespoons virgin olive oil

1 teaspoon minced garlic

1 teaspoon sugar

¼ cup lemon juice (about 1 lemon)

Salt and freshly cracked black pepper to taste

2 firm but ripe avocados, peeled, pitted, and each cut into 6 wedges

2 oranges, peeled and separated into segments

½ red onion, very thinly sliced

½ head romaine lettuce, cut into short, thin strips

METHOD

1. In a small bowl, make the dressing: Whisk together the chopped olives, olive oil, garlic, sugar, lemon juice, salt, and pepper.

2. In a large bowl, combine the avocados, orange segments, and onion. Pour the olive dressing over the avocado mixture and toss lightly. Serve on a bed of the cut romaine.

Serving Suggestion:

I would serve this with Grilled Sausage Skewers with Fresh Apricots, Jalapeños, and Chipotle Vinaigrette and Whole Grill-Roasted Banana (page 288).

Green Bean Salad with Corn, Basil, and Black Olives

Serves 8 as salad

Another great summer salad. Easy to make, colorful, delicious, it goes with anything. Also, unlike your greens-based salads, it keeps for several days. The key to success here is having ultra-fresh vegetables and blanching them in boiling (not just hot) water only long enough to tenderize them and bring out their color without destroying their crispness and flavor.

2 pounds fresh green beans, trimmed

3 ears corn, husked and desilked

½ red bell pepper, diced small

1 small red onion, diced small

½ cup pitted Kalamata or other cured black olives, roughly chopped

⅓ cup finely chopped fresh basil

1 teaspoon minced garlic

1 cup extra-virgin olive oil

3 tablespoons balsamic vinegar

3 tablespoons lemon juice (about 1 lemon)

3 dashes Tabasco sauce

2 teaspoons salt or to taste

Freshly cracked black pepper to taste

METHOD

1. Put a huge pot of water on the stove over high heat and fill your other largest pot half full of ice water. When the water on the stove comes to a rolling boil, add about half the green beans and blanch for 2 minutes. Remove the beans and immediately plunge them into the ice water. Allow water to return to boil, then repeat with the second half of the green beans.

2. Refill the pot with fresh water and bring to a boil. Add the ears of corn and blanch for about 1 to 2 minutes—the corn should still be crisp. As soon as the corn is cool enough to handle, cut the kernels off the cobs.

3. In a large bowl, combine the beans, corn, and all the remaining ingredients and toss thoroughly. This salad will keep, covered and refrigerated, for about 3 days.

Serving Suggestions:

As I said, this goes well with anything, but in particular you might try serving it as a vegetable/salad with Smoked Roasted Leg of Lamb with Chile-Garlic Rub (page 138), "The Greatest": Grill-Roasted Prime Rib (page 144), or Grilled Chicken in the Style of Vulcan (page 171).

HOW CAN OIL BE A VIRGIN?

The terminology of olive oils can be confusing. *Virgin* sort of makes sense as a description, since it implies untouched purity. But then we are thrown a curve with *extra-virgin,* a term along the lines of "a little bit pregnant." I mean, isn't something either virgin or not virgin?

In fact, what the various grades of olive oil signify is the amount of acid in the oil, less acid being more desirable. Olive oil is made by squeezing olives, then removing the water from the liquid that results. Oil from the initial pressing that has less than 1 percent acidity is extra-virgin; oil with less than 2 percent acidity is virgin. Neither can be refined or treated except for filtering.

The rest of the oil is refined to remove excess acidity. Since this process creates a virtually colorless oil with little taste, some virgin or extra-virgin is added back in to restore flavor and color. The end product of this is labeled either simply olive oil, or (just for a little more confusing terminology) "pure" olive oil.

Red Potato and Cucumber Salad with Mango

Serves 8 as side dish

Combining fruits and vegetables in salads is standard practice all over the tropical world. This particular combination, with its mangoes, curry, and ginger, is Indian inspired. If good-quality ripe mangoes aren't available, you may substitute papayas.

METHOD

1. Blanch the potatoes in boiling water to cover until just cooked through, about 8 minutes. Drain, allow to cool to room temperature, and cut in half.

2. Cut the cucumbers in half lengthwise, then slice ½ inch thick.

3. In a large bowl, combine the potatoes, cucumbers, and all the remaining ingredients. Toss well and serve.

Serving Suggestions:

Try serving this with Grilled Quail with Cardamom, Ginger Sauce, and Grilled Scallions (page 192) and Chile-Soaked Grilled Chicken with Indonesian Catsup (page 180).

8 Red Bliss potatoes about the size of golf balls or slightly larger

2 medium-sized cucumbers, peeled and seeded

2 ripe mangoes, peeled, pitted, and diced

1 cup fresh orange juice (about 2 oranges)

1 tablespoon minced ginger

2 tablespoons Simple Dry Masala (page 203); you may substitute 2 tablespoons prepared curry powder

¼ cup lemon juice (about 1 lemon)

¼ cup chopped fresh mint

Salt and freshly cracked black pepper to taste

Simple Dry Masala

2 tablespoons ground cumin

2 tablespoons paprika

1 teaspoon ground turmeric

1 tablespoon crushed coriander
seeds

1 teaspoon cayenne pepper

1 tablespoon ground ginger

1 tablespoon ground cinnamon

1 teaspoon dry mustard

METHOD

Place all ingredients in a medium-size skillet and heat over medium heat, shaking skillet until the first tiny wisp of smoke appears, 2 to 3 minutes. Let cool, cover well, and store in a cool, dark place.

Roast Beet and Carrot Salad with Lemon-Mint Dressing

If the dinner you are planning is missing a strong-sounding, really colorful salad course, look no further. Vegetable salads with beets are popular in the Middle East, and here we give a little twist by roasting the vegetables at high heat to add flavor, then tossing them with a dressing featuring lemon, garlic, and mint. A little offbeat, but it's a great way to dress up everyday ingredients.

Try to dress this dish close to serving time in order to keep the colors clear. Mixing the ingredients together earlier won't affect the taste much, but the beets do tend to bleed when tossed.

½ pound carrots, cut into pieces about the size of wine corks

1 pound beets, preferably small ones about the size of golf balls, unpeeled, with 1 inch of stems left on

2 tablespoons virgin olive oil

Salt and freshly cracked black pepper to taste

DRESSING:

½ cup virgin olive oil

¼ cup lemon juice (about 1 lemon)

1 teaspoon brown sugar

1 tablespoon ground cumin

1 teaspoon finely minced garlic

2 tablespoons chopped fresh mint

1 tablespoon paprika

4 scallions, minced (both green and white parts)

½ pound spinach, stems removed, well washed, and sliced into thin ribbons about the size of crayons

METHOD

1. Preheat the oven to 450°F. Rub the carrots and beets with oil, sprinkle them with salt and pepper, and lay them out on separate baking sheets or pans. Place both in the preheated oven.

2. Roast the vegetables until easily pierced through with a fork. This should take 30 to 40 minutes for the carrots, and anywhere from 30 to 90 minutes for the beets, depending on their size. As the vegetables are done, remove them from the oven and allow to cool.

3. When the beets are cool enough to handle, pop them out of their skins by trimming the root end and applying pressure at the top; the skin should slide off easily. If you have used large beets, halve or quarter them so they are just slightly larger than the carrot pieces.

4. Mix together all dressing ingredients in a large bowl. Add the roasted beets and carrots and toss together well. Make a bed of the sliced spinach and serve the salad on top of the bed.

Serving Suggestions:

This salad goes very well with a strong-tasting fish like tuna or bluefish.

Pumpkin Salad with Cilantro and Toasted Cumin

Serves 4 as salad

4 cups pumpkin, cleaned, seeded, and cut into 1-inch cubes

2 tablespoons cumin seeds

1 red onion, thinly sliced

1 tablespoon minced fresh red or green chile pepper of your choice

¼ cup raisins

2 teaspoons minced garlic

¼ cup lemon juice (about 1 lemon)

¼ cup chopped fresh cilantro

½ cup extra-virgin olive oil

Salt and freshly cracked black pepper to taste

Although the pumpkin originated in the Americas, it was one of the first items to gain popularity in other countries as part of the great food exchange that followed the voyages of Columbus. Most people think of that Columbian exchange as an interchange of foods between Europe and America, but it was actually far more complex than that. The pumpkin, for example, quickly took hold in Equatorial Africa and today is used in many ways in the cuisines of that area. This dish is an unusual, fast, and healthy side dish for any time.

METHOD

1. Bring a stockpot of water to a rolling boil, add the pumpkin cubes, and cook until they are easily pierced by a fork but still offer some resistance, 5 to 6 minutes.

2. Meanwhile, toast the cumin seeds in a small skillet over medium heat, watching carefully and shaking frequently to prevent burning, until they just begin to release a little smoke, 2 to 3 minutes.

3. Drain the pumpkin, add the toasted cumin seeds and all the other ingredients, and toss well.

Serving Suggestions:

I think this goes particularly well with a pork dish like Roast Pork Tenderloin with Orange–Red Onion Salsa (page 153) or Fried Pork Salad with Cabbage and Avocados (page 158).

Turnip and Bread Salad with Minted Yogurt Dressing

Serves 4 as salad

3 turnips the size of baseballs (about ½ pound in all)

2 cups day-old French bread cut into 1-inch cubes

¼ cup virgin olive oil

Salt and freshly cracked black pepper to taste

DRESSING:

½ cup virgin olive oil

¼ cup lemon juice (about 1 lemon)

½ cup plain yogurt

2 teaspoons minced garlic

¼ cup chopped fresh mint

Salt and freshly cracked black pepper to taste

1 cucumber, diced medium

1 red onion, diced medium

2 ripe tomatoes, diced medium

½ cup chopped fresh parsley

1 head romaine lettuce, leaves broken into quarters

1 large pomegranate, split and seeds picked out (optional)

Cold vegetable salads of this type are very common in the Middle East, so I have used two ingredients very common in that part of the world, turnips and yogurt. To me, this lemony concoction is a good example of how common ingredients can come together to make a new and unique flavor—at least to those of us in the West. The pomegranate seeds aren't essential, but if you can find them, the crunchy little sweet-sour seeds are a great addition.

This dish is best served shortly after it is made, but it will last for a day or two, covered and refrigerated.

METHOD

1. Place the turnips in a large saucepan and add enough cold water to cover by 1 inch, along with a pinch of salt. Bring to a boil over high heat, reduce the heat to low, and cook until easily pierced with a fork but not mushy, 10 to 12 minutes. Remove from the heat, allow to cool, and cut into bite-size chunks; you should have about 1 cup of chunks.

2. Preheat the oven to 350°F. In a large bowl, toss the bread cubes with the ¼ cup of olive oil, sprinkle with salt and pepper, and toast on a baking sheet in the oven until golden brown, 15 to 18 minutes, shaking occasionally.

3. In a medium-size bowl, combine the dressing ingredients and whisk until well blended.

4. In a large bowl, combine the diced turnips, toasted bread cubes, cucumber, red onion, tomatoes, and parsley and toss well. Pour the dressing over this mixture, toss again, and serve on a bed of the romaine lettuce. Sprinkle with pomegranate seeds for garnish.

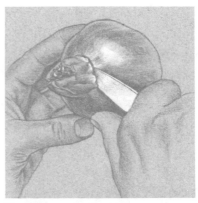

Stemming pomegranate

Scoring pomegranate skin

Breaking fruit into quarters

Serving Suggestions:

On a hot summer day, this unique and refreshing salad goes well with London Broil "Smoke Gets in Your House" Style with Lime-Marinated Red Onions and Chunky Pineapple Catsup (page 148), along with Mexican Corn Pudding (page 398).

Lentil Salad with White Grapes and Carrots

1 cup dried green lentils

2½ cups water

1 teaspoon salt

DRESSING:

1 teaspoon minced garlic

¼ cup chopped fresh cilantro

1 tablespoon ground coriander

1 tablespoon ground cumin

6 tablespoons virgin olive oil

½ cup lemon juice (2 lemons)

Salt and freshly cracked black
pepper to taste

2 carrots, sliced ¼ inch thick

1 red onion, diced small

1 red bell pepper, cut into very
thin strips

1 cup seedless white grapes, cut
in half

These days, legumes are getting all sorts of attention as we try to incorporate more of them into our diets. This is a good trend, because legumes in general and lentils in particular have long had a bad rap as being good only as "health food." Wrong. This dish, for example, more than proves that lentils are great-tasting. Their earthy flavor is a perfect background for a spicy cumin/coriander-accented dressing which is gentled by sweet, juicy grapes and crunchy carrots.

METHOD

1. In a medium-size saucepan, combine the lentils, water, and salt. Bring to a boil, reduce the heat to a simmer, cover, and cook until the lentils are soft but not mushy, 40 to 60 minutes. (You may need to add a bit more water if the lentils become too dry during cooking.) Drain the lentils and allow to cool to room temperature.

2. In a small bowl, combine all the dressing ingredients and mix well.

3. In a large bowl, combine the lentils, carrots, onion, bell pepper, and grapes. Pour the dressing onto the mixture and mix well. This salad will keep, covered and refrigerated, for 3 to 4 days.

Serving Suggestion:

I would serve this salad with any type of seafood; it is particularly good with any red snapper recipe.

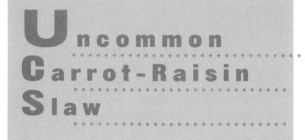

Uncommon Carrot-Raisin Slaw

Makes about 3 cups,
enough for 4 as side dish

2 cups shredded carrots

¼ cup raisins

1 red bell pepper, thinly sliced

¼ cup chopped fresh parsley

1 tablespoon cumin seeds
(you may substitute
ground cumin)

½ cup white vinegar

¼ cup honey

Salt and freshly cracked black
pepper to taste

It seems like the coleslaw vehicle is becoming more and more popular as chefs all over try to be more creative with vegetables. Here some North African flavors creep in with the cumin and raisins. This is a nicely sweet slaw that works well as a foil for hot dishes.

METHOD

In a large bowl, combine the carrots, raisins, and red pepper and toss. Add the parsley and cumin and toss again. Add the vinegar, honey, salt, and pepper, toss one more time, and serve.

Serving Suggestions:

I would serve this as a side dish accompanying K.C.'s Grilled Killer Jamaican Party Beef from Hell (page 286) or Chile-Rubbed Grilled Turkey Sandwich with Smoky Red Onion Salsa (page 190) and a Savory Watermelon and Pineapple Salad (page 220).

Green Mango Slaw

A little twist on an old American standby, coleslaw. Crunchy cabbage is replaced by green tropical fruit, the vinegar becomes lime juice, and an old summer-meal war-horse becomes a sleek new breed.

METHOD

1. Peel the mangoes and cut the flesh away from the large inner seed. Shred the sections of mango as you would cabbage for coleslaw.

2. Combine the mangoes with all the remaining ingredients and mix well.

Serving Suggestions:

Like the classic version, this slaw is great with grilled fish or fried foods of any variety.

Makes about 4 pints

3 green or semi-ripe mangoes (you may substitute green papayas)

---

1 large carrot, grated

½ red bell pepper, very thinly sliced

¼ cup pineapple juice

¼ cup mayonnaise

---

2 tablespoons sugar

¼ cup lime juice (about 2 limes)

---

3 dashes Tabasco sauce

Salt and freshly cracked black pepper to taste

Arugula **S**alad with **O**ven-Dried **T**omatoes, **O**lives, and **B**lue Cheese

This is a salad with a lot of tastes and textures. I really like the distinctive, slightly bitter taste of arugula, which stands up well to other strong flavors. In this case, we match it with brine-cured black olives and blue cheese and it still doesn't get pushed into the background. To complete the scene, we bring in some tomatoes that have been oven-dried with an easy method that concentrates their taste wonderfully without drying them out.

VINAIGRETTE:

1 teaspoon minced garlic

1 tablespoon Dijon mustard

¼ cup balsamic vinegar

2 tablespoons chopped fresh oregano, thyme, or mixture of both

Pinch sugar

¾ cup extra-virgin olive oil (approximately)

Salt and freshly cracked black pepper to taste

3 bunches arugula (about 1 pound), stemmed, washed, and well dried

Salt and freshly cracked black pepper to taste

1 cup Kalamata or other brine-cured black olives, pitted if desired

6 ounces blue cheese of your choice, crumbled into large chunks

8 oven-dried plum tomatoes (see box)

METHOD

1. In a small mixing bowl, combine all the vinaigrette ingredients except the olive oil, salt, and pepper and whisk together. Slowly drizzle in the olive oil, whisking, until the dressing has the right acidity for your taste. Season with salt and freshly cracked black pepper.

2. Place the arugula in a large bowl, dress lightly with the vinaigrette, season with salt and pepper, and toss well. Arrange on 4 plates and top each with ¼ of the olives, blue cheese, and dried tomatoes.

Serving Suggestions:

This would go well before a light fish entrée like Grilled Pompano with Lemon-Cinnamon Sauce (page 89), Scallop and Nectarine Skewers with Grilled Red Pepper–Lime Sauce (page 124), or Jennie's Crab Cakes with Funny Red Tartar Sauce (page 126).

OVEN-DRYING TOMATOES

To dry plum tomatoes, split them in half lengthwise, place them on a large drying rack set on top of a baking sheet, and sprinkle with salt and pepper and a bit of finely chopped rosemary or thyme. Place in a 200°F oven for 6 to 8 hours, depending on the size and ripeness of the tomatoes. The tomatoes should be shriveled up and reduced to about half their original size, but not leathery.

Parsley Salad with Bulgur, Mint, and Tomatoes

Wait, you say, isn't this just another recipe for tabbouleh? Well, yes, it is, but in the title I'm doing my part to try to right a culinary wrong. The stuff that passes for tabbouleh in these parts would be looked at strangely by a person who grew up with the dish in his or her homeland. In the original version, tabbouleh is just what I have called it here—a salad in which parsley is the major player and bulgur is an accent. This is okay with me because I have always liked parsley and think its virtues have been overshadowed by its ubiquitous use as a garnish. I recommend that you use lettuce leaves for eating utensils here, but if you insist on not having any fun, you can always use forks.

Serves 6 as salad

⅓ cup bulgur (medium-fine grain if you have a choice)

1 cup water

3 cups finely chopped fresh parsley

3 ripe tomatoes, diced small

1 red onion, diced small

1 cucumber, peeled and diced small

¼ cup finely chopped fresh mint

1 teaspoon minced garlic

⅓ cup extra-virgin olive oil

½ cup lemon juice (about 2 lemons)

2 to 6 dashes Tabasco sauce, depending on your taste for heat

1 head romaine lettuce leaves, washed and dried

M E T H O D

Rinse the bulgur and soak in the cup of water for 30 minutes. Drain, squeeze out excess water with your hands, and place in a large bowl. Add all the remaining ingredients except lettuce and toss well. Serve with lettuce leaves for scooping up and eating the salad.

Serving Suggestions:

If you want to blow away your friends who are unfamiliar with the depth, range, and incredible flavors of Middle Eastern cuisine, I suggest you serve this with any or all of the following: Roast Beet and Carrot Salad with Lemon-Mint Dressing (page 204), Turnip and Bread Salad with Minted Yogurt Dressing (page 208), Avocado and Orange Salad with Black Olive Dressing (page 199), Lentil Salad with White Grapes and Carrots (page 210), Big Sky's Grilled Sweet Lemon Salad with Parsley (page 222), Couscous with Raisins and Parsley (page 276), and Middle Eastern–Style Crisp Bread (page 404). If you have guests from the Middle East, sprinkle some of the Persian-Style Nut Rub (page 384) on top of the bread and watch their eyes widen as you re-create a dish from their homeland. For a drink, try Tim's Sparkling Limeade (page 452).

TARAS BULGUR

Also known as cracked wheat, bulgur is made by boiling whole wheat grains until they are partially cooked, then drying them and grinding them. Bulgur comes in various degrees of coarseness; the type found in most supermarkets is medium fine, which is just right for this recipe. Prevalent in Middle Eastern cooking, particularly Turkish, bulgur can also be substituted for rice in any pilaf recipe.

Watercress Salad with Grilled Asparagus and Red Onion

Serves 4 as salad

Sometimes, when spring is happening just right, the arrival of the first asparagus coincides exactly with the dusting off of the grill for its first session of the warm weather season. Asparagus on the grill is easy, and the slight char flavor, slow-cooked red onions, and Asian-flavored salad complement this delicate spring vegetable perfectly.

20 spears asparagus, trimmed

2 red onions the size of baseballs, each cut into eight slices

2 tablespoons virgin olive oil

2 tablespoons sesame oil

2 tablespoons soy sauce

1 tablespoon minced ginger

2 tablespoons white vinegar

5 dashes Tabasco sauce

2 bunches watercress, carefully washed and roughly chopped

1 red bell pepper, halved and thinly sliced

Freshly cracked white pepper to taste

METHOD

1. Blanch the asparagus in a large pot of boiling water for 2 minutes, then plunge immediately into a large pot of ice water.

2. Over a low, slow fire, cook the onions until soft and brown, about 7 minutes per side.

3. Meanwhile, over the same low fire, cook the asparagus until slightly brown, 3 to 4 minutes, rolling it around occasionally to brown evenly.

4. Combine the grilled onions, asparagus, and all the other ingredients in a large bowl and toss lightly.

Serving Suggestions:

I would keep the meal vegetarian and serve this with Sweet and Spicy Lo Mein Noodles (page 274) and Mangoes, Cucumbers, and Red Onion in Vinegar with Toasted Sesame Seeds (page 350).

Savory Watermelon and Pineapple Salad

1½ cups large watermelon chunks, seeded

1½ cups large pineapple chunks

1 red onion, thinly sliced

1 tablespoon chopped fresh oregano (you may substitute parsley)

6 tablespoons lime juice (about 3 limes)

2 tablespoons red wine vinegar

Originally from Africa, the watermelon is said to be the most widely eaten fruit in the world. Always refreshing on a hot day, it is served as street food from Lima, Peru, to Bangkok, Thailand. Here the melon is combined with the more firm-textured pineapple and the oregano common to Latin cuisines to create a light and savory complement to any meal.

I first got the idea of using watermelon in a savory way from my Grandfather Wetzler, who used to put salt and pepper on his. I've done it ever since myself but was wary of springing it on my customers until I saw a watermelon and red onion salad on the menu at Hamersley's Bistro in Boston. As is often the case, eating at another restaurant was the birth of an idea. This is not the first inspiration I've gleaned from my friend Gordon Hamersley, and I'm sure it won't be the last.

METHOD

It couldn't be simpler—just mix and serve.

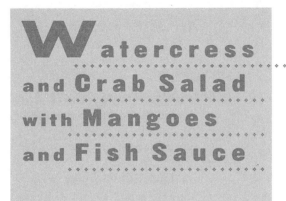

Watercress and Crab Salad with Mangoes and Fish Sauce

Serves 4 as salad or appetizer

If you can lay your hands on some high-quality crabmeat, whether it's Maine, rock, blue, dungeness, king, or whatever, this is a good way to use it. There is a lot going on in this dish, but the delicate nature of the crab still predominates, while the mango provides a sweet touch that I like with the rich crab. This dish is also delicious served without the crabmeat.

2 bunohes wateroress, stemmed, washed, and drained

1 cup thinly sliced Napa cabbage

¼ cup chopped fresh cilantro

¼ cup coarsely grated carrots

2 ripe mangoes, peeled, pitted, and cut into bite-size pieces

DRESSING:

1 tablespoon chopped fresh basil

1 tablespoon chopped fresh mint

2 tablespoons sesame oil

2 tablespoons fish sauce

¼ cup lime juice (about 2 limes)

2 tablespoons sugar

4 dashes Tabasco sauce

1 teaspoon minced garlic

Salt and freshly cracked white pepper to taste

1 pound fresh crabmeat

METHOD

1. In a large bowl, combine the watercress, cabbage, cilantro, carrots, and mango and toss well.

2. In a small bowl, combine all the dressing ingredients and mix well. Pour the dressing over the watercress mixture and toss well. Transfer to a serving platter and arrange the crabmeat on top.

Serving Suggestion:

Serve this dish with Grilled Foie Gras on Toast (page 62) for a rich dinner.

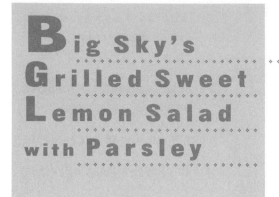

Big Sky's Grilled Sweet Lemon Salad with Parsley

Serves 4 as small salad

4 lemons, ends cut off, sliced very thinly, seeds removed

¼ cup sugar

1 bunch flat-leaf parsley, well washed and stems removed

¼ cup extra-virgin olive oil

Salt and freshly cracked black pepper to taste

This is one of those dishes that cooks come up with when they are just kind of playing around because they are all set up for service and have nothing else to do. The cook in this case is a former sous-chef at The Blue Room named Big Sky, aka Michael Peternell. He created this to go on a platter with a couple of other salads and dips. Simple, quick, and easy, this is another dish that proves that tasty, innovative food does not need to be either expensive or complicated to be successful.

METHOD

1. In a small bowl, combine the lemon slices and sugar, mix well, and allow to sit for 2 hours.

2. Remove the lemon slices and grill them over a medium-low fire until slightly brown, about 1 minute per side. (It is important to have a very clean grill grid so the lemons do not stick to it.)

3. Remove the lemon slices from the grill, combine with the remaining ingredients, mix well, and serve.

Malaysian Fruit Salad

In Malaysia, 80 percent of which is still covered with rain forest, there are dozens of luscious fruits. Throughout the country there are stands selling skewers of spiky, orange-red rambutans, purplish, apple-size mangosteens, and beadlike chiku.

One of the local specialties is rojak, a refreshing salad in which a sweet and slightly spicy sauce is mixed with fruits such as starfruit (carambolas), water apples, pineapple, semi-ripe mangoes and papayas, and a vegetable or two, such as cucumber or yam beans. This is my version of rojak, in which I have substituted readily available fruits. It may sound odd, but try it and I bet you'll be serving it throughout the summer. Make sure the mango and papaya you use are not completely ripe, as they will mush up too much when you mix them with the other fruits.

½ pineapple, peeled and cored

1 semi-ripe mango, peeled and pitted

1 semi-ripe papaya, peeled and seeded

2 cucumbers, peeled and seeded

DRESSING:

1 teaspoon finely minced ginger

¼ cup packed light or dark brown sugar

2 tablespoons white vinegar

2 tablespoons lime juice (about 1 lime)

¼ cup orange juice (about ½ orange)

¼ cup tamarind water (see Pantry, page 465)

¼ cup unsalted roasted peanuts, roughly chopped

2 tablespoons chopped fresh cilantro

2 tablespoons chopped fresh mint

4 to 6 dashes Tabasco sauce

3 dashes fish sauce (available in Asian markets) (optional)

METHOD

1. Cut the fruit and cucumber into bite-size chunks. Place in a large bowl.

2. In a medium-size bowl, combine all the dressing ingredients and mix well.

3. Pour the dressing over the fruits, mix well, and serve.

Sesame Shrimp and Mango Salad with Ginger-Soy Vinaigrette

Serves 4 as appetizer or salad

1 pound medium-size (16/20 count) shrimp, shelled and deveined

2 ripe or semi-ripe mangoes, peeled, pitted, diced medium

1 red bell pepper, diced small

1 green bell pepper, diced small

1 red onion, finely chopped

¼ cup thinly sliced scallions (7 to 8 scallions), including green and white parts

3 tablespoons sesame oil

GINGER-SOY VINAIGRETTE:

½ cup virgin olive oil

¼ cup soy sauce

2 tablespoons white vinegar

¼ cup lime juice (about 2 limes)

1 tablespoon minced ginger

3 to 5 dashes Tabasco sauce

1 teaspoon freshly cracked white pepper (you may substitute black pepper)

I just can't get enough of mangoes and shrimp, so here I mix them together with an Asian-flavored vinaigrette for a salad that makes a great lunch dish or dinner appetizer. If you want to make the dish a bit simpler, you can use only one type of cabbage, but I think the mixture of red and green, combined with the pink shrimp and yellow mango, makes an especially attractive dish.

¼ head red cabbage, thinly sliced

¼ head green cabbage, thinly sliced

¼ cup sesame seeds, toasted in 350°F oven for 4 to 5 minutes, for garnish (optional)

1 lime, cut into wedges, for garnish (optional)

8 sprigs fresh basil, for garnish (optional)

METHOD

1. Blanch the shrimp in boiling water for 2 minutes, drain, and slice in half lengthwise. In a large bowl, combine the shrimp, mangoes, red and green bell peppers, onion, scallions, and sesame oil and toss well.

2. In a small bowl, combine all the vinaigrette ingredients and whisk together well.

3. Mix together the red and green cabbage, make a bed of it on 4 individual plates or a large platter, and spoon the shrimp and mango salad over it. Pour the vinaigrette over the salad and mix lightly. Sprinkle with the sesame seeds and garnish with lime wedges and basil sprigs if desired.

Serving Suggestions:

For a very special meal, I would serve this before some red meat, such as London Broil "Smoke Gets in Your House" Style (page 148), "The Greatest": Grill-Roasted Prime Rib (page 144), or Skewered Steak with Guava-Soy Glaze and Grilled Pineapple (page 146).

Amilcar's Grilled Shrimp and Avocado Salad

Serves 4 as salad

Working with food all the time, cooks tend to become very creative about their lunch. In fact, most restaurant cooks don't really stop to eat; they just throw together whatever is on their cutting board at the time and turn it into something. I got the idea for this dish from Amilcar, one of my co-workers, who put all these ingredients together and ate it as a sandwich. Kind of a salad, kind of a salsa, kind of a side dish, it's got shrimp and avocado and tastes good, so call it anything you want.

3 ears corn, husked and desilked (you may substitute 1½ cups frozen corn)

1 pound medium-size (16/20 count) shrimp, shelled and deveined

3 ripe but firm avocados, peeled, pitted, and diced large

1 red onion, diced small

1 red bell pepper, diced small

⅓ cup virgin olive oil

⅓ cup red wine vinegar

¼ cup lime juice (about 2 limes)

1 tablespoon minced garlic

1 teaspoon minced fresh red or green chile pepper of your choice

1 tablespoon ground cumin

¼ cup chopped fresh oregano

Salt and freshly cracked black pepper to taste

METHOD

1. Blanch the corn in boiling water for 1 minute. Cut off the kernels and allow them to cool to room temperature.

2. Meanwhile, season the shrimp with salt and pepper, thread onto skewers, and grill over a medium-hot fire for 3 to 4 minutes per side, or until opaque throughout. Remove from the fire and allow to cool to room temperature.

3. In a large bowl, combine the corn and shrimp with all the remaining ingredients and toss well.

Serving Suggestion:

I might serve this with Your Favorite Real Grilled Cheese Sandwich (page 268) for a nice, light summer lunch.

Grilled Shrimp and Black Bean Salad with Papaya

I like using cold grilled food in salads the next day—it gives the salad a unique smoky dimension. In this case, we use black beans as the base of the dish, add some grilled shrimp for a rich, smoky taste, and use the sweet, musky undertone of papaya to harmonize with the classic Mexican flavors of lime, cilantro, and cumin. Of course, if you don't have any leftover shrimp, you can always grill some fresh.

Serves 6 as main-course salad

½ pound dried black beans

½ teaspoon salt

2 teaspoons minced garlic

2 ripe papayas, peeled, seeded, and diced (you may substitute mangoes or ½ pineapple)

1 red bell pepper, diced

1 red onion, diced

DRESSING:

¼ cup chopped fresh cilantro

1 tablespoon ground cumin

1 tablespoon chili powder

1 teaspoon minced garlic

¼ cup virgin olive oil

½ cup lime juice (about 4 limes)

1 pound medium-size (16/20 count) shrimp, shelled and deveined

Salt and freshly cracked black pepper to taste

1 small head green cabbage, thinly sliced

METHOD

1. Soak the black beans in cold water to cover for 5 hours or overnight, then drain and rinse well.

2. Place the beans in a large saucepan and add enough cold water to come about 1½ inches above the beans. Add the salt and garlic, bring the water to a boil over high heat, then reduce the heat to low and simmer, uncovered, for 1 to 1½ hours, or until the beans are tender but not mushy. Drain the beans and rinse under cold water for 1 minute to stop the cooking process, then drain again.

3. Place the beans in a large bowl, add the papayas, bell pepper, and onion, and mix well.

4. In a medium-size bowl, combine the dressing ingredients and whisk together well. Pour this dressing onto the bean mixture, toss well, and set aside.

5. Thread the shrimp onto skewers, sprinkle with salt and pepper, and grill over a medium-hot fire for 3 to 4 minutes per side or until completely opaque throughout.

6. Remove the shrimp from the skewers and toss with bean mixture. Serve on a bed of the thinly sliced cabbage.

Serving Suggestions:

Try this one with Big Jim's Grilled Chicken Thighs with Garlic and Herbs (page 186) or Grilled Chicken Breasts with Red Cabbage Slaw and Cilantro-Pecan Pesto (page 176).

Cold Grilled Tuna Salad with Spinach, Cashews, and Five Spices

1 pound cold grilled tuna or any other leftover fish

1½ pounds spinach, well washed and roughly chopped

1 red bell pepper, halved and sliced into thin strips

1 red onion, halved and sliced into thin strips

½ cup cashews

DRESSING:

1 teaspoon minced fresh red or green chile pepper of your choice

1 teaspoon minced garlic

1 teaspoon minced ginger

2 tablespoons soy sauce

1 tablespoon molasses

¼ cup sesame oil

¼ cup virgin olive oil

6 tablespoons white vinegar

¼ teaspoon ground cinnamon

¼ teaspoon ground cloves

¼ teaspoon Szechuan peppercorns (you may substitute white or black peppercorns)

½ teaspoon crushed star anise

This spicy treatment is a great way to spark up last night's left-over grilled fish. The heaviness of the chilled fish is lit up by a very pungent, intensely aromatic, Asian-flavored dressing. By adding spinach, we get a full-flavored, filling dish that is also healthful. So next time you're grilling tuna for dinner, buy a little extra, grill it, and set it aside for tomorrow.

METHOD

1. In a large bowl, crumble the tuna into bite-size chunks. Add the spinach, bell pepper, and onion and toss.

2. Toast the cashews in a single layer on a baking sheet in a 350°F oven until lightly browned, 5 to 7 minutes. Allow to cool, chop roughly, and set aside.

3. In a small bowl, combine all the dressing ingredients and mix well. Pour over the spinach-tuna mixture, toss well, and garnish with toasted cashews.

Quick and Easy Sautéed Leafy Greens with Lime and Chiles

6 tablespoons virgin olive oil

1½ pounds spinach, well washed, dried, and cut into thin strips

1 teaspoon minced garlic

¼ cup lime juice (about 2 limes)

1 tablespoon red pepper flakes (or less, depending on your taste for heat)

1 teaspoon sugar

Salt and freshly cracked black pepper to taste

Here is a quick and tasty way to consume your daily quotient of leafy greens. We specify spinach, but you can substitute Swiss chard, collards, mustard greens, beet greens, or kale. Lime juice and hot pepper flakes add some piquancy and heat. The trick here is to cook the greens very quickly over high heat, so if you don't have a large sauté pan, you may need to do this in two batches.

METHOD

1. In your largest sauté pan, heat the oil over high heat until very hot and just beginning to smoke. Add the spinach and stir furiously until the spinach has turned bright green and become slightly wilted, about 1 minute. Add the garlic and cook for 20 seconds more.

2. Add the lime juice, red pepper flakes, sugar, salt, and pepper and cook, still stirring vigorously, for an additional 10 to 15 seconds. Remove from the heat and serve at once.

MOTHER KNOWS BEST

Sometimes it seems almost impossible to get a handle on how to eat healthfully.

There are, however, some facts that seem beyond dispute. Fat is not healthful, so limit your intake. The same goes for red meat—you don't have to forgo it, but you should eat less of it.

And, finally, the advice we all got from our parents: Eat your vegetables. As science catches up with mother lore, we are finding that orange and green leafy vegetables in particular contain high amounts of beta carotene and other chemicals that help fight modern health problems like cancer and heart disease.

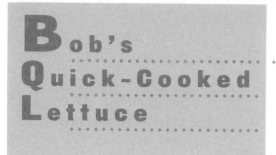

Bob's Quick-Cooked Lettuce

Serves 4 as side dish

1 head lettuce of your choice (big romaine is best)

1 tablespoon sesame oil

1 tablespoon peanut oil

1 red onion, thinly sliced

1 teaspoon minced garlic

1 teaspoon minced ginger

1 teaspoon red pepper flakes

2 tablespoons soy sauce

Pinch freshly cracked white (or black) pepper

I was once asked, for a newspaper story, to create a meal with ingredients purchased at my local convenience store. Along with sausage quesadillas and a fruit chutney, I prepared an Asian-style sautéed lettuce. For this I received a tremendous hard time from my fellow cooks—how could anyone even consider cooking lettuce, they scoffed.

Fortunately, my colleague Roberto Sargento secretly slipped me an Indonesian lettuce recipe that he had come across. From Java, the original dish is known as *oseng oseng h'sau,* and this is my adaptation. It goes to show that almost anything has been cooked somewhere in the world.

This is a good use for lettuce that is a little wilted and also for those big outside leaves—a new addition to the green vegetable lineup, great with fish and chicken.

METHOD

1. Separate the lettuce into individual leaves and tear them in halves or thirds, depending on the size of the leaves.

2. In a large sauté pan, heat the oils over high heat until hot but not smoking. Add the onion and sauté, stirring, for 1 minute. Add the lettuce leaves and continue to sauté, stirring, for 1 additional minute. Add the garlic and ginger and continue to sauté, still stirring, for 30 seconds.

3. Remove the pan from the heat, add the red pepper flakes, soy sauce, and white pepper, stir well, and serve.

Fried Green Tomatoes with Sweet and Hot Dressing

The movie *Fried Green Tomatoes* has introduced this southern dish to a wide audience. Some people have told me they don't believe it's really that big a deal, but the truth is that in early and late summer, when green tomatoes are plentiful, this fried treatment suddenly turns up all over the South. In this version the molasses in the spicy dressing soothes the tart bite of the underripe fruit (yes, tomatoes are fruit), and I have added some cumin for an additional earthy taste.

Serving Suggestions:

This is an outstanding side dish with heavy meats. Try it with "The Greatest": Grill-Roasted Prime Rib (page 144), Smoked Roasted Leg of Lamb with Chile-Garlic Rub (page 138) or Grilled Pork Chops with Green Apple–Chipotle Salsa (page 156).

DRESSING:

¾ cup virgin olive oil

¼ cup lime juice (about 2 limes)

2 tablespoons molasses

2 tablespoons white vinegar

¼ cup chopped fresh cilantro

1 teaspoon minced garlic

1 tablespoon minced fresh red or green chile pepper of your choice

4 green tomatoes the size of baseballs

1 cup yellow cornmeal

2 tablespoons ground cumin

Salt and freshly cracked black pepper to taste

⅓ cup vegetable oil for frying

METHOD

1. In a small bowl, whisk together all the dressing ingredients until well blended. Set aside.

2. Trim the top and bottom ends from the tomatoes, then cut each tomato into 5 or so slices about ½ inch thick.

3. In a large bowl, combine the cornmeal, cumin, salt, and pepper and mix well. Dredge the tomato slices in the cornmeal mixture and shake to remove the excess.

4. In the largest sauté pan you have, heat half of the vegetable oil over high heat until hot but not smoking. Add half the tomato slices and fry until golden, about 2 minutes per side. Drain on several thicknesses of paper towel. Repeat with the remaining tomato slices. Serve with the dressing.

GREEN TOMATO ESCUTCHEON

Since tomatoes are native to the Americas, there were none in Italy until after the voyages of Columbus. Even after tomatoes were introduced into Italy, it was a long time before ripe red tomatoes shed their reputation as poisonous and insinuated themselves firmly into the core of Italian cuisine.

Before that happened, however, cooks in northern Italy had taken to slicing up green tomatoes, breading them, and sautéing them. So, as it turns out, the fried green tomatoes that we think are prototypically southern actually boast a long Italian heritage as well. I guess some dishes are so good that people just dream them up independently all over the world.

New Potato Hash Browns with Caramelized Onions

16 new potatoes slightly larger than golf balls

2 tablespoons olive oil

1 large yellow onion, thinly sliced

6 tablespoons peanut or vegetable oil

Salt and freshly cracked black pepper to taste

1/4 cup chopped fresh parsley

Here the dark onions add a sweet counterpart to the crispness of the fried potatoes. When cooking the onions, the darker you can get them the better they will taste.

METHOD

1. Bring a small stockpot of water to a rolling boil. Add the new potatoes and cook until they are easily pierced by a fork but still offer some resistance, 14 to 25 minutes, depending on the size of the potatoes. Drain, cut into quarters, and reserve.

2. In a large sauté pan, heat the olive oil until hot but not smoking. Add the onion and cook over medium heat, stirring constantly, for 6 to 10 minutes, until well browned. Remove from the heat and set aside.

3. In a large sauté pan, heat the peanut oil until hot but not smoking. Add the potatoes and cook, stirring occasionally, until they are well browned, 5 to 8 minutes. Remove from the heat, add the onions, and mix well. Season with salt and pepper, sprinkle with parsley, and serve.

Orange-Glazed Carrots and Mangoes

Serves 4 as side dish

1 pound carrots, peeled and trimmed

1 tablespoon unsalted butter

1 firm mango, peeled, pitted, and thinly sliced

¼ cup golden raisins

½ cup orange juice (about 2 oranges)

2 tablespoons brown sugar

1 lime, halved

Salt and freshly cracked black pepper to taste

Sometimes my sister Susan asks me to come up with dishes for her kids that are healthful, easy, and that they will actually eat. It's a tall order, but here is a variation on a suggestion I made that actually fits all of these requirements. The natural sweetness of the carrots, orange juice, and raisins makes a nice contrast to the tang of slightly underripe mangoes.

METHOD

1. Blanch the carrots in boiling water for 4 minutes, drain, cut into long sticks, and set aside.

2. In a large sauté pan, melt the butter over medium heat. Add the mango and raisins and cook, stirring, for 2 minutes. Add the orange juice and brown sugar, stir to dissolve the sugar, and add the carrots. Cook for 1 minute, stirring to make sure the vegetables are well coated with glaze, and remove from the heat.

3. Squeeze the lime over the vegetables, sprinkle with salt and pepper, toss, and serve.

Arabian Summer Vegetables with Feta

In the heat that predominates in most Arabic countries, collections of vegetables served cold are a common sight. This particular combination is a sort of quick pickle, in which the vegetables sit in the dressing for a while to allow all the flavors to mingle properly. Set off by crisp romaine and rich feta cheese, this salad is just right for those days when it's too hot to cook. You might also want to try it as a pita stuffing mix.

1 cucumber, thinly sliced

1 red onion, halved and thinly sliced

1 red bell pepper, halved and thinly sliced

1 green bell pepper, halved and thinly sliced

2 ripe tomatoes, each cut into 8 wedges

1 small head cauliflower, separated into large florets

1 large carrot, thinly sliced

1½ cups red wine vinegar

½ cup olive oil

1 tablespoon minced garlic

1 tablespoon minced fresh red or green chile pepper of your choice

Salt and freshly cracked black pepper to taste

½ cup chopped fresh parsley

¼ cup chopped fresh mint

1 cup black olives (Kalamata or other variety of your choice)

1 head romaine lettuce, washed and sliced into ribbons

½ pound feta cheese

METHOD

1. Place the cucumber, onion, bell peppers, tomatoes, cauliflower, carrot, vinegar, oil, garlic, and chile pepper in a very large bowl, mix well, season with salt and pepper, and let the whole lot marinate for at least 1 hour or up to 8 hours. (After that, the vegetables may begin to get a little mushy.)

2. Just before serving, stir in the parsley, mint, and olives, place the mixture on a bed of the sliced romaine, and crumble feta cheese over the top.

Serving Suggestions:

Make this a part of an Arab-style no-meat buffet extravaganza, along with Avocado and Orange Salad with Black Olive Dressing (page 199), Red Potato and Cucumber Salad with Mango (page 202), Turnip and Bread Salad with Minted-Yogurt Dressing (page 208), Parsley Salad with Bulgur, Mint, and Tomatoes (page 216), Salty Persian-Style Pickled Turnips and Onions (page 254), and Spicy Roasted Red Pepper Dip with Grilled Pita (page 66).

Grilled Sweet Potatoes with Molasses Glaze

Serves 4 as side dish

3 large sweet potatoes, scrubbed but not peeled

2 tablespoons vegetable oil (approximately)

2 tablespoons unsalted butter

¼ cup molasses

These are like giant, sweet steak fries. I love sweet potatoes cooked just about any way, but this is my absolute favorite—the rich, mellow taste of the sweet potato takes on the smoky flavor of the grilling fire and a touch of added sweetness from the molasses glaze. This method can be used with almost any root vegetable; the cooking time will vary, but the way of testing for doneness is the same.

METHOD

1. Preheat the oven to 350°F, lightly oil the sweet potatoes, and bake on a baking sheet for 35 to 50 minutes, or until they are easily pierced by a fork but still offer some resistance. When they are done, remove them from the oven, cool them in the refrigerator for about an hour, then cut them into quarters lengthwise.

2. Meanwhile, combine the butter and molasses in a small saucepan and heat over very low heat until the butter has melted. Mix well and set aside.

3. Grill the sweet potatoes over a medium-hot fire, turning every 2 minutes, for a total of about 6 minutes, or until they are warmed through and slightly toasted. Just before removing the potatoes from the grill, paint them lightly with molasses-butter mixture.

Serving Suggestion:

An easy side dish to make while the grill is fired up anyway, these potatoes taste great with just about anything, especially pork.

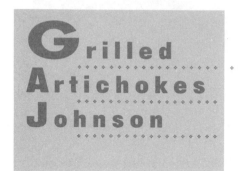

Grilled Artichokes Johnson

Serves 6 as side dish

4 to 6 large globe artichokes

½ cup extra-virgin olive oil

Kosher salt and freshly cracked black pepper to taste

3 lemons, halved

This is another addition to the "Johnson" line of grilled dishes, continuing the legend that began with Grilled Clams Johnson and continues with Grilled Hearthbread Johnson. For a dish to earn the coveted Johnson moniker, it must be grilled; it must be easy to prepare; it must be both very creative and very tasty; and it must be created by my high school amigo, cooking colleague, and all-around snappy dresser, Steve "Ice Cream" Johnson, chef de cuisine at Hamersley's Bistro in Boston.

Like Clams Johnson (see *The Thrill of the Grill*), this is a straightforward preparation, but I'll never forget the first time Steve cooked these artichokes at a small get-together at his house. Even my niece and nephew, Tommy and Lizzie, were clamoring for more.

METHOD

1. Cut off the top third of each artichoke, remove the sharp tips from the remaining leaves, and trim the bottom slightly so that it is even all the way around.

2. In a small stockpot, bring 3 quarts of water to a boil. Cook the artichokes in the boiling water for about 20 minutes, or until the outer leaves will pull away easily with a sharp tug. Drain the artichokes and rinse them in cold water to stop the cooking process.

3. Cut the artichokes in half lengthwise, brush them lightly with olive oil, and sprinkle with salt and pepper. Place the artichokes on the grill, cut sides down, and grill them for about 10 minutes, or until the cut sides are well browned. Remove the artichokes, coat them liberally with the remaining olive oil, and squeeze the lemons over them. Serve accompanied by a bowl of kosher salt for sprinkling.

Serving Suggestions:

Serve this with Jennie's Crab Cakes with Funny Red Tartar Sauce (page 126) and Corn-Crusted Panfried Shrimp with Sweet and Hot Seared Onions (page 22).

CHANGING WINE INTO KOOL-AID

In the columns and books of some wine experts, you will find this advice: "Never, *never* serve artichokes when serving wine." Other experts, however, think this is nonsense. What goes on here?

Well, what goes on is genetics. For a certain percentage of the population, eating globe artichokes causes any liquid drunk immediately afterward to taste intensely sweet, so that wine drunk following artichokes is reminiscent of Kool-Aid. For those without this genetic disposition, artichokes have no effect whatsoever on the taste of liquids. Check it out to see what happens for you.

Grilled Spring Onions with Fried Garlic-Ginger Sauce

Serves 5 as appetizer

10 spring onions, rare ripes, or scallions, including green and white parts

3 tablespoons sesame oil

Salt and freshly cracked white or black pepper to taste

The spring onion that I'm talking about here looks like a scallion but has a golf ball–size bulb on the end. Don't fret if you can't lay your hands on these—you can use a lot of different types of onions for this recipe because any onion is going to taste good when you grill it. I do like spring onions best for this treatment, though, because the bulb stays a bit raw in the center, so you get a sweet raw onion flavor mixed with the char on the outside.

METHOD

1. Rub the onions lightly with sesame oil and sprinkle with salt and pepper.

2. Place the onions on the grill over a medium fire, with the bulbs of the onions over the hotter portion of the fire. Grill, turning occasionally, until the whites are golden and the leaves are slightly crisp, 4 to 5 minutes. Remove from the grill and serve with Fried Garlic-Ginger Sauce for dipping.

Okay, so maybe this isn't the dish you cook on a first date, but it is great for family and friends. It makes a wonderful side dish with any kind of seafood, but also goes well with just about any dish in this book. If you ever see spring onions in the market and don't get them, you are making a real mistake.

Fried Garlic-Ginger Sauce

Makes about 1 cup

This sweet-sour soy glaze has strong overtones of garlic and ginger. For some people, it is a real savior when they get to the raw center of the grilled spring onions. But even if you love raw onions, you'll like them better dipped in this sauce.

¼ cup sesame oil

5 large cloves garlic, sliced into thin slivers

2 tablespoons minced ginger

½ cup soy sauce

¼ cup white vinegar

1 tablespoon brown sugar

1 teaspoon red pepper flakes

1. In a 10-inch sauté pan, heat the sesame oil over medium heat until hot but not smoking. Add the garlic slivers and cook until golden brown, 1 to 2 minutes, stirring constantly to prevent burning. Add the ginger and continue to cook, stirring, for an additional minute.

2. Remove the pan from the heat and allow to cool. Add all the remaining ingredients and stir well. This sauce will keep, covered and refrigerated, for 1 week.

Grilled Onion Rings

4 yellow onions about the size of softballs

¼ cup virgin olive oil

Salt and freshly cracked black pepper to taste

There's a saying among cooks that if you want to make people hungry, all you have to do is apply some high heat to onions. Simple and quick, these smoky, sweet onion rings go well with just about anything. You might want to try grilling red onions too.

METHOD

1. Peel the onions, cut off the ends, slice them about ¾ inch thick, and separate them into individual rings.

2. In a medium-size bowl, combine the onion rings and olive oil, mix until the rings are fairly uniformly covered, and sprinkle with salt and pepper.

3. Lift the rings out of the bowl (don't dump the contents of the bowl onto the grill or the excess oil will flare up) and grill the onions over a medium-hot fire until they are golden, 4 to 5 minutes per side.

Serving Suggestion:

You can't go wrong with these, no matter what else you are serving.

A MANY-LAYERED THING

A relative of the lily, the onion is one of those ingredients that is used in cooking in just about every country around the world. There are many types of onions, the most familiar to Americans being the yellowish round Spanish or "regular" onion and the red or Italian onion.

Over the past few years, however, other regional onions—sweeter, juicier, and more distinct in flavor than Spanish or red—have begun to enter the American seasonal larder. Among these, my favorites are three varieties named for the places from which they come: big gold Walla Walla onions from the Washington city of the same name; Maui onions from the Hawaiian island, which are particularly sweet and shaped like flattened ovals; and light yellow Vidalia onions from Vidalia, Georgia. All are excellent in this recipe.

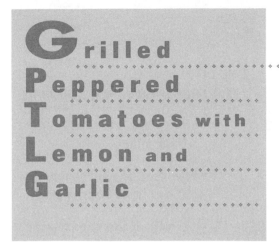

Grilled Peppered Tomatoes with Lemon and Garlic

Serves 4 as salad
or side dish

4 vine-ripened tomatoes

¼ cup freshly cracked black
pepper

¼ cup extra-virgin olive oil

2 tablespoons lemon juice
(about ½ lemon)

¼ cup chopped fresh parsley,
basil, or mixture of both

2 teaspoons minced garlic

3 dashes Worcestershire sauce

6 dashes Tabasco sauce

This dish is a fine demonstration of the fact that really good produce needs very little done to it to create a great-tasting dish; simply let the taste of the vegetable shine through. Since the quality of the dish depends completely on the quality of the tomatoes, make sure you get vine-ripened ones.

METHOD

1. Stem the tomatoes and cut them into quarters. Sprinkle them with pepper and grill over a hot fire for about 2 minutes, turning occasionally, or until they are lightly browned.

2. Remove the tomatoes from the grill and place them in a bowl. Add all the remaining ingredients, toss gently, and serve.

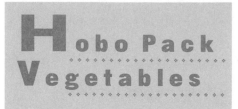

Hobo Pack Vegetables

1 large sweet potato, quartered

1 white potato, cut into ½-inch-thick slices

1 whole head of garlic, unpeeled, sliced in half horizontally

1 large yellow onion, quartered

1 carrot, cut into large chunks

½ large red bell pepper, cut into large chunks

½ small eggplant, cut into bite-size chunks

4 sprigs fresh rosemary

Salt and freshly cracked black pepper to taste

¼ cup virgin olive oil

Every chef has many influences on his or her cooking style, some going back to an early age. When I was a twelve-year-old Boy Scout filling foil packets with vegetables and catsup and sticking them in the coals of the campfire, it never occurred to me or anyone else that this would be the inspiration for a cookbook recipe. But the dynamics of cooking with live coals left a distinct impression on my mind, and I still enjoy the unpredictability and unique character of this technique. It's always a dramatic moment when you open the foil package that has been hidden for half an hour in the mysteries of the fire. Continuing along the hobo pack line started with Hobo Pack Chicken in *The Thrill of the Grill,* here is an all-veggie version. I have provided about 25 percent more vegetables than you will actually need for four portions because a certain amount of loss due to burning is unavoidable if you want to be sure the potatoes get cooked through. My particular favorites are the garlic and the burned parts of the potatoes.

M E T H O D

1. Arrange half of the vegetables on a large sheet of extra-heavy-duty aluminum foil, add 2 sprigs of rosemary, sprinkle with salt and pepper, and drizzle with 2 tablespoons of olive oil. Cover with a second sheet of foil and roll the edges of the 2 sheets together, closing the pack. Cover the entire pack with a second layer of foil and fold the edges together well. Repeat this process with the remaining vegetables.

2. Build a medium-hot fire, place the packs on the bottom of the fire or grill, and pile coals up all around them. Cook for 35 to 45 minutes, depending on the intensity of the coals. Remove from the coals, unroll the foil, and serve at once.

Serving Suggestions:

This versatile preparation goes well with nearly everything, as you'll see from the serving suggestions for other recipes in this book. It's especially good with grilled large pieces of meat and fish.

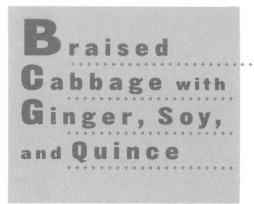

Braised Cabbage with Ginger, Soy, and Quince

While we were traveling in Southeast Asia, my co-author fell in love with quince. So now he is always asking me why, if I'm such an international guy, I never cook anything with quince. Not one to back down from a challenge, I developed this Asian-flavored version of the classic braised sweet-and-sour cabbage. I have to agree that the quince adds an excellent texture, a certain smoothness, and a nice, aromatic quality.

Serves 6 as side dish

2 tablespoons sesame oil

2 tablespoons virgin olive oil

1 small head (about 2 pounds) green cabbage, cored and cut into thin strips

2 tablespoons minced ginger

2 quinces, cored and cut into bite-size chunks

½ cup white vinegar

½ cup water

½ cup sugar

⅓ cup soy sauce

1 tablespoon ground coriander

Pinch ground star anise

Freshly cracked white pepper to taste

METHOD

1. In a large sauté pan, heat the sesame and olive oils over medium heat until hot but not smoking. Add the cabbage and cook, stirring occasionally, for 3 minutes.

2. Add the ginger and quince and cook, stirring frequently, for 2 minutes more. Add all the remaining ingredients, bring to a boil, reduce the heat to low, and simmer, covered, for 15 minutes or until the quince is soft.

Serving Suggestions:

I would serve this along with Grilled Chicken in the Style of Vulcan (page 171), Peach-Parsley Relish (page 352), and Grilled Hearthbread Johnson (page 406).

WHENCE QUINCE?

Once widely used in the United States as a preserved fruit, the quince is now a rarity here. This decline in popularity is probably due to the fact that it has an unusually dry texture for a fruit and does not develop much sugar even when completely ripe. To my mind, however, these drawbacks are compensated for by the distinctly tropical, musky perfume of this aromatic fruit, as well as by the fact that its texture causes it to soak up flavors like a sponge. Quinces are generally available in the fall and on through Christmas.

Spicy Pumpkin and Tomato Dish

Serves 4 to 6
as side dish

Here's another recipe that is West African by inspiration. As my education in African cuisines continues to develop, I am increasingly taken by the similarities between the cuisines of that continent and the southern cooking of my childhood. It's really not that much of a mystery, of course—cooks in the antebellum South were mostly Africans, and they brought their techniques, foods, and flavors with them. This dish, for example, could have been served to me either somewhere in Africa or in a school cafeteria in the South.

¼ cup virgin olive oil

2 cups pumpkin, seeded, cleaned, and cut into 1-inch cubes

1 yellow onion, thinly sliced

1 ripe tomato, diced small (about 1 cup)

⅓ cup Simple Dry Masala (page 203) *or* ¼ cup prepared curry powder

2 cups water

Salt and freshly cracked black pepper to taste

METHOD

1. In a large sauté pan, heat the oil over medium-high heat until hot but not smoking. Add the pumpkin and sauté, stirring occasionally, for 3 minutes, until it has acquired a slight sear. Add the onion and cook, stirring frequently, for another 4 minutes.

2. Add the tomato, masala, and water and bring to a boil. Reduce the heat and simmer for 20 to 25 minutes, until the pumpkin is easily pierced with a fork but still offers some resistance. The mixture will be rather soupy. Season to taste with salt and pepper.

Deep-Fried Plantain Rounds

Serves 4 as side dish

2 green plantains, peeled and cut into 2-inch rounds
----
2 cups vegetable oil

Salt and freshly cracked black pepper to taste

This is one of my favorites. Fried plantains are great with a whole range of Caribbean and African-inspired dishes or just as a snack by themselves. Make sure you use green plantains, even though they are somewhat of a nuisance to peel. Ripe ones are too mushy for this preparation.

METHOD

1. Heat the oil in a small saucepan until hot but not smoking. Drop the plantain rounds into the hot oil 3 or 4 at a time and cook until well browned, 2 to 3 minutes. Remove and drain.

2. Set each fried plantain on a flat side and, using a rolling pin, frying pan, or whatever else you think will work, squash it as flat as you can. It should have a circular shape.

3. Return the flattened plantain sections to the hot oil 3 or 4 at a time and cook until the entire surface is golden brown, about 2 minutes. Remove the plantains from the oil, drain, and season liberally with salt and pepper. Serve hot or at room temperature.

Smashing plantains

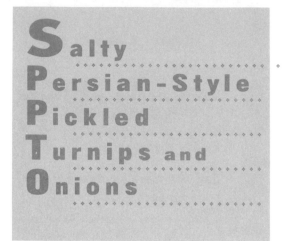

Salty Persian-Style Pickled Turnips and Onions

Makes about 4 cups

I know turnips may not be the most popular vegetable, but prepared this way they make a great snack. During the summer I like to put out a bowl of these during cocktail hour.

This Persian-inspired recipe is the result of buying too many local turnips one fall. I planned to use them in the restaurant during the winter, but our basement doesn't have desirable root cellar characteristics. What we were going to do with a hundred pounds of turnips? I sent the cooks searching for ideas, and somewhere along the line we learned that turnips are a very popular pickle in the Middle East, particularly in Iran. So here is the East Coast Grill's take on a pickle that dates way back.

1 turnip the size of a softball (about 1½ pounds), peeled and cut into long slices about the size of your little finger

½ pound pearl onions, peeled and left whole, *or* 2 red onions, cut into ½-inch pieces

1 beet the size of a golf ball, peeled and sliced as thick as quarters

5 cloves garlic, thinly sliced

2 tablespoons crushed coriander seeds

2 tablespoons fennel seeds

1 tablespoon cumin seeds

1 tablespoon freshly cracked black pepper

3 cups water

2 cups white vinegar

3 tablespoons kosher salt

2 tablespoons sugar

METHOD

1. In a small stockpot of boiling salted water, blanch the vegetables in turn, removing each with a slotted spoon as its time is up: The turnip slices should be blanched for 3 minutes, the onions for 2 minutes, and the beet slices for 1 minute. Drain all the vegetables and place them in a large bowl or giant glass jar.

2. Combine all the remaining ingredients and bring to a boil over medium heat. Pour this hot mixture over the vegetables and use a plate or other weight to make sure that all vegetables are covered by the liquid.

3. Cover the bowl or jar well and place in the refrigerator. Allow to sit for 4 days, then eat. This mixture will keep, covered and refrigerated, for 1 month.

Serving Suggestions:

Serve these with Middle Eastern salads for a very special hot summer salad combination, or put a bowl of them out with **Middle Eastern–Style Crisp Bread (page 404)** and **Grilled Pita (page 67)** for cocktail snacks.

IN A PRETTY PICKLE

I love pickles. Fortunately, before refrigeration pickling was a major means of preserving food, and therefore pickles of some sort exist in just about every cuisine in the world. They are easy to make and provide a superior vehicle for weird ingredients and exotic flavors. You can use the general method in this recipe to pickle just about any vegetable you want, varying the spices you add to enhance the vegetables. Use your imagination—the wilder, the better. You'll find that pickles are excellent items to have on hand, whether to add a new dimension to salads and relishes or just to chew on while sharing a few drinks with friends.

Señor Rossi's Cuban-Style Yucca

Serves 6 as side dish

2½ pounds yucca, peeled and diced medium

¾ to 1 cup chicken stock or water

1 tablespoon minced garlic

Salt and freshly cracked black pepper to taste

¼ cup extra-virgin olive oil for drizzling

¼ cup lime juice (about 2 limes)

While hanging out in Costa Rica, I've had the good fortune of enjoying many a meal with my fellow *hombre de negocios,* Juan Carlos Rossi. Juan is a world traveler and a connoisseur of many of the finer things in life, food being among the top three.

When Juan eats, whether it's in an expensive New York restaurant or a cozy local joint in downtown San José, the conversation is the same: meals past, present, and future. His descriptions are so poetic and inspiring that several times I have been moved to try to re-create a dish that he has described. But any meal is comprised not only of the food but of the time and place where it was consumed, and my attempts at re-creating his visions have never lived up to his elaborate reveries, with the exception of this one. I saw the steam coming off the yucca, tasted the garlic against the starchy background, sensed the lime and olive oil. Add some salt and freshly cracked pepper, and you can experience a true culinary transference.

METHOD

1. Place the yucca in a large saucepan with lightly salted water to cover. Bring to a rapid boil over high heat, reduce the heat to medium, and cook for about 20 minutes, or until the yucca is easily pierced with a fork but still offers a bit of resistance.

2. Drain well and place in a large bowl. Add the stock or water and the garlic and mash with potato masher until smooth. Season with salt and pepper, drizzle with olive oil and lime juice, and serve.

Serving Suggestions:

Serve this dish (and eat it) as you would serve and eat mashed potatoes. If you like your mashed potatoes really smooth and creamy, try adding a couple of tablespoons of heavy cream to this dish.

Black Bean Dip with Fried Sweet Plantains

Makes 4 to 5 cups

One day when I was making black bean soup in the East Coast Grill, it turned out much too thick. Since it was too late in the day to adjust it, I did what any cook would do—changed it from a soup to a dip. As it often turns out in the world of food, out of failure came a new creation.

I like black beans both for their own intrinsic taste and for the fact that they are an interesting way to pass on other flavors. Here they are cooked with beer and chiles and served with fried sweet plantains. I prefer a dark or amber beer, which complements the earthy taste of the black beans, but you can use whatever suits your fancy. If you don't feel like making fried plantains, you can always use tortilla chips.

2 tablespoons vegetable oil

1 large red onion, diced small

2 tablespoons minced garlic

1 pound (about 2 cups) dried black beans, rinsed well, covered with 6 cups cold water, and allowed to stand overnight

2 bottles beer of your choice

1 cup white vinegar

3 cups cold water

¼ cup tomato catsup

1 tablespoon ground cumin

1 tablespoon chili powder

1 tablespoon dry mustard

1 teaspoon ground cinnamon

1 tablespoon minced fresh red or green chile pepper of your choice

1 cup sour cream

½ cup chopped fresh cilantro

¼ cup lime juice (about 2 limes)

Salt and freshly cracked black pepper to taste

METHOD

1. In a large saucepan, heat the oil over medium-high heat until hot but not smoking. Add the onion and cook, stirring occasionally, until it begins to turn dark, about 5 to 7 minutes. Add the garlic and cook, stirring, for an additional 30 seconds. Add the drained beans, beer, vinegar, and water and bring the mixture to a boil. Reduce the heat to low and simmer for about 1½ hours, stirring occasionally, until the beans are mushy, adding more beer or water if the mixture becomes too dry.

2. Remove from the heat, add the catsup, cumin, chili powder, mustard, cinnamon, and chile pepper, and mix well. Allow to cool slightly (about 20 minutes), then purée the mixture in a blender or food processor until very smooth.

3. With the mixture still in the blender or food processor, add the sour cream, cilantro, lime juice, salt, and pepper. Blend briefly, just until well mixed. If the mixture is too thick, thin it with more beer. This mixture will keep, covered and refrigerated, about 4 days.

(continued)

Fried Sweet Plantains

◆ ◆

**Serves 8 as appetizer
or side dish**

To prepare plantains this way, they have to be dead ripe. If only green ones are available, you should use the method on page 253. Either way is fine. You will find that this preparation results in plantains that are a bit more floppy than the chips made from the green variety, so I suggest you spoon the dip onto them and eat them with a fork.

In a large sauté pan, heat the oil over medium heat until hot but not smoking. Add as many plantain slices as will fit easily in a single layer, and fry until just lightly browned, about 1 minute per side. As they brown, remove them to paper towels to drain, then sprinkle well with salt and pepper. Repeat until all the plantain slices are fried.

4 ripe (yellow-black) plantains, peeled and cut on a severe slant into ½-inch slices

¼ cup vegetable oil

Salt and freshly cracked black pepper to taste

Basic Black Beans

1 pound (about 2 cups) dried black beans

3 tablespoons peanut or other vegetable oil

2 large yellow onions, diced small

2 tablespoons minced garlic

1 teaspoon chili powder

1 teaspoon ground cumin

4 to 10 dashes Tabasco sauce, depending on your taste for heat

1 teaspoon sugar

¼ cup white vinegar

2 cups water

1 bottle beer of your choice

Salt and freshly cracked black pepper to taste

A staple in much of the warm-weather world, black beans are delicious by themselves, as ingredients in salsas and salads, or served with rice. This dish stores very well, so cook a double batch and keep some in the refrigerator.

METHOD

1. Soak the beans in cold water overnight or for at least 5 hours, then drain and rinse well.

2. In a large saucepan, heat the oil over medium-high heat until hot but not smoking. Add the onions and sauté, stirring occasionally, until just transparent, 5 to 6 minutes. Add the garlic and sauté, stirring a few times, for 1 more minute.

3. Add all remaining ingredients except the salt and pepper and bring to a simmer.

4. Add the beans, bring it all back to a simmer again, then reduce the heat to low and cook, covered, for 3 hours or until the beans are tender. If you think additional liquid is needed, stir in some more beer. Season to taste and serve.

All-Purpose Rice and Beans

Each Latin country has its own version of this culinary dynamic duo. In Cuba and Puerto Rico, for example, the rice and beans are combined in the same dish, while in Mexico they are usually eaten separately, at different points in the meal. In this version we cook the black beans and rice separately, then mix them together at the end. If you prefer, you can set them out in separate bowls and allow your guests to mix them in the proportion they find best. Many variations of this dish use oregano as the main herb, but we like the flavor of cilantro a bit better with the earthy taste of black beans.

2 tablespoons virgin olive oil

1 yellow onion, diced small

2 teaspoons minced garlic

1 recipe Basic Black Beans (page 261) *or* 2 16-ounce cans black beans

¼ cup white vinegar

5 to 10 dashes Tabasco sauce, depending on your taste for heat

¼ cup finely chopped fresh cilantro

3 cups cooked long-grain rice (preferably cooked in chicken stock)

Salt and freshly cracked black pepper to taste

METHOD

1. In a large sauté pan, heat the oil over medium-high heat until hot but not smoking. Add the onion and sauté, stirring occasionally, until transparent, 5 to 7 minutes. Add the garlic and sauté, stirring occasionally, for an additional 2 minutes.

2. Add the black beans, vinegar, and Tabasco. Bring the mixture to a boil, then reduce heat to low, cover, and simmer for 5 minutes, stirring occasionally.

3. Add the cilantro and rice, mix well, and serve accompanied by Tabasco or other hot pepper sauce.

THE PERFECT DUET

To me, black beans and rice is the ultimate example of the unconscious healthfulness of "peasant cuisines" around the world. Unconscious because it is a dish devised not in a calculated effort to be healthful but rather in an attempt to be as tasty and satisfying as possible given the ingredients available to indigenous cooks. Healthful because the rice-beans marriage creates a dish that is low in fat, high in complex carbohydrates, and—maybe best of all—the perfect complement of proteins. Because of this, the tasty combination provides a nearly ideal dietary base.

(continued)

Rice is the staple food for more than half of the world's population. In fact, it is so central to the diet of much of Asia that in several languages the word for rice is the same as the word for food or meal.

For those of us who grew up with "instant" rice, the many varieties now readily available in this country are a revelation. In fact, Americans are rapidly increasing their consumption of rice as we learn that this grain is not only tasty but also healthful—full of complex carbohydrates, low in fat, and cholesterol-free.

Rice is generally divided into three types, depending on size: *Long-grain* rices are at least three times as long as they are wide and generally cook up separate and fluffy. They are by far the most popular in America. *Medium-grain* rices are less than two times as long as they are wide and cook up tender and moist but a little sticky. *Short-grain* rices cook up very moist and tender.

Within these designations there is a huge range of rice varieties, including the popular Italian *arborio,* from which risotto is made, and the sweet *glutinous* or *sticky rice* used in many East Asian desserts. Of course, rice can also be divided into the two camps of *white,* from which both hull and bran have been removed, and *brown,* from which only the hull has been removed, with the bran left on.

In recent years aromatic rices, with their pronounced, nutty aromas and distinctive flavors, have begun to appear in stores around this country. Among the more popular types of aromatic rices are the following:

- *Basmati.* Perhaps the best known and most popular of the aromatic rices, basmati is grown in India and Pakistan, where it is considered a luxury food. It is particularly long and thin, and as it cooks it grows longer rather than fatter. With its pronounced, perfumy aroma, it adds a distinctive touch to any rice dish, particularly pilafs.

- *Jasmine.* This long-grain variety used to be grown only in Thailand but now is being grown in the U.S. as well. It has a particularly silken texture and a jasmine-like fragrance.

- *Texmati.* Grown in Texas, this long-grain is a hybrid of aromatic and regular long-grain varieties and has a nutty flavor and aroma similar to—but less pronounced than—that of basmati.

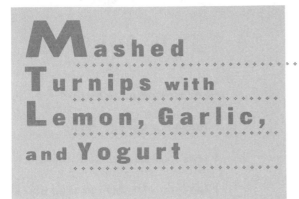

Mashed Turnips with Lemon, Garlic, and Yogurt

Serves 4 as side dish

1½ pounds turnips, peeled and diced into ½-inch chunks

¼ cup plain yogurt

¼ cup lemon juice (about 1 lemon)

1 tablespoon minced garlic

¼ cup chopped fresh curly parsley

Salt and freshly cracked black pepper to taste

I truly like turnips. Turnips have a slightly stronger flavor than many other root vegetables but still have all the old-fashioned charm that we associate with the underground vegetable clan. Mashing them with lemon, garlic, and yogurt gives us a kind of Middle Eastern mashed potatoes.

METHOD

1. In a small stockpot of boiling water, cook the turnips until easily pierced with a fork, 6 to 8 minutes. Do not overcook.

2. Drain well, place in a large bowl, and add the remaining ingredients. Mash roughly with a potato masher, adjust the seasonings, and serve at once.

Grilled Eggplant and Pepper Sandwiches with Basil and Black Olive Spread

Makes 4 sandwiches

Not like the sandwiches Mom used to make for lunch, this hearty, savory vegetable version gives new definition to the term. This is a member of the new ultra-chic Northern Italian line of sandwiches, which may be new to us but are probably eaten in some form by regular folks from Iran to Greece and everywhere in between.

¼ cup virgin olive oil

1 teaspoon minced garlic

1 teaspoon kosher salt

1 teaspoon freshly cracked black pepper

1 large eggplant, unpeeled, ends trimmed, and sliced lengthwise into planks about ½ inch thick (4 to 5 planks)

2 large red bell peppers, quartered

8 slices good, heavy bread, about 1 inch thick

BLACK OLIVE SPREAD:

½ cup pitted Kalamata or other black olives

1 teaspoon minced garlic

¼ cup extra-virgin olive oil

3 tablespoons balsamic vinegar

Salt and freshly cracked black pepper to taste

¼ cup fresh basil, cut into long, thin strips

METHOD

1. In a small bowl, mix the olive oil, garlic, salt, and pepper. Rub the eggplant and peppers lightly with this mixture.

2. Now for some serial grilling: Put the eggplant on the grill over a medium-hot fire and grill it until golden brown, 3 to 4 minutes per side; after about 2 minutes, add the peppers and grill until slightly charred, 2 to 3 minutes per side; about 1 minute into the peppers, add the bread slices and grill until just toasted, 1 to 2 minutes per side. If you're a genius, everything will be done at the same time.

3. Combine all the spread ingredients and purée in a food processor or blender until smooth.

4. Slather some of the spread onto the toasted bread, layer with grilled eggplant and peppers, and sprinkle with basil.

Serving Suggestion:

With this sandwich I would serve Spinach, Avocado, and Papaya Salad with Orange-Cumin Dressing (page 198).

SEX, LIES, AND EGGPLANT

Recently there has been a lot of talk among cooks about the sex of eggplants. This may lead you to think that chefs will do anything to spice up the time they spend in the kitchen, but in fact there is a practical reason for this salacious vegetable gossip. The rumor is that male eggplants (detectable mainly by the lack of an "innie") have fewer seeds and are therefore less bitter than the female variety. However, according to Harold McGee, author of the wonderful *On Food and Cooking* (Collier, 1984) and *The Curious Cook* (North Point, 1990), eggplants have no sex. The main variable in the number of seeds is simply age—the younger (and smaller) the eggplant, the fewer the seeds and the less bitter. So much for Eggplant Peyton Place.

Your Favorite Real Grilled Cheese Sandwich

Serves 4 special friends

1 pound cheese of your choice

8 slices bread of your choice

⅓ cup condiment of your choice (mayonnaise, mustard, Inner Beauty Hot Sauce, etc.)

¼ cup extra-virgin olive oil

From my early years, I had a firm grip on the meaning of "grilled" and knew that for something to qualify for this moniker, it had to be cooked over real fire. For this reason, it was always confusing to me when people served things like grilled cheese sandwiches that didn't meet that cardinal criterion.

So here it is, a real grilled cheese sandwich or, as it is known around my sister's house, "cheese on bread." As you can see, it is in some ways a blank canvas for you to do with as you wish. If it's lunchtime, serve with a green salad and a beer.

METHOD

1. Slice the cheese fairly thick, divide it among 4 slices of bread, and slather with your favorite condiment. Top with the remaining slices of bread and brush the outsides with olive oil. Wrap each sandwich in an 8" × 10" sheet of aluminum foil.

2. Grill the sandwiches over a low, low fire for about 5 minutes per side. Remove from the grill, unwrap, and return to the grill to brown the bread, which should take 2 to 3 minutes per side.

TOP 10 CHEESE-ON-BREAD ADD-ONS

A quick poll among our friends shows that the top 10 most popular additions to this perennial favorite are avocados, bacon, garden-fresh tomatoes, sliced red onions, minced chile peppers, chutney, salsa Mexicana, pimentos, arugula, and black olives.

Rice Pilaf with Lime Zest and Almonds

Serves 4 as side dish

Pilaf has a long tradition in the cuisines of the Middle East. The term generally refers to main dishes made of rice combined with other ingredients, from eggplant to chicken. In this version rice maintains its starring role, with nuts, raisins, and spices adding their various flavors. Lime zest is not a traditional pilaf ingredient, but I like the underlying tartness it provides. When making this pilaf, be sure to grind the cardamom seeds well; also be careful not to use the white pith of the lime zest, which is very bitter.

This dish is an excellent accompaniment to just about anything; I particularly like it with grilled fish.

1 tablespoon vegetable oil

1 yellow onion, diced small

2 tablespoons pine nuts

1 cup long-grain rice (preferably Basmati)

2 cups chicken stock or water

1 teaspoon red pepper flakes

4 cardamom seeds, removed from pods and finely ground

1/3 cup golden raisins

2 teaspoons finely minced lime zest (about 1 large lime)

1/2 teaspoon ground cinnamon

1 teaspoon salt

1/4 cup blanched slivered almonds, toasted in a 400°F oven for 5 minutes, or until lightly browned

METHOD

1. In a large sauté pan or saucepan, heat the oil until hot but not smoking. Add the onion and pine nuts and sauté until the onions are soft and the pine nuts slightly browned, 5 to 7 minutes. Stir in the rice and cook, stirring frequently, an additional 4 to 5 minutes.

2. Add all the remaining ingredients except the almonds and stir well. Turn the heat to low, cover, and simmer until all the liquid has been absorbed, 15 to 18 minutes. Remove from the heat, fluff with a fork, stir in the almonds, and serve at once.

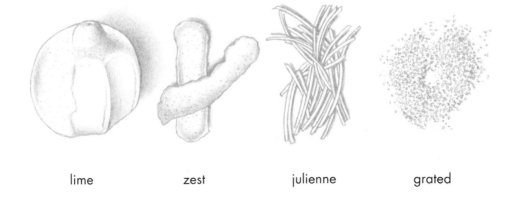

lime   zest   julienne   grated

Coconut Rice

Serves 4 as side dish

In the humid tropics, rice is the central staple and is prepared in a bewildering variety of ways. This is your basic coconut rice which we saw served all over Southeast Asia, either by itself or as an accompaniment to roasted chicken, duck, or pork. It goes beautifully with a huge range of dishes, providing a good counterpoint to spicy foods as well as a velvety-rich accompaniment to nonspicy preparations.

2 tablespoons peanut oil

1 small yellow onion, diced small

1 cup long-grain rice of your choice

1 cup chicken stock

1 cup coconut milk, unsweetened canned, or prepared by method on page 458

Salt and freshly cracked black pepper to taste

METHOD

1. Preheat oven to 350°F. In a large sauté pan, heat the oil over medium-high heat until hot but not smoking. Add the onion and sauté, stirring frequently, until just transparent, about 5 minutes.

2. Add the rice and continue to cook, stirring frequently, for 1 minute. Add the chicken stock and coconut milk, bring to a simmer, and add salt and pepper.

3. Cover the pan tightly, put it in the oven, and bake for about 18 minutes. All the liquid should be absorbed and the rice should be cooked through but not mushy.

Elmer's Salvadoran Pickled Cabbage

1 small head green cabbage, cored and very thinly sliced

1 small red onion, thinly sliced

1 carrot, thinly sliced

1 small green papaya, peeled, seeded, and cut into long, thin slices

1½ teaspoons minced garlic

¾ cup white vinegar

¼ cup pineapple juice

Salt and freshly cracked black pepper to taste

Elmer Sanchez, the talented day chef at the East Coast Grill, is fond of taking dishes from his country and adding a little something extra. Here he has transformed the Salvadoran pickled cabbage dish known as *cortido* by adding a bit of fresh green papaya. It reminds me of the coleslaw with pineapple that my grandmother used to make. In El Salvador this dish is often served as an accompaniment to *pupusas,* a snack made of masa flour stuffed with vegetables or meat. Let this dish sit for at least 12 hours for the cabbage to soften and the flavors to mingle.

METHOD

Mix all the ingredients together well and let stand, covered and refrigerated, for about 12 hours, stirring occasionally. Will keep, covered and refrigerated, about 4 days.

Serving Suggestion:

Serve this as you would serve coleslaw, with just about anything.

Sweet and Spicy Lo Mein Noodles

Serves 4 as entrée

This Asian-style cold noodle dish is the creation of Andy Husbands, chef at the East Coast Grill, where it was an instant hit. The recipe given here for the sweet and hot sauce makes about 3 cups, although you need only 1 cup for the noodles. You can cut the recipe, but I recommend you make the whole batch. It's an excellent all-purpose sauce, keeps for several weeks covered and refrigerated, and is an outstanding glaze for strong-flavored fish and grilled pork dishes of all kinds—just brush it on during the last minute or so. Think of it as your Asian version of A-1 Sauce.

1 pound lo mein noodles

2 tablespoons sesame oil

SWEET AND HOT SAUCE:

2 tablespoons sesame oil

1 tablespoon minced ginger

1 teaspoon minced garlic

6 tablespoons cider vinegar

¼ cup firmly packed brown sugar

½ cup molasses

1 tablespoon dry sherry

½ cup soy sauce

2 tablespoons rice wine vinegar

1 to 2 tablespoons minced fresh red or green chile pepper

2 tablespoons cornstarch

2½ tablespoons cold water

1 red bell pepper, cut into strips ¼ inch wide

1 green bell pepper, cut into strips ¼ inch wide

½ red onion, cut into strips ¼ inch wide

3 scallions, cut diagonally into strips ½ inch wide

1 small carrot, cut into pieces half the size of marbles

METHOD

1. Bring a stockpot of lightly salted water to a rolling boil. Add the noodles and boil, stirring frequently, until they are tender but still offer some resistance to the tooth, 1½ to 2 minutes. Drain, run under cold water until cool, drain again, and place in a large bowl. Add the sesame oil, toss well to coat the noodles, cover, and refrigerate.

2. Make the sauce: In a sauté pan, heat the sesame oil over medium-high heat until hot but not smoking. Add the ginger and garlic and sauté, stirring frequently, until golden brown, 2 to 3 minutes. Add all the remaining sauce ingredients except the cornstarch and water, bring the mixture to a boil, and let simmer for 3 minutes, stirring frequently.

3. In a small bowl, combine the cornstarch and water and whisk together well. Whisk this mixture into the simmering sauce, allow the sauce to return to a boil, and simmer for 5 minutes more, stirring frequently. Remove from the heat, allow to cool to room temperature, cover, and refrigerate.

4. In a large bowl, combine the noodles with the bell peppers, onion, scallions, and carrot and mix until they are well intertwined. Add 1 cup of the sweet and hot sauce, mix well, and serve.

Serving Suggestions:

For an Asian flavor fest, serve this with Sweet and Hot Sesame-Spinach Condiment (page 362) and Watercress and Crab Salad with Mangoes and Fish Sauce (page 221).

Couscous with Raisins and Parsley

3 cups instant couscous (about 1 box)

3½ cups boiling water

1 tablespoon cumin seeds

½ cup raisins

½ cup chopped fresh parsley

¼ cup virgin olive oil

¼ cup lemon juice (about 1 large lemon)

I have always been slightly confused about couscous because the word has more than a single meaning. It is the name of the national dish of Morocco, a huge meal consisting of an aromatic stew and the accompanying semolina-based pasta—which is also called couscous.

Couscous is perhaps the smallest member of the pasta family and is made from the same ingredients as its larger cousins. It originated with the Berbers of North Africa, and the traditional way of making it is exact and painstaking. Today couscous is available in a precooked form, and preparing it is as simple as pouring hot water over it and allowing it to sit for a while.

This form, along with people's increasing eagerness to include more grains in their diets, is helping to bring couscous into many American kitchens. Although purists may cringe at the evolved uses of couscous, particularly in this country, it still remains a great all-purpose grain that can be used creatively in many ways. This quick and easy salad or side dish, which goes well with just about anything, is just a small indication of the many uses of this North African pasta.

METHOD

1. Put the couscous in a large heatproof bowl. Pour the boiling water over, cover, and allow to sit for about 15 minutes, then fluff with a fork.

2. Meanwhile, toast the cumin seeds in a sauté pan over medium heat, watching carefully and shaking frequently to prevent burning, until they just begin to release a little smoke, 2 to 3 minutes.

3. Put the couscous in a large bowl, add the cumin seeds and all the remaining ingredients, and mix well.

Serving Suggestions:

Use this where you might have used rice before, or try it in combination with a relish like Peach-Parsley Relish (page 352), Apple-Apricot Chutney (page 346), or North African Chile Pepper Condiment (page 360) as a meal in itself.

COUS COUS COUS

When the Berbers of North Africa first started making couscous, it was not pasta but coarsely ground wheat. Over the years this evolved into the granular semolina pasta that we know as couscous today.

To prepare couscous in the traditional Arab manner, you must first soak it in cold water, then work it by hand to separate the grains, then steam it, then allow it to rest, and then steam it again, usually over an aromatic stew of meat and vegetables so it absorbs the flavors of the stew. The instant couscous available in the U.S. today has already been taken through the first steaming, so allowing it to absorb boiling water will bring it to the final stage.

Couscous has many advantages, including the fact that it is healthful, it tastes really good, and it adapts itself to pairing with many flavors. Not least of all, it is fun to say.

EAT THE HEAT: DISHES FOR THRILL SEEKERS

◼

Lava-Soaked Very Rare Steak Salad with Grilled Cabbage and Galangal ▪ Grilled Shell-On Giant Shrimp with Hot Peanut-Chile Butter ▪ K.C.'s Grilled Killer Jamaican Party Beef from Hell with Sweet Grilled Bananas ▪ Grilled Sausage Skewers with Fresh Apricots, Jalapeños, and Chipotle Vinaigrette and Whole Grill-Roasted Banana ▪ Grilled Fiery White-Peppered Chicken Wings ▪ Chile-Steamed Mussels with Ginger and Lemongrass ▪ Gingered Crab in Chile Sauce ▪ Scrambled Eggs with Fresh Oysters and Chiles ▪ Spicy Hard-Cooked Eggs in Coconut Milk with Chiles

These dishes are for those of you who think that the greatest culinary experience in the world would be drinking molten lava. In other words, this is for all you chile heads out there.

More than perhaps any other single ingredient, chile peppers have come into their own in America in the past few years. Not long ago the only kind of chiles you could find in supermarkets were dried red pepper flakes, which most people used almost exclusively on pizza. Today, however, dried and fresh chiles of every variety are showing up all over the country, and Americans have begun to appreciate the liveliness that a little heat can add to food.

I guess in a way it makes sense that people were slow to appreciate the glories of the chile. After all, the main thing that chiles contribute to our taste experience is pain. That's right, pain. Barry Green, a scientist at the Monell Sensory Institute in Philadelphia, has spent the past several years studying chiles. He has found that capsaicin, the active ingredient in these fiery little pods, affects not the taste receptors in the mouth, but the pain receptors. This might seem a bit odd, but it is also true of many of our other favorite spices, from mustard to horseradish to black pepper to onions and even garlic.

Green's findings fit right in with the theories of Paul Rozin, a psychologist from the University of Pennsylvania, who speculates that people eat chile peppers because of what he calls "benign masochism," the ability to experience the roller-coaster thrill of the body's reaction to danger but with no actual physical threat. Rozin also suggests that chile peppers may stimulate the production of endorphins, the body's own internal pleasure drug.

Whatever the reason we like them, there are certainly plenty of chiles to choose from, and confusion runs rampant over their names and their natures. I have spent a lot of time testing and tasting fresh chiles, and my conclusion is that you should not worry about finding a particular pepper called for in some recipe. While dried chiles do have very distinct flavor characteristics, fresh chiles contribute mostly heat, not flavor, so you can easily substitute one for another.

Because of this—and because calling for specific chiles is too complicated and tends to scare people off—I generally call for the "fresh chile of your choice" in a recipe, rather than specifying one variety. This allows you to follow my one piece of advice about chiles: Choose a pepper that you like and is readily available where you live, then get to know it. Only after a fair amount of experimentation will you know just how hot that particular chile makes a given dish and how much you like to put in. When you have weaseled all of the culinary secrets out of that particular pepper, you might want to consider striking up an acquaintance with a second variety; on the other hand, you might want to stick to a familiar relationship.

Now that I have said all this, I have to add the exceptions. Although substituting one chile for another is generally a fine practice, you may want to avoid it when cooking traditional Mexican cuisine. In that culture, centuries of experience have led to a very fine appreciation of the subtle nuances of flavor differentiation among various dried chiles. Also, there are two peppers that I sometimes call for in recipes and for which I would advise you to make no substitutes: the chipotle and the habañero. The chipotle is a jalapeño that has been dried and then smoked, and it is available both in dry form or (more commonly) canned in a vinegar sauce. The habañero, or Scotch Bonnet as it is known in the Caribbean, is the hottest chile pepper known to humankind and has a singular floral, nasal heat that lights up every cavity in your head. You can substitute for these two just as for all other peppers, but doing so is not as successful because of their very special characteristics.

So if you are one of those folks who just can't get enough fire in your food— or if you're a risk taker who is into culinary experimentation—dig into the dishes in this chapter. I guarantee you'll soon be sweating and panting and otherwise enjoying your chile high.

Lava-Soaked Very Rare Steak Salad with Grilled Cabbage and Galangal

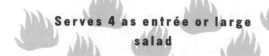

Serves 4 as entrée or large salad

1 pound top round (about 1 inch thick), cut into 4 equal portions

$\frac{1}{2}$ cup minced fresh red or green chile pepper of your choice

$\frac{1}{4}$ cup vegetable oil

$\frac{1}{4}$ cup lime juice (about 2 limes)

Salt and freshly cracked black pepper to taste

1 small head green cabbage (about the size of a cantaloupe), cored and quartered

2 tablespoons sesame oil

Salt and freshly cracked white pepper to taste (you may substitute black pepper)

$\frac{1}{4}$ cup virgin olive oil

$\frac{1}{4}$ cup pineapple juice

$\frac{1}{4}$ cup white vinegar

2 tablespoons minced galangal (you may substitute ginger)

$\frac{1}{4}$ cup chopped fresh cilantro

$\frac{1}{4}$ cup chopped fresh mint

Here's a collision of textures and flavors resulting in a burst of sensations that will lead to tingling brows and flushed faces. Not for everyone, this dish features small pieces of beef that have been seared hard, soaked in chiles, then surrounded by crunchy, smoky cabbage; sweet, pungent galangal; and aromatic cilantro and mint. What I like best about this recipe is that by heavily searing the meat and then cutting it into small pieces, you get a strong meat presence without actually using a lot of beef. Also, the chunks are small enough to become supercharged with sear and chiles.

If you want to avoid chopping all the chiles, you may substitute 1 cup of your favorite hot sauce for the lava mixture in Step 1. I particularly recommend Vietnamese chile-garlic paste.

METHOD

1. Combine the top round, chile peppers, vegetable oil, lime juice, salt, and pepper and mix well. Place in a bowl just large enough to fit, so that the liquid is completely covering the meat. Cover very tightly and refrigerate for at least 8 but no more than 24 hours.

2. Rub each cabbage quarter with sesame oil and sprinkle with salt and white pepper. Grill the cabbage over a medium fire until well browned on all sides, 2 to 3 minutes per exposed surface. (The idea is to give the cabbage some sear and color; don't try to cook it completely.) Remove the cabbage from the grill, cut it into thin strips (julienne), and place in a large bowl.

3. Remove the meat from the lava mixture, discard the remaining liquid, and grill the meat over a hot fire for 2 to 3 minutes, rolling the chunks around a bit so they get a good, heavy char on the surface.

4. Remove the meat from the grill, cut into pieces about the thickness of a bottle cap, and add to the sliced cabbage. Add all the remaining ingredients, toss well, and serve.

GALANGAL: THE COMEBACK KID

Virtually unknown to American cooks until the past few years, the pungent and aromatic root called galangal is an important spice in the cooking of East Asia, particularly in Southeast Asia and Indonesia. It also provides an interesting illustration of the way foods come and go in different cultures.

During the Middle Ages, galangal was very well known to European cooks and ranked in popularity with ginger, which was used in copious quantities by cooks all over the continent. With the coming of the Renaissance and the attendant rejection of strong flavors in cooking, however, galangal fell so far out of favor that we basically forgot about it. It is only recently, with Americans' newfound interest in the bold flavors of non-European cuisines, that this spice has begun to be reintroduced to our larder.

Grilled Shell-On Giant Shrimp with Hot Peanut-Chile Butter

Grilling shrimp is easy, and they have a taste that goes well with all kinds of wild flavors. This dish, which is almost like a shrimp relish, takes advantage of the peanut-chile combination that is well known in parts of Africa and was brought to northern Brazil by African slaves.

2½ pounds giant shrimp (8 to 10)

2 tablespoons virgin olive oil

¼ cup salt

¼ cup freshly cracked black pepper

¼ pound butter

2 tablespoons minced garlic

3 tablespoons minced fresh red or green chile pepper of your choice

½ cup lemon juice (about 2 lemons)

¼ cup roughly chopped roasted unsalted peanuts

½ cup chopped fresh parsley

METHOD

1. Slice the shrimp down the back with a serrated knife about ⅓ of the way through, so that the flesh is exposed but the shrimp are still whole. Devein them, but do not remove the shells from the shrimp. Put them into a large bowl along with the olive oil, salt, and pepper, and toss until the shrimp are well coated.

2. Over a medium-hot fire, grill the shrimp for 4 to 5 minutes per side, or until they are opaque all the way through. Remove and set aside in a large bowl.

3. In a small saucepan, combine the butter, garlic, and minced chile pepper over very low heat and cook until the butter has melted. Remove from the heat, add the lemon juice, and toss well.

4. Pour this mixture over the shrimp and toss well. Add the peanuts and parsley, adjust the seasonings, toss well, and serve.

Serving Suggestions:

Try this with Lentil Salad with White Grapes and Carrots (page 210) and Savory Watermelon and Pineapple Salad (page 220). Grilled Onion Rings (page 246) are also nice with these shrimp.

K.C.'s Grilled Killer Jamaican Party Beef from Hell with Sweet Grilled Bananas

Serves 8 as appetizer

2 pounds flank steak, skirt steak, or top round

HOT PEPPER PASTE:

½ cup finely chopped habañero peppers (about 15 habañeros) *or* 1 cup Home-Style Inner Beauty Hot Sauce, bottled or homemade (page 355), or other habañero-based hot sauce

6 tablespoons lime juice (about 3 limes)

¼ cup chopped fresh cilantro

Salt and freshly cracked black pepper to taste

2 tablespoons butter

2 tablespoons molasses

4 bananas, cut in half lengthwise but not peeled

Okay, I know that this one will appeal to only a very small number of you readers. The rest of you will think that I am out of my mind for even suggesting that someone might eat this, much less enjoy it. So if you're not one of the few, one of the brave, one of that small group who seek an altered state of consciousness through heat, stop here, do not go forward, because this dish is totally out of control.

This is a second-generation member of the East Coast Grill's infamous "... from Hell" line of volcanic and potentially lethal dishes. It was created when K.C., our chef, became frustrated because two customers in the same week actually finished a full dose of Pasta from Hell. In response, he developed this recipe. To this day I can count on one hand the customers who have eaten this dish and returned to eat it again. Fresh habañeros provide the power, while grilled bananas provide a momentary modicum of relief. This, my friends, is the final frontier.

METHOD

1. Slice the flank steak on a slant as thinly as possible. Place each piece of steak between 2 sheets of plastic wrap, and pound until ¼ inch thick, or about the thickness of a beer bottle cap. (This should result in rounds of steak 3 to 5 inches in diameter.)

2. Make the hot pepper paste: In a small bowl, combine the habañero peppers, lime juice, cilantro, salt, and pepper and mix well. Rub the steak rounds with about ⅔ of this paste and reserve the remainder.

3. Grill the steak rounds over high heat for about 1 to 2 minutes per side, or until they are medium rare. Brush liberally with the remaining hot pepper paste.

4. Meanwhile, combine the butter and molasses in a small saucepan and heat over very low heat until the butter is just melted. Grill the bananas over a medium-hot fire until they are golden brown, 2 to 3 minutes. Brush with the molasses-butter mixture and cook for another 30 seconds. Remove from the grill and serve with the party beef.

BEAT THE HEAT: CHILE ANTIDOTES

There are two things that relieve the self-inflicted pain of a chile overdose: cold and milk products. Cold, however, will abate the pain only for a few seconds until your mouth warms up again, whereas certain molecules in milk products actually bind with molecules of capsaicin (the "heat" in chile peppers) and flush them away.

In any case, here are a few antidotes that we have come across over the years. Despite scientific evidence that some of them are next to useless, each has its firm adherents. As with chile peppers themselves, I encourage you to try them all and find what works best for you.

Ice cubes
Chocolate
Milk
Cornbread or other breads
Sugar
Vintage port (has the advantage of being undetectable as an antidote; just tell your friends you like to sip port throughout the meal)
Orange Creamsicle (possibly the #1 antidote, since it combines milk products and cold)
Frozen Brandy Alexander

Grilled Sausage Skewers with Fresh Apricots, Jalapeños, and Chipotle Vinaigrette and Whole Grill-Roasted Banana

Serves 4 as entrée

2 pounds hot sausage of your choice, cut into 8 pieces

4 fresh apricots, pitted and halved (you may substitute small peaches)

8 whole jalapeños, stemmed

VINAIGRETTE:

¼ cup canned chipotle peppers (see Pantry, page 457)

¼ cup lime juice (about 2 limes)

¼ cup molasses

1 tablespoon ground cumin

¼ cup chopped fresh cilantro

Salt and freshly cracked black pepper to taste

Here's a whammer hot-sweet combination, with the hot sausage of your choice on a skewer with apricots and jalapeños. If that doesn't faze you, then the sledgehammer of the chipotle vinaigrette surely will. Since I know some of you will overdo it, I've included a Whole Grill-Roasted Banana as an instant heat antidote.

I prefer a cured sausage like kielbasa or linguica in this dish, but you may use raw sausage if that's your preference. If you do use raw sausage, however, you must first blanch it in boiling water for 3 to 4 minutes, let it cool to room temperature, and then proceed with the recipe.

METHOD

1. Thread the sausages, apricots, and jalapeños alternately onto skewers. (I prefer 8 small skewers rather than 4 large ones because they are easier to deal with.) Grill the skewers over a medium fire, turning occasionally, until the peppers and apricots are browned, 6 to 8 minutes.

2. In a food processor or blender, combine all the vinaigrette ingredients and purée. Serve the skewers topped with the vinaigrette and accompanied by ¼ of the grill-roasted banana.

Serving Suggestions:

These fiery skewers are good with Cheesy Cornbread (page 394) and All-Purpose Rice and Beans (page 262).

CHILE MYTH #742

Since chile peppers cause sensations of burning when you eat them, most people assume these little pods will somehow damage the stomach if you eat too many of them too often. But when scientists at Baylor College of Medicine in Houston, Texas, ran experiments to check this out, it turned out that even when ground jalapeños were funneled directly into people's stomachs, no damage was caused. So eat in good health.

Whole Grill-Roasted Banana

Place the unpeeled banana on the grill over a medium fire and cook until black but not burned, 8 to 10 minutes, turning occasionally.

1 ripe to very ripe banana, unpeeled

Grilled Fiery White-Peppered Chicken Wings

20 chicken wings, cut at the joint (save wing tips for stock or discard them)

¼ cup freshly cracked white pepper

2 tablespoons salt

½ cup soy sauce

¼ cup lime juice (about 2 limes)

2 tablespoons minced ginger

2 teaspoons minced garlic

2 tablespoons minced fresh red or green chile pepper of your choice

1 tablespoon sugar

2 tablespoons chopped fresh basil

2 tablespoons chopped fresh cilantro

I like to grill chicken wings for three reasons. First, they are easy and fast; second, they have an almost limitless versatility as to the flavors you can combine with them; and third, you have to pick them up with your hands to eat them. That kind of sets the mood for the rest of the meal, letting folks know right up front that they can relax.

In this dish the wings are coated with white pepper—preferably freshly cracked, but if not you'll still be all right—and everything else is added after the wings are cooked. It's sort of like post-marinating, applying the flavors after cooking instead of before in order to preserve their individual dimensions. As you take your first bite, see how many different, clearly defined tastes you get.

METHOD

1. Sprinkle the wings with pepper and salt. Grill over a medium-hot fire until they are well browned, 5 to 7 minutes, turning a couple of times. Take the largest wing off the fire and check for doneness by eating it.

2. Remove the wings from the grill and place in a large bowl. Add all the remaining ingredients, toss well, and serve.

Serving Suggestions:

Try these with Watercress and Crab Salad with Mangoes and Fish Sauce (page 221) and Savory Watermelon and Pineapple Salad (page 220).

CHILE SECRET WEAPON

In the often-macho world of chile lovers, a constant source of puzzlement is the age-old question "Why can he eat hotter food than I can?" Barry Green, a scientist at the Monell Sensory Institute in Philadelphia, has found at least part of the answer.

As every heat aficionado worth his habañero knows, the burn of chile peppers continues to increase in intensity as long as you keep eating. But Green has discovered that if you *stop* eating chiles—even for as little as 2 to 5 minutes—the phenomenon known as desensitization kicks in. So the next bite you take of hot food will taste only a fraction as hot as the first bite.

Like the secret of the atom, this bit of scientific lore can be used for good or for evil. Imagine yourself taking a buddy on a first visit to a Mexican restaurant. When the waitperson sets down a bowl of spicy salsa with chips, you dig right in, but warn your friend the tyro chile eater that it might be too hot for him or her. After a few bites of salsa you lay off and just chat for a few minutes until the entrées arrive. Assuming you both have the same dish, your friend will probably find it incendiary, while you, with your newly desensitized palate, can just shrug and say, "Ah, I've had a lot hotter." The legend continues.

Chile-Steamed Mussels with Ginger and Lemongrass

Like squid—another inexpensive, delicious, and nutritious denizen of the ocean—mussels have recently begun to gain popularity in the U.S. Here we steam the tasty little mollusks in an Asian-flavored broth with a hefty portion of chiles to provide some searing heat.

2 tablespoons sesame oil

2 stalks lemongrass, tough upper leaves and outer stalk removed and reserved, inner portion of bulb (bottom third of stalk) very finely minced

2 tablespoons minced ginger

2 tablespoons minced fresh red or green chile pepper of your choice

1 cup orange juice (about 2 oranges)

¼ cup lime juice (about 2 limes)

Salt and freshly cracked white pepper to taste (you may substitute black pepper)

4 pounds mussels, shells well scrubbed and beards removed

4 scallions, including white and green parts, thinly sliced

¼ cup chopped fresh cilantro

METHOD

1. In a small stockpot, heat the sesame oil over medium-high heat until hot but not smoking. Add the lemongrass and sauté, stirring occasionally, for 3 minutes.

2. Add the ginger and chile and cook 1 additional minute, stirring a few times.

3. Add the orange juice, lime juice, salt, pepper, and mussels and bring to a boil. Turn the heat to low, cover, and cook for 3 to 5 minutes, or until all mussels have opened. (Discard any that fail to open.)

4. Place ¼ of the mussels in each of 4 bowls, pour ¼ of the broth into each bowl, and sprinkle with scallions and cilantro.

Serving Suggestions:

This is a great summertime first course. I would serve it with just about anything.

SHOWING YOUR MUSSEL

Most of the mussels that come to market are farmed on ropes strung out into the ocean, which these mollusks grab onto with their byssal threads, commonly known as "beards." The beards must be removed before cooking. You can usually pull them off with your fingers; for more stubborn ones, use a pair of pliers. Mussels on the East Coast of the U.S. have a deep, rich, slightly sweet flavor. For my money, the specimens from Cape Cod are the best that I have tasted anywhere in the world. A note of caution, though: Be sure you know the origin of the mussels you buy because they are very susceptible to toxins.

Gingered Crab in Chile Sauce

Serves 4 as appetizer

¼ cup vegetable oil

8 fresh live blue crabs, claws separated and bodies chopped in half

1 tablespoon virgin olive oil

1 tablespoon sesame oil

3 tablespoons minced ginger

2 tablespoons minced garlic

¼ cup minced fresh red or green chile pepper of your choice

½ cup pineapple juice

¼ cup white vinegar

¼ cup tomato catsup

¼ cup soy sauce

¼ cup lime juice (about 2 limes)

½ cup chopped fresh cilantro

In Southeast Asia crab is a very popular food, and they have all kinds, from the giant Sri Lankan hairy crab to the prehistoric horseshoe crab to a small, blue-spotted variety that resembles the blue crab I know from my Tidewater, Virginia, youth. Unlike here, where the meat is generally picked out, over there cooks just chop the crab into a couple of pieces, cook it, and let the customer deal with it. That's fine with me; when given the chance, I'd just as soon eat with my hands.

This is my version of a common Malaysian/Singaporean way of serving crabs. Break out the old tablecloth and T-shirts for this one because you're going to destroy the serving area. One characteristic that both Asian and blue crabs have in common is that they go great with cold beer.

METHOD

1. In your largest sauté pan, heat the vegetable oil over medium heat until hot but not smoking. Working in batches, add the crab claws and half-bodies in a single layer and fry until the color changes, 2 to 3 minutes. Remove and drain on several layers of paper towels. Repeat until all claws and half-bodies have been fried. Discard the oil.

2. In the same pan, heat the olive and sesame oils over medium heat until hot but not smoking. Add the ginger, garlic, and chiles and sauté, stirring, for 2 minutes. Add the pineapple juice, vinegar, catsup, and soy sauce and bring to a boil. Add the crab and cook for 4 to 5 minutes, stirring frequently.

3. Remove the mixture from the heat, add the lime juice and cilantro, stir well, and serve.

Serving Suggestions:

This particular preparation goes well with Red Potato and Cucumber Salad with Mango (page 202) and any grilled pork dish. For a really exotic dinner, I'd serve it with Raw Beef with Ginger and Cardamom and Grilled Chile-Garlic Toast (page 40) and Sesame Shrimp and Mango Salad with Ginger-Soy Vinaigrette (page 224).

WHAT A CRAB

I am a big fan of the American blue crab from my childhood days in the Tidewater area of Virginia. Among my favorite early memories are the summer fests when we would all sit at a huge picnic table sucking and picking the tender white meat from crabs we had caught earlier in the day, using chicken necks on a string as bait. This technique has been discovered by my niece and nephew, and when I visit my sister's family at the riverfront house where they spend the month of August, I love to see them out on the dock early in the morning dangling pieces of string in the water. The trick of the method, for those of you who might be thinking of trying it, is to wait until the crab has a lock on the chicken neck, then very gently lift the string, bringing the unwary crab just far enough above the bottom so you can slide your net underneath him with a lightning move. It sounds easy, but those crabs are a lot faster than they look.

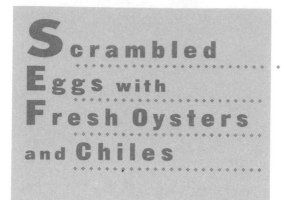

Scrambled Eggs with Fresh Oysters and Chiles

¼ cup all-purpose flour

1 teaspoon salt

1 teaspoon freshly cracked white pepper (you may substitute black pepper)

1 cup shucked oysters (10 to 12 oysters)

3 tablespoons virgin olive oil

1 tablespoon sesame oil

1 tablespoon minced ginger

¼ cup chopped scallions (both white and green parts)

1 tablespoon minced fresh red or green chile pepper of your choice

2 tablespoons soy sauce

4 large eggs, lightly beaten

Salt and freshly cracked white pepper to taste

I am constantly amazed by way-out food combinations that sound so weird it's hard to figure out why people eat them. Being a fan of huevos rancheros, I'm no stranger to the combination of chiles and eggs, but throw in oysters and I had my doubts. When I actually encountered this dish in Singapore, though, it turned out to be one of my favorites.

The key here is super-fresh oysters. In this version, I cook them a little more than they do in Singapore and cut down on the chiles for our less-than-asbestos palates. But whether it's a case of jet lag or a hangover that's getting you down, this dish definitely possesses remarkable restorative powers.

METHOD

1. In a medium-size bowl, combine the flour, salt, and pepper and mix well.

2. Drain the oysters and lightly dredge them through the flour mixture.

3. In a large sauté pan, heat the olive and sesame oils until hot but not smoking. Add the oysters and fry until slightly browned, 2 to 3 minutes. Remove and set aside.

4. Add the ginger, scallions, and chile and cook, stirring, 1 additional minute. Stir the soy sauce into the eggs, add to the pan, and scramble until as dry as you like; I like eggs a bit runny, which means I scramble them for about 2 minutes. Season to taste and serve.

Serving Suggestion:

For a sure hangover cure, serve this with a double batch of Chris's Bloody Marys (page 448).

TO THE BRAVE GO THE SPOILS

So there we were, on our first night in Singapore, suffering from jet lag but nevertheless busily checking out the street food scene. It was 2:00 A.M. and we were in the heart of Newton Circus, one of the city's organized collections of street food vendors that reflect the incredible cultural diversity of Singapore.

We were watching a guy toss a couple of raw eggs into a wok smoking hot with oil, followed by some giant raw oysters, soy sauce, ginger, herbs, and an extra-large handful of chopped chiles to torture the tourists. Before I could say, "I've changed my mind," this chile-laden egg-oyster thing was looking up at me from a plate. This dish may not sound great, but that's nothing compared to the way it looked, and my buddy was cracking up as I took my first bite. The ginger and herbs were the first things I tasted, the consistency was a little like brains, with a distinct, partially cooked oyster flavor, and then whammo! the chiles kicked in.

The oysters were meaty and delicious, and with the eggs to bind them together a bit and the power of the chiles—well, I lost my jet leg and became quite a fan of this common street food. It goes to show, once again, that being adventurous pays off, and you should never judge anything until you have actually tasted it.

Spicy Hard-Cooked Eggs in Coconut Milk with Chiles

3 tablespoons virgin olive oil

1 small red onion, diced small

1 tablespoon minced ginger

1 teaspoon minced garlic

1 tablespoon minced fresh red or green chile pepper of your choice

1 tablespoon brown sugar

½ cup pineapple juice

6 tablespoons lime juice (about 3 limes)

1 cup coconut milk, unsweetened canned, or prepared by method on page 458

4 dashes Worcestershire sauce

3 tablespoons prepared curry powder *or* Sweet and Hot Masala #7 (page 388)

Salt and freshly cracked black pepper to taste

8 hard-cooked eggs, shelled

When you travel to other countries, you find that foods that seem completely bizarre to you are just ordinary, everyday dishes to the people of that culture. In Malaysia, for example, curried hard-boiled eggs are a very common Muslim street food. Whenever I saw people selling them, I would make a face, until finally the guy who was showing us around politely pointed out that we Westerners also eat some pretty strange things. Cheese, for example, appeared to him to be nothing but milk that was so rotten it had become solid, a totally disgusting thing.

I appreciated his insight so much, I grabbed a couple of the eggs. They were really tasty and reminded me of the curried deviled eggs that were a highlight of my grandmother's Fourth of July picnics.

These eggs are best eaten hot, but they are also fine at room temperature or even cold. (The sauce will congeal a bit if you serve them cold, but the great taste will still be there.) You can try to eat them with your fingers, as if you were in Malaysia, but I suggest a knife and fork.

METHOD

1. In a large sauté pan, heat the oil over medium-high heat until hot but not smoking. Add the onion and sauté, stirring frequently, for 3 to 4 minutes. Add the ginger, garlic, and chile and sauté, stirring, for 1 additional minute.

2. Add the brown sugar, pineapple juice, and lime juice and cook, stirring occasionally, for 5 minutes. Add the coconut milk, Worcestershire sauce, curry powder, salt, and pepper. Bring to a boil, reduce the heat to low, and simmer for 10 minutes; the mixture should thicken slightly.

3. Add the whole shelled eggs, cook for 3 minutes, and serve.

Serving Suggestions:

Serve these with Quick and Easy Sautéed Leafy Greens with Lime and Chiles (page 231) and Coconut Rice (page 272), and if you close your eyes you can imagine yourself in Johore Bahru, gateway to Malaysia.

THE FLAVOR OF PAIN

When you handle chile peppers, they are not hot to the touch, so why do we experience them as ''hot'' when we eat them? The answer is not a very comforting one—it turns out that chiles manage to confuse our poor little brains.

To understand this phenomenon, you first have to understand that capsaicin, the active ingredient in chile peppers, stimulates not the taste buds but the pain sensors in our mouths. It also helps to know that our bodies contain not just one type of pain sensor but several different sets of sensors that respond to different types of pain. It so happens that capsaicin stimulates the same subset of pain fibers that respond to painfully high temperatures. Consequently, our brains become slightly addled and translate this particular chemical pain as heat.

Cardamom Chicken Stew in the Indian Style ▪ African-Style Chicken Stew with Squash ▪ Malay-Style Chicken and Sweet Potato Stew with Coconut Milk, Ginger, and Chiles ▪ Garlicky Fried Pork and Chicken Stew ▪ Elmer's Stewed Pork Ribs with Chunks of Corn ▪ Pork and Pumpkin Stew with Tripe and Cornmeal Dumplings ▪ Pork Stew with Chiles and Peanuts ▪ Aromatic Southeast Asian Pork Stew ▪ North African Lamb Stew with Sweet Potatoes and Couscous ▪ Paella à la Diplomate ▪ Seafood Mixed Grill with Lobster, Clams, Oysters, Corn, and Sausage ▪ Cary's New Year's Eve Rice Stew Thang

LET'S GET STEWED IN A STRANGE AND EXOTIC WAY

■

Every culture in the world seems to have some version of the one-pot meal, which is usually a variation on the soup or stew theme. To me, making soups and stews is a special craft because the origins of a dish often lie in the cook's ability to use things that are otherwise discarded. With their extra latitude for experimentation, soups and stews, more than other dishes, seem to take on the character of the individual cook.

In any case, stew-type dishes provide a great way to discover and explore the typical ingredients and flavor combinations of various cuisines. Since most of the dishes in this chapter are inspired by the food of hot-weather countries, there is usually something added at the last minute—citrus juice, fresh herbs, toasted spices, coconut milk—to enliven the dish with the well-defined flavors typical of these cuisines. You will also find a take-off on the classic Brunswick stew of the American South; a grilled variation on the New England clambake; and a kind of modernized take on the jambalaya of New Orleans. One-pot dishes are all about homeyness, after all, so how could I not include some American regional examples?

You will notice that whenever a recipe here contains meat, the meat is well seared over high heat before it goes into the pot. This is a key step. It creates a nice brown crust that prevents the meat from turning an unappetizing gray as it stews. More importantly, this crust is also very flavorful. The interaction of the high heat and the meat causes the same Maillard reaction that takes place when you grill meat over a live fire (see page xxvi), and the brown sear that should cover the exterior of the meat when you finish searing has a complex taste that lends flavor to the entire stew.

Each of the dishes in this chapter is enough for a meal in itself. In case you feel like putting out a real banquet, however, we have provided menu suggestions. Remember that these are just what they say they are—suggestions. Feel free to mix and match with abandon.

When all is said and done, I guess I find a special attraction in throwing all the ingredients for a meal into one big pot. It has a communal, gathered-around-the-fire kind of feel to it—and it's a lot easier for whoever has to clean up the dishes. So drag out your biggest pot and let's get stewed.

Cardamom Chicken Stew in the Indian Style

This exotic dish will give your house the aroma of an Indian bazaar. Its preparation demonstrates several techniques commonly used with spices. The first is a dry rub in which cardamom, salt, and pepper are rubbed on the chicken prior to sautéing. The second is the sautéing of whole spices to release their oils and intensify their flavors. The third is the toasting of several ground spices to create a powdered spice mix known as a masala. Like the most famous of these mixtures, garam masala, the mix we create here is added at the last moment, just prior to the completion of cooking. All of this adds up a certain smooth richness countered by pungent lime juice and aromatic cilantro as well as the spice mix.

Banquet Suggestions:

Apple-Apricot Chutney (page 346), Mangoes, Cucumbers, and Red Onion in Vinegar with Toasted Sesame Seeds (page 350), Sweet Potato–Onion Pancakes (page 45), Indian-Style Grill Bread (page 400), and Rice Pilaf with Lime Zest and Almonds (page 270).

Serves 4 as entrée

12 chicken thighs

1 tablespoon salt

1 tablespoon freshly cracked black pepper

2 tablespoons ground cardamom

¼ cup virgin olive oil

2 yellow onions, thinly sliced

2 teaspoons ground cinnamon

15 whole cloves

2 tablespoons minced ginger

2 tablespoons minced garlic

2 tablespoons minced fresh red or green chile pepper

2 white potatoes, peeled and cut into quarters lengthwise

4 cups chicken stock

2 cups coconut milk, unsweetened canned, or prepared by method on page 458

1 tablespoon each ground cumin, ground coriander, and chili powder

1 teaspoon ground turmeric

⅓ cup chopped fresh cilantro

¼ cup lime juice (about 2 limes)

Salt and freshly cracked pepper

METHOD

1. Preheat the oven to 350°F. Sprinkle the chicken thighs with salt, pepper, and cardamom. In a large sauté pan, heat the olive oil over medium heat until hot but not smoking. Add the chicken thighs, skin sides down, and cook until the skins are well browned, 4 to 6 minutes. Flip over and cook an additional 2 minutes on the other side. Remove the thighs and place in a large ovenproof casserole.

2. Add the onions, cinnamon, cloves, ginger, garlic, and chile to the sauté pan and cook, stirring frequently, until the onions are translucent, 5 to 7 minutes. Transfer to the casserole.

3. Add the potatoes, chicken stock, and coconut milk to the casserole, place in the oven, and bake for 40 minutes to 1 hour, or until the chicken thighs are cooked through. To check for doneness, cut into one of the thighs; when the juices run clear, the chicken is done.

4. Meanwhile, in a separate pan, toast the cumin, coriander, chili powder, and turmeric over medium heat, stirring or shaking frequently, until they just barely begin to smoke, 4 to 5 minutes. Be careful not to burn the spices.

5. When chicken is done, remove the casserole from the oven, add the toasted spices, cilantro, and lime juice, season with salt and pepper, and serve.

CARDAMOM

Although it originated in southern India and Sri Lanka, cardamom quickly became one of the most popular spices in ancient Europe when the trade routes were established and the flavors of the East became available. Apicius, the 1st-century Roman cook and epicure, recommended cardamom as a digestive aid for his fellow countrymen. This slightly sweet, uniquely flavorful spice will grow only in the tropics, and India is still the largest producer.

African-Style Chicken Stew with Squash

Serves 4 as entrée

This recipe uses many of the flavors of East African cooking. We have provided a simple spice rub for everyday use, as well as a more authentic, more complex spice paste inspired by the classic berberé of Ethiopia. You might want to first try the simpler version, then make the East African mix when you feel like spending some time with your spices. With the chicken, squash, and ginger, this creates a one-pot dinner that is both earthy and rich; for a slightly sour finish, we throw some lemon juice in the pot, which I think works well with the ginger.

SPICE RUB:

3 tablespoons paprika

1 tablespoon cayenne pepper

1 tablespoon dry mustard

1 teaspoon ground cloves

¼ cup vegetable oil (approximately)

1 3½-pound chicken, cut into 8 pieces

2 large yellow onions, thinly sliced

2 tablespoons minced garlic

1 tablespoon minced ginger

1 butternut or 2 small acorn squash, peeled and cut into small chunks

2 ripe tomatoes, diced small

1½ quarts chicken stock

¼ cup lemon juice (about 1 lemon)

Salt and freshly cracked black pepper to taste

METHOD

1. Make the spice rub: In a small bowl, combine all the ingredients and mix well. Rub the chicken pieces well with the spice mix, reserving about ¼ cup. (You may substitute the more complex East African Spice Mix #3, page 380.)

2. Heat the oil in a large, wide stockpot over low heat until it is hot but not smoking. Add the chicken pieces and cook slowly (resisting the temptation to turn the heat to high, which would burn the spice rub) until well browned, 8 to 10 minutes, adding a bit more oil if needed. Remove and set aside.

3. Add the onions to the pan in which the chicken was cooked, turn the heat to medium high, and cook until soft, about 8 minutes. Add the garlic and ginger and cook, stirring occasionally, for 1 additional minute.

4. Add the squash, tomatoes, and chicken stock, along with the browned chicken, and bring to a boil. Reduce the heat to low, cover, and simmer for 35 to 40 minutes, or until a peek inside one of the chicken pieces shows no traces of pink.

5. Add the lemon juice, season with salt and pepper, and serve.

Banquet Suggestions:

Black-eyed Pea Fritters with Joey's Seared Collards (page 52), Grilled Onion Rings (page 246), Red Potato and Cucumber Salad with Mango (page 202), and Deep-Fried Plantain Rounds (page 253).

Malay-Style Chicken and Sweet Potato Stew with Coconut Milk, Ginger, and Chiles

Serves 6 to 8 as entrée

½ cup all-purpose flour

1 teaspoon cayenne pepper

1 teaspoon ground cinnamon

1 teaspoon ground cloves

2 2½-pound chickens, each cut into 8 pieces

½ cup vegetable oil (approximately)

2 large yellow onions, thinly sliced

3 tablespoons minced ginger

2 tablespoons minced garlic

5 tablespoons prepared curry powder

2 tablespoons minced fresh red or green chile pepper of your choice

2 quarts chicken stock

4 sweet potatoes, peeled and cut into large chunks

1 cup coconut milk, unsweetened canned, or prepared by method on page 458

¼ cup chopped fresh cilantro

I think some folks perceive stews as somewhat difficult, but to me the fact that you get a whole meal in one pot makes them easier, on the whole, than other types of dishes. Besides, the simmering time gives you a break to relax, talk with your guests, have a beer, whatever.

This particular one-pot meal is similar to the strongly flavored sauced dishes of Malaysia, minus the heavy dried fish flavor, which is ubiquitous in Malaysian cooking but which I dropped because it's too strong for those of us who are not used to it.

This stew is versatile because it can be used as either a hot-weather or cold-weather dish.

METHOD

1. In a small bowl, combine the flour, cayenne, cinnamon, and cloves and mix well.

2. Dredge the chicken pieces in the spiced flour. In a large, wide stockpot, heat the oil over medium-high heat until hot but not smoking. Add the chicken pieces in a single layer, being careful not to crowd the pan—work in batches if necessary. Cook until well browned, 3 to 4 minutes per side. As the chicken is browned, remove to a platter.

3. Reduce the heat to medium, add the onions, and cook until they just begin to color, about 5 minutes. Add the ginger, garlic, curry powder, and chile and cook, stirring constantly, for 1 minute more. Add the stock, the browned chicken, and the sweet potatoes, return to a simmer, and cook for about 1 hour, covered, until a peek inside one of the pieces of chicken shows that it is cooked through.

4. Add the coconut milk and continue to cook for 1 minute. Remove from the heat, add the cilantro, mix well, and serve.

Banquet Suggestions:

Coconut Rice (page 272), Green Mango Slaw (page 213), Quick and Easy Sautéed Leafy Greens with Lime and Chiles (page 231), Cucumber-Ginger Relish (page 354), Equatorial Wine Cooler Blanco (page 451).

Garlicky Fried Pork and Chicken Stew

Serves 6 to 8 as entrée

¼ cup virgin olive oil

7 cloves garlic, thinly sliced

6 chicken thighs

1½ pounds pork tenderloin or loin, cut into ½-inch cubes

Salt and freshly cracked black pepper to taste

1 yellow onion, thinly sliced

1 tablespoon minced ginger

2 ripe tomatoes, diced small

½ cup soy sauce

1 cup white wine vinegar

2 quarts chicken stock or water

1 cup coconut milk, unsweetened canned, or prepared by method on page 458 (optional)

This dish is kind of a weird combination of the traditional Western tomato-garlic stewing process with the Eastern staples of ginger, soy, and vinegar. It's the sort of dish that happens when cultures collide, and fittingly enough, its inspiration comes from the Philippines. With centuries of strong Western influence—first from the Spanish who sailed to Asia from Mexico, then from the United States after the Spanish-American War—this Pacific island nation developed a cuisine that stands out among Asian countries for its frequent adaptation of Western foodways, such as the heavy use of tomatoes, frequent frying, and, as in this case, stewing. The sweet and sour treatment we give this stew is also somewhat typical of Philippine cooking, in which sourness has been developed to a point of great subtlety.

METHOD

1. In a large sauté pan, heat the oil over medium-high heat until hot but not smoking. Add the garlic slices and sauté, stirring, until brown, 2 to 3 minutes. Remove and set aside.

2. Sprinkle the chicken thighs and pork cubes with salt and pepper. Put the thighs in the sauté pan with the hot oil and brown well on all sides, about 8 minutes. Remove and set aside. In the same pan, brown the pork cubes on all sides, about 4 minutes. Add the onion and cook, stirring frequently, for another 5 minutes.

3. Add the ginger, tomatoes, soy sauce, vinegar, and stock or water. Bring the mixture to a boil, reduce the heat to low, and simmer, covered, for 30 to 35 minutes, or until the chicken is cooked through.

4. Add the coconut milk if desired, stir well, and season with salt and pepper to taste.

Banquet Suggestions:

Savory Watermelon and Pineapple Salad (page 220), Bob's Quick-Cooked Lettuce (page 232), Grilled Sweet Potatoes with Molasses Glaze (page 240), Red Onion–Tamarind Chutney (page 344), Coconut Rice (page 272), and Mashed Banana with Lime-Coconut Milk and Mango Sauce (page 414).

Elmer's Stewed Pork Ribs with Chunks of Corn

The hard-working and friendly day chef at the East Coast Grill, Elmer Sanchez, makes this soup every once in a while for his kitchen mates. He says it's his version of a soup his mom makes back in El Salvador, called *sopa del rey*, or "soup of the king." It's a very hearty soup, and all the folks in the kitchen like it because, with all those bones and chunks of corn on the cob, there's a lot of handling involved.

Serves 6 to 8 hungry folks as entrée

4 pounds country-style pork ribs

Salt and freshly cracked black pepper to taste

¼ cup virgin olive oil

3 large yellow onions, thinly sliced

3 tablespoons minced garlic

3 tablespoons ground cumin

2 tablespoons chili powder

2 tablespoons minced fresh red or green chile pepper of your choice

3 green plantains, peeled and each cut into 5 pieces

2 sweet potatoes, peeled and cut into chunks the same size as the plantain chunks

3 quarts chicken, pork, or beef stock

5 ears corn, husked, desilked, and each cut into 5 pieces

½ cup chopped fresh cilantro

3 limes, quartered

METHOD

1. Sprinkle the ribs with salt and pepper. In the largest soup pot that you have, heat the oil over high heat until hot but not smoking. Add the ribs in batches so that they cover the bottom of the pan in a single layer without touching, and brown well, about 4 minutes per side. Remove and set aside. Continue until all the ribs are browned.

2. Reduce the heat to medium, add the onions, and sauté until just translucent, 5 to 7 minutes. Add the garlic, cumin, chili powder, and chile pepper and cook, stirring, for 2 minutes.

3. Add the browned ribs and all the remaining ingredients except the corn, cilantro, and limes. Bring to a boil, reduce the heat to low, and simmer, uncovered, for 1 hour. Add the corn and continue to cook an additional ½ to 1 hour, or until the pork ribs are tender. Season to taste with salt and pepper, stir in the cilantro, and serve with limes for squeezing.

Banquet Suggestions:

All-Purpose Rice and Beans (page 262), Cheesy Cornbread (page 394), Elmer's Salvadoran Pickled Cabbage (page 273), Jicama-Pineapple Salsa (page 338), and Dark Rum–Flavored Flan (page 422).

Pork and Pumpkin Stew with Tripe and Cornmeal Dumplings

In this dish we use tripe to add some great texture to the pork-pumpkin combination that is common in cuisines from Africa, Asia, the West Indies, and South America. Of course, if you either don't like tripe or don't feel like dealing with processing it, you can leave it out.

This particular dish has a definite Latin beat to it, and I've added simple cornmeal dumplings to soak up some of the rich flavors. They are kind of a Latin version of the dumplings my grandma used to float on top of her beef stew.

TRIPE:

1 cup kosher salt

1 cup white vinegar

1 pound honeycomb tripe

STEW:

2 pounds pork butt, cut into 2-inch chunks

Salt and freshly cracked black pepper to taste

½ cup virgin olive oil

3 yellow onions, diced large

3 tablespoons minced garlic

2 tablespoons minced fresh red or green chile pepper of your choice

2 pounds pumpkin meat, cut into 1-inch chunks (about 5 cups) (you may substitute acorn or butternut squash)

3 ears corn, husked, desilked, and each cut into 5 pieces

3 quarts chicken or pork stock

1 cup white vinegar

½ cup chopped fresh parsley

¼ cup chopped fresh oregano

METHOD

1. Mix together the cup of salt and the cup of vinegar. Pour ⅓ of this mixture into a large bowl. Add the tripe and scrub it violently with a brush as if you were doing laundry the old-fashioned way. Rinse the tripe thoroughly with cold water. Repeat the process twice more with the remaining vinegar-salt mixture.

2. After the third rinsing, put the tripe in a large bowl, cover with cold water, and allow to sit, covered and refrigerated, for 12 to 24 hours, changing the water at least once.

3. Drain the tripe and put it in a large saucepan. Cover with water and bring to a boil over high heat. Reduce the heat to low and simmer for 1½ hours, adding more water as necessary. Drain, allow the tripe to cool to room temperature, and dice it small.

4. Sprinkle the pork chunks liberally with salt and pepper. In a large, wide stockpot, heat the oil over medium-high heat until hot but not smoking. Add the pork chunks in batches just large enough to cover the bottom of the pot without touching, and sauté until well browned on all sides, which will take 8 to 10 minutes. Remove and set aside.

ALL THAT TRIPE

Count me among those folks who enjoy tripe. As a professional cook, I feel that I should know how to cook all the parts of the animals I deal with, not just the popular parts. So I have always eaten dishes containing tripe—the stomach lining of cows—whenever I find them on menus, and several years ago I started a tradition of cooking a big batch of tripe soup for my annual New Year's Day party. Among other things, tripe is high in B vitamins. I believe it is this quality that accounts for its high standing as a hangover cure. In any case, if it is dealt with properly, which basically means laundering it, the strong initial flavor of tripe largely disappears, leaving a meat with an unusual texture that I think adds real interest to a dish.

(continued)

5. Add the onions and cook until translucent, stirring occasionally, 5 to 7 minutes. Add the garlic and chile and cook 1 additional minute.

6. Add the tripe, pumpkin, corn, stock, and vinegar, along with the browned pork chunks. Bring to a boil, reduce the heat to low, and simmer until the pork chunks are tender, about 1½ hours. (After an hour, start making the dumplings so you can put them in for the final 15 minutes.)

7. Add the parsley and oregano, adjust the seasonings, stir well, and serve.

Banquet Suggestions:

Chile-Yucca Fritters (page 50), Amilcar's Grilled Shrimp and Avocado Salad (page 226), Jicama-Pineapple Salsa (page 338), Grilled Onion Rings (page 246), and Mashed Banana with Lime-Coconut Milk and Mango Sauce (page 414).

Cornmeal Dumplings

◇ ◇

Makes about 12 dumplings

1. In a large bowl, combine the corn-meal, flour, baking powder, salt, and cumin and whisk together well.

2. In a separate bowl, combine the remaining ingredients and whisk together well.

3. Add the wet mixture to the dry mixture slowly and evenly, stirring constantly.

4. Using a large wooden spoon, shape the dough into 12 equal football shapes. Poach the dumplings in lightly salted boiling water for about 15 minutes, or add to the stew for the final 15 minutes of cooking time. Serve 2 dumplings with each bowl of stew.

1 cup yellow cornmeal

½ cup all-purpose flour

1 teaspoon baking powder

1 teaspoon salt

1 tablespoon ground cumin

3 large eggs

½ cup milk

3 tablespoons butter, melted

Pork Stew with Chiles and Peanuts

Serves 4 to 6 as entrée

Where I grew up in Virginia, pork and peanuts represent major food groups, and their relationship is a particularly close one. Because of this, I always find it interesting to see these two ingredients used together outside the context of the American South. My reaction is provincial, since this combination is popular worldwide, from Africa to China to South America. In fact, this particular dish was inspired by a Peruvian pork and peanut stew.

2 tablespoons vegetable oil

1 pound boneless pork loin or butt, trimmed of excess fat and cut into ½-inch cubes

Salt and freshly cracked black pepper to taste

1 medium yellow onion, diced

2 tablespoons minced garlic

1 tablespoon paprika

1 teaspoon minced fresh red or green chile pepper of your choice

2 teaspoons ground cumin

2 pounds potatoes, peeled and diced small

½ cup unsalted roasted peanuts, roughly chopped

2 quarts chicken stock or water

1 tablespoon sugar

Lime quarters, for garnish (optional)

Whole cilantro leaves, for garnish (optional)

METHOD

1. In a large sauté pan, heat the oil over medium-high heat until hot but not smoking. Sprinkle the pork cubes with salt and pepper and brown on all sides, which should take 5 to 7 minutes. Remove and set aside.

2. Drain all but 1 tablespoon of fat, add the onion, and sauté over medium heat, stirring occasionally, until translucent, 5 to 7 minutes. Add the garlic, paprika, chile, and cumin and cook, stirring, for 1 additional minute.

3. Add all the remaining ingredients except the limes and cilantro and bring just to a boil. Reduce the heat to very low and simmer, stirring occasionally, for about 45 minutes, or until the pork is quite tender. Garnish with lime quarters and cilantro if desired.

Banquet Suggestions:

Black-eyed Pea Fritters with Joey's Seared Collards (page 52), Green Grape–Parsley Relish (page 77), Grilled Onion Rings (page 246), and Your Basic Cornbread (page 393).

Aromatic Southeast Asian Pork Stew

This is a dish for a very cold winter day when you need a stick-to-your-ribs kind of thing. The idea is to use the same technique used by Texans for authentic chili (meaning no tomato, no beans), simmering heavily browned meat in a spice-filled liquid. Of course, we are changing the venue here by adding the aromatic ingredients characteristic of Southeast Asian cooking, so what we end with looks a lot like rendang, a traditional spicy beef dish with gravy from Malaysia.

As with all stewlike preparations, one of the keys here is to brown the meat heavily. So disconnect the smoke alarm, because if you're doing it right, it will be going off.

Serves 6 to 8 as entrée

STOCK:

2 tablespoons sesame oil

1 piece ginger the size of your index finger, unpeeled, roughly chopped

5 stalks lemongrass, roughly chopped

1 tablespoon minced garlic

1 gallon chicken stock

¼ cup vegetable oil

2 pounds pork butt or loin, cut into 1-inch cubes

Salt and freshly cracked white pepper to taste

2 yellow onions, diced

¼ cup minced garlic

¼ cup minced peeled ginger

2 tablespoons minced red or green chile pepper of your choice

¼ cup soy sauce

¼ cup white vinegar

3 tablespoons fish sauce (available in Asian markets) (optional)

2 tablespoons crushed coriander seeds

3 tablespoons brown sugar

1 cinnamon stick *or* 2
   tablespoons ground
   cinnamon

2 tablespoons prepared curry
   powder *or* Simple Dry
   Masala (page 203)

GARNISH:

3 limes, halved

¼ cup chopped unsalted roasted
   peanuts

½ cup chopped fresh cilantro

METHOD

1. Make the stock: Heat the sesame oil in a small stockpot over medium-high heat until hot but not smoking. Add the ginger, lemongrass, and garlic and sauté for 2 minutes, stirring occasionally. Add the chicken stock, bring to a boil, and reduce the heat to low. Simmer the mixture for 1 hour, then remove it from the heat, strain, discard the solids, and return the liquid to the pot.

2. In a large sauté pan, heat the vegetable oil over high heat until hot but not smoking. Season the pork cubes with salt and pepper and add enough to the pan to form a single layer without crowding. Sear the cubes, turning often, until they are very well browned on all sides, 6 to 8 minutes. Add the browned pork to the stockpot and continue to sear the pork in batches until it has all been browned, adding each batch to the stockpot as it is done.

(continued)

3. Drain all but a thin coating of fat from the pan. Reduce the heat to medium, add the onions, and sauté, stirring often, until they are just slightly brown, 5 to 7 minutes. Add the garlic, ginger, and chile, reduce the heat to medium-low, and cook for an additional 1 to 2 minutes. Add the soy sauce and vinegar and stir well to dissolve any stuck-on bits from the bottom and sides of the pan. Add to the stockpot.

4. Add the fish sauce, coriander, brown sugar, cinnamon, and curry powder to the stockpot and bring the mixture to a simmer over high heat. Reduce the heat to low and simmer for 1½ to 2 hours, or until the pork is very tender and easily pierced through with a fork. Ladle into bowls over rice, squeeze half a lime into each bowl, and sprinkle peanuts and cilantro over the top.

Banquet Suggestions:

Quick and Easy Sautéed Leafy Greens with Lime and Chiles (page 231), Green Mango Slaw (page 213), Southeast Asian Onion-Tomato Condiment (page 364), and Panfried Banana Fritters with Molasses-Rum Sauce (page 428).

North African Lamb Stew with Sweet Potatoes and Couscous

This is basically a lamb stew like Mom used to make, but borrowing the flavors of a Moroccan tagine, which is also a type of stew. Maybe I should say it's like the lamb stew that Mom used to make if you grew up in Morocco. In any case, it makes a great centerpiece for a North African–inspired dinner.

Serves 6 to 8 as entrée

2 pounds lamb stew meat, cut into ½-inch cubes

Salt and freshly cracked black pepper to taste

2 to 3 tablespoons vegetable oil

2 yellow onions, thinly sliced

6 cloves garlic, cut into thin slivers

¼ cup red wine vinegar

3 quarts chicken stock

1 20-ounce can chickpeas, drained and rinsed well

¼ cup apricot preserves

1 stick cinnamon *or* 1 teaspoon ground cinnamon

3 medium *or* 2 large sweet potatoes, peeled and cut into ½-inch cubes

2 tablespoons whole coriander seeds

2 tablespoons whole cumin seeds

1 tablespoon red pepper flakes

1 tablespoon ground fenugreek

½ cup raisins

¼ cup chopped fresh cilantro

1 lemon, halved

(continued)

METHOD

1. Sprinkle the lamb with salt and pepper. Coat the bottom of the largest and heaviest sauté pan that you own with vegetable oil, and heat over medium-high heat until the oil is hot but not smoking. Add a single layer of the lamb cubes and sear until browned on all sides, about 4 minutes per side. Transfer to a large stockpot. Repeat this process until all the lamb has been browned.

2. In the same pan, sauté the onions over medium-high heat, stirring constantly to prevent burning, until they are well browned and beginning to caramelize, 8 to 10 minutes. Add the garlic and sauté for 1 additional minute. Add the vinegar and continue to cook for 2 to 3 minutes, stirring up any browned bits from the bottom of the pan. Transfer to the stockpot.

3. Add the chicken stock, chickpeas, apricot preserves, and cinnamon stick and bring the mixture to a boil. Reduce the heat to low and simmer for 1 hour. Add the sweet potatoes and continue to cook until the potatoes are easily pierced with a fork and the stew has thickened slightly, about ½ hour more.

4. Toast the coriander and cumin seeds in a sauté pan over medium heat, watching carefully and shaking frequently to prevent burning, until they just begin to release a little smoke, 2 to 3 minutes. Grind in a spice mill or coffee grinder, or crush under the bottom of a sauté pan.

5. Add the crushed seeds and red pepper flakes to the stew, along with the fenugreek, raisins, and cilantro. Squeeze the lemon into the stew and stir until well combined. Serve on top of a mound of couscous.

Banquet Suggestions:

Couscous with Raisins and Parsley (page 276), Peach-Parsley Relish (page 352), Roast Beet and Carrot Salad with Lemon-Mint Dressing (page 204), and Grilled Peppered Tomatoes with Lemon and Garlic (page 247).

TO MAKE INSTANT COUSCOUS

To make instant couscous, follow the directions on any boxed mix. If you are feeling adventurous, make a flavored broth to use instead of the plain water called for on the box. To do this, use ¾ water and ¼ orange juice, and add ½ teaspoon each of ground coriander, ground cumin, minced garlic, and minced fresh ginger. Bring to a boil and allow to simmer for 10 minutes, then strain and use as directions indicate for water.

If you have a bit more patience, you might want to follow the advice of Paula Wolfert, the author of several truly outstanding cookbooks and an authority on couscous. Paula correctly insists that steaming couscous—even the instant variety—adds greatly to its flavor and texture. To find out for yourself, layer a strainer with cheesecloth, add about half the couscous, set it in a pan over water, seal the joint between strainer and pan with a length of cheesecloth, and bring the water to a boil. Let it sit until steam is coming out of the top of the couscous, then add the remainder of the couscous and again wait until steam comes out of the top.

Paella à la Diplomat

Like many other "national dishes" that have caught the imagination of the public, paella has many definitions and encompasses many varieties. It is safe to say, however, that paella is a Spanish rice dish flavored with saffron and usually containing small amounts of chicken, sausage, and/or seafood, along with garlic, onions, tomatoes, and perhaps other vegetables such as peas or artichokes, all depending on the area of Spain and the individual cook.

Many Americans have rather warped ideas of what paella is, and for many years I was right there among them. That was because I was introduced to the dish by Jorge, the Cuban chef at the Diplomat Hotel in Hollywood, Florida, where I worked for a while very early in my career. Every Saturday afternoon during my time at the hotel, I would follow Jorge's instructions and prepare "paella" for the staff dinner. It was only years later that I discovered that true paella usually had seafood in it (far too expensive for staff dinners), was flavored with saffron (ditto), and contained neither black beans nor chiles. Nevertheless, over the years I have made modifications to old Jorge's recipe, and now I like to think of it as the Cuban evolution of a classic dish.

6 chicken thighs

Salt and freshly cracked black pepper to taste

½ cup virgin olive oil

2 yellow onions, diced small

2 red bell peppers, diced small

2 green bell peppers, diced small

3 tablespoons minced garlic

3 tablespoons minced fresh red or green chile pepper of your choice

2 cups uncooked rice of your choice

1 pound kielbasa, chorizo, or linguica, cut into large chunks

1 pound medium-size (16/20 count) shrimp, shelled and deveined

12 littleneck clams

1 ripe tomato, diced small

1½ cups canned or cooked black beans (page 455)

3 quarts chicken stock

1 cup chopped fresh parsley

½ cup lemon juice (about 2 lemons)

METHOD

1. Sprinkle the chicken thighs with salt and pepper. In a large stockpot, heat the oil over medium heat until hot but not smoking. Add the chicken thighs, skin sides down, and cook until very well browned, 6 to 7 minutes. Flip over and cook an additional 2 minutes. Remove and set aside.

2. Add the onions to the pot and cook over medium heat until just translucent, 5 to 7 minutes. Add the bell peppers, garlic, and chile and cook, stirring frequently, for 4 minutes. Add the rice and cook, stirring constantly, for 2 minutes. Add the sausage, shrimp, clams, tomato, beans, and chicken stock. Bring to a boil, reduce the heat to low, cover, and cook for 15 to 20 minutes, or until the liquid is completely absorbed.

3. Remove from the heat, add the parsley and lemon juice, stir well, and serve.

Banquet Suggestions:

Elmer's Salvadoran Pickled Cabbage (page 273), Savory Watermelon and Pineapple Salad (page 220), Grilled Onion Rings (page 246), Orange-Chipotle Salsa (page 337), Watermelon Daiquiris (page 447), and Simple All-Purpose Mixed Fruit (page 410).

Seafood Mixed Grill with Lobster, Clams, Oysters, Corn, and Sausage

Serves 4 hearty eaters as entrée

8 new potatoes

2 small lobsters (1½ pounds each)

4 ears corn (do not husk)

½ pound linguica, chorizo, kielbasa, or other spicy cured sausage

12 oysters, scrubbed

12 littleneck clams, scrubbed

Lemon quarters for garnish

Melted butter for dipping

In tropical areas, seafood and live fire have a harmonious relationship. Some folks are surprised that this relationship can travel as far north as New England in the summertime. Some people are also surprised at the robust influence the Portuguese have had on New England cooking; one of their major contributions is the combination of seafood and sausage. Here is an example in which the region's abundant seafood is combined with spicy sausage to make for a New Wave version of the classic beach clambake. The hearty combination of corn, potatoes, lobsters, sausage, oysters, and clams is an outstanding feast that makes me proud to live in Boston.

Approximate Grilling Times for Each Ingredient

Corn: 25 minutes
Lobster claws: 15 minutes
Lobster tails, sausage, and potatoes: 10 minutes
Oysters: 8 minutes
Clams: 5 minutes

METHOD

1. Blanch the potatoes in boiling water until they can easily be pierced with a skewer, 12 to 15 minutes.

2. Prepare the lobsters: Kill them by quickly pushing the point of a sharp French knife into the heads just between the eyes. Cut off the claws and tails and set aside the bodies and legs to use for stock. Split the tails almost in half lengthwise, cutting through the meat but leaving the shells just connected. Crack the claws just slightly with a knife handle or nutcracker.

3. Build a small fire off to one side of your grill. Let the fire reach its hottest point, then allow it to die down to medium-low. When the fire is at the right temperature, place the ears of corn on the grill and cover the grill. You will want to cook the ears for a total of about 25 minutes, and you should roll them around each time you add something new to the grill so that they cook evenly.

4. After about 10 minutes, move the corn to the side of the grill surface and put the cracked lobster claws on the center of the grill. Add a little fuel to the fire at this point, then cover the grill.

5. After another 5 minutes, move the lobster claws to the side of the grill and replace them with the lobster tails, spread out on the grill flesh side down. Place the sausage and potatoes next to the lobster tails and cover the grill again.

6. After another 2 or 3 minutes, add the oysters. You will probably need to add a few coals at this point, then cover again.

7. After another 3 minutes, add the littleneck clams to the grill and cover again.

8. In about 5 minutes, check all of your ingredients. The littleneck clams and the oysters should have popped open, which indicates that they are done. (If any fail to open, discard them.) The potatoes should be nicely browned, as should the ears of corn. The lobster meat should be completely opaque, and the sausage should be brown clear through. If any ingredient is not completely done, leave it on the fire for a few minutes more. You will need a few minutes to set out all the ingredients that are done anyway.

9. Serve accompanied by crusty bread, lemon quarters, and melted butter for dipping. If you wish, try mixing a little white wine and chopped fresh parsley with the butter and bathing the oysters and clams in it.

Cary's New Year's Eve Rice Stew Thang

Serves 6 as entrée

3 tablespoons virgin olive oil

6 boned chicken thighs (about 1½ pounds of thighs with bone in)

Salt and freshly cracked black pepper to taste

2 yellow onions, diced small

4 stalks celery, diced small

1 red bell pepper, diced small

2 tablespoons minced garlic

2 tablespoons minced fresh red or green chile pepper

1 pound linguica, chorizo, andouille, or kielbasa, sliced about as thin as poker chips

2 ripe tomatoes, diced small

2 quarts chicken stock

2 pounds medium-size (16/20 count) shrimp, shelled and deveined

3 cups rice of your choice

3 bay leaves

6 whole cloves

¼ cup lemon juice (about 1 lemon)

½ cup chopped fresh curly parsley

Heavy stews in which rice is mixed with both meat and seafood exist in many cultures. The jambalaya of Creole cuisine and Spain's paella are well-known examples. In fact, jambalaya is said to be an interpretation of paella, with more than a little influence from the African-American cooks of New Orleans.

This particular variation on that culinary theme comes from my partner, Cary Wheaton, who serves it at her justly famed New Year's Eve dinners. It is hearty and filling and delicious, goes great with champagne, and I have also been known to make some sandwiches out of it the next day when I really didn't feel up to cooking.

METHOD

1. In a large saucepan, heat the oil over medium-high heat until hot but not smoking. Sprinkle the chicken thighs with salt and pepper and cook, skin sides down, until the skins are well browned, about 7 minutes.

2. Add the onions and cook, stirring occasionally, until they are translucent, 5 to 7 minutes. Add the celery, bell pepper, garlic, chile, sausage, and tomatoes and cook, stirring frequently, for an additional 4 minutes.

3. Add the chicken stock, bring to a simmer, reduce the heat, and cook, uncovered, for 30 minutes. Add the shrimp, rice, bay leaves, and cloves and continue to simmer, covered, for an additional 20 minutes, stirring occasionally.

4. Remove from the heat and remove the bay leaves if desired. Add the lemon juice and parsley, mix well, season with salt and pepper, and serve.

Banquet Suggestions:

Arugula Salad with Oven-Dried Tomatoes, Olives, and Blue Cheese (page 214), Hobo Pack Vegetables (page 248), Cheesy Cornbread (page 394), Chunky Corn and Tomato Salsa (page 340), and A Peach Shortcake for Lizzie (page 430).

Mango-Tomatillo Salsa ▪ Orange-Chipotle Salsa ▪ Jicama-Pineapple Salsa ▪ Chunky Corn and Tomato Salsa ▪ Apricot-Anise Chutney ▪ Red Onion–Tamarind Chutney ▪ Apple-Apricot Chutney ▪ Lime-Raisin Chutney ▪ Eggplant Chutney ▪ Mangoes, Cucumbers, and Red Onion in Vinegar with Toasted Sesame Seeds ▪ Red Onion–Chile Relish with Lime and Basil ▪ Peach-Parsley Relish ▪ Cucumber-Tomato Relish with Oregano and Cinnamon ▪ Cucumber-Ginger Relish ▪ Home-Style Inner Beauty Hot Sauce ▪ Homemade Worcestershire Sauce ▪ Mango-Chipotle Catsup ▪ North African Chile Pepper Condiment ▪ Hot Vietnamese Ginger-Lime Condiment ▪ Sweet and Hot Sesame-Spinach Condiment ▪ Southeast Asian Onion-Tomato Condiment ▪ Tangerine Chile Oil ▪ Savory Orange-Chile Marmalade ▪ Vietnamese Dipping Sauce (Nuoc Cham) ▪ Mango-Chile Sambal

SALSAS, CHUTNEYS, RELISHES, CONDIMENTS, AND OTHER STUFF LIKE THAT

I have always loved the intensely flavored "little dishes" of the world. Halfway between a condiment and a side dish, these combinations of fruits, vegetables, spices, herbs, and chiles offer an ideal way to put strong, loud tastes into your food while sampling the typical flavor combinations of the equatorial world.

Salsas are the "little dishes" most familiar to Americans, but in nearly every country where the weather is hot, you will find something similar. From the chutneys of India and the sambals of Indonesia, to the blatjangs of southern Africa and the harissas of North Africa, to the pickles and relishes of the American South and the salsas of Mexico and Latin America, these healthy, simply prepared dishes add intense flavor to any meal.

As we Americans continue to slowly shift our diets away from a heavy reliance on meat and include more grains and legumes, these little dishes are just the thing to combat blandness and boredom. They can convert a simple bowl of rice, couscous, or pasta into a flavor explosion without adding any unhealthful fat or cholesterol. Of course, they also make great accompaniments to that piece of meat or fish you toss on the grill.

We have included a range of these little dishes here. Many, such as Jicama-Pineapple Salsa and Mango-Tomatillo Salsa, explore the flavors of the tropical fruits and vegetables newly available to Americans; others, such as Peach-Parsley Relish and Eggplant Chutney, combine familiar ingredients in unusual ways; and still others, such as Mango-Chipotle Catsup or Savory Orange-Chile Marmalade, are new versions of familiar condiments. What they all have in common are the three main traits of the world's "little dishes": they're healthful, they're easy to make, and they are packed with intense, loud flavors.

So get out your knife, your cutting board, and your favorite mixing bowl, and get down with these intense flavors and bold taste combinations. With one of these on the table, you'll never have to eat boring food again.

Mango-Tomatillo Salsa

Makes about 3 cups

1 12-ounce can tomatillos, drained

¼ cup pineapple juice

¼ cup orange juice

¼ cup white vinegar

4 teaspoons minced garlic

1 teaspoon red pepper flakes

¼ cup chopped fresh cilantro

¼ cup lime juice (about 2 limes)

3 small *or* 2 large ripe but firm mangoes, peeled, pitted, and diced small

1 red onion, diced small

1 red bell pepper, diced small

Have you been getting bored with putting out the same old tired tomato salsa with the chips? Well, next time bring this out for your friends, and you'll be the envy of the neighborhood, admired for your culinary adventurism. This is your basic *salsa verde*, but the mango adds a sweet taste to the sourish salsa. You may substitute papayas for the mangoes. This one is great with any type of seafood, particularly shrimp and scallops.

METHOD

1. In a blender or food processor, purée the tomatillos, pineapple and orange juices, vinegar, garlic, red pepper flakes, cilantro, and lime juice.

2. Put the mangoes, onion, and bell pepper in a medium-size bowl, add the purée, and mix well.

Orange-Chipotle Salsa

Makes about 4 cups

I think the flavors of oranges and chipotle peppers work well together, so I use the combination a lot. Here is a straightforward mix of orange sections and chopped chipotles accented with cumin and fresh oregano, which gives a nice earthy taste.

This is an outstanding table salsa, one of my all-time favorites. I recommend that you make a huge batch of it on Friday night and use it with grilled chicken for dinner; put it on a sandwich for Saturday's lunch; set it out as a dip with chips at cocktail time that evening; and finish it up by making totally unique scrambled eggs for Sunday brunch. Great weekend.

2 cups orange sections, peeled, pith and seeds removed (about 2 oranges)

1 red onion, diced small

½ red bell pepper, diced small

1 teaspoon minced garlic

1 tablespoon cumin seeds

3 tablespoons minced canned chipotle peppers (see Pantry, page 457)

¼ cup chopped fresh oregano

1 cup lemon juice (about 4 lemons)

Salt and freshly cracked black pepper to taste

METHOD

In a large bowl, combine all the ingredients and mix well. This will keep about 4 days, covered and refrigerated.

Jicama-Pineapple Salsa

When asked to describe a jicama, I usually say that it's a cross between an apple and a potato and that it's best eaten raw. From my perspective the best feature of the jicama is its texture—its ability to remain crisp for a long time even when soaked with liquid—which makes it ideal for salsas. Here it is combined with smooth-textured pineapple and mixed with citrus juices, chiles, and cilantro to complete the de rigueur salsa flavor combo. The texture of this salsa makes it a good partner for fish, but with the pineapple, it also works well with pork.

1 jicama about the size of a softball, peeled, diced medium

½ pineapple, peeled, cored, diced large

½ red bell pepper, diced small

½ green bell pepper, diced small

½ red onion, diced small

1 teaspoon minced garlic

1 cup freshly squeezed orange juice (about 4 oranges)

½ cup lime juice (about 4 limes)

½ cup chopped fresh cilantro

1 tablespoon minced fresh red or green chile pepper of your choice

Salt and freshly cracked black pepper to taste

METHOD

In a large bowl, combine all the ingredients and mix well. This salsa will keep, covered and refrigerated, about 1 week.

Chunky Corn and Tomato Salsa

A salsa is a salsa is a salsa (as opposed to a chutney, a sambal, and so on) mainly because it uses ingredients common to Central and Latin America. Here we combine three of our favorite indigenous foods of the Americas—tomatoes, corn, and chile peppers—in a hot and flavorful salsa. You can serve this with just about anything and not go wrong. Try it with a pork dish just for starters.

Makes about 4 cups

3 ears corn, husked and desilked

3 ripe garden tomatoes about the size of baseballs, diced small

1 tablespoon minced fresh red or green chile pepper of your choice

¼ cup chopped fresh oregano

¼ cup lime juice (about 2 limes)

½ cup tomato juice

Salt and freshly cracked black pepper to taste

METHOD

1. Blanch the corn in boiling water for 1 to 2 minutes, then cut off the kernels. You should have slightly more than 2 cups of kernels.

2. Combine the corn with all the other ingredients and mix well. This salsa will keep, covered and refrigerated, for 4 or 5 days.

DOIN' THE SALSA

In the past few years, Americans have increasingly been turning to "ethnic" (which as far as I can tell means anything other than northern European) cuisines in their search for flavor without fat. In fact, we have already changed our diet considerably in that direction since the benighted fifties. In those Eisenhower years, seasonings in general were looked upon as rather suspect. Garlic, for example, was considered almost risqué, and olives were most often found in cans in the "gourmet" section of the supermarket. Fortunately, overnight shipping, immigration, and widespread travel have opened our supermarkets and our minds to other cuisines over the past decades. As evidence, consider that salsa recently surpassed tomato catsup as the most popular condiment in the country.

Apricot-Anise Chutney

Makes about 3 cups

Fresh apricots are hard to come by, particularly ones of good quality, because they are among the most perishable of fruits. But if you can find them, you will enjoy one of the most luscious, fragrant, delicate tastes in the fruit world. If you find a lot, use a few to make this flavorful chutney. I usually don't recommend chutneys with fish, but for some reason that I can't explain, this one works. It is a definite winner with bluefish or tuna. On the other hand, by chance I once had it on a hot dog and it was delicious that way, too.

2 tablespoons vegetable oil

2 large yellow onions, diced small

6 fresh apricots, each pitted and cut into 8 wedges

¼ cup packed brown sugar

¼ cup white sugar

2 tablespoons molasses

¼ cup golden raisins

1 teaspoon salt

½ teaspoon freshly cracked white pepper (you may substitute black pepper)

1 teaspoon crushed star anise

Pinch ground mace

½ cup white vinegar

2 tablespoons lemon juice (about ½ lemon)

METHOD

1. Heat the oil in a large sauce-pan over medium heat until hot but not smoking. Add the onions and sauté until translucent, 5 to 7 minutes.

2. Add the apricots and cook, stirring frequently, for 4 minutes.

3. Add all the remaining ingredients except ¼ cup of the vinegar and the lemon juice. Turn the heat to low and simmer, uncovered, for 1 hour, stirring occasionally and watching to be sure the mixture does not burn.

4. Remove from the heat, add the remaining vinegar and the lemon juice, and mix thoroughly. Serve at room temperature. This chutney will keep, covered and refrigerated, for several weeks.

PRIMA DONNA FRUIT

Apricots originated somewhere in western Asia, were brought to Europe by the armies of Alexander the Great, and have had a rather perilous existence in the Western world ever since. These fruits need a cold winter in order to set, but since they bloom very early in the spring, a late frost will often destroy the blossoms. If the weather happens to be too wet or too hot, the fruit will rot. If picked before they are fully ripe—which must be done in order to ship the fruit by ordinary means—they never develop their full, luscious flavor.

Despite all this, sometimes you run across a specialty store or fruit stand that has good fresh apricots, and you'll find that the fruit is worth seeking out despite its difficult nature.

Red Onion— Tamarind Chutney

Makes about 5 cups

¼ cup virgin olive oil

6 red onions, thinly sliced

2 ripe tomatoes, diced small

1 tablespoon minced garlic

1 tablespoon minced ginger

¼ cup tamarind paste (available in Latin and Indian markets)

½ cup molasses

1 cup white vinegar

½ cup pineapple juice

1 tablespoon ground turmeric

1 tablespoon ground cinnamon

3 to 6 dashes Tabasco sauce, depending on your taste for heat

Salt and freshly cracked black pepper to taste

Tamarind, the fruit of a tropical tree, originated in Africa but today is central to the cooking of Indonesia and Malaysia. We Westerners are probably most familiar with the uniquely tart taste of this fruit from Worcestershire sauce, in which it is a primary ingredient. I particularly like tamarind's tartness when matched up with the rich sweetness of molasses.

This chutney takes a few minutes of preparation, so it makes sense to make a relatively big batch while you're at it. Like all chutneys, it goes well with almost anything, but I recommend you try it with red meat.

METHOD

1. In a large sauté pan, heat the oil until hot but not smoking. Add the onions and sauté for 7 to 9 minutes, stirring frequently, until they are browned.

2. Add the tomatoes, garlic, and ginger and cook an additional 2 minutes. Add all the remaining ingredients, bring to a boil, reduce the heat, and simmer for about 5 minutes. Remove from the heat, let cool to room temperature, and serve. This chutney will keep, covered and refrigerated, for 2 to 3 weeks.

TAMARIND MIGRATION

Tamarind originated in the dry savannas of tropical Africa. In fact, according to Dr. Noel Vietmeyer of the National Academy of Sciences, tamarind trees and their fruit were so important to the people of what is now Senegal that they named their capital city after it; Dakar, the name of the city, is also the word for tamarind in the local language.

The word *tamarind*, however, comes from an Arabic name. The tree acquired this moniker after Arab traders introduced it into Asia. Indians took to the tamarind with such enthusiasm that the Arabs began calling it *tamar-u'l-Hind*, loosely translated as ''date of India.'' Today India is the only country that exports large amounts of tamarind.

Apple-Apricot Chutney

Although it is very flavorful and has a little bit of a bite, this chutney doesn't have all that much heat and therefore makes a good accompaniment to any very spicy hot dish. I think the sourness of the apples and the sweetness of the apricots work well together, and the tomato just seems to meld it all together. Unity in diversity—that's a good chutney.

2 tablespoons virgin olive oil

1 yellow onion, thinly sliced

1 ripe tomato, diced small

2 green apples such as Granny Smiths, cored and diced small

½ cup dried apricots, diced

1 tablespoon minced ginger

1 tablespoon minced garlic

1 teaspoon minced fresh red or green chile pepper of your choice

1 cup white vinegar

½ cup packed brown sugar

½ cup orange juice

METHOD

1. In a large sauté pan over medium heat, heat the oil until hot but not smoking. Add the onion and cook, stirring, until translucent, 5 to 7 minutes.

2. Add the tomato, apples, apricots, ginger, garlic, and chile and cook, stirring, 2 more minutes.

3. Add the vinegar, sugar, and orange juice and bring to a simmer, stirring constantly. Remove from heat. Cool to room temperature. This chutney keeps, covered and refrigerated, up to 2 weeks.

Serving Suggestions:

Serve with any pork or chicken dish.

Lime-Raisin Chutney

2 tablespoons vegetable oil

12 limes, ends removed, quartered, then very thinly sliced

1 tablespoon minced garlic

¼ cup minced fresh ginger

2 cups raisins

2½ cups white vinegar

2 cups packed brown sugar

1 cup water

2 tablespoons minced fresh red or green chile pepper of your choice

2 tablespoons each crushed coriander seeds, crushed mustard seeds, and crushed cumin seeds

Salt and freshly cracked black pepper to taste

Limes and lime juice are used so extensively in the cooking of the tropics that they take on the status of a seasoning rather than just another ingredient. In this Indian-inspired chutney, I use the limes without peeling them, which makes for a dish that is quite tart as well as spicy and hot. It's a little unusual, but it tastes great.

Grilled bluefish or tuna match up well with this chutney, as does chicken. I also like to purée a bit of it and add it to barbecue sauce.

METHOD

1. In a large stockpot or sauté pan, heat the oil until hot but not smoking. Add the limes and sauté for 5 minutes, stirring frequently. Add the garlic and ginger and cook 1 minute more.

2. Add all the remaining ingredients and cook until the mixture is thick and slightly gooey, about 1 hour. This mixture will keep, covered and refrigerated, about 10 days.

Eggplant Chutney

This dish is similar to the traditional *brinsal blatjang* of southern Africa. (Blatjangs are the chutneys of southern Africa, and *brinsal* simply means "eggplant.") Here we grill the eggplant, which is more typical of Indian cooking, so we call it a chutney. Since the blatjangs are descendants of chutneys brought to southern African from Asia, it is just another example of "what goes around comes around."

Makes about 5 cups

3 large eggplants

¼ cup virgin olive oil

Freshly cracked black pepper to taste

2 large yellow onions, thinly sliced

1 tablespoon minced garlic

2 tablespoons minced ginger

1 tablespoon red pepper flakes

1 small ripe tomato, chopped fine

¼ cup molasses

½ cup packed brown sugar

1 teaspoon chili powder

1 teaspoon ground cumin

1 cup white vinegar

¼ cup lemon juice (about 1 lemon)

METHOD

1. Cut the ends off the eggplants, then slice them lengthwise into planks ½ to 1 inch thick, leaving the skins on. Brush the planks with about 2 tablespoons of the olive oil, sprinkle with black pepper, and grill over a medium-low fire, turning once, until brown, about 5 minutes per side. (You may broil until brown, 5 to 7 minutes per side, if grilling is not possible.) Allow to cool to room temperature, then chop into bite-size chunks, skin and all.

2. In a large sauté pan, heat the remaining 2 tablespoons of olive oil over medium heat until hot but not smoking. Add the onions and sauté until beginning to color slightly, 5 to 7 minutes. Add the eggplant and all remaining ingredients except the vinegar and lemon juice, and continue to cook, stirring, until well blended, 2 to 3 minutes. Remove from the heat, add the vinegar, and mix well.

3. Allow the mixture to cool to room temperature. Just before serving, stir in the lemon juice. This mixture will keep, covered and refrigerated, up to 3 weeks.

Serving Suggestions:

This chutney is a good choice for serving with beef tenderloin and also has an affinity for pork or fowl. You might try it with Faux Hokien-Style Ginger Roast Chicken (page 172), or use it to add even more flavor to a meal of Malay-Style Chicken and Sweet Potato Stew with Coconut Milk, Ginger, and Chiles (page 308).

Mangoes, Cucumbers, and Red Onion in Vinegar with Toasted Sesame Seeds

Makes about 2 cups

¼ cup sesame seeds

1 ripe mango, peeled, pitted, and thinly sliced

1 cucumber, unpeeled, halved and then cut into finger-size spears

1 red onion, thinly sliced

½ cup red wine vinegar

Salt and freshly cracked white pepper to taste

This is a relish typical of those that are served with the hot and spicy dishes of Indian cuisine. It's cool and refreshing, and the toasted sesame seeds add a unique nutty flavor. This one goes well with anything, especially dishes with a lot of spices. If you see a mango in the supermarket, definitely pick it up and try this dish. I'm betting it will become a staple for you.

METHOD

1. Toast the sesame seeds in a sauté pan over medium heat, watching carefully and shaking frequently to prevent burning, until they just begin to release a little smoke, 2 to 3 minutes. Set aside.

2. Combine all the remaining ingredients in a large bowl and mix well. Just prior to serving, sprinkle liberally with sesame seeds.

Red Onion–Chile Relish with Lime and Basil

3 red onions, halved and thinly sliced

1 tablespoon minced fresh red or green chile pepper of your choice

1 tablespoon sugar

¹/₂ cup lime juice (about 4 limes)

3 tablespoons chopped fresh basil

Salt and freshly cracked black pepper to taste

Here's a good example of how the payoff from relishes far exceeds the investment of time. This one might take all of 10 minutes to make from start to finish and uses ingredients you are likely to find in your pantry on any given day. Both delicious and versatile, it goes great with any grilled fish or roast meat. Just the thing to have in the refrigerator when you come home late from work and want a tasty meal without much effort.

METHOD

In a large bowl, combine all the ingredients and mix well. Will keep, covered and refrigerated, for about 4 days.

Peach-Parsley Relish

Makes about 4 cups

3 ripe but firm peaches, pitted and thinly sliced

¼ cup roughly chopped fresh parsley

½ red bell pepper, thinly sliced

½ green bell pepper, thinly sliced

3 teaspoons minced garlic

2 tablespoons balsamic vinegar

2 tablespoons extra-virgin olive oil

Salt and freshly cracked white pepper to taste

In the tropics, fruits like mangoes and papayas are often served as a kind of salad, with lime juice or vinegar for tartness and local herbs for intensity of flavor. This is sort of a Mediterranean version, made with the balsamic vinegar, olive oil, and parsley integral to Italian and Spanish cooking.

For this recipe it's best to use firm peaches that will hold their shape. However, if the ones you are using are underripe, add a teaspoon or so of sugar to compensate for their lack of sweetness.

I like this relish with simple grilled or smoked fish because its fresh tastes complement the smokiness well.

METHOD

In a large bowl, combine all the ingredients and mix well. This relish is best eaten the day is it made but will keep, covered and refrigerated, for a day or two.

Cucumber–Tomato Relish with Oregano and Cinnamon

2 cucumbers, halved and thinly sliced

1 red onion, halved and thinly sliced

1 ripe tomato, diced small

1 teaspoon minced garlic

¼ cup chopped fresh oregano (you may substitute fresh marjoram, thyme, or any combination of these herbs)

2 tablespoons fresh mint

1 teaspoon ground cinnamon

½ cup red wine vinegar

¼ cup virgin olive oil

Salt and freshly cracked black pepper to taste

Cinnamon gives this Mediterranean relish a definite Greek spin, showing that as you move south and east in the Mediterranean, the use of spices becomes more pronounced. The fresh oregano and mint also add strong, earthy flavors to the mix of vegetables.

You might serve this as an accompaniment to fish with rather delicate flavors, like snapper or halibut. If you add a half cup or so of roughly chopped feta cheese, this can also serve as a refreshing small salad course.

METHOD

In a large bowl, combine all the ingredients and mix well. This relish is best used the day it is made but will keep, covered and refrigerated, for 2 to 3 days.

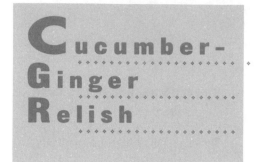

Cucumber-Ginger Relish

This classic Asian-style relish features the sweet, pungent taste of ginger matched with the crisp freshness of cucumber. Since this relish is cool and rather sweet, it's a great antidote for spicy foods. I would definitely pair this one with seafood.

1 cucumber, cut in half lengthwise and very thinly sliced

½ red bell pepper, thinly sliced

½ red onion, thinly sliced

1 tablespoon minced ginger

½ cup white vinegar

3 tablespoons sugar

¼ cup chopped fresh cilantro

Salt and freshly cracked white or black pepper to taste

METHOD

In a medium-size bowl, combine all the ingredients and mix well. This relish will keep, covered and refrigerated, for 2 to 3 days.

Home-Style Inner Beauty Hot Sauce

12 to 15 habañero (Scotch Bonnet) chile peppers, roughly chopped

1 ripe mango, peeled, pitted, and mashed

1 cup cheap yellow prepared mustard

¼ cup packed brown sugar

¼ cup white vinegar

1 tablespoon each prepared curry powder, ground cumin, and chili powder

Salt and freshly cracked black pepper to taste

This style of hot sauce, widely used in the West Indies, is basically habañero peppers (also known as Scotch Bonnets), fruit, and yellow mustard, with a few other ingredients thrown in. Use this recipe as a guideline. Habañeros are at the top of the chile pepper heat scale, so feel free to substitute other peppers of your choice.

Funnel the sauce into an old pint liquor bottle, then let your imagination run free as to what whopper you can lay on your guests regarding its origins. If you're having trouble, here's a start: "One day in Jamaica I was in this dingy bar and met this old guy who . . ." and you take it from there.

METHOD

Mix all the ingredients together and stand back. This will keep, covered and refrigerated, until the year 2018. Be careful, though: If it spills, it will eat a hole in your refrigerator. If you ever want to dispose of it, call the local toxic waste specialists.

WARNING

Hottest sauce in North America. Use this to enhance dull and boring food. Keep away from pets, open flames, unsupervised children, and bad advice. This is not a toy. This is serious. Stand up straight, sit right, and stop mumbling.

Be careful not to rub your nose, eyes, or mouth while working with habañeros. You may actually want to wear rubber gloves while chopping and mixing—these babies are powerful.

Homemade Worcestershire Sauce

One of my favorite recreational cooking activities is trying to re-create prepared foods that we use all the time—catsups, mustards, and the like—but I never took on Worcestershire sauce until I had dinner at Emeril Lagasse's fine New Orleans restaurant, Emeril's, and tasted his version. It inspired me to play around and come up with my own, which I bottled and gave away as Christmas presents. Feel free to roam here, making your own adaptations and changes. Although tamarind is the base for the real thing, don't let the lack of it stop you.

Makes about 6 cups

2 tablespoons virgin olive oil

1 yellow onion about the size of a softball, thinly sliced

1 cup shrimp shells *or* 1 teaspoon chopped anchovies *or* 1 teaspoon chopped sardines (optional)

1 tablespoon minced garlic

1 tablespoon minced ginger

1 tablespoon minced fresh red or green chile pepper

2 cups white vinegar

1 cup beer of your choice

1 cup pineapple juice

½ cup molasses

3 tablespoons tomato paste

2 whole cloves

1 tablespoon ground cumin

2 tablespoons freshly cracked black pepper

1 shot brown liquor of your choice (Scotch, bourbon)

¼ cup soy sauce

1 lime, very thinly sliced

1 cup tamarind water (see Pantry, page 465)

METHOD

1. In a large saucepan, heat the oil over medium-high heat until hot but not smoking. Add the onion and sauté, stirring frequently, until slightly browned, 7 to 9 minutes. Add the shrimp shells or anchovies or sardines if you are using them, along with the garlic, ginger, and chile, and cook, stirring, for 2 minutes.

2. Add all the remaining ingredients, bring the mixture to a boil, reduce the heat to low, and simmer gently for 2 hours.

3. Strain the mixture, pushing on the solids with a wooden spoon to extract all the liquid. The sauce should have about the same consistency as the standard Lea & Perrins sauce. This sauce will keep, covered and refrigerated, for several months.

Serving Suggestions:

Although most people use this sauce with meat, you ought to try it on seafood too.

THE SAUCE WITH THE FUNNY NAME

When I was a kid, I considered Worcestershire sauce a food group unto itself. I ate it on everything. Not only did I love the taste, but I also enjoyed the fact that it was a mysterious food, since no one had any idea what it was made of. When I asked my father how it got its name, he said that when a waiter brought the sauce to some southern guy eating at Delmonico's in New York, he said, "What's this here sauce?"

As it turns out, Worcestershire sauce was just the earliest example of my natural attraction to the foods of warm-weather climates, since it has its origins among the tamarind sauces prevalent in the Near East. The original recipe was brought back to England by Sir Marcus Sandy, a retired British officer who had served in India, and he asked two grocers in his native town of Worcester to make up a batch for him. The grocers—Mr. Lea and Mr. Perrins—obliged, and eventually the product came to the market as Lea & Perrins Worcestershire Sauce in 1838. Its popularity has since spread around the world, and people who would never think of eating anchovies or tamarind paste are almost as addicted to the stuff as I was as a child.

Mango-Chipotle Catsup

Makes about 2 cups

2 tablespoons vegetable oil

1 red onion, diced small

3 ripe mangoes, peeled, pitted, and cut into bite-size chunks

½ cup packed brown sugar

½ cup red wine vinegar

2 or 3 canned chipotle peppers (see Pantry, page 457), depending on your taste for heat

¼ cup molasses

Salt and freshly cracked black pepper to taste

To my mind, catsup is a smooth, chutney-like sauce based on a particular fruit or vegetable, with some vinegar in it. In this I think I am fairly close to the form that catsup took in Europe and America in colonial days when it had just been imported from its original home in Asia, where it was a salty, fish-based condiment. As catsup begins to regain its standing as an all-purpose condiment based on many things other than tomatoes, we chefs are having fun pushing and pulling out the more standard ingredients but leaving the form recognizable, which is just what I have done here.

METHOD

1. In a large saucepan, heat the oil over medium-high heat until hot but not smoking. Add the onion and cook, stirring occasionally, until well browned, 7 to 9 minutes.

2. Add the mangoes, brown sugar, vinegar, chipotle peppers, and molasses. Bring to a boil, reduce the heat to low, and simmer, stirring occasionally, until well thickened, about 1 hour. Be careful not to allow the mixture to burn.

3. Remove the mixture from heat, allow to cool somewhat, then purée in a food processor or blender. Season with salt and pepper. This catsup will keep, covered and refrigerated, for about 2 weeks.

Serving Suggestions:

This is good with grilled sausage subs (try substituting it for Inner Beauty Hot Sauce on Fenway Sausage Bombs—Fully Loaded in the Style of George, page 166) or a hearty fish such as a grilled tuna steak.

PLAYING CATSUP

It seems to me that the subject of catsup is worth a book in itself. This condiment, which we now think of as a tomato-vinegar sauce that comes in a bottle and sits on every table in America, actually originated in Asia as a salty, fish-based sauce. When Europeans brought it back from the Asian lands they had colonized, they converted it into a vinegar-based sauce larded with spices. From there they proceeded to make catsup out of everything from nuts to horseradish, grapes to mushrooms, and even tomatoes. This process not only provided them with very flavorful condiments for daily use, but also served as a way to preserve things in those days before refrigeration.

North African Chile Pepper Condiment

Makes about ½ cup

¼ cup minced fresh red chile pepper of your choice

1 teaspoon minced garlic

2 tablespoons white vinegar

¼ cup virgin olive oil

1 tablespoon caraway seeds

1 tablespoon ground cumin

2 tablespoons chopped fresh cilantro

Salt and freshly cracked black pepper to taste

The harissas of northeastern Africa have a basic similarity, within which regional and local variations take on great significance. The essential basis is a relish of chile peppers, olive oil, and salt. After that, North African cooks may add garlic, caraway, and/or cumin. In this Tunisian-inspired version, caraway seeds provide a subtle flavor undertone. My buddy Moncef Meddeb told me one night that this mixture is pretty close to the real thing, and he should know, because not only is he a talented chef, he's also Tunisian.

This is a great addition to stews, tastes fantastic with couscous (page 276), and can also be used as you might use any other hot condiment. How about trying it to spice up a bloody Mary? Or in a cocktail sauce? See. There are lots of ways to use it.

METHOD

Combine all the ingredients in a food processor or blender and purée. Or combine in a mortar and pound to a paste. The mixture will keep, covered and refrigerated, about 1 month.

Hot Vietnamese Ginger-Lime Condiment

This concentrated sauce is a more pungent version of a table sauce that I enjoyed with squab in a fancy French restaurant in, of all places, Ho Chi Minh City. When I asked the waiter what the ingredients were, he just sighed and said, "Lots of lime juice." Right. Anyway, I'm pretty close to my memory here, and if you're not having squab, then try it with any rare red meat.

Makes about 1 cup

2 tablespoons minced fresh ginger

1 tablespoon Vietnamese chile-garlic paste (you may substitute 1½ teaspoons minced garlic combined with 1½ teaspoons minced fresh chile pepper)

2 tablespoons fish sauce (available in Asian markets)

2 tablespoons soy sauce

1 tablespoon brown sugar

¼ cup lime juice (2 to 3 limes)

2 tablespoons chopped fresh cilantro

METHOD

In a medium-size bowl, combine all the ingredients and mix well. This condiment will keep, covered and refrigerated, for 5 to 6 days.

Sweet and Hot Sesame-Spinach Condiment

Makes about 2 cups

2 pounds fresh spinach, washed very well

1 cup soy sauce

1 cup white vinegar

¼ cup sugar

3 tablespoons sesame oil

1 tablespoon minced garlic

3 tablespoons minced ginger

1 tablespoon freshly cracked pepper (white if you have it)

5 to 10 dashes Tabasco sauce, depending on your taste for heat

¼ cup sesame seeds, toasted for 3 minutes in a 350°F oven

This is a variation on a Japanese side dish called oshitashi, which is basically chilled spinach. When I've eaten a lot of fat in recent meals and start to feel saturated, I head for a sushi bar to eat raw fish and a cold spinach salad. I figure it's a yin-yang kind of thing. In any case, it's a tasty way to get all those important leafy greens into your diet.

This particular preparation has a lot of concentrated flavor, so you won't need much. Also, you'll be amazed how much the spinach shrinks when cooked. The spinach can be cooked ahead, but combine it with the sauce as close to serving time as possible.

I would have this as a side dish with raw fish or any strong-flavored grilled fish like tuna, bluefish, or mackerel.

METHOD

1. Blanch the spinach for 1 minute in boiling water, drain, and rinse in very cold water for 1 minute to stop the cooking process. Put in a large bowl and set aside.

2. In a small saucepan over medium heat, combine the soy sauce, vinegar, and sugar. Bring to a boil, reduce the heat, and simmer until reduced in volume by about half, 35 to 50 minutes. Remove from the heat and allow to cool.

3. Add all the remaining ingredients except the sesame seeds to the blanched spinach and mix well. Add the soy reduction and mix well again. Sprinkle with toasted sesame seeds and serve.

Southeast Asian Onion-Tomato Condiment

Makes about 4 cups

This dish features fish sauce, the all but indispensable condiment of Southeast Asian cooking, along with basil and mint, classic herbs used in the region. You can make this dish without the fish sauce, of course, but to me the fermented sauce cuts a bit of the rawness of the onions and mellows the heat of the chile peppers as well. In any case, it really does serve much the same function as salt; it's not so much that you notice it as a separate flavor, but that it enhances other flavors. Without it, the dish loses a certain depth.

This rough-and-ready condiment is great with any grilled food. It's particularly good with seafood like shrimp or scallops.

2 yellow onions, halved and thinly sliced

3 small *or* 2 large ripe tomatoes, diced small

1 tablespoon minced garlic

3 tablespoons minced fresh red or green chile peppers of your choice

½ cup lime juice (about 4 limes)

1 tablespoon minced fresh ginger

¼ cup fish sauce (available in Asian markets)

2 tablespoons brown sugar

3 tablespoons chopped fresh basil

2 tablespoons chopped fresh mint

¼ cup chopped fresh cilantro

Salt and freshly ground white pepper to taste

METHOD

In a large bowl, mix all the ingredients together. This preparation will keep, covered and refrigerated, for 4 to 5 days.

Tangerine Chile Oil

Makes about 1 quart

Peels of 4 tangerines (save fruit for other use)

1 quart virgin olive oil

8 to 10 fresh serrano or other fresh red or green chile peppers of your choice

There was a time when flavored oils were all the rage, so I felt we had to make some to use at the East Coast Grill to keep up with the Joneses. We had been working with tangerine peel, which is pretty potent, when our former chef K. C. O'Hara thought of adding chiles to make a more explosive brew. I think it really works because both the tangerine and the chile flavors come through clearly.

Use this as part of a dressing, or dip grilled bread into it as a wild appetizer.

METHOD

1. Place the peels on a baking sheet and dry for 3 hours at 200°F. Allow to cool to room temperature, cut into thin strips, and place in a large glass jar or plastic container. Add the olive oil.

2. Split the chiles into quarters and add to the oil-peel mixture. Allow to sit, tightly covered, for a week for the flavors to infuse into the oil. You can start using the oil at this point, although as you allow it to sit for more time, the flavors in the oil will intensify. The oil will keep, covered and refrigerated, for up to 6 months.

Savory Orange-Chile Marmalade

What makes this a marmalade? I guess it's the fact that we leave the rinds on the oranges. Otherwise, it could easily be a chutney or preserve. In fact, this makes perfect sense. As Nick Zappia, the ace general manager of our restaurants, points out, marmalades can be used just like chutneys, but people don't think of it. Partly that's because folks tend to serve marmalade right out of the refrigerator, when it's hard and cold and fit for use only on toast and crumpets. Don't do this. Instead, be adventurous and try using marmalade in new ways. Purée a quarter cup and add it to your own barbecue sauce for a unique citrus flavor, or combine it with equal parts of vinegar and use it as a last-minute ham glaze.

Like more conventional marmalades, this spicy version makes an excellent gift. It goes well with pork or chicken dishes of any variety.

6 oranges, cut in half and sliced as thinly as possible, seeds removed but peels left on

3 tablespoons each chili powder, ground cumin, and ground coriander

1 tablespoon ground cinnamon

1½ cups orange juice (about 6 oranges)

1 cup cider vinegar

2 tablespoons minced fresh red or green chile pepper of your choice

2 cups sugar

¼ cup molasses

METHOD

1. Blanch the orange slices in boiling water for 5 minutes. Remove from the heat, drain, and let cool.

2. In a large, deep saucepan, toast the chili powder, cumin, coriander, and cinnamon over medium heat, stirring constantly, until they just begin to smoke, about 2 minutes. Be careful—they will burn quickly if you don't take them off right after the first little wisp of smoke appears.

3. Immediately add the orange juice and vinegar and stir well. Add the orange slices, chile pepper, sugar, and molasses, mix thoroughly, and bring to a boil. Reduce the heat to low and simmer the mixture, stirring once in a while, until the oranges are slightly gooey, about 45 minutes. (The mixture will still be quite wet.) If the mixture begins to stick, add more orange juice. This mixture will keep, covered and refrigerated, for 3 to 4 weeks.

Vietnamese Dipping Sauce (Nuoc Cham)

Makes about 3½ cups

½ cup fish sauce (available in Asian markets)

¼ cup lime juice (about 2 limes)

½ cup sugar

3 tablespoons Vietnamese chile-garlic paste (you may substitute 1½ tablespoons minced garlic plus 1½ tablespoons minced fresh chile)

2 tablespoons minced ginger

½ cup thinly sliced scallions

1 cup warm water

¼ cup white vinegar

This is a version of the classic Vietnamese table sauce known as nuoc cham. My buddy Binh Duong, a talented and irrepressible chef, restaurateur, cookbook author, and general all-round bon vivant, calls it the catsup of Vietnam, and when I visited there I understood what he means. It is found on every table and is used in conjunction with an incredibly wide range of dishes in that country. I put some ginger and scallions in this version to give it a little body, but if you're using it as an ingredient in other recipes, just leave those two out.

METHOD

In a small bowl, combine all the ingredients and mix together well. This mixture will keep, covered and refrigerated, for several months.

LEARNING TO LOVE FISH SAUCE

Remember the story of the green eggs and ham? Well, I know I've said it before, but I will say it again: If you try fish sauce, you will learn to really like it. Each country in Southeast Asia has its own variety of fish sauce, but my guess is that our untrained taste buds won't pick up the subtle differences. Vietnamese Dipping Sauce is a good choice for your first experiment with fish sauce because the strength of the other flavors tends to push the fish taste to the background a bit.

Mango-Chile Sambal

Sambals are elusive little things, changing meaning and composition depending on where you are in the world. If you're eating this one, you're in Malaysia.

This is my attempt to copy a sambal that was served with a grilled fish in a restaurant just outside Melacca. The chef's name was Charlie, and he was good enough to let me buy him a couple of beers while he helped me struggle to understand what a sambal meant to him. I think this is pretty close.

METHOD

1. In a large sauté pan, heat the oil over medium-high heat until hot but not smoking. Add the onion and cook, stirring occasionally, until it is more or less translucent, about 5 minutes.

2. Add the garlic, ginger, lemongrass, and chile and cook, stirring constantly, for 1 additional minute. Add the mangoes, vinegar, molasses, and fish sauce and cook, stirring constantly, for 3 minutes. Add the nutmeg, mix well, and season with salt and pepper. Serve hot or cold. This sambal will keep, covered and refrigerated, for 5 to 7 days.

Makes about 2 cups

2 tablespoons sesame oil

1 red onion, diced small

1 teaspoon minced garlic

1 teaspoon minced ginger

1 teaspoon lemongrass, tough upper leaves and outer stalk removed and reserved, inner portion of bulb (bottom 1/3 of stalk) very finely minced, *or* 1 teaspoon minced lemon peel

2 tablespoons minced fresh red or green chile pepper of your choice

2 ripe mangoes, peeled, pitted, and diced small

1/4 cup white vinegar

1/4 cup molasses

2 tablespoons fish sauce (available in Asian markets) (optional)

Pinch ground nutmeg

Salt and freshly cracked black pepper to taste

Simple Dry Masala • East Coast Grill Masala • Jake's All-Purpose Barbecue Rub • Latin-Style Spice Rub • East African Spice Mix #3 • North African Spice Rub • Middle Eastern Spice Rub • Persian-Style Nut Rub • Sweet Anise Rub • Spice Rub for Oily Fish • Sweet and Hot Masala #7 • Coconut-Ginger Wet Spice Mix

SPICE RUBS

I first heard the term *spice rub* as a kid growing up in Virginia. The culinary masters who introduced me to this concept were the good ol' boys who showed up at my family's house every year in late July for the annual all-night pig roast. When the pit had been dug, the fire had burned down to the proper stage, and the pig was about to commence its long hours of slow cooking, the pit master would take out a plastic bucket full of a reddish powder that he called "mah secret spice rub" and vigorously rub handfuls of it all over the beast.

As the pig slowly cooked, the rub formed a crispy, flavor-packed crust on the outside. When the pig finally came off the fire, the contrast between the rich, moist, juicy interior meat and the spicy, super-flavorful crunch of the crust was fantastic. Barbecue quickly became one of my favorite foods, and I took a permanent shine to the technique of "rubbing" as a way to add great flavor and texture to a dish.

Years later, when I became intrigued with the spice mixtures of the world, I drew on my youthful barbecue experience and used the characteristic flavor combinations of these classics to make rubs. From the earthy spice blends of North Africa and the Middle East to the fiery roasted and ground masalas of India to the pungent wet spice mixtures of Thailand, traditional spice mixes inspired me to make all kinds of rubs suitable for use on meat, fowl, fish, game, and even vegetables.

The spice blends from which I have drawn inspiration are found all over the hot-weather world, but Indian cooks are probably the most prolific creators of these mixtures, which in that country are known as masalas. Each region of India has its own masalas, and each masala has its own particular uses and history. Unfortunately, we Westerners have lumped all of these complex blends together under the generic heading of "curry powder." To be accurate, the yellowish mixture that we know as curry powder is only one among many masalas of southern India.

In fact, hidden beneath the single English term *curry* is a whole world of wonderful spice blends, a world that American cooks are just beginning to understand and explore. We call Sri Lankan spice mixtures curries, for example, but they differ from Indian versions in that the spices are typically toasted until dark. In Thailand spice blends known as kaengs are an important part of the cuisine. Kaengs differ from Indian spice mixtures in that they are usually not cooked separately but instead are mixed with coconut milk or other liquid to form a wet paste prior to use in cooking. Kaengs, however, are also known in the English-speaking world as (you guessed it) "curries."

The five-spice powder of China; the gulai of Sumatra, in which spices are cooked together with coconut milk to form a wet paste; the moles and recadoes of Mexico; the complex spice blends of the Maghreb (Tunisia, Algeria, and Morocco), the best known being *ras el hanout*, comprising at least twenty individual spices; Ethiopia's berberé; the zug and baharat of the Middle East, chile-based mixes that share cardamom and cumin in addition to other ingredients—these are only a few of the characteristic spice mixes of the world. Creatively crafted, rich in vibrant flavors and robust aromas, and based in deep culinary understanding of their effects on the ingredients with which they are used, these astonishingly imaginative blends provide vivid examples of the way that spices can add diversity and deep, complex flavor to food.

From what I have been able to discover, most of these classic spice blends are seldom used as rubs. Instead, they serve as flavorings for a whole range of dishes, from soups to stews to condiments. The technique of rubbing has been pretty much restricted to Cajun blackening and barbecue in the American South; to curing—for example, the salt or pepper rubs used on prosciutto, pastrami, or gravlax; and to some wet spice pastes, such as those of the Yucatán in Mexico. Using the world's time-honored spice mixtures as the inspiration for rubs adds a whole new dimension to the technique, providing an ideal way to add bold flavors to all kinds of food with little effort and great effect.

This chapter includes recipes for a few rubs that I have come up with. They are all inspired by the characteristic flavor combinations of the cuisines of what I call the Spice Zone, that band around the earth that is the home of hot weather and most of the world's spices. The North African Spice Rub that I have included, for example, might or might not exist in this form in North Africa. Whether it does or not, all of the individual spices and their cumulative flavor as a mix are true to the spirit of the region's cuisine.

These spice mixes can be used not only as rubs but as flavor enhancers for soups, stews, and most any other dish, as well as for sprinkling on foods after cooking, like salt and pepper. When you do use these mixtures as rubs, though, you will find that the procedure couldn't be easier. Just take small handfuls of the mix and rub it over the entire surface of the food you are going to cook, using a bit of pressure to make sure that a good layer adheres to the food. Don't bother with brushes or other types of applicators; bare hands are really your best tools. Also, once you've started to cook, don't worry if the rub begins to turn dark brown. This is what happens to spices when they are cooked, especially if you are using a high-heat cooking method such as grilling or sautéing. As long as the spices don't begin to smoke, you are in the clear.

When you have become familiar with the flavors and properties of these mixtures and the individual spices they are composed of, you might find it fun and rewarding to try toasting your own combination of spices, grinding them into a powder, and using it as a rub.

Since there are few hard-and-fast rules about spice use, I advise you to use either my spice blends or the traditional ones mentioned above as your models and slowly take off from there. However, there are some simple guidelines to follow. Use a smaller proportion of the highly aromatic spices, such as clove, nutmeg, and cinnamon; a higher proportion of the more earthy spices, such as coriander, cumin, and paprika, which provide a base for the mixture; and go heavy or light on the chile peppers depending on your taste for heat. You should also be careful to create an overall balance between the sweetness of spices like cardamom, the heat of chiles, and the aromaticity of spices like cinnamon.

Whichever spice rub you use, I predict that once you try this technique you'll become as addicted to it as I am. As the pit masters of my youth knew well, there is no quicker or easier way to add big flavor to a simple food than by coating it with a carefully balanced mixture of spices. It's also a great way to experience the flavors of other lands. Simple, healthful, flavorful, quick, and exotic—you just can't ask much more of a cooking technique.

Simple Dry Masala

Makes a little more than
¹/₂ cup

This simple spice mixture can be substituted for prepared curry powder in any recipe. Since the spices are probably fresher to begin with and are toasted and mixed together closer to the time that you actually use them, you will get much brighter, more distinct flavors than with the packaged variety.

2 tablespoons ground cumin

2 tablespoons paprika

1 teaspoon ground turmeric

1 tablespoon crushed coriander seeds

1 teaspoon cayenne pepper

1 tablespoon ground ginger

1 tablespoon ground cinnamon

1 teaspoon dry mustard

METHOD

Place all the spices in a medium-size sauté pan and heat over medium heat, stirring, until the first tiny wisp of smoke appears, 2 to 3 minutes. Remove from the heat immediately.

Covered and stored in a cool, dark place, this rub will keep for about 6 weeks.

East Coast Grill Masala

¼ cup ground cumin

¼ cup prepared curry powder

¼ cup chili powder

2 tablespoons ground allspice

2 tablespoons cayenne pepper

2 tablespoons salt

2 tablespoons freshly cracked black pepper

1 tablespoon ground cinnamon

Known at the East Coast Grill as our own special masala, this mixture is the base seasoning for many of the dishes that we cook. I particularly like to use it on things that fly or swim.

METHOD

Just mix the ingredients together well and use. Covered and stored in a cool, dark place, this rub will keep for about 6 weeks.

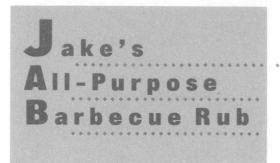

Jake's All-Purpose Barbecue Rub

Makes about 2½ cups

1 cup paprika

¼ cup ground cumin

¼ cup packed brown sugar

¼ cup chili powder

¼ cup salt

¼ cup freshly cracked black pepper

2 tablespoons cayenne pepper

1 teaspoon ground cloves

This is the latest in a five-year evolution of the barbecued rib rub we use at Jake & Earl's Dixie Barbecue. The nuances in this state-of-the-art version were added by our fine pit master, Randall. A little sweet, a little hot, with just a hint of clove, this rub can be used on just about anything.

METHOD

Mix all the ingredients together and rub to your heart's content. Covered and stored in a cool, dark place, this rub will keep for about 6 weeks.

Latin-Style Spice Rub

Featuring the cumin, chile, coriander, and cinnamon that are characteristic of much of Latin American cookery, this rub is particularly good on pork and chicken. Makes sense, since those are the main meats of the region. As ethnobotanist Gary Nabhan said in a different context, "Ethnic cuisines are not just floating in the sky; they have a direct connection to the land people have lived on for centuries."

Makes about 1 cup

¼ cup cumin seeds (you may substitute ground cumin)

¼ cup chili powder

2 tablespoons crushed coriander seeds

1 tablespoon ground cinnamon

1 tablespoon brown sugar

2 tablespoons salt

1 tablespoon red pepper flakes

2 tablespoons freshly cracked black pepper

METHOD

Toast the cumin seeds in a small sauté pan over medium heat, shaking constantly, for 2 to 3 minutes, or until they just start to smoke. Combine with all the remaining ingredients and grind to a powder in a spice mill, coffee grinder, or mortar and pestle. Covered and stored in a cool, dark place, this rub will keep for about 6 weeks.

East African Spice Mix #3

Makes about 1½ cups

Add this to the long line of special spice mixtures that are responsible for the characteristic flavors of certain cuisines. This particular mix is modeled on an East African combination, the classic Ethiopian spice mix known as berberé. Here we turn it into a wet spice by adding the tropical staples ginger and orange juice.

This spice mix is most appropriate for soups (or *wats*, for you Ethiopian food fans out there) or as a rub, in which guise I would try it with roast chicken or roast lamb.

1 tablespoon crushed cardamom seeds

1 teaspoon ground cloves

1 tablespoon ground cinnamon

1 tablespoon ground nutmeg

1 tablespoon ground fenugreek

1 tablespoon ground cumin

2 tablespoons ground coriander

2 tablespoons fennel seeds

¼ cup paprika

¼ cup cayenne pepper

2 tablespoons kosher salt

2 tablespoons freshly cracked black pepper

2 tablespoons virgin olive oil

2 tablespoons minced ginger

2 tablespoons minced garlic

1 cup red wine

½ cup red wine vineger

½ cup orange juice

METHOD

1. In a large sauté pan, combine all the dry ingredients and sauté over medium heat for 2 to 3 minutes, shaking and stirring constantly. If the mixture starts to smoke, remove from the heat immediately. Remove from the pan and set aside.

2. Rinse and dry the sauté pan, add the olive oil, and heat until hot but not smoking. Add the ginger and garlic and sauté, stirring fre-quently, for 1 minute. Add the wine, vinegar, and orange juice, bring to a boil, and cook until reduced in volume by about half, 5 to 8 minutes. (This will take longer if you are using a smaller sauté pan.)

3. Remove from the heat, stir in the toasted dry spice mixture, and mix well. This mixture will keep, covered and refrigerated, for up to 2 months.

North African Spice Rub

The use of caraway and cumin marks this as a distinctively North African rub. It is actually quite similar to the North African Chile Pepper Condiment (page 360), but this version is constituted entirely of dried spices for easy rubbing. It's excellent on lamb or a hearty fish like bluefish or mackerel.

¼ cup caraway seeds

¼ cup cumin seeds

2 tablespoons coriander seeds

1 tablespoon red pepper flakes

2 tablespoons salt

2 tablespoons whole black peppercorns

METHOD

In a large sauté pan, lightly toast all the ingredients, shaking constantly to prevent burning, for 2 to 3 minutes, or until they begin to brown a tiny bit. Allow to cool to room temperature, then grind roughly with a mortar and pestle, spice mill, or coffee grinder, leaving some coarseness to the mixture. Covered and stored in a cool, dark place, this rub will keep for about 6 weeks.

Middle Eastern Spice Rub

Makes about 1 cup

2 tablespoons crushed coriander seeds

2 tablespoons crushed cumin seeds

¼ cup paprika

1 tablespoon cayenne pepper

1 tablespoon ground allspice

2 tablespoons ground cinnamon

1 tablespoon ground ginger

1 teaspoon ground cloves

When spice mixtures are discussed, the intricate and varied masalas of India always seem to get the most attention. They are indeed wonderful, but if you walk into any Persian market, you will realize that the cooks of the Middle East are also serious devotees of the craft. This recipe is a variation on a mixture called baharat, which is used in the Middle East as an all purpose spicer-upper. To facilitate its use as a dry rub, I have increased the paprika a bit. This mixture is great as a rub on grilled or roasted chicken and will give the bird a crisp, flavorful crust.

METHOD

Combine all the ingredients in a non-stick sauté pan and heat over medium heat for 2 to 3 minutes, stirring constantly with a wooden spoon. The heat will bring out flavors of the individual spices and blend them together. This mixture will maintain its potency for about 6 weeks if stored in an airtight container in a cool, dark place.

Persian-Style Nut Rub

Makes about 1 cup

¼ cup sesame seeds

¼ cup ground pistachios

----

2 tablespoons ground almonds

¼ cup finely chopped fresh oregano

----

1 tablespoon ground allspice

Salt and freshly cracked black pepper to taste

Here is a variation on the zaatar spice mixture that is used in the Middle East for a variety of culinary purposes. This version, like those of Saudi Arabia and the Gulf States, features ground nuts. I've left out the sumac (a sour, earthy-tasting spice that is quite difficult to find in the U.S.) and have substituted fresh herbs for the dried thyme usually used in Middle Eastern versions. I like the fresh herbs with nuts.

This rub is great for coating grilled fish or chicken; it creates a nice seared crust with a unique nutty flavor.

METHOD

1. Using a nonstick sauté pan, roast the sesame seeds, pistachios, and almonds separately over medium heat, shaking the pan frequently to prevent burning, until they are lightly browned, 4 to 5 minutes each.

2. When all the nuts are roasted, combine them with the remaining ingredients and, using a coffee grinder or blender, process until fine, about the consistency of coarse meal.

SUMAC

Sumac generally refers to a powder made by grinding the dried seeds of a Mediterranean plant of the same name. The term may also refer to the seeds themselves or to juice pressed from the seeds, both of which are also used in cooking.

In any of these forms, sumac is used to add a fruity tartness to dishes, providing the sour taste so well loved by Middle Eastern cooks but with less harshness than vinegar, lemon juice, or lime juice. It is used on all types of grilled fish and meat, mixed with yogurt and herbs as a sauce, added to stews, salads, and marinades, and in general is used as widely as we use lemon juice.

As modern communications and air transport continue to shrink the global village, it is becoming increasingly rare to find ingredients that are used exclusively in one area of the world. Sumac, however, is one such product. Virtually ubiquitous in Arab and Middle Eastern (particularly Lebanese) cooking, it is virtually unknown in the West, available only in Middle Eastern stores in a few large cities.

Sweet Anise Rub

Makes about 1 scant cup

15 star anise

Seeds from 5 cardamom pods

1 teaspoon whole cloves

¼ cup salt

¼ cup freshly cracked black pepper

¼ cup sugar

Star anise has an intense flavor, so in this rub it is nicely balanced with salt and pepper. This is an excellent rub for large cuts of meat like leg of lamb, pork roast, or beef roast, as well as for whole chicken or turkey. On smaller cuts, however, the salt is a little too intense; if you want to use it on a pork chop or chicken thigh, cut down the salt by about half.

Covered and placed in a cool, dark place, this mixture will keep about 6 weeks.

METHOD

1. In a spice grinder or coffee grinder, grind together the anise, cardamom seeds, and cloves until fine.

2. Place this mixture in a sauté pan over medium heat and heat briefly, 2 to 3 minutes, shaking fairly constantly to prevent burning.

3. Remove from the heat, add the remaining ingredients, and mix well.

Spice Rub for Oily Fish

Makes about 1 cup

2 tablespoons fennel seeds

2 tablespoons coriander seeds

2 tablespoons freshly cracked
    pepper (white if available)

2 teaspoons ground cinnamon

2 teaspoons ground turmeric

2 teaspoons cayenne pepper

2 tablespoons dry mustard

¼ cup salt

I know it doesn't sound all that appetizing to talk about "oily" fish, but that's what they are, so why not say it? This rub is particularly good on bluefish, tuna, or mackerel because they have the character to stand up to a strong-flavored mix of spices.

Covered and stored in a cool, dark place, this rub will keep for about 6 weeks.

METHOD

In a medium-size bowl, combine all the ingredients and mix thoroughly.

Sweet and Hot Masala #7

Makes about 1 cup

While working in my restaurant kitchen preparing daily specials, I often make spice mixtures like this in small amounts to be used for a specific dish. I call them masalas, which is what spice mixtures are called in India, curry being a specific type of masala used mostly in the south.

This particular blend is strong on the sweeter flavors of cardamom, cinnamon, and cloves. I use it as a dry rub on grilled chicken, but it can also be used to add a little spice to a stew or soup just prior to serving. When you are making it, the smell of the spices being heated adds a distinctive touch of the dramatic and the exotic to your kitchen.

5 tablespoons whole cardamom seeds

1 stick cinnamon *or* 1 tablespoon ground cinnamon

7 whole cloves *or* 1 teaspoon ground cloves

1 tablespoon dried chile pepper of your choice

3 tablespoons coriander seeds

¼ cup cumin seeds

1 tablespoon ground turmeric

2 tablespoons whole black peppercorns

1 tablespoon whole white peppercorns (you may substitute black)

METHOD

In a large sauté pan, combine all the ingredients and cook over medium-low heat, shaking frequently, until the mixture begins to take on a darker color, 2 to 3 minutes. Remove from the heat, allow to cool to room temperature, then grind in a spice blender, coffee grinder, or blender. If you keep this mixture tightly covered and store it in a cool, dark place, it will stay potent for up to 6 weeks.

Coconut-Ginger Wet Spice Mix

In countries where a lot of spices are used, it is common to take a dry spice mix and convert it into a wet one, which allows you to add even more flavors. Here we build on Sweet and Hot Masala #7, using coconut milk as the agent of change. With the addition of ginger and lime, the mixture begins to take on a Southeast Asian character. This is the one to use as a powerful flavor enhancer in any Near or Far Eastern soup or stew.

2 tablespoons sesame oil

----

2 tablespoons minced ginger

----

1 tablespoon minced garlic

½ cup coconut milk, unsweetened canned, or prepared by method on page 458

----

2 tablespoons tamarind water (see Pantry, page 465)

----

1 tablespoon grated lime peel

----

1 cup Sweet and Hot Masala #7 (page 388)

METHOD

1. Heat the sesame oil in a large sauté pan over medium heat until hot but not smoking. Add the ginger and garlic and cook, stirring frequently, for 1 minute.

2. Add the coconut milk, bring to a simmer, then reduce the heat to low. Add the tamarind water and stir well, then add the lime peel and Sweet and Hot Masala #7 and stir until the spice mix is fully dissolved. Remove from the heat, allow to cool to room temperature, then cover and refrigerate. This mix will keep, covered and refrigerated, for about 1 week.

Your Basic Cornbread ▪ **Cheesy Cornbread (aka Hopper's Choice)** ▪ **Chile Quesadilla Bread** ▪ **Mexican Corn Pudding** ▪ **Indian-Style Grill Bread** ▪ **Indian-Style Griddle Bread** ▪ **Middle Eastern–Style Crisp Bread with Toasted Sesame Seeds** ▪ **Grilled Hearthbread Johnson**

BREADS

Because I grew up in the South, I tend to like breads made with cornmeal. I like the taste and texture of these breads, and I also like the fact that they are similar to the breads of Africa—another reminder that southern food is largely a variant of African cooking.

I also enjoy grilling and traveling in equatorial countries, which means I go for breads cooked on the grill and breads that remind me of exotic climes. In this department, Middle Eastern and Indian flatbreads are my favorites.

Here are a handful of such breads, ranging from the very simple, such as Your Basic Cornbread, to the somewhat more difficult, such as Middle Eastern–Style Crisp Bread. Whichever one you choose, they are all excellent, healthful accompaniments to the recipes in this book.

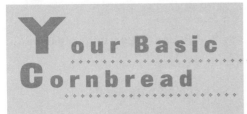

Your Basic Cornbread

4 cups all-purpose flour

2 cups yellow cornmeal

1¼ cups sugar

1 teaspoon salt

2 tablespoons baking powder

4 large eggs

3 cups milk

1½ tablespoons vegetable oil

½ cup melted butter

Sometimes the only thing you really want with a spicy meal is a good, plain, hearty hunk of old-fashioned cornbread, and this is the version that I like best. A bit on the sweet side, it goes great with just about everything, particularly with hot and spicy foods.

METHOD

1. Preheat the oven to 350°F. Lightly grease an 8" × 12" × 2" baking pan.

2. Sift together the flour, cornmeal, sugar, salt, and baking powder.

3. In a separate bowl, mix together the eggs, milk, and oil.

4. Pour the wet ingredients over the dry ingredients, then add the melted butter. Stir until just barely mixed.

5. Pour the batter into the greased pan and bake for approximately 1 hour, or until the top of the cornbread is brown and a cake tester inserted in the center comes out clean.

Cheesy Cornbread (aka Hopper's Choice)

This slightly dense cornbread has a lot going for it—a little crunchy texture from the fresh corn kernels, a subtle bite from the black and red peppers, the smooth richness of cheese, even a trace of sour from the buttermilk and lemon juice. All together, these flavors make for a cornbread that is unusual enough to be interesting but not too strange for everyday eating. After all, it's the odds-on favorite of Hopper, the son of Blue Room chef Michael Peternell.

Makes 9 generous pieces

1 cup all purpose flour

1 cup yellow cornmeal

2 teaspoons salt

½ teaspoon freshly cracked black or white pepper

½ teaspoon cayenne pepper

2 tablespoons sugar

2 teaspoons baking soda

1 cup buttermilk

2 large eggs

⅔ cup grated Monterey Jack or Cheddar cheese

1 tablespoon lemon juice

2 tablespoons unsalted butter, melted

2 ears corn, husked, desilked, blanched in boiling water for 30 seconds, and kernels removed (you may substitute 1 cup frozen corn)

M E T H O D

1. Preheat the oven to 450°F and grease a 9" × 9" × 2" baking pan.

2. In a large bowl, combine the flour, cornmeal, salt, pepper, cayenne, sugar, and baking soda and mix very well.

3. In a separate bowl, combine the buttermilk, eggs, cheese, and lemon juice, beat together lightly, and pour into the flour mixture. Mix a few strokes, then add the melted butter and corn kernels and stir just until combined. Be careful not to overbeat.

4. Pour the batter into the baking pan and bake until the top is well browned and a toothpick inserted in the center comes out clean, about 40 minutes.

Serving Suggestions:

This is good with any spicy food, particularly of Latin origin. It is a real helper with super-hot dishes like K.C.'s Grilled Killer Jamaican Party Beef from Hell with Sweet Grilled Bananas (page 286) or Scrambled Eggs with Fresh Oysters and Chiles (page 296). It's also good with grilled shrimp dishes like Grilled Shrimp with Green Mangoes and Red Lime Sauce (page 118).

Chile Quesadilla Bread

One large pan

Quesadilla bread is the creation of Rosemary Mack, the truly talented original baker at the East Coast Grill. This bread goes great with spicy Latin food, so I decided to add a little Latin twist by throwing in some chili powder. I liked it a lot, so here it is. With eggs, butter, and sour cream in abundance, this is a heavy, soft, rich bread, dense and delicious.

3 cups all-purpose flour

1 tablespoon baking powder

1 tablespoon salt

1 tablespoon freshly cracked white pepper (you may substitute black pepper)

1 tablespoon chili powder

12 large eggs, separated

½ cup sugar

1 pound unsalted butter, melted

3 cups (about 12 ounces) grated Monterey Jack cheese (you may substitute sharp Cheddar cheese)

1 cup sour cream

METHOD

1. Preheat the oven to 375°F and grease a 12" × 17" × 2" baking pan.

2. Sift together the flour, baking powder, salt, pepper, and chili powder. Set aside.

3. In a large bowl, beat the egg yolks and sugar together until light. In a separate bowl, beat the egg whites until they form stiff peaks, then fold into the yolk mixture.

4. Working steadily, fold into the egg mixture the dry ingredients, the melted butter, the grated cheese, and finally the sour cream. You will have to be a little aggressive to be sure everything gets well blended, but try to be as gentle as you can at the same time.

5. Pour the batter into the greased pan and bake for 20 to 30 minutes, or until the top is golden brown and a cake tester inserted into the center comes out clean.

6. Let the bread cool slightly in the pan, then turn it out onto a wire rack to cool completely.

Mexican Corn Pudding

This is kind of a takeoff on the bread soufflés popular in Virginia in colonial days. You can think of it either as rich, free-flowing cornbread or as a variation on the traditional spoonbread of the South. Or you can think of it as bread pudding in which you don't have to use previously baked bread. In any case, it makes a perfect accompaniment to spicy hot foods.

Serves 8 as side dish

2 cups water

2½ cups milk

1½ cups yellow cornmeal

1 teaspoon salt

1 tablespoon sugar

1 cup corn kernels (about 2 small ears, husked, desilked, blanched in boiling water for 30 seconds, and kernels removed) *or* 1 cup frozen corn

½ red bell pepper, diced small

2 tablespoons butter, melted

½ cup farmer's cheese or small-curd cottage cheese (you may substitute grated Cheddar cheese)

2 tablespoons finely chopped fresh cilantro

5 large eggs

1 tablespoon baking powder

2 teaspoons minced fresh red or green chile pepper of your choice

Salt and freshly cracked black pepper to taste

METHOD

1. Preheat the oven to 425°F and grease a 3-quart casserole dish or medium-size cast-iron skillet.

2. In a large saucepan, combine the water and milk and bring to a boil. Add the cornmeal, salt, and sugar, reduce the heat to medium-low, and whisk for 1 or 2 minutes, or until the mixture thickens. (If the mixture thickens immediately and becomes difficult to stir, add another ¼ to ½ cup of water.) Remove from the heat, whisk in the corn kernels, red bell pepper, butter, farmer's cheese, and cilantro, and set aside.

3. In a large bowl, whisk the eggs together with the baking powder until frothy. Add the chile and whisk into the warm cornmeal mixture until thoroughly blended. Add salt and pepper, pour the mixture into the casserole dish or skillet, and bake for 25 to 30 minutes, or until the top is just golden brown.

Serving Suggestions:

You might want to serve this with Grilled Striped Bass with Sweet Tomato Salsa and Glazed Mango (page 84) or Grilled Swordfish with Spicy Shrimp Salsa (page 78).

Indian-Style Grill Bread

Tandoori is a method of cooking in which food is cooked in a big clay oven, called a tandoor, with a charcoal fire at the bottom. In India food cooked in a tandoor is often accompanied by bread known as nan, along with some sort of pickle and maybe a cucumber-tomato relish. Nan is cooked by slapping the dough onto the interior walls of the tandoor. Since most of us don't have tandoors, my version of nan is baked in a regular oven, then given a little charred flavor at the end by flashing on a hot grill.

4 cups all-purpose flour plus extra for working
- - - - - - - - -
1 teaspoon sugar
- - - - - - - - -
1 tablespoon baking powder
- - - - - - - - -
1 teaspoon salt
- - - - - - - - -
2 large eggs
- - - - - - - - -
½ cup milk
- - - - - - - - -
½ cup plain yogurt
- - - - - - - - -
2 tablespoons virgin olive oil (approximately)
- - - - - - - - -
2 tablespoons poppy seeds (optional)

METHOD

1. In a large bowl, combine the flour, sugar, baking powder, and salt and mix well.

2. In a separate bowl, combine the eggs, milk, and yogurt and mix well. Make a well in the center of the dry ingredients and pour the liquid ingredients into it. Incorporate the dry ingredients into the liquid gradually, sweeping in from the sides of the well with a wooden spoon, until they are well mixed.

3. Moisten your hands with olive oil, gather the dough into a ball, and place it on a well-floured surface. Knead the dough for 8 to 12 minutes, sprinkling lightly with flour every once in a while so it doesn't stick to your hands. If you are using the poppy seeds, sprinkle them over the dough as you knead so they become incorporated. The dough should be elastic and smooth and easily formed into a ball. Sprinkle the dough with flour, wrap it in plastic wrap, and allow it to sit for 3 hours.

4. Put 2 large baking sheets in the oven and preheat the oven to 500°F. Divide the dough into 6 equal balls, moisten your hands with oil, and by stretching, pulling, or throwing the dough back and forth in your hands, shape each ball into an oval ¼ to ½ inch thick.

5. Place the ovals on the hot baking trays (don't burn yourself—remember not to handle hot pans with damp cloths because moisture conducts heat) and return the trays to the oven. Bake until firm, 6 to 7 minutes. To serve, rub lightly with olive oil and grill over a medium-hot fire until slightly browned, about 1 minute per side.

Indian-Style Griddle Bread

Makes about 12 small breads

3 cups whole-wheat flour plus extra for working

1 tablespoon salt

1 cup water

1 tablespoon vegetable oil

This is my version of a chapati, the staple bread of everyday life in India. A common street food, chapatis are tortilla-like little breads that are cooked on hot griddles and eaten with melted clarified butter (ghee) and perhaps a pickle relish. They are simple and fairly quick to make and go well with soups or stews. In India chapatis are often used as eating utensils.

METHOD

1. In a large bowl, mix the flour and salt until well combined. Add the water slowly, mixing as you add. If the resulting dough is too stiff to work, add a bit more water.

2. Turn out onto a well-floured surface and knead until elastic, 5 or 6 minutes. Oil very lightly, wrap in plastic wrap, and set aside for about 2 hours.

3. Separate the dough into a dozen golf ball–sized balls. On a well-floured board, roll out each ball into a very thin (about ⅛ inch thick) oval.

4. In a medium-size cast-iron skillet with no oil or butter, cook each oval briefly over medium heat on both sides until well browned, 1½ to 2 minutes per side.

Serving Suggestions:

These breads are ideal for dishes that require something to sop up the gravy, like African-Style Chicken Stew with Squash (page 306), Cardamom Chicken Stew in the Indian Style (page 304), or North African Lamb Stew with Sweet Potatoes and Couscous (page 323). For a snack I would serve these little guys accompanied by butter and a pickle like Salty Persian-Style Pickled Turnips and Onions (page 254) or any kind of chutney or relish, from Red Onion–Tamarind Chutney (page 344) to Mangoes, Cucumbers, and Red Onion in Vinegar with Toasted Sesame Seeds (page 350).

Middle Eastern–Style Crisp Bread with Toasted Sesame Seeds

Makes 8 flatbreads

2¼ cups warm water

1 tablespoon sugar

1 envelope active dry yeast

7 cups sifted all-purpose flour plus extra for working

1 tablespoon coarse salt plus extra for sprinkling

¼ cup vegetable oil

1 egg yolk mixed with 2 tablespoons water

¼ cup sesame seeds, toasted in a 350°F oven until brown, about 5 minutes

This is a variation on the crispy, cracker-like bread known as lavash in Armenia and Iran and lawausha in Afghanistan. Since it is already crisp, it will keep for several weeks, and with its curvy shape and irregular bubbles, it looks dramatic on the table. This bread is great eaten by itself, used as a dipping tool, or set out with olives and cheeses as a simple appetizer.

METHOD

1. In a small bowl, combine the water and 1 teaspoon of the sugar and sprinkle the yeast on top. Allow to sit until the yeast blooms, about 10 minutes.

2. Meanwhile, in a large bowl, combine the flour, remaining 2 teaspoons sugar, and salt and mix well. Make a well in the middle of the flour mixture and pour in the yeast mixture and vegetable oil. Gradually incorporate the flour mixture, stirring it in with your hands or a wooden spoon until you have a dough of uniform texture.

3. Turn the dough onto a lightly floured board and knead with floured hands for 8 to 10 minutes, or until it is smooth and elastic. Shape into a ball and put into a lightly oiled bowl. Allow to stand, covered, in a warm, draft-free place until it has doubled in bulk; this will take about 2 hours.

4. Put 2 large baking sheets into the oven and preheat the oven to 425°F. Punch down the dough and divide it into 8 balls of approximately equal size, each about the size of a lemon. Roll each ball into a flat, oval shape about 8" × 12" × ¼". Brush the ovals with the egg wash and sprinkle with the toasted sesame seeds and a bit of coarse salt.

5. Place 2 ovals on each of the hot baking sheets (don't burn yourself—remember not to handle hot pans with damp cloths because moisture conducts heat), prick each one 5 or 6 times with a fork, and bake for about 8 minutes, or until golden brown and crisp. Be careful not to let them burn. Remove from the oven. The breads will have a dip-and-sway contour studded with large bubbles.

6. Repeat Step 5 with the remaining 6 balls of dough. This bread will last at least a week, covered.

Serving Suggestions:

Try this as a dipping tool for Spicy Pumpkin Dip (page 68), Parsley Salad with Bulgur, Mint, and Tomatoes (page 216), or Big Sky's Grilled Sweet Lemon Salad with Parsley (page 222).

Grilled Hearthbread Johnson

6 tablespoons extra-virgin olive oil (approximately)

1 tablespoon minced garlic

1 teaspoon minced fresh herbs (rosemary, basil, or thyme, alone or in combination)

2 teaspoons salt

1 teaspoon freshly cracked black pepper

1¼ cups warm water

1 envelope active dry yeast

1 teaspoon sugar

3¼ cups all-purpose flour

Here's yet another addition to the body of cooking that carries the name Johnson, from my close amigo Steve "Maurice" Johnson. From a day spent in the goose-fat capital of France to a laid-back grill party at the beach, from a white-tablecloth dinner to an all-night pig roast, if an event involves food, Steve is there. Just about any type of food makes him happy—really happy. So happy that he has been known to go on at length about a meal or a dish or even an ingredient, whether in person, over the phone, or even on my answering machine.

Fortunately for me, Steve became interested in grilling pizzas and researched the topic with his usual thoroughness. This dough recipe is the result of his efforts. Infused with fruity oil, fresh herbs, and garlic, the dough is reminiscent of focaccia, and I like to use it as an all-purpose hearthbread. If you are like me and only want to make dough every once in a while, you can make a double batch of this recipe, form it into loaves, wrap them in plastic wrap, and toss them in the freezer. They will defrost at room temperature in a couple of hours, three at the most.

1. In a small sauté pan, heat 2 tablespoons of the oil over medium heat until hot but not smoking. Turn the heat to low, add the garlic, herbs, salt, and black pepper, and cook, stirring occasionally, until the garlic has softened, about 5 minutes. Remove from the heat and set aside.

2. Place the warm water in a large mixing bowl, sprinkle the yeast and sugar over the water, and allow to sit until the yeast blooms, about 10 minutes.

3. Add the flour all at once to the liquid yeast mixture. Without mixing, pour the oil over the top of the flour. Mix with your hands or a large wooden spoon until the ingredients are well combined and form a sticky mass.

4. Turn the dough out onto a lightly floured surface and knead until it is smooth, shiny, and elastic, 3 or 4 minutes. Form the dough into a ball, place in a lightly oiled bowl, cover with a damp cloth, and let it rise until doubled in bulk, about 1½ hours.

5. When the dough has doubled in bulk, punch it down, knead it for about 2 minutes, then divide it in half. Form each half into a smooth, round ball, place on a floured surface, cover with a damp cloth, and allow to sit for about 5 minutes, so both you and the dough have a chance to relax.

6. Roll each dough ball into a round about 10 inches in diameter and ½ inch thick, flouring the work surface and the dough lightly as necessary. Set aside, cover with a damp cloth, and allow to rise for 20 minutes.

7. To grill the breads, brush each round lightly with olive oil, sprinkle with salt, and grill, oiled sides down, over a medium-low fire for about 8 minutes. Brush the exposed sides with oil, flip the breads over, and grill for an additional 8 minutes, or until both sides are deep golden brown, with little grill marks. To check for doneness, thump with your finger; the bread should sound slightly hollow. Remove and eat.

Simple All-Purpose Mixed Fruit ▪ Mangoes with Lime and Ginger ▪ Grilled Peaches with Blue Cheese and Sweet Balsamic Glaze ▪ Mashed Banana with Lime-Coconut Milk and Mango Sauce ▪ Roast Pineapple with Lime and Molasses ▪ Really Sweet Carrots Cooked in Milk ▪ Grilled Banana Splits ▪ Banana-Papaya Fool ▪ Dark Rum–Flavored Flan ▪ Banana-Guava Bread Pudding with Rum Sauce ▪ Andy's Rice Pudding ▪ Panfried Banana Fritters with Molasses-Rum Sauce ▪ A Peach Shortcake for Lizzie ▪ Sargento's Labor-Intensive Lime Pie with Coconut Crust and Mango Topping ▪ Blue Room Chocolate-Bourbon-Pecan Tart with Gentleman Jack Hard Sauce ▪ Banana-Rum Ice ▪ Limon Ice ▪ Mango Ice ▪ Watermelon Ice

SWEETNESS AND LIGHT: DESSERTS

The way I see it, desserts should pretty much fall into one of two camps: Either they should be really, really sweet or they should be just plain fruit. Since this opinion is consistent with the practice In most hot-weather countries, many of the desserts here are inspired by the same cuisines that influenced the rest of the book.

However, I am a lot less opinionated about desserts than about other parts of the meal. In this end-of-the-meal territory I also tend to have more allegiance to the dishes of my youth, so you will also find here some renditions of plain old American desserts that I just happen to like.

One thing is true of every dessert that I have included: Whether directly inspired by spicy cuisines or not, they make excellent endings to spicy, highly flavored meals.

Simple All-Purpose Mixed Fruit

Serves 4

1 small cantaloupe, peeled and seeded

1 ripe banana, peeled

1 ripe papaya, peeled and seeded

1 cup blueberries or other berries

Juice of 1 orange

6 tablespoons lime juice (about 3 limes)

2 tablespoons honey

I love fresh fruit, and I'm always looking for ways to get more of it into my daily diet. This dish is a take-off on the mixed-fruit platters that you get for breakfast in almost any tropical country. Following the usual equatorial method, I use lime juice with the fruit, and here I add orange juice for an additional citrus taste and some sweetness. This would finish off a big, hearty meal very nicely.

METHOD

Cut all the fruit into bite-size chunks. Combine all the ingredients in a large bowl and toss well.

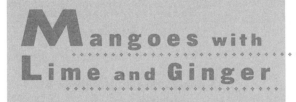

Mangoes with Lime and Ginger

3 ripe mangoes, peeled, pitted, and thinly sliced (save the pits for me; they are excellent for gnawing)

----

2 teaspoons minced ginger

¼ cup lime juice (about 2 limes)

----

2 ounces rum

Fresh mint leaves for garnish (optional)

I'm serious about this—mangoes are my absolutely favorite fruit. I'll admit they can be a little tough to deal with, but they are well worth the hassle. We usually see only one or two types in our supermarkets, but in fact there are as many varieties of mangoes as there are of apples. In this simple but fantastic dessert, lime, ginger, and rum are good complements to the mellow sweetness of the well-named ''king of fruits.''

METHOD

1. Combine the mangoes and ginger and mix well.

2. Just before serving, pour the lime juice and rum over the mango-ginger mixture. Garnish with mint leaves if desired.

LIME ROUTES

Historically, limes followed a roundabout route on their way to the United States. First cultivated in southern India, limes were brought to Persia, Palestine, and Egypt by Arab traders during the Middle Ages. Europeans discovered them during the Crusades and carried them back to southern Europe. From there, limes came to the Americas on the ships of Spanish explorers—it is believed that Columbus carried lime seedlings on his second voyage in 1493—and to the United States with the Spanish settlers of St. Augustine in 1565.

Grilled Peaches with Blue Cheese and Sweet Balsamic Glaze

Serves 4 as appetizer or dessert

1 cup good-quality balsamic vinegar

2 tablespoons sugar

1 tablespoon freshly cracked black pepper

3 peaches, halved and pitted

2 tablespoons virgin olive oil (approximately)

4 ounces blue cheese of your choice, crumbled

Here is a somewhat refined dessert for ending an ambitious dinner. If you want to be a little highbrow, bring out the vintage port for this one. You might want to make a double batch of the balsamic glaze while you're at it, since it is also excellent brushed on grilled chicken or fish just before they come off the grill.

METHOD

1. In a small saucepan, combine the vinegar, sugar, and pepper and bring to a boil. Reduce the heat to low and simmer, stirring occasionally, for 45 minutes to 1 hour, or until reduced in volume by about two-thirds. At this point, the glaze should be thick enough to coat the back of a spoon.

2. Rub the peach halves with olive oil and grill over a medium to medium-low fire until just slightly charred, 8 to 10 minutes. Brush the tops with the glaze and grill for another 2 to 3 minutes, or until the glaze begins to caramelize slightly.

3. Remove the peaches from the grill, brush on another layer of glaze, and cut into thick slices. Place the slices on individual plates, crumble cheese over them, and serve.

HOW DO YOU THINK OF THAT STUFF?

People often ask chefs how they think of their recipes. In my experience, there are only so many ways to put different ingredients together, which means there is almost always a precedent for any recipe you create. After that, it's often a matter of fooling around to see what tastes good.

This recipe is a good example. I was teaching a class on grilling for Claudia McQuillan at Bristol Farms in Los Angeles and was doing the standard demonstration of all the different things you can grill. Grilled fruit always seems to interest people the most, and I was grilling the usual pineapple and bananas. There was a peach on hand, so I figured I might as well throw it on the grill too. I was using a balsamic glaze on something else; some blue cheese had been set out as part of a fruit and cheese platter; and one of the students asked what they would taste like together.

At first it seemed a little too far out, but then I realized that fruit and cheese is a classic combination; and balsamic always goes well with the char taste of grilled food. So why not fruit, cheese, and balsamic all together? As it turned out, this was one of those rare combinations you stumble onto that is good enough to become a standard part of your cooking repertoire.

Mashed Banana with Lime-Coconut Milk and Mango Sauce

Serves 8

8 to 10 overripe bananas (4 cups after puréeing)

½ cup coconut milk, unsweetened canned, or prepared by method on page 458

¼ cup lime juice (about 2 limes)

MANGO SAUCE:

1 ripe mango, peeled, pitted, and diced small

¼ cup sugar

¼ cup water

1 drop vanilla extract

Salt to taste

I like the sweetest of fruits, and I like them even better when they are served with additional sugar, so it's easy to see how this recipe became one of my favorites. It is my version of a dessert served in an old, beat-up sub shop run by Samoans on the outskirts of Lahani on the Hawaiian island of Maui. When I was working in a hotel restaurant there, a buddy and I used to make regular stops at this shop for a snack on the way to work. My buddy liked the sandwiches, but this dessert was what brought me back. Rich and sweet, it is easy to make and slightly unusual. If it doesn't appeal to you as a dessert, you can always try it before you go to work.

BANANA FREEZIN'

It's difficult to store bananas once they reach the proper overripe state, with blackened skins. So, unless you know exactly when you will be making this, it is easiest to ripen the bananas until almost totally black, then freeze them. When you want to make this recipe, allow the bananas to thaw about two-thirds of the way, then proceed.

METHOD

1. Peel the bananas and press through a coarse sieve or purée in a blender or food processor. Add the coconut milk and lime juice and mix well. Cover and refrigerate.

2. Make the mango sauce: In a large saucepan, combine the mango, sugar, and water. Over medium-high heat, bring the mixture just to a simmer. Remove from the heat and purée in a blender or food processor. Add the vanilla and just a pinch of salt. Cover and refrigerate.

3. When ready to serve, place a generous amount of the banana mixture in a stemmed glass and top with the mango sauce.

MANGOES SAMOAN STYLE

- - - - - - - - - - - - - - - - - - -

The mango sauce here calls for ripe mangoes, but the authentic Samoan version calls for semi-ripe ones. In fact, I was always a bit puzzled that the Samoan proprietors of the shop where I first tasted this sauce invariably used mangoes with a little crunch to them, despite the easy availability of ripe mangoes, which seemed more appropriate to a dessert. Later I learned that Samoans generally prefer to eat fruit in a semi-ripe state—a preference that they say was developed because the many small animals on the island provided too much competition for mangoes once they were fully ripe.

- - - - - - - - - - - - - - - - - - -

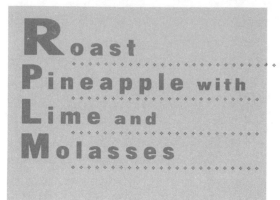

Roast Pineapple with Lime and Molasses

Serves 6

1 ripe pineapple

2 tablespoons vegetable oil

Salt and freshly cracked black pepper to taste

¼ cup molasses

¼ cup butter

¼ cup lime juice (about 2 limes)

Native to South America, the pineapple gained quick favor with European explorers of the fifteenth century, who often compared its flavor to a combination of quince and melons. Today it is one of the most widespread of all tropical fruits, popular from Europe to China. Here we roast it to bring out its inherent sweetness, then slap on a thin coat of lime-molasses glaze for some complementary flavors.

METHOD

1. Preheat the oven to 500°F. Remove the top and bottom of the pineapple and cut it into 6 slices, each about 1 inch thick.

2. Rub the pineapple slices lightly with oil, sprinkle lightly with salt and pepper, place in a single layer on a baking sheet, and roast for 15 minutes. Flip the slices over and roast for an additional 10 minutes. The pineapple should be lightly browned on both sides.

3. While the pineapple is roasting, combine the molasses, butter, and lime juice in a small saucepan and heat over low heat, stirring frequently, until the butter is melted.

4. Remove the pineapple from the oven, brush on the butter-molasses mixture, and serve.

Serving Suggestions:

This makes an excellent dessert with roasts of any kind. I would also suggest trying it after Grilled Orange Rabbit with Green Sauce and Toasted Pecans from Hell (page 168), Grilled Pork and Shrimp-Stuffed Chiles with Sweet Soy Glaze (page 55), or Rosemary-Cumin Grilled Lamb Skewers (page 143).

Really Sweet Carrots Cooked in Milk

Serves 6 to 8

Among the many reasons I appreciate the food of tropical climes is my intense sweet tooth. I like my iced tea really sweet; I like flans and gooey stuff; and super-sweet seems to be a common characteristic of hot-weather desserts. I think sweetness actually helps balance the meal, especially one that is hot and spicy. That certainly is the case with the halvas of India, which are intensely sweetened vegetables cooked in milk and served as desserts. If you're tired of having the same old desserts, try this pudding-like version of halva.

1½ pounds carrots

1½ quarts milk

1 cup heavy cream

1 tablespoon crushed cardamom

1 teaspoon ground cinnamon

5 threads saffron (optional)

½ cup white sugar

½ cup packed brown sugar

1 teaspoon salt

¼ cup raisins

OPTIONAL GARNISHES:

1 cup heavy cream, whipped

½ cup crushed toasted pistachios

METHOD

1. Grate, shred, or finely chop the carrots and place them in a large, heavy-bottomed saucepan. Add the milk, cream, cardamom seeds, cinnamon, and saffron if desired. Bring to a boil over medium heat, reduce the heat to a simmer, and cook for about 1 hour, or until most of the liquid is gone.

2. Add the white and brown sugars, salt, and raisins and cook for an additional 10 minutes, or until all liquid has been absorbed.

3. Remove from the stove, place in a bowl, and either serve hot or cover and refrigerate for 2 to 3 hours, then serve cold. If desired, top with whipped cream and sprinkle with crushed pistachios.

Grilled Banana Splits

Grilled desserts? Okay, this one may be stretching the idea a bit, but it does work, and its taste is unique and delicious. You can substitute mangoes, strawberries, or most any other sweetish fruit for the raspberries.

¼ cup lime juice (about 2 limes)

2 tablespoons molasses

4 ripe bananas, unpeeled, halved lengthwise

RASPBERRY SAUCE:

1 pint fresh raspberries, halved (you may substitute frozen)

2 tablespoons sugar

2 tablespoons Triple Sec

1 pint ice cream of your choice

½ cup chopped pecans or other nuts

1 cup heavy cream, whipped

METHOD

1. In a small bowl, combine the lime juice and molasses and mix well.

2. Place the banana halves on the grill, cut sides down, over a medium fire and grill for about 4 minutes, or until they are just golden. Flip the bananas over, paint the cut sides with the lime-molasses glaze, and grill, glazed sides up, for an additional 2 minutes. Remove from the grill.

3. Meanwhile, in a blender or food processor purée the raspberries, sugar, and Triple Sec until well blended. Serve the bananas topped with ice cream, raspberry sauce, nuts, and whipped cream as desired.

Banana-Papaya Fool

Serves 6 to 8

Although fools were originally made with gooseberries, today any type of stewed or puréed fruit mixed with custard or cream can be called by the name.

2 ripe bananas, peeled

1 large ripe papaya, peeled, seeded, and cut into ½-inch chunks

1 tablespoon dark rum

2 tablespoons plus ¼ cup sugar

1 cup heavy cream

½ cup toasted shredded coconut (optional)

½ pint raspberries (optional)

METHOD

1. In a large bowl, combine the bananas, papaya, rum, and 2 tablespoons of sugar and toss well.

2. Put about half of this fruit mixture into a food processor or blender and purée until smooth. Stir back into the remaining fruit and mix well.

3. In a large bowl, whip the heavy cream until it holds soft peaks, then add the remaining ¼ cup of sugar about 1 tablespoon at a time, continuing to whip, until the cream is quite stiff.

4. Fold the fruit mixture into the whipped cream and serve, either in individual small bowls or in a single large bowl. Garnish with toasted coconut and/or raspberries if desired.

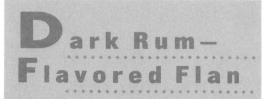

Dark Rum—Flavored Flan

Serves 4

1 12-ounce can evaporated milk

¼ cup sugar

2 large eggs plus 1 egg yolk

¼ cup heavy cream

2 tablespoons dark rum

2 tablespoons brown sugar (approximately)

In the heat of the Caribbean, fresh dairy products have traditionally been hard to come by, so the custard known as flan uses evaporated milk in place of the cream of European versions. Here we steer a middle course, using evaporated milk for authenticity and a touch of heavy cream for smoothness. Any liqueur may be substituted for the rum—Guaro, the sugarcane liqueur, is particularly fine.

METHOD

1. Preheat the oven to 350°F. In a medium-size bowl, whisk together all the ingredients except the brown sugar until thoroughly combined. Pour through a strainer, then ladle into 4 large (8-ounce) ramekins. Place the ramekins in a small roasting pan and add hot water to the pan until it comes halfway up the sides of the ramekins.

2. Bake in the preheated oven for about 50 minutes, or until a cake tester inserted in the center of a flan comes out wet but clean. Remove the flans from the water bath and refrigerate them for at least 1 hour or up to 24 hours.

3. Just before serving, sift the brown sugar onto the tops of the flans. You want a very thin layer that completely covers the tops of the custards. Put the flans on a baking sheet and slide under the broiler for about 2 minutes, or until the brown sugar is completely melted. Watch carefully to be sure the sugar does not burn.

Banana-Guava Bread Pudding with Rum Sauce

Here's a tropical turn on a down-home dessert originally designed to use up bread that had been around a bit too long. I use cornbread in my version because I think its slightly rich flavor matches up best with the sweet banana and guava, but feel free to use whatever type of bread you like, and don't bother to remove the crusts. Guava paste is available in most Latin stores, but if you can't find it, you can substitute two mashed ripe peaches.

2 cups stale bread crumbled into small chunks (about 3 pieces of cornbread or 5 slices of bread)

3 large bananas, peeled and sliced ¼ inch thick (just a bit thicker than poker chips)

⅓ cup guava paste (see Pantry, page 459)

CUSTARD:

4 large eggs, beaten

1 quart milk

2 cups sugar

1 tablespoon vanilla extract

1 teaspoon ground nutmeg

1 tablespoon ground cinnamon

¼ cup butter, melted

METHOD

1. Grease a 2-quart casserole dish or medium-size baking pan and preheat the oven to 350°F.

2. Place half of the bread chunks in the casserole dish, spread the bananas and guava paste evenly over the bread, then cover with the remaining bread chunks.

3. In a medium-size bowl, combine all the custard ingredients and pour into the casserole dish. Let stand at room temperature for 15 minutes.

4. Cover the casserole with aluminum foil, place in a large baking dish, and fill with enough hot water to come about 2 inches up the sides of the casserole. Bake for about 30 minutes, or until the custard has begun to firm up and has the consistency of slightly runny Jell-O. Remove the foil and continue to cook for about 30 minutes more, or until the custard is quite firm. To test, insert a spoon into the custard; no liquid should collect around it. Serve warm with whipped cream or chilled with warm Rum Sauce.

Rum Sauce

◇ ◇

Makes about 2 cups

1. In a small saucepan, combine the butter and sugar and cook over low heat, stirring frequently, until the butter is completely melted and the sugar is dissolved.

2. Remove the mixture from the heat and let it cool to room temperature. Add the eggs and mix for 1 minute. Add the rum and mix until thoroughly incorporated.

¼ cup butter

1 cup sugar

2 large eggs, beaten

½ cup dark rum

Andy's Rice Pudding

Andy Husbands, the chef at the East Coast Grill, constantly comes up with unusual ideas for the menus, and he always does the research to back them up. Just to keep him sharp, I occasionally ask for his reason for pairing one item with another in a particular dish. He might reply that he was inspired by a common dish from an area of Brazil that was settled successively by Portuguese and Africans.

Andy has spent a lot of time looking into the culinary influence of the slave trade in particular. This dish, which he conceived, is inspired by the mingling of foodways that resulted from the trading triangle of the 17th century: molasses from the Caribbean to the U.S.; rum from the U.S. to Europe; slaves from Africa to the Caribbean. Not that you really need to understand the origins of a dish to enjoy it, but it always comes in handy if the dinner conversation is getting tired.

In any case, this pudding is rich, mellow, and spicy all at the same time, so it's great even if you have no clue to its origins.

2 cups cooked rice

¼ cup golden raisins

2 ripe mangoes, peeled, pitted, and diced small

4 large eggs, well beaten

2 cups milk

1 teaspoon each ground nutmeg, ground allspice, and ground cinnamon

Small pinch ground mace

2 tablespoons butter, melted

¼ cup white sugar

¼ cup packed brown sugar

¼ cup molasses

1 tablespoon vanilla extract

¼ cup lime juice (about 2 limes)

METHOD

1. Grease a 4-quart casserole dish and preheat the oven to 350°F.

2. Place the rice and raisins in the casserole dish. In a large bowl, combine the remaining ingredients and mix well.

3. Pour the egg-milk mixture over the rice and, without mixing, bake in the preheated oven for approximately 30 minutes, or until the mixture has started to firm up. Stir well, return to the oven, and continue to bake until the pudding is as firm as you like, about 10 minutes more (I prefer it to jiggle a bit when it is shaken). Serve warm or cold.

Panfried Banana Fritters with Molasses-Rum Sauce

SAUCE:

¼ cup rum (dark is best)

¼ cup molasses

¼ cup unsalted butter

Pinch ground nutmeg

1 tablespoon lime juice

BATTER:

3 large eggs

¾ cup milk

2 cups all-purpose flour

1 teaspoon baking powder

Pinch salt

1½ cups vegetable or peanut oil for frying (approximately)

4 ripe bananas, peeled and sliced diagonally about ½ inch thick (about 5 pieces per banana)

Bananas and rum are among the most classic of tropical taste combinations, and I use them together often. Here we make hot, sweet fritters, then top the whole with a sauce of rum, molasses, and lime. Besides being a great dessert, banana fritters are also excellent for breakfast or, for you night owls, as a midnight snack with espresso.

Make sure you use bananas that are good and ripe for this recipe because their sweetness is essential to the dish. The batter may be a little thicker than you expect, but it's actually supposed to be like that—the consistency of pancake batter.

METHOD

1. Make the sauce: In a small saucepan, combine the rum and molasses and bring to a simmer over medium heat. Remove from the heat, add the remaining sauce ingredients, and stir until the butter is melted and the ingredients are well combined. Set aside until the fritters are made; if the butter starts to separate out, whisk over low heat until it is recombined.

2. Make the batter: In a large bowl, combine the eggs and milk and whisk together well. In a separate bowl, combine the flour, baking powder, and salt. Add the dry ingredients to the wet in 3 more or less equal parts, beating until smooth after each addition.

3. Make the fritters: Pour the oil into a heavy sauté pan until about 2/3 inch deep and heat over medium heat until hot but not smoking. Dip 3 or 4 banana pieces into the batter and drop into the hot oil. (When the banana hits the oil, it should bubble vigorously; if it does not, your oil is not hot enough.) Cook until well browned, about 3 minutes per side. Remove the fritters from the oil and set on several thicknesses of paper towels to drain. Repeat until all the bananas have been fried. Serve hot, accompanied by the molasses-rum sauce.

A Peach Shortcake for Lizzie

Serves 8 as dessert

My classic American shortcake features peaches, the fruit of choice in the South. I then add bourbon to "doll it up" a bit. My niece Lizzie, who lives up North, took a real liking to my version and insists that it be made on every occasion at which she is honored, from birthdays to eighth-grade graduation.

I prefer more peaches than cake, so the shortcakes here are a bit smaller than you might be used to.

8 to 10 large ripe peaches, peeled, pitted, and sliced into 8 wedges

½ cup brown sugar

¼ cup bourbon *or* 2 tablespoons lemon juice

SHORTCAKES:

2 cups all-purpose flour

¾ teaspoon salt

1 tablespoon baking powder

2 tablespoons sugar plus extra for sprinkling

½ cup unsalted butter

¾ cup light cream plus 2 tablespoons for brushing

1 teaspoon vanilla extract

1 cup heavy cream

1 to 2 tablespoons confectioners' sugar

METHOD

1. Preheat the oven to 450°F. In a large bowl, combine the peach slices, brown sugar, and bourbon or lemon juice. Cover and allow to macerate while you make the shortcakes.

2. Make the shortcakes: In a large bowl, combine the flour, salt, baking powder, and 2 tablespoons of sugar and mix well. Cut the butter into this mixture either by hand, with 2 knives or a pastry mixer, or in the food processor using a few quick pulses. Whichever method you use, the butter should be cut in until the mixture resembles coarse cornmeal, with only a few slightly larger pieces.

3. Add ¾ cup light cream to this mixture all at once and stir until you have a dough that just holds together. Knead the dough gently in the bowl by rolling and folding it 6 to 8 times, then turn it out onto a lightly floured surface and gently roll into a rectangle about 10" × 5" × 1" thick.

4. Cut the dough into 8 rectangles of roughly equal size, brush with the remaining 2 tablespoons of cream, and sprinkle lightly with sugar. Bake the rectangles on an ungreased baking sheet until the tops are lightly browned, 12 to 15 minutes. Remove and set aside to cool.

5. Combine the vanilla and heavy cream and whip until the cream holds soft peaks, sprinkling in confectioners' sugar during the last minute or two.

6. To assemble, cut each shortcake in half horizontally, spoon peaches and syrup on the bottom half, top with a generous amount of whipped cream, and replace the top.

Sargento's Labor-Intensive Lime Pie with Coconut Crust and Mango Topping

At some point, most cooks decide whether they are going to be bakers or line cooks. It's hard to do both well because the required mind-sets are radically different. Bob Sargent, a former chef at The Blue Room, is unique in that he can easily switch from one to the other. This is a dessert Bob developed during the summer months, when mangoes were peaking and limes were inexpensive; that's the line cook mentality sneaking in.

This pie takes some time to make, but lime, mango, and coconut form a trop-ical standard, and the combination of the crunchy, sweet crust with the tart limey filling and the fresh mango top-ping is wonderful. Incidentally, this is an excellent way to use up any overripe mangoes you might happen to have hanging around the kitchen.

CRUST:

1 cup coconut flakes (sweetened type is okay)

1 cup fine graham cracker, gingersnap, or vanilla wafer crumbs (crumb the crackers or cookies in a food processor or blender)

¼ cup sugar

½ cup butter, melted

LIME FILLING:

4 large egg yolks

½ cup all-purpose flour

Pinch salt

2 cups sugar

1 cup very thinly sliced limes, seeded, peels left on

1½ cups water

¼ cup butter, cut into 8 or 10 pieces

MANGO TOPPING:

¾ cup sugar

3 tablespoons cornstarch

½ cup cold water

1½ cups ripe mango chunks (2 small or 1 large mango)

Make the crust:

1. Preheat the oven to 450°F. Spread the coconut flakes on an ungreased baking sheet and bake until just golden brown, 5 to 7 minutes.

2. In a large bowl, combine the toasted coconut flakes, cracker crumbs, and sugar and mix well. While stirring with a fork, pour in the melted butter and continue to mix until well combined.

3. Press the mixture into a 9-inch pie pan. Allow it to rest for 1 hour in the refrigerator, then preheat the oven to 350°F. Bake the pie crust until light golden, 5 to 10 minutes, checking often to prevent scorching. Remove to a rack and allow to cool to room temperature.

Make the lime filling:

1. In a medium-size bowl, combine the egg yolks, flour, salt, and 1 cup of the sugar, mix well, and set aside.

2. Place the limes and 1½ cups water in a medium saucepan and bring to a boil over medium heat. Reduce the heat to low and simmer for 10 minutes, or until the lime peels are very soft. Add the remaining 1 cup of sugar and continue to simmer, stirring frequently, for 5 minutes.

3. Carefully stir about ½ cup of the lime mixture into the egg yolk–flour mixture until well combined.

Stir this mixture into the rest of the lime mixture and cook over low heat, stirring constantly, until clear, 8 to 10 minutes. The mixture should be thick enough so that, if you draw a line through it on the back of a spoon, the line maintains a distinct edge for several seconds. (Be careful not to overcook, or the acid in the limes will cause the mixture to thin out too much.)

4. Remove the mixture from the heat, whisk in the butter until melted, and allow to cool to room temperature. Pour into the prepared coconut pie shell.

(continued)

Make the topping:

In a medium-size saucepan, combine the sugar, cornstarch, water, and ½ cup of the mango and cook over medium heat, stirring constantly, until bubbling and thick, 5 to 8 minutes. Remove from the heat and stir in the remaining mango chunks. Allow to cool to room temperature, spread on top of the lime filling in the pie shell, cover, and refrigerate. Serve chilled.

Blue Room Chocolate-Bourbon-Pecan Tart with Gentleman Jack Hard Sauce

Serves 8

CRUST:

1 cup unsalted butter

½ cup sugar

½ cup crushed pecans

2 cups all-purpose flour

1 teaspoon vanilla extract

¼ teaspoon ground nutmeg

½ teaspoon ground cinnamon

1 teaspoon salt

1 large egg

FILLING:

1 ounce unsweetened chocolate

¾ cup dark corn syrup (you may substitute light)

¾ cup molasses

¼ cup unsalted butter, melted

2 ounces Gentleman Jack or other bourbon

2 teaspoons salt

2 teaspoons vanilla extract

3 large eggs

¼ cup all-purpose flour

1 cup pecans

This recipe was created by Jim Stringer, former pastry chef at The Blue Room, for a dessert contest sponsored by Jack Daniel's bourbon. The contest raises funds for the James Beard House in New York, so it's definitely for a good cause. Besides, as any Southerner knows, a good bourbon can give Scotch a run for its money any day, and I'm happy to spread that knowledge through recipes or by any other means.

Like many pastry chefs, Mr. Stringer insists that there are so many variables in any kitchen—or on any given day—that it doesn't make sense to give exact times in recipes. I forced him into it, but he agreed only on the condition that we tell you that the times are only approximations and you should rely more on the evidence of your eyes and hands than on the clock. Good advice for any recipe, actually.

(continued)

Make the crust:

Using an electric mixer, cream the butter and sugar together until very light, 4 to 5 minutes. Add all the remaining crust ingredients and mix just until well combined. Work the dough by hand in the bowl until it is smooth and elastic, 2 to 3 minutes, adding small amounts of flour as necessary. Allow the dough to rest in the refrigerator for 30 minutes, covered, then press into a tart or pie pan with your fingers.

Make the filling:

1. Combine the chocolate, corn syrup, and molasses in a stainless steel bowl. Bring a saucepan of water to a boil, remove the saucepan from the heat, and place the bowl on top of the saucepan to melt the chocolate, stirring occasionally. While the chocolate is melting, combine all the remaining filling ingredients in a separate mixing bowl and stir well. When the chocolate has melted, combine the 2 mixtures and stir well.

2. Preheat the oven to 375°F. Pour the filling into the prepared pie or tart pan and bake for approximately 40 minutes, or until the center of the pie is firm and no longer jiggles when shaken.

Make the hard sauce:

Cream the butter with an electric mixer until very soft, 8 to 10 minutes. When the butter is light and fluffy, add the confectioners' sugar and continue whipping for 8 to 10 minutes more, or until the hard sauce is extremely light and fluffy. Whisk in the bourbon. Serve at room temperature alongside the tart so that people can spoon on as much as they want.

HARD SAUCE:

½ cup unsalted butter

1½ cups confectioners' sugar

1½ tablespoons Gentleman Jack or other bourbon

Banana-Rum Ice

Makes about 6 cups

1 cup water

½ cup sugar

4 ripe bananas, peeled and roughly chopped

¼ cup dark rum

Bananas may seem a rather odd ingredient for an ice, but their taste and texture make for a very sweet, smooth dessert. In keeping with my penchant for classic tropical combinations, I add some rum to this cool dessert.

METHOD

1. Combine the water and sugar in a small saucepan, bring to a simmer over medium heat, and cook and stir until the sugar is dissolved, 2 to 3 minutes.

2. In a food processor or blender, combine the bananas and rum and purée well. Add the sugar water and whirl until well mixed. Pour the mixture into a 9" × 12" baking pan and freeze overnight or until solid (at least 3 hours).

3. Break the frozen mixture into chunks and purée in a food processor until smooth. Return to the freezer for at least 15 minutes but no more than 2 hours before serving.

BANANA GEOMETRY

I was fascinated when I discovered years ago that bananas are a tripartite fruit, which means that they are made up of three sections. To check this out, take a peeled banana and apply even pressure to the sides of the fruit with your fingers; the banana will naturally divide lengthwise into three parts. This is a great trick to show a kid about seven years old.

On a recent trip to Malaysia, where there are more than 100 varieties of bananas, I discovered that this is only the beginning of banana geometry; the exterior of this fruit is a kind of geometric chameleon. Unripe bananas on the plant are triangular in shape, and as they mature, they gradually become five-sided (on the exterior). Finally, when they are ripe and soft, they take on a round shape.

Limon Ice

1 oup water

1 cup sugar

¼ cup lime juice (about 2 limes)

¼ cup lemon juice (about 1 lemon)

I always find the tartness of citrus refreshing, particularly after a spicy meal. So here I combine those two old favorites, lemon and lime, in a sweet-tart tribute to the sno cones that turn up at every carnival and minor league ball game around the country. If you're making a batch for adults, try adding a few shots of tequila.

METHOD

1. Combine the water and sugar in a small saucepan, bring to a simmer over medium heat, and cook and stir until the sugar is dissolved, 2 to 3 minutes.

2. Add the lime juice and lemon juice to the mixture and mix well. Pour the mixture into a 9" × 12" baking pan and freeze overnight or until solid (at least 3 hours).

3. Break the frozen mixture into chunks and purée in a food processor or blender until smooth. Return to the freezer for at least 15 minutes but no more than 2 hours before serving.

Mango Ice

Makes about 1 quart

1 cup water

1 cup sugar

2 large ripe mangoes, peeled, pitted, and roughly chopped

2 tablespoons lime juice (about 1 lime)

I love ices because they are basically a less sweet version of the Sno-Kones that I doted on during my childhood summers. They make a simple, light, and refreshing ending to a spicy meal and lend themselves to fruit combinations of all types. Here we use the classic tropical lime-mango duo.

Ices tend to become grainy a few hours after they are puréed, so it's best to keep them in their frozen block form until just a couple of hours before you plan to serve them.

METHOD

1. Combine the water and sugar in a small saucepan, bring to a simmer over medium heat, and cook and stir until the sugar is dissolved, 2 to 3 minutes.

2. Combine the mangoes and lime juice in a food processor or blender and purée until smooth. Add the sugar water and whirl until well mixed. Pour the mixture into a 9" × 12" baking pan and freeze overnight or until solid (at least 3 hours).

3. Break the frozen mixture into chunks and purée in a food processor until smooth. Return to the freezer for at least 15 minutes but no more than 2 hours before serving.

Watermelon Ice

½ cup water

½ cup sugar

3 cups watermelon chunks, seeded

¼ cup Campari or other liqueur or liquor (optional)

2 tablespoons lemon juice (about ½ lemon)

Also known as sorbets, ices are basically frozen, sweetened fruit juices and purées. You can't get much simpler than that, and if you get the proportions right, you get both coolness and an intense fruit taste. My friend Jack Bishop suggested adding Campari to this watermelon ice for a deeper color and extra flavor. I think it works really well.

METHOD

1. Combine the water and sugar in a small saucepan, bring to a simmer over medium heat, and cook and stir until the sugar is dissolved, 2 to 3 minutes.

2. In a food processor or blender, combine the watermelon, Campari or other liquor (if desired), and lemon juice and purée well. Add the sugar water and whirl until well mixed. Pour the mixture into a 9" × 12" baking pan and freeze overnight or until solid (at least 3 hours).

3. Break the frozen mixture into chunks and purée in a food processor until smooth. Return to the freezer for at least 15 minutes but no more than 2 hours before serving.

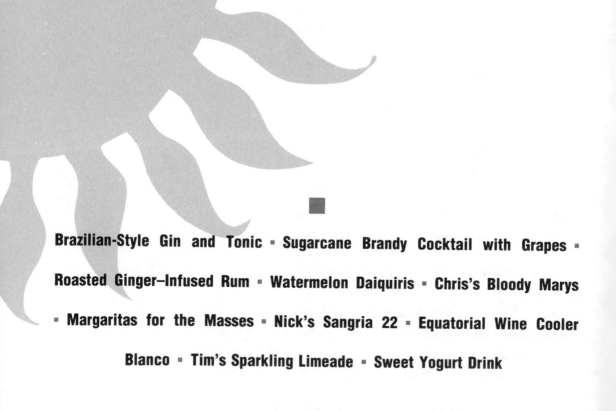

Brazilian-Style Gin and Tonic ▪ Sugarcane Brandy Cocktail with Grapes ▪

Roasted Ginger–Infused Rum ▪ Watermelon Daiquiris ▪ Chris's Bloody Marys

▪ Margaritas for the Masses ▪ Nick's Sangria 22 ▪ Equatorial Wine Cooler

Blanco ▪ Tim's Sparkling Limeade ▪ Sweet Yogurt Drink

DANCE TO THE MUSIC: A FEW BEVERAGES

■

Wine sings a very nice song, but it ain't got that tropical beat. What I mean is, wine is great, but sometimes I think we overemphasize it at the expense of the many other drinks of the world. In many hot-weather regions, wine is not a major player, and folks have come up with a whole range of other beverages, both alcoholic and non, which are great for serving with spicy food or for just hanging out. These drinks naturally tend to center on products that originate in the tropics, like rum and sugarcane brandy, lime juice and tequila, and I've included some of my favorites here. But, as with everything else, you can't neglect your roots, so I've also thrown in my favorite Bloody Mary recipe and a couple of pitcher drinks in which wine combines with fruit.

Brazilian-**S**tyle **G**in and **T**onic

½ lime, cut into 8 wedges

1 teaspoon sugar

1 cup ice (about 8 cubes)

2 ounces gin

6 ounces tonic

To me, the key to a great gin and tonic is lots of lime. When I'm at home, I always use half lime juice in the mix. Here is a technique I borrowed from Brazil, where lime wedges and sugar are muddled together in a glass to get a big lime flavor.

METHOD

Put the lime pieces and sugar in a large glass and muddle vigorously for 1 minute. Add the ice, gin, and tonic, mix well, and get laid back.

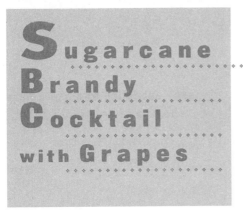

Sugarcane Brandy Cocktail with Grapes

Makes 1 drink

10 to 15 red or green seedless grapes

2 teaspoons sugar

Ice cubes

2 ounces cachaça (you may substitute gin or vodka)

This is a version of the classic Brazilian cocktail known as caprahina, which is lime wedges muddled together with the sugarcane brandy known as cachaça poured over the top. I first tasted this version, in which grapes are substituted for the limes, in a Brazilian restaurant in New York City. Try this one on a hot summer day.

METHOD

Put the grapes and sugar in a highball glass and crush and muddle them with a spoon for about 1 minute. Add ice cubes to the top of the glass, pour in the cachaça, and stir well.

Muddling grapes

CACHAÇA

One of the bonuses of working in restaurant kitchens is that they are truly multicultural meeting places. Over my years working in Boston restaurants, I've had the good fortune to work beside and become friends with a lot of Brazilians. Along the way I've learned a lot about their food customs, and late at night I've also learned a fair amount about Brazilian drinking customs. If you ever go out for a pop with a Brazileño, the odds are better than even that you will run into a powerful spirit known as cachaça (ka-SHA-sa). This distilled sugarcane beverage, which varies in quality from throat-burning firewater to fine aged brandy, is also drunk all over Latin America and Portugal, where it is known as *agua dente.*

Roasted Ginger—Infused Rum

Makes 1 quart

2 unpeeled pieces of ginger, each the size of your index finger

1 quart rum (dark is best)

Infused liquors seem to be getting very big these days, and here's a slightly spicy, smooth-drinking version that combines ginger and rum. These two are old tropical partners, and the result is excellent on the rocks with a squeeze of fresh lime. It also makes a great "Dark and Stormy" when combined with ginger beer, if you're into that kind of drink. I used to make this with raw ginger, but it was always a bit harsh. Bob Sargent, a former chef at The Blue Room, played around with roasting the ginger, and it is so much smoother that it's definitely worth the effort.

METHOD

1. Roast the ginger in a 450°F oven until it has softened slightly and the skin has puckered, 20 to 25 minutes. (It should feel somewhat like an undercooked potato.)

2. Remove the ginger from the oven and allow it to cool. When it is cool enough to handle, peel and slice it thinly.

3. Empty out some space in the rum bottle by pouring yourself and a friend a drink, then add the ginger to the bottle. Leave for a week, then drink.

Watermelon Daiquiris

2 cups well-packed, seeded
watermelon flesh

2 cups ice (about 16 cubes)

2 tablespoons sugar

4 ounces golden rum

1 lime, halved

Mint sprigs for garnish

While traveling in Malaysia, I found an incredible variety of fruit and fruit juices sold at little stands located in markets, in alleyways, by the side of the road, just about anywhere. My favorite was watermelon juice; not too sweet or thick, it tasted great. When I got back to the U.S., I thought of a way I could make it just a bit better—add a little rum. So here is it, what I consider a superlative summer cocktail.

METHOD

Throw the first 4 ingredients into a blender and purée well. Squeeze half a lime into each drink and garnish with a mint sprig.

Chris's Bloody Marys

2 quarts Clamato juice

1 quart gin or vodka

21 dashes Worcestershire sauce

5 to 10 dashes Tabasco sauce, depending on your taste for heat

Juice of 6 limes

2 teaspoons sugar

Salt and freshly cracked black pepper to taste

When I was growing up, Sunday noontime always meant one thing—Bloody Marys. This ritual always confused me, as it seemed like a particularly odd combination. As is the way with family rituals, however, this one got passed along, the son slowly acquiring key information about how to live his life, hard facts learned through years of sometimes painful experience. In this case, the lessons are to use a bit of sugar to balance the acid of the tomato, and to use Clamato juice as the base; it's lighter and makes for a less heavy experience, and you really can't taste the clam juice at all. I forgo the horseradish, but you can easily add it if you want. If you want to make a smaller batch, the booze to juice ratio is 1 to 2. If you want a balanced meal, you can always add a celery stick.

METHOD

In a large pitcher, mix all the ingredients well. Pour over ice and garnish with lime wedges if desired.

Margaritas
for the Masses

Serves 20 to 25 close
friends

So let's say it's time for your big summer blow-out party and you're not sure what to serve for beverages. Here's the answer. This margarita is strictly for huge crowds, its potency slightly diffused but still tangy and not exactly alcohol-free. It is designed to be served on the rocks, and the kosher salt is for the optional ring around the glass; you'll find that if you run the lime wedge around the top of the glass, it will help the salt stick.

3½ cups fresh lime juice (about 25 limes)

1½ cups fresh lemon juice (about 6 lemons)

3 egg whites

2 cups sugar

1 quart Cointreau or Triple Sec

2 quarts tequila of your choice (but at least 1 quart should be gold)

2 cups kosher salt

8 limes, cut into rounds, for garnish

METHOD

1. In a large mixing bowl, whisk together the lime juice, lemon juice, and egg whites until frothy.

2. Put the egg white–citrus juice mixture into a gallon jar and add the sugar and enough water to fill the jar. Shake well. This is your sour mix.

3. At this point, you have two options: (a) combine the sour mix and the liquors in a huge punch bowl, mix, and serve; or (b) mix individual margaritas to order, combining 4 parts sour mix, 2 parts tequila, and 1 part Cointreau or Triple Sec for each drink.

Nick's Sangria 22

1 big pitcher—about 8 drinks

Personally, I am a beer guy, but for those who like wine but think spicy food overpowers it, this is the answer, a great drink with spicy food and hot weather—sweet and fruity, cool and tasty. This is the creation of Nick Zappia, the general manager of the East Coast Grill and the Blue Room. Everyone always asks Nick why he calls it Sangria 22, but he just grins a mysterious grin and shakes his head. It doesn't have 22 ingredients, and Nick swears it has nothing to do with the 33 on the Rolling Rock bottle, so it remains a mystery.

2 oranges, halved and thinly sliced

2 lemons, halved and thinly sliced

2 limes, halved and thinly sliced

½ cup superfine sugar

Juice from 2 lemons

1 bottle cheap red wine

1 cup orange juice

1 cup sparkling water

METHOD

Put the fruit, sugar, and lemon juice into a large pitcher and bruise lightly with a wooden spoon for about 15 seconds. Add the wine, orange juice, and sparkling water, and pour over ice.

Equatorial Wine Cooler Blanco

For a crowd

Sometimes when you're having a lot of people over, you want to mix up a big batch of drinks that are suitably refreshing, have a little alcoholic kick, but don't knock everybody out after one glass. Here's just the ticket—a cooler that is basically an equatorial fruit salad mixed with white wine. Tastes great, looks good, and has a discreet punch.

3 limes, halved, then thinly sliced

2 oranges, halved, then thinly sliced

½ pineapple, peeled, then thinly sliced

1 mango or papaya, peeled, seeded, and thinly sliced

½ cup superfine sugar

1 cup lime juice (about 8 limes)

2 bottles cheap white wine

1 quart mango or other tropical fruit juice

METHOD

In a large bowl, combine the fruit, sugar, and lime juice and mash the fruit for about 15 seconds with a large wooden spoon. Add the wine and mango juice and serve over ice.

Tim's Sparkling Limeade

Makes about 5 cups

12 limes

1 cup sugar

½ cup water

1 quart sparkling water

Mint sprigs for garnish (optional)

In the summertime it's time to slow down a bit and make the real thing. Squeezing limes is a pain but it's also kind of therapeutic, and the results are definitely worth the effort. My friend Tim Wheaton, a college soccer coach who is constantly searching for beverages that will revive his charges, created this version of the classic limeade.

METHOD

1. Remove the green zest from the limes using a vegetable peeler, then juice the limes.

2. In a small saucepan, combined the sugar, ½ cup of water, and the lime zest. Bring to a boil, stirring frequently, and boil for 1 minute, stirring to fully dissolve the sugar.

3. Let the mixture cool, then strain it and discard the lime zest. Combine this sugar syrup with the lime juice and sparkling water, mix well, and pour over crushed ice. Garnish with mint sprigs if desired.

Sweet Yogurt Drink

¾ cup plain yogurt

4 teaspoons sugar

2 tablespoons cold water

½ teaspoon lime juice

4 ice cubes

Like almost everything else in India, the drinks are surprising. One day while eating lunch on vacation there years ago, I worked my way through a soft drink that contained as much salt as Coca-Cola does sugar, followed by freshly squeezed orange juice heavily laced with black pepper, and ending up with sweet lassi, a delicious cold yogurt drink that was thirst-quenching, sweet, and a bit sour at the same time. It tasted great and had the added advantage of providing some relief from the incredibly hot food we were eating.

This is my adaptation of that drink. Since Indian yogurt, made from water buffalo milk, is very creamy, it is best not to use low-fat yogurt here.

METHOD

1. In a blender or food processor, combine the yogurt, sugar, water, and lime juice and blend until the sugar has dissolved.

2. Add ice cubes and blend or pulse until the ice is chopped but not completely dissolved, about 1 minute.

PANTRY OF THE HOT SUN

■

Over the past decade or so, hundreds of ingredients from the tropical world, once exotic and difficult to find, have appeared in specialty shops, produce stands, and supermarkets all across the United States. This has come about partly because of the continued influx of immigrants from around the world, who bring their recipes and foodways with them and create a demand for the ingredients of their native countries; partly because of the increasing openness and appetite of American cooks and diners for more unusual and flavorsome ingredients; and partly because of our ability to quickly and efficiently transport ingredients to our shores from around the world so they are both relatively fresh and relatively inexpensive by the time they get here.

Whatever the reasons, the increasing availability of ingredients from hot-weather cultures has greatly expanded the repertoire of American cooks, allowing us to experiment with and experience the flavor footprints of many other cultures. To help in this process, we have included here some notes on a few of the ingredients used in this book with which American cooks may be unfamiliar or which we think are particularly interesting.

Achiote: A name often given to the spice made from the seeds and surrounding pulp of the annatto tree (see below), *achiote* may also be used to describe a paste made from ground annatto to which herbs and other ingredients, such as sour orange, are sometimes added.

Allspice: The dried, unopened, but mature bean of an evergreen tree, allspice, along with chile peppers and vanilla, completes the trio of important spices that originated in the American sector of the Spice Zone. Outside the U.S., it is called pimiento, a name that seems to have derived from the desperate desire of Spanish explorers to find something close to black pepper—which they knew as *pimienta*—in the New World. These reddish beans are slightly larger than peppercorns and have an aromatic flavor slightly on the sour side. Many folks think that they taste like a combination of cinnamon, cloves, and nutmeg with a sort of peppery background—hence, the name allspice.

Anise seed: Small, brown, and fuzzy, anise seeds have a sweet, aromatic, licorice flavor. They are often confused with star anise but are more subtle in flavor, and in fact the two are completely unrelated. Anise originated

in the Middle East and these days is grown in Russia, India, and Europe as well. It is widely used to flavor aperitifs and in Mediterranean-style fish stews and sausages.

Annatto: Annatto is a spice made from the seeds and surrounding pulp of a small, bright-orange evergreen tree that grows throughout the Caribbean, Mexico, and South and Central America. The spice is valued more for its brilliant orange-red color than for its taste and is widely used in Caribbean cooking, particularly in Puerto Rico, Jamaica, and Cuba, where it is sautéed in oil or lard, which is then used in many dishes. In my opinion paprika is an acceptable substitute for this spice.

Black Beans: Also known as turtle beans, these smooth-surfaced little legumes are a fixture of South and Central American cuisines, particularly those of Mexico, Cuba, and Brazil. They are available canned or dried in the "ethnic foods" sections of most U.S. supermarkets. The canned beans are perfectly acceptable, but are a bit mushy and don't have the full flavor of dried ones cooked according to the recipe on page 261.

Carambola: The fruit of a small tree native to Indonesia, carambola is also known as starfruit because in cross-section its five pronounced ridges give it the shape of a five-pointed star. Carambola has orangy-yellow skin and yellow flesh that is sweet, juicy, and rather crisp in texture.

Caraway: Some experts claim that caraway, the small seed of a plant of the parsley family originally from the area around Turkey and Iran, was the first spice used in Europe. Today it is used from Germany to England to Scandinavia to flavor bread, liquor, and the preserved cabbage dish known as sauerkraut.

Cardamom: A sweet, aromatic spice that is a member of the ginger family, cardamom is the second most expensive spice in the world (after saffron). This is largely because the pods, each of which contains 15 to 20 of the pungent seeds, must still be harvested by hand. There are three varieties of cardamom, green, white, and brown, but the white pods are actually just bleached green ones. Both white and green are preferable to the brown, which is considerably less aromatic and perfumey. Originally from southern India and Sri Lanka, cardamom is widely used in spice mixtures throughout India, where it is also sometimes chewed to aid digestion or is added to tea. In the Middle East cardamom is chewed as a sweet and is added to coffee to mellow the bitterness. In northern Europe the spice adds sweetness and a touch of the exotic to breads and rolls.

Chile Peppers: Members of the *Capsicum* genus, the fiery little pods known as chile peppers are the featured New World contribution to the Spice Zone. After their "discovery" by the Europeans who came to the Americas in the 15th century, chiles spread around the globe, becoming inextricably entwined in the cuisines of many countries. To me they are indispensable ingredients. The varieties of chiles are many and bewildering—red, green, fresh, dried, superhot, sweet, you name it. Since there are more than 2,000 varieties of chiles, each with its own heat level and individual flavor, we will make no attempt to catalogue them here. In fact, you will notice that when I call for fresh chiles in a recipe, I generally refrain from specifying which variety you should use. Instead, I call for a certain amount of "red or green chile pepper of your choice." This is because I think it is most rewarding to locate a particular variety of chile that you enjoy and that is readily available in your area, then develop a relationship with it. That way you will get to know just how hot a dish will be if you add x amount of your favorite chile. There are, however, a couple of chiles whose taste and heat are so distinctive that they really should be used when specifically called for in a recipe. I include the chipotle and the habañero (see both below) in this category.

There are many excellent books that deal with chiles in some detail, of which I particularly recommend *The Whole Chile Pepper* by Dave Dewitt and Nancy Gerlach (Little, Brown, 1990), *The Great Chile Book* by Mark Miller with John Harrison (Ten Speed Press, 1991), *Authentic Mexican* by Rick Bayless (Morrow, 1989), and *Red Hot Pep-*

pers by Jean Andrews (Macmillan, 1993).

Chipotle Chile Pepper: Chipotles, which are dried, smoked jalapeño chile peppers, are flat and wrinkled, with a dark reddish-brown color, and about 1 to 1½ inches long. Chipotles have a unique smoky, imposing flavor that goes with everything, and (particularly important for novice chile users) a consistent level of heat. They usually are found canned, packed *en adobo,* a sauce of onions, tomatoes, vinegar, and spices. You may also find them dried. To use the dried variety, place them in very hot water and allow to soak for 40 minutes to reconstitute. In a real pinch, you may substitute a mixture of 1 puréed fresh pepper of your choice, 1 teaspoon ketchup, and 1 drop Liquid Smoke for each chipotle called for.

Cilantro: Also known as fresh coriander, Mexican parsley, or Asian parsley, cilantro is a pungent, very distinctive, highly aromatic herb that is central to the cooking of Mexico, Latin America, and Southeast Asia. Almost unknown in the United States a decade ago, it is now readily available. Since drying largely destroys the aromatic nature of cilantro, it is worth the effort to get the fresh herb.

Cinnamon (aka Cassia): Cinnamon is the dried inner bark of a bushy evergreen tree native to Sri Lanka. Its cousin the cassia tree, native to Myanmar (Burma), grows considerably taller and therefore gives a higher yield and a less expensive product. Because of this,

chances are better than 50 percent that when you're eating a cinnamon bun in this country, you are really having a cassia bun.

Cloves: Cloves are the dried, unopened buds of an evergreen tree native to the Moluccas, the small cluster of Pacific islands known as the Spice Islands. Easily cultivated throughout the tropics, especially Africa and the West Indies, cloves are recognized as perhaps the most fragrant of all spices. They have a warm flavor that is at once sweet-fruity and peppery-pungent.

Coconut Milk: A simple preparation, coconut milk is made by steeping fresh coconut meat in hot water and then pressing until all the liquid is extracted. It is a daily cooking staple throughout Southeast Asia and Indonesia, where in every market you will find a vendor with a mechanical extractor making coconut milk of various grades. As with olive oil, the first pressing is the most expensive and desirable, the second less so, and so on.

While it is quite easy to make your own coconut milk, good quality canned versions are also available in most Asian or Caribbean markets. Just be sure that you do *not* buy the sweetened type such as Coco Loco—that stuff is good only for making blender drinks, never for cooking.

A health note: Being the extract of a nut, coconut milk has quite a high fat content. I recommend that you think of it as you would a well-marbled steak; don't eat it every day, but when you do, go for the real thing. However, for those who need to watch their diets, many Indian and Asian markets now carry an acceptable low-fat canned version, with about ¼ of the fat. For an even lower fat substitute, you can follow the suggestion of Dave DeWitt in *World of Curries* (Little, Brown, 1993) and combine about ½ teaspoon of coconut extract with 1 cup of milk. It is nowhere near as full-bodied or full-flavored as the real thing, but it will do the trick in a pinch.

To make your own coconut milk, follow this simple process: Husk a coconut, break the meat into smallish pieces, and place equal quantities of coconut meat and boiling water in a food processor or blender. Purée well, then remove the resulting mixture from the blender or processor and strain it through cheesecloth, pressing to extract all the liquid. Discard the solids and what you have left is coconut milk. It will keep, covered and refrigerated, for about 10 days.

Coriander Seeds:
Like the leaves and stems (commonly known as cilantro, see above), the small, yellow-brown seeds of the coriander plant are widely used in Asian and Latin cooking. Lightly toasted and ground to a powder, the fruity, warm, spicy, flowery seeds are an essential ingredient in curry powders, as well as many chutneys and sambals. Toasting whole coriander seeds prior to using them brings out their flavor and aroma. To do so, simply heat a sauté pan over medium heat and place the seeds in it. Toast, watching carefully and shaking frequently to prevent burning, until they just begin to release a little smoke, 2 to 3 minutes. If

the recipe calls for ground coriander, this is the point at which you grind them in a spice mill or coffee grinder. If you don't have either of those tools, you can easily crush the seeds with the bottom of the sauté pan you used to toast them.

Cumin:
With their distinctive nutty flavor, cumin "seeds" are actually the ripe fruit of an annual herb of the same name. They are an integral part of the cooking of India and are also widely used in Latin, African, and Middle Eastern cuisines. Their taste is similar to their cousin caraway, but more musty. The common cumin seed is greenish yellow, but there is also a black variety, which has a sweeter, more refined, more complex flavor and is expensive and difficult to locate. As with other spice seeds, toasting cumin prior to use brings out its flavor and aroma. To toast the seeds, follow the directions given above for coriander seeds.

Fennel:
The dried seed of a perennial herb, fennel has a predominantly licorice-like flavor, with a slightly bitter aftertaste. The plant from which it comes is similar in appearance to celery, and the leaves, stalks, and bulb are all used in cooking, as are the seeds. Like many spices throughout history, fennel seeds were valued for their medicinal properties and were used, among other things, as aphrodisiacs and to settle upset stomachs.

Fenugreek Seeds:
From an annual herb of the pea family, fenugreek seeds look like tiny nuggets and their flavor when ground is slightly sweet and spicy,

but mainly bitter. Native to Western Asia but long grown all around the Mediterranean, this spice is commonly used in the spice blends of India, but in the West has traditionally been used mostly in medicines.

Fish Sauce: Fish sauce is an essential ingredient in the cuisines of Southeast Asia. When used properly, it works much like salt in Western cooking, adding real depth of flavor without standing out as an individual taste. Known as nuoc mam in Vietnam, nam pla in Thailand, and nam pa in Laos, this thin, brownish sauce is made by packing anchovies or other small fish in salt and allowing them to ferment for 3 months or more, then drawing off the accumulated liquid. The resulting sauce can quickly become addictive. In Vietnam, nuoc mam is served with most meals and is the primary ingredient in the ubiquitous table sauce known as nuoc cham, for which a recipe is given on page 462.

Five-Spice Powder: True to its name, five-spice powder—one of the best known of the Asian spice blends—contains five spices: star anise, pepper, fennel seeds, cloves, and cinnamon (although the ''true,'' or original, powder contains cassia, a close relative of cinnamon). This mixture is very aromatic and quite powerful in flavor, though with little heat.

Galangal: Many people think of galangal as a kind of East Asian version of ginger. This comparison does have some validity, since it is a root spice with rhizomes (knobs) that bear a close resemblance to ginger. However, galangal is slightly thinner and smoother-skinned than its better-known cousin, with a creamy white or yellowish interior and a unique, delicate flavor that has more perfume and less bite. Galangal is used widely in East Asian cooking and is particularly important in the cuisines of Indonesia and Malaysia, where the flowers of the plant are also used in salads. You can substitute fresh young ginger root for galangal if necessary.

Ginger: The underground stem, or rhizome, of a perennial tropical plant, ginger is the personification of pungency. It originated in Southeast Asia but now is cultivated throughout the tropics. It was one of the most popular spices in Europe during the Middle Ages, when it was appreciated for its ability to assist digestion. Best known for its sweet, sharp, aromatic quality, ginger root is used today in cuisines around the world, either fresh or cured, dried, and powdered. The dried version, which increases in pungency when heated, is very useful for smoothing out spice mixtures.

Guava Paste: Guavas, originally from Brazil but now found all over the tropical world, have a very distinctive, intense aroma and a sweet-tart taste. Unfortunately, they do not travel well, but you can still enjoy the taste of guava by using a paste made from the flesh of the fruit. It has a super-sweet, concentrated guava taste and is found in 1-pound cans in Latin markets.

Habañero Chile Pepper: Also known as the Scotch Bonnet in the Caribbean, the habañero is generally acknowledged as the hottest commercially available chile pepper in the world. This baby, with its Scoville heat rating of up to 300,000 (compared with the jalapeño's 2,500 to 5,000 Scoville units), will take you places you've never been before. It has a unique floral flavor and an over-the-top nasal heat that is quite different from the flat, back-of-the-throat heat of many other chile peppers. Because of this, when a recipe specifically calls for habañeros, we recommend that you make a real effort to locate them rather than substituting other varieties. These peppers sometimes show up unpredictably in various markets, and if you happen upon them, buy a bunch and freeze them for later use, which will not damage them or reduce their heat or flavor. If you can't find habañeros, you may substitute Inner Beauty Hot Sauce or any of the other habañero/Scotch Bonnet–based sauces, using about 1 tablespoon of sauce for each pepper called for in the recipe. The habañero is a short, fat, lantern-shaped pepper, about 1 to 1½ inches long and 1 inch in diameter, and may range in color from yellow to red-orange to green to white. A word of caution: When working with habañeros, be sure to wear gloves, and if you get any of the juice on your skin, wash it off with a mild bleach solution, which neutralizes the capsaicin. Also be sure you don't rub your eyes or other sensitive areas while working with the peppers, and wash your hands well after you're done. If you ever fail to follow these precau-

tions, you will know why we are stressing them.

Hoisin Sauce: One of the most popular sauces of Chinese cooking, hoisin is a thick, sweetish, dark red mixture that is particularly well liked in southern China. It is made from soybeans, garlic, vinegar, sugar, flour, chile pepper, and various spices, and is widely used as a table dipping sauce and in marinades. It can be found in all Chinese markets and many supermarkets.

Jalapeño Chile Pepper: I think the jalapeño deserves special mention as the best-known and most widely consumed fresh chile pepper in the United States. Plump and bullet-shaped, it has a sleek and shiny exterior and grows 1 to 1½ inches long. Although relatively low on the heat scale, it still packs a decent punch. It comes in both red and green varieties. The red is a bit more difficult to locate, but I find it has a richer flavor. You may also find jalapeños pickled (*en escabeche*).

Jicama: The jicama is a bulbous root vegetable with thin brown skin, a refreshing crisp, crunchy texture, and a sweetish taste that lies somewhere between an apple and a potato. It is widely used in the cooking of Mexico, Latin America, and throughout the Pacific Rim. In the United States the jicama has become increasingly familiar over the past few years as Latin and Asian ethnic cuisines have gained in popularity, and can be found in many urban supermarkets. Peel its skin off with a knife, cover it with water, and jicama will keep, covered and refrigerated, for up to 2 days.

Kosher Salt: A coarse-grained sea salt that contains natural iodine, kosher is the only type that I use. I particularly like it in relishes because it dissolves more quickly than iodized salt and because to me it taste better than the free-flowing variety. Besides, it's more fun to sprinkle this stuff on with your fingers than to shake the standard variety out of a shaker.

Lemongrass: Grown throughout tropical Asia, lemongrass provides a fresh, lemony, extremely aromatic flavor that is essential to the cuisines of Thailand and Vietnam. Lemongrass stalks have bulbs at the base like scallions, topped by long, thin, gray-green upper leaves. To prepare lemongrass, remove the stems above the bottom third (the bulb) and reserve them for use in broths, soups, or teas. Remove the outer leaves from the bottom third of the stalk, and inside you will find a tender core. Mince this core very finely as you would ginger or garlic and add to dishes as directed. Lemongrass can be found in Asian markets and is increasingly available in supermarkets. Although not nearly as aromatic, dried lemongrass is an acceptable substitute.

Mace: Mace is a spice made from the bright red membrane that surrounds the nutmeg seed. The membrane is dried and then ground, although it can occasionally be found whole. Highly aromatic and slightly milder in flavor than nutmeg, mace is a familiar spice

in Southeast Asian and Caribbean cooking.

Mango: A luscious, fragrant fruit, the mango comes in as many different varieties as the apple and is a daily staple in more than half of the world. It originated somewhere in Southeast Asia, possibly Myanmar, but today is grown as a cash crop throughout the humid tropics, from India to Mexico to Central and South America and the Caribbean. When mangoes are ripe, the flesh is bright orange and very juicy, with a rich, sweet-tart flavor. Like the papaya, the mango is used not only as a fruit when ripe, but also as a vegetable in its green state—either cooked or added raw to salads and relishes. Due to the fruit's large pit and slippery flesh, the flesh of the mango can be somewhat difficult to get at, but it is well worth the effort.

Mustard: Mustard is made from the seeds of an annual plant of the cabbage family. The seeds come in three main varieties: brown, black, and white. Mustard seeds are used whole in some cuisines, but the most common way to use them is ground to a powder, which may either be used as a seasoning in itself or combined with liquids to make prepared mustards. Mustard has been used in southern Mediterranean cuisines since at least the days of the Roman Empire, appearing as a sauce ingredient in a cookbook by the Roman gourmand Apicius. Who knows, maybe vendors served mustard along with the Roman equivalent of hot dogs at the Colosseum.

Nuoc Cham: In Vietnam fish sauce, or nuoc mam, is served with most meals and is the primary ingredient in the sauce known as nuoc cham. There are as many subtle variations in the sauce as there are Vietnamese cooks, but here is the version I like:

For about 3½ cups of nuoc cham, whisk together the following ingredients in a large bowl: ½ cup fish sauce, ¼ cup lime juice, ½ cup sugar, 3 table-spoons Vietnamese chile-garlic paste, 2 tablespoons minced ginger, ½ cup thinly sliced scallions, 1 cup water, and ¼ cup white vinegar. This sauce will keep, covered and refrigerated, for about 2 months.

Oils: In addition to the flavorful sesame oil (see below), I recommend you keep three separate oils on hand in your pantry: first, an inexpensive, all-purpose vegetable oil for tasks like brushing vegetables before grilling or oiling baking pans, where the taste of the oil has little relevance; second, a good-quality virgin olive oil for general cooking use, where the oil will affect the dish but not be featured; and finally, a bottle of excellent extra-virgin olive oil, to be used in a miserly fashion, making its appearance only for those dishes in which the fruity taste of the oil is a star player.

Papaya: The papaya, which looks somewhat like a melon in the shape of a pear, is native to the Caribbean (where it is also known as the pawpaw) and is found in tropical regions throughout the world. The rind is pale green when unripe, becoming yellow when ripe; the musky-flavored, aromatic interior fruit ranges in color from greenish yellow when underripe to bright orange or red when fully ripe. In the center of the fruit is a core of black seeds in a kind of slick gelatin; the seeds are edible but are usually discarded. Papayas can grow to 20 pounds in size and are used by tropical cooks as a vegetable when green and a fruit when ripe. They are variously used as salad or salsa ingredients, cooked in soups, or eaten raw as a kind of snack food with just a squeeze of lime juice. Papayas are sold in the U.S. in Latin markets, specialty stores, and supermarkets.

Paprika: Paprika is a deep red powder made from dried, nonpungent chile peppers. Although it varies somewhat in taste from Spain to Morocco to India to Hungary, the flavor of this spice is always mild relative to other chiles. Outside Hungary, where it is widely used in large quantities, paprika is valued as much for the color it lends to dishes as for its taste. Paprika should be bought in small quantities because the powder goes stale quite quickly.

Peppercorns: There is no spice as popular around the world as the berry of the plant *Piper nigrum,* also known as pepper. True peppercorns come in three colors, depending on when they are harvested and dried. *Green peppercorns* are harvested while still unripe. Used fresh, they have an incomparable fresh, hot taste. When dried, green peppercorns become *black peppercorns,* the variety most familiar around the world. *White peppercorns* are berries that have been allowed to fully ripen on the vine, at which point they become red in color. After harvesting, this outer red coating is peeled off, and the inner white corn is dried. (So-called *pink peppercorns* are actually the berries of a South American tree, not of *Piper nigrum*.) Within each of the three color categories, there is a wide variety of peppers with various nuances of taste depending on where they were grown and the method by which they were dried.

In general, I suggest using black pepper. However, in some Southeast Asian–inspired recipes and seafood dishes, I think the slightly more aromatic, less robust nature of white pepper works better.

Whatever color you use, the difference between freshly cracked peppercorns and preground pepper is enormous. I can't emphasize enough how important it is that you use freshly cracked whenever pepper is called for in this book. It has a major impact on every dish. In fact, I strongly recommend that you make a dish of freshly cracked black pepper a permanent fixture next to the dish of kosher salt on your kitchen counter and your dining room table.

Plantain: A tropical relative of the banana, the plantain is always cooked before being eaten, which is why it is sometimes called "cooking banana." In its green state, it has the starchy quality of a potato, but by the time it is ripe (the skin will be black) the starch has turned to sugar. In its ripe state the plantain is used in desserts or as snack food; in its green state it is most often cut into

rounds and deep-fried (page 253). Popular in the West Indies, Central America, Africa, and Asia, it keeps for a long time and is a wonderfully adaptable ingredient with which to experiment. Plantains are most easily found in Latin and West Indian markets.

Pomegranate Molasses: As the name implies, pomegranate molasses is thick syrup of concentrated pomegranate juice, with the deep, rich sweetness and sour undertones of the fruit from which it is made. It is available in Middle Eastern stores.

Quince: The quince has an unusually dry texture for a fruit and does not develop much sugar even when completely ripe. These drawbacks are compensated for by the distinctly tropical, musky perfume of this fruit. Its high pectin content also makes it useful for jams and jellies. Nevertheless, while once quite popular in the United States as a preserved fruit, the quince is now a rarity in this country.

Rice Wine Vinegar: See Vinegars.

Roasted Red Bell Peppers: Roasting bell peppers is an easy way to add a rich, smoky flavor to any dish. At first the technique might seem odd, since it involves burning the exterior of the pepper, which goes against cooking instinct. However, the result is wonderful. To roast bell peppers, put them on the grill over a hot fire and roll them around until the skins are completely dark and well blistered. Remove from the grill, pop into a brown paper bag, seal the bag, and allow the peppers to cool for about an hour. (This facilitates removal of the skins.) After an hour remove the peppers from the bag and roll them around in your hands, caressing the skins into falling off. Tear the peppers in half, remove the inner cores and seeds, and run the peppers gently under cold water to remove any remaining charred pieces of skin. Put into a small container, add olive oil to cover, cover the container, and refrigerate. They will keep up to 2 weeks stored in this manner.

Scotch Bonnet Pepper: See Habañero Chile Pepper, page 460.

Sesame Oil: Popular in Asian cooking, sesame oil is made from roasted sesame seeds and has a pronounced nutty, almost burned flavor. It is usually used for flavoring rather than straight cooking, often in combination with other, less intensely flavored oils.

Shrimp Paste: Known as belacan in Malaysia, mam tom in Vietnam, gapi in Thailand, and trasi in Indonesia, this paste of fermented, dried shrimp is a key ingredient in the cuisines of Southeast Asia. It is particularly important in the cooking of Malaysia and Indonesia, where it is virtually ubiquitous. Despite its very widespread use, however, it is used rather sparingly in each individual dish, as Western cooks use salt or pepper.

Star Anise: Named for its shape, star anise is the dried seed pod of an evergreen tree that grows in China and northern Vietnam. With its deep licorice flavor and its eight-pointed, star-shaped pods, it is one of the more exotic spices readily available to American cooks. Star anise is both stronger and slightly harsher than anise seed, a spice with which it is often confused, even though the two spices are totally unrelated. (As far as I can tell, they have similar names only to confuse us.) Star anise is an essential ingredient in Chinese five-spice powder and is frequently used in Vietnamese cooking as well as that of other Southeast Asian countries.

Tabasco: Tabasco is the name for both a particular chile pepper and the most popular hot sauce in the U.S. The pepper is shaped like a blunt jalapeño with a wrinkled skin, is fairly high in the heat range, may be red, yellow, or orange, and is about 1 to 1½ inches long. The famous sauce made from this pepper plus vinegar and salt has been manufactured by the McIlhenny family on Avery Island off the coast of Louisiana, since about 1872. It has a nice flavor, packs a respectable punch, and, since it is available everywhere, makes a good substitute for chiles in a pinch.

Tahini: An oily paste made of ground raw white sesame seeds, tahini is a staple ingredient in the cooking of the Middle East. In Asia cooks use a very similar paste, but theirs is made from toasted sesame seeds.

Tamarind: Tamarind trees, which reach heights up to 70 feet, grow in the tropics throughout the world. Their fruit consists of pods from 3 to 6 inches long, covered with brown, furry skin and containing a dark pulp along with several seeds. The pulp has a tart, sweet-sour taste and is used in chutneys, curries, confections, stews, syrups, and drinks of all varieties throughout the tropical world. Tamarind is most easily located in paste form in Asian and Indian markets; it may also be found fresh or as a syrup.

When used in recipes, tamarind is usually diluted to make tamarind water. To make tamarind water from syrup, combine 1 tablespoon syrup with ½ cup hot water and stir well. If using paste, combine a chunk about the size of a golf ball with ½ cup very hot water, allow to sit for 10 minutes, press through a strainer or fine sieve, and discard the solids. If using fresh pods, peel the pods and follow the instructions for paste. If you can't locate tamarind, a mixture of equal parts molasses, fresh lime juice, and Worcestershire sauce is a valiant effort at approximating the flavor.

Tomatillo: The tomatillo is a tart Latin American staple that looks like a small unripe tomato with a papery brown husk. It is cooked and used in sauces and salsas in Latin cuisine and is widely available in the United States canned as well as fresh.

Tomatoes, Oven-Dried: Drying tomatoes concentrates their flavor and makes them even sweeter. You can buy sun-dried tomatoes in most specialty markets these days, but it takes very little effort to dry your own in the oven. To dry plum tomatoes, split them in half lengthwise, place them on a large drying rack set on top of a baking sheet, and sprinkle with salt and pepper and a bit of finely chopped rosemary or thyme. Place in a 200°F oven for 6 to 8 hours, depending on the size and ripeness of the tomatoes. The tomatoes should be shriveled up and reduced to about half their original size.

Turmeric: Turmeric is the dried, powdered underground stem of the turmeric plant, which grows in tropical climates throughout the world. The bright yellow color of this spice is its claim to fame, and in fact it has long been used as a dye for cloth. Widely used in Indian spice mixtures, its flavor is strongly medicinal, bitter, slightly metallic, and earthy; a little of this spice goes a long way, but when properly used it adds an indefinable edge to spice mixes.

Vanilla: Vanilla is the fruit (bean) of a climbing perennial plant in the orchid family. Another New World spice, it had many different uses in pre-Columbian Aztec culture and became very popular in Europe when brought there by the Spanish. Vanilla beans grow in humid tropical rain forests, and their distinctive taste results from curing the beans when slightly underripe. Although vanillin, the key flavor element in vanilla, can be reproduced chemically, synthetic vanilla lacks the flavor nuances of the bean. Vanilla beans can be used fresh, or to make your own liquid vanilla, follow this simple recipe: Split 3 beans, scrape out the seeds, and add them to about ½ cup of your favorite liquor. Bring the seeds and liquor to a simmer, reduce the heat, and simmer gently for 25 minutes or so. Strain, discard the seeds, and keep the liquid covered in the refrigerator. Another way to preserve beans is to cut them in half, cover them with sugar, and store in a covered jar; this has the added advantage of creating sugar with a wonderfully subtle vanilla flavor.

Vietnamese Chile-Garlic Paste: The name says it—this is a paste from Vietnam made of red chile peppers ground up with garlic. It has an incendiary flavor all its own and also makes a suitable substitute for fresh chile peppers in any recipe where garlic is an acceptable addition.

Vinegars: Vinegars are created by a double fermentation process. During the first part of the process, the sugars in liquids like apple juice and grape juice are turned to alcohol. In the second part, yeast cells are introduced into the liquid and turn the alcohol to acetic acid, which gives you vinegar. I find vinegars to be excellent flavor balancers, helping to bring other strong tastes into harmony, so I use many of them. These are the ones I use most often:

- *White, or distilled, vinegar.* Like vodka, this garden-variety vinegar is made from grains. It is the least subtle of vinegars, made through a quick distillation process.

- *Red wine vinegar.* The name says it—it's made from red wine. It varies wildly in quality, depending on the wine you start with and the aging process used. The most expensive red wine vinegars are aged in wooden vats.

- *Rice wine vinegar.* The Asian version of red wine vinegar, this is made from fermented rice water and has a beautifully delicate, subtle taste.

- *Balsamic vinegar.* Balsamic is a mellow, complex, distinctly flavored red wine vinegar. It is aged in wooden casks, and the contents of several different casks are combined during the aging process to create the final product.

Yucca: Yucca (aka cassava and manioc), is one of the most popular starchy tubers in the tropical world. It has a tough outer skin and crisp, white flesh and may range in length from 6 to 12 inches, with a diameter of up to about 3 inches. It has the consistency of a crisp potato, but with a little spicy bite. Originally from Brazil and still used in many forms there, the yucca has become a major staple in much of Africa, and most yucca grown for export is produced on that continent.

WHERE TO GET IT ALL

■

Thanks to modern air transport and this country's increasing appreciation of food in all its variety, American supermarkets now routinely stock items that only a few years ago would have been considered rare and exotic. Fresh chile peppers, for example, used to be found only in the Southwest and in a few specialty stores in the nation's largest cities. Today you would be hard pressed to find a town or city anywhere in the country that doesn't have at least one store that carries at least one type of fresh chile.

Happily, this development means that most of the ingredients in this book can be found either in supermarkets or in specialty stores throughout the country. And if some are not available in your area, you can be sure that you can get them by mail order.

To make it easier for you to find the more unusual items used in this book, below is a list of sources for various types of ingredients. They are listed alphabetically by city within each category. I encourage you to send for some of the catalogues—they are very entertaining to look through and can be great sources of ideas for cooking.

GENERAL SOURCES

Each of these four places has a large selection of ingredients, both fresh and prepared, from all over the world. They all have mail-order catalogues, so that you can buy a wide variety of ingredients from a single source if you wish.

Rafal Spice Company
2521 Russell Street
Detroit, MI 48207
(800) 228-4276
In Michigan:
(313) 259-6373

Balducci's
11-02 Queens Plaza S.
Long Island City, NY 11101-4908
(800) 225-3822

Dean & DeLuca
560 Broadway
New York, NY 10012
(800) 221-7714
In New York:
(212) 431-1619

G. B. Ratto, International Grocers
821 Washington St.
Oakland, CA 94607
(800) 325-3483
In California:
(800) 228-3515

**C a r i b b e a n
I n g r e d i e n t s**

California Sources:

Caribbean Delites
1057 East Artesia Blvd.
Long Beach, CA 90805
(213) 422-5594

La Preferida, Inc.
4615 Alameda St.
Los Angeles, CA 90056
(213) 232-4322
Contact: Ivan Bayona

Rosado's International Foods, Inc.
1711 Little Orchard, Ste. B
San Jose, CA 95125
(408) 298-2326

Florida Sources:

J.R. Brooks and Son, Inc.
P.O. Drawer 9
18400 SW 256th St.
Homestead, FL 33090-0009
(800) 423-4808
(800) 327-4833 (Outside Florida)
(800) 338-1022 (Canada)

Goya
1900 N.W. 92nd Ave.
Miami, FL 33172
(305) 592-3150

Jamaica Groceries &
Spices
9587 S.W. 160th St.
Miami, FL 33157
(305) 252-1197

Temptations-Caribbean
Harvest
P.O. Box 170105
Miami, FL 33017

West Indian Food
Specialties
6035 Miramar Parkway
Miramar, FL 33023
(305) 926-6418

Other Sources:

La Preferida, Inc.
3400 West 35th St.
Chicago, IL 60632
(312) 254-7200

Dekalb World Farmers
Market
3000 East Ponce de Leon
Decatur, GA 30034
(404) 377-6410

La Palma
2884 24th St.
San Francisco, CA 94110
(415) 647-1500

Toronto Caribbean
Corner
57 Kensington Ave.
Toronto, Ont. M3T 2K2
(416) 593-0008

Mexican/Latin American Ingredients

CMC Company
P.O. Drawer B
Avalon, N J 08202
(800) CMC-2780

Tropical Foods, Inc.
2101 Washington St.
Boston, MA 02119
(617) 422-7439

El Coloso Mareket
102 Columbia St.
Cambridge, MA 02139
(617) 491-1361

La Casa del Pueblo
1810 South Blue Island
Chicago, IL 60608
(312) 421-4640

El Original Supermercado
Cardenas
3922 North Sheridan Rd.
Chicago, IL 60607
(312) 254-7200

La Preferida, Inc.
3400 West 35th St.
Chicago, IL 60632
(312) 254-7200

Hernandez Mexican
Foods
2120 Alamo St.
Dallas, TX 75202
(214) 742-2533

Johnnie's Market
2030 Larimer St.
Denver, CO 80205
(303) 297-0155

Algo Espcial
2628 Bagley St.
Detroit, MI 48216
(313) 237-0295

Hi-Lo Market
415 Centre St.
Jamaica Plain, MA 02130
(617) 522-6364

The Grand Central
Market
317 South Broadway
Los Angeles, CA 90013
(213) 622-1763

International Groceries
and Meat Market
5219 Ninth Ave. (between
39th and 40th Streets)
New York, NY 10018
(212) 297-5514

Latin American Products
142 West 46th St.
New York, NY 10036
(212) 302-4323

Casa Hispania
International Food
Market
P.O. Box 587
73 Poningo St.
Port Chester, NY 10578
(914) 939-9333

Tropicana Market
5001 Lindenwood St.
St. Louis, MO 63109
(314) 353-7328

Casa Sanchez
2778 24th St.
San Francisco, CA 94110
(415) 282-2400

Coyote Cocina
1364 Rufina Circle #1
Santa Fe, NM 87501
(800) 866-HOWL

**Great Southwest Cuisine
Catalog**
223 North Gaudalupe St.,
Ste. 197
Santa Fe, NM 87501
(800) GREAT-SW

Josie's Best
1130 Agua Fria St.
P.O. Box 5525
Santa Fe, NM 87501
(505) 983-6520

Goya Foods
100 Seaview Dr.
Secaucus, NJ 07904
(201) 348-4900

Americana Grocery
1813 Columbia Rd. N.W.
Washington, DC 20009
(202) 265-7455

Casa Pena
1636 17th St. N.W.
Washington, DC 20009
(202) 462-2222

**General Asian
Ingredients**

De Wildt Imports
R.D. 3
Bangor, PA 18013
(215) 588-0600
(800) 338-3433

Ming's Market
85-91 Essex St.
Boston, MA 02111
(617) 338-1588

New England Food
225 Harrison Ave.
Boston, MA 02111
(617) 426-8592

Sun Sun Company
18 Oxford St.
Boston, MA 02111
(617) 426-6469

Star Market
3349 North Clark St.
Chicago, IL 60657
(312) 472-0599

**Yee Sing Chong
Company, Inc.**
977 North Broadway
Los Angeles, CA 90012
(213) 626-9619

Keesan Imports
9252 Bird Rd.
Miami, FL 33165
(305) 551-9591

**Southeastern Food
Supply**
400 N.E. 67th St.
Miami, FL 33431
(305) 758-1432

**Kam Kuo Food
Corporation**
7 Mott St.
New York, NY 10013
(212) 571-0330

**China Bowl Trading Co.
(Chinese and Japanese)**
160 Lackawanna Ave.
Parsippany, NJ 07054
(201) 335-1000
(800) 526-5051

The Chinese Grocer
209 Post St. at Grant Ave.
San Francisco, CA 94108
(415) 982-0125
(800) 227-3320

**Southeast
Asian
Ingredients**

Bangkok Grocery
1021 West Lawrence Ave.
Chicago, IL 60640
(312) 784-0001

Tan Viet Market
10332 Ferguson Rd.
Dallas, TX 75228
(212) 324-5160

Bangkok Market, Inc.
4804-6 Melrose Ave.
Los Angeles, CA 90029
(213) 626-9619

Bangkok Market
106 Mosco St.
New York, NY 10013
(212) 349-1979

A Taste of Thai
P.O. Box AX
Old Saybrook, CT 06475
(800) 243-0897

Anzen Importers
736 N.E. Martin Luther King,
Jr., Blvd.
Portland, OR 97232
(503) 233-5111

Lao Market
3125 9th St. N.
St. Petersburg, FL 33704
(813) 821-5492

Da Hua Market
623 H Street N.W.
Washington, DC 20001
(202) 371-8880

**Nancy's Speciality
Market**
P.O. Box 327
Wye Mills, MD 21679
(800) 4-Nancy-1

Middle Eastern Ingredients

**Sahadi Importing
Company, Inc.**
187 Atlantic Ave.
Brooklyn, NY 11201
(718) 624-4550

**Gourmet Treasure
Hunters**
10044 Adams Ave., Ste. 305
Huntington Beach, CA 92646
(714) 964-3355

**C & K Importing
Company**
2271 West Pico Blvd.
Los Angeles, CA 90006
(213) 737-2970

Sultan's Delight
P.O. Box 140253
25 Croton Ave.
Staten Island, NY 10314-
0014
(718) 720-1557

Indian Ingredients

India Tea and Spice, Inc.
453 Common St.
Belmont, MA 02178
(617) 484-3737

Bazaar of India
1810 University Ave.
Berkeley, CA 94703
(415) 548-4110

International Grocer
3411 Woodward
Detroit, MI 48201
(313) 831-5480

K. Kalustan
123 Lexington Ave.
New York, NY 10016
(212) 685-3451

Spices and Chiles

Vanns Spices Ltd.
1238 East Joppa Rd.
Baltimore, MD 21286
(410) 583-1643

Cuisine Express
1784 Deer Trail Rd.
Boulder, CO 80302
(303) 444-4302

Jody Cooper
Chile-of-the-Month
HCR 64, Box 18
Chimayo, NM 87522
(505) 351-2223

Pendery's, Inc.
1221 Manufacturing St.
Dallas, TX 75207
(800) 533-1870

Spice It Up
R.R. #2, Box 1732
21 North St.
East Rindge, NH 03461

El Paso Chile Co.
100 Ruhlin Court
El Paso, TX 79922
(915) 544-3434

House of Spices
76-17 Broadway
Jackson Heights, NY 11373
(718) 476-1577

The Spice Merchant
P.O. Box 524
Jackson Hole, WY 83001
(307) 733-7811

Spice House
1048 N. Old World 3rd St.
Milwaukee, WI 53201
(414) 272-0977

Nature's Key Products
P.O. Box 1146
New Hyde Park, NY 11040

Adrianna's Bazaar
2152 Broadway
New York, NY 10023
(212) 877-5757

Hot Stuff
227 Sullivan St.
New York, NY 10012
(800) 466-8206

**Spices of Vermont
(Indian)**
Rte. 7, P.O. Box 18
North Ferrisburg, VT 05473
(802) 425-2555

**Frontier Cooperative
Herbs**
P.O. Box 299
Norway, IA 52318
(319) 227-7991

KCJ Vanilla Co.
P.O. Box 126-MG
Norwood, PA 19074

Cinnabar
1134 West Haining St.
Prescott, AZ 86301
(602) 778-3687
(800) 824-4563

**Los Chileros de Nuevo
Mexico**
P.O. Box 6215
Santa Fe, NM 87502
(505) 471-6967

Market Spices
85A Pike Place Market
Seattle, WA 98101
(206) 622-6340

Exotic Produce

Suwanee Sweet Organics
Rte. 1, Box 116
Jennings, FL 32053
(904) 938-2046

Frieda's By Mail
P.O. Box 58488
Los Angeles, CA 90058
(213) 627-2981

Malibu Greens
P.O. Box 6286
Malibu, CA 90265
(800) 383-1414

Sources for Inner Beauty Hot Sauce

Le Saucier
Quincy Market, North
Canopy
Boston, MA 02109
(617) 868-9139

Mo' Hotta, Mo' Betta
P.O. Box 4136
San Luis Obispo, CA 93403
(800) 462-3220

Index

ABOUT THE AUTHORS

Chris Schlesinger and John Willoughby are the co-authors of *The Thrill of the Grill* (Morrow, 1990) and *Salsas, Sambals, Chutneys & ChowChows* (Morrow, 1993) and are regular contributors to *The New York Times*. The short story is: These are two guys who like to cook food and drink beer with friends in places where the weather is hot. Then they write about it. Here's the long story:

Chris Schlesinger is the chef and co-owner of the East Coast Grill, Jake and Earl's Dixie Barbecue, and The Blue Room, all located in Cambridge, Massachusetts.

Chris was born and raised in Virginia, where he first developed his lifelong devotion to barbecue, spicy food, and live-fire cookery. He entered the food-service industry at the age of eighteen, when he dropped out of college to become a dishwasher. After graduating from the Culinary Institute of America in 1977, Chris cooked in over thirty restaurants, having the opportunity to work with some of the most innovative chefs in New England during the first blossoming of nouvelle cuisine. In 1986, he and partner Cary Wheaton opened the East Coast Grill, the first of their restaurants. This was followed by Jake and Earl's in 1989 and The Blue Room in 1991.

John Willoughby writes about food, health, and travel from his home in Cambridge, Massachusetts.

John grew up in rural Iowa, directly across the road from a traditional working farm. After graduating from Harvard University in 1970, he spent seventeen years working in various human-services positions. During this time, he also worked part-time for two years in the kitchen of the East Coast Grill. In 1989, Willoughby became a full-time writer, joining the staff of *Cook's* magazine as feature writer. John is senior editor of *Cook's Illustrated* and a regular contributor to *Metropolitan Home, Eating Well,* and *Boston Magazine*. His work has also appeared in *Men's Health, GQ, The New York Times,* and various major metropolitan newspapers.